Voices in the Dark

ALSO BY PAUL KANE

*The* Hellraiser *Films and Their Legacy*
(McFarland, 2006)

# Voices in the Dark

*Interviews with Horror Writers, Directors and Actors*

PAUL KANE *and*
MARIE O'REGAN

*Foreword by* ANNE BILLSON

McFarland & Company, Inc., Publishers
*Jefferson, North Carolina, and London*

All photographs and images used in this book are from private collections or picture libraries and are used solely for the advertising, promotion, publicity and review of the specific motion pictures, books and individuals they illustrate with all rights reserved. They have not been reproduced for advertising or poster purposes, nor to create the appearance of a specially licensed or authorized publication. Grateful acknowledgment is made to the following for the use of their material. While every effort has been made to trace and acknowledge all creators and copyright holders, the author apologizes for any errors or omissions and, if informed, will be glad to make corrections in any subsequent editions.

Maggie Ellis and Jo Cadoret (Film London), Amanda Boyle, Helen Giles, Kate Meyers and Tracy Brimm (Forward Films), Sean Garrehy (Little Brown/Orbit), Sarah Pinborough, Tracy Heydweiller (Leisure Books), Peter Medak, Greg Goldstein and Ted Adams (IDW), Gordon Correll, Jo Fletcher and Edward Bettison, Silvia Baglioni, Damon D'Amato, Caitlin Raynor (Headline Books), Andy Gould, Kate Harvey (Bloomsbury), Dave McKean and Chris Riddell, Mike and Lin Carey, Mickey Choate and Joe Hill, Dara Hoffman (Gauntlet Press), Richard Christian Matheson, Steve Niles, Richard Chizmar and Brian Freeman (Cemetery Dance Publications), Eric Red, Mick Garris, John Gullidge, Kathi and Tom Holland, Graham Masterton, Meghan Tillett (Grand Central), Tim Sullivan, Christa Campbell, William Malone, Fiona Carpenter (Pan Macmillan), Aine Leicht, Ryan Meyer and John Carpenter, Sandy King, Magnet Releasing, Vincent Chong, Mark Chadwick and Peter Crowther (PS Publishing) and Dominic Harman.

Parts of the following interviews were published in the magazines listed, reprinted with kind permission from the publishers: Clive Barker (*DeathRay* #3, *SFX* #163, *Writers' Forum* #78, *Dreamwatch Presents Total Sci-Fi* online), Mike Carey (*DeathRay* #5, *Writers' Forum* #74), Neil Gaiman (*Writers' Forum* #75, *FantasyCon Souvenir Booklet* 2006), James Herbert (*Writers' Forum* #76), Shaun Hutson (*The Dark Side* #134), Joe R. Lansdale (*The Dark Side* #135), Mick Garris (*DeathRay* #7), Stuart Gordon (*DeathRay* #1), William Malone (*The Dark Side* #131) Tim Sullivan (*The Dark Side* #126), Christa Campbell (*Red Scream* Special Obituary Issue), Zach Galligan (*TV Film Memorabilia* #5), Ron Perlman (*TV Film Memorabilia* #12).

LIBRARY OF CONGRESS CATALOGUING-IN-PUBLICATION DATA

Voices in the dark : interviews with horror writers, directors and actors /
Paul Kane and Marie O'Regan ; foreword by Anne Billson.
p. cm.
Includes index.

ISBN 978-0-7864-4634-6
softcover : 50# alkaline paper ∞

1. Horror films—United States—History and criticism. 2. Horror films—Great Britain—History and criticism. 3. Screenwriters—United States—Interviews. 4. Screenwriters—Great Britain—Interviews. 5. Authors, American—20th century—Interviews. 6. Authors, English—20th century—Interviews. 7. Motion picture producers and directors—United States—Interviews. 8. Motion picture producers and directors—Great Britain—Interviews. 9. Motion picture actors and actresses—United States—Interviews. 10. Motion picture actors and actresses—Great Britain—Interviews. I. Kane, Paul, 1973- II. O'Regan, Marie.
PN1995.9.H6V65 2011 791.43'615—dc22 2010036433

British Library cataloguing data are available

© 2011 Paul Kane and Marie O'Regan. All rights reserved

*No part of this book may be reproduced or transmitted in any form
or by any means, electronic or mechanical, including photocopying
or recording, or by any information storage and retrieval system,
without permission in writing from the publisher.*

Front cover: *The Fog* (1980, AVCO Embassy Pictures; courtesy John Gullidge)

Manufactured in the United States of America

*McFarland & Company, Inc., Publishers
Box 611, Jefferson, North Carolina 28640
www.mcfarlandpub.com*

To horror fans ... everywhere.

# Table of Contents

*Acknowledgments* .................................................. viii
*Foreword by Anne Billson* ........................................ 1
*Introduction* ....................................................... 3

## PART ONE: WRITERS

Clive Barker ................ 7
Mike Carey .................. 18
Neil Gaiman ................. 28
James Herbert ............... 40
Joe Hill .................... 50
Shaun Hutson ................ 61
Joe R. Lansdale ............. 70
Graham Masterton ............ 80
Richard Christian Matheson .. 88
Steve Niles ................. 96
Sarah Pinborough ............ 108

## PART TWO: DIRECTORS

John Carpenter .............. 117
Mick Garris ................. 123
Stuart Gordon ............... 133
Tom Holland ................. 144
William Malone .............. 153
Peter Medak ................. 165
Eric Red .................... 171
Tim Sullivan ................ 181
Rob Zombie .................. 191

## PART THREE: ACTORS

Christa Campbell ............ 201
Zach Galligan ............... 210
Betsy Palmer ................ 220
Ron Perlman ................. 229
Alex Vincent ................ 239

*Index* ............................................... 247

# *Acknowledgments*

Thanks go to the following for their help with organizing and securing the interviews for this book: Erik Kritzer; Rehana Razvi; Ed Peters; Mick Garris; David Bidwell of The Monster Company (*www.themonstercompany.co.uk*); Katie James; Angie and Ryan of Big Deal Pro; Sarah Martin; George Walkley; Bryn Hammond; Hillary Golding; and Samantha Smith.

# *Foreword by Anne Billson*

Horror gets a bad press. At best, it's regarded with scorn, like a spotty adolescent habit, a refuge in fantasy which needs to be outgrown so we can face facts and grow up. At worst, it's viewed as a corrupting influence which ought to be stamped out, especially when society's moral guardians or publicity-seeking backbenchers are on the lookout for a scapegoat to drum up tabloid outrage. More than a thousand years after *Beowulf*, more than 400 years after *Titus Andronicus*, more than 100 years after *Dracula* and after a century of cinema, horror remains perhaps the most despised and reviled of genres, one that has yet to be accorded even that limited measure of respect occasionally bestowed on crime stories or science fiction.

In fact, horror often overlaps with both crime and science fiction, not to mention other genres such as romance, the historical yarn, comedy and social realism. Because what its unthinking critics don't understand—and what a perusal of the following pages will make clear—is that "horror" is a versatile term. It can be applied to Gothic fiction, ghost stories, fantasy, morality tales, Grand Guignol, psychothrillers and outright splatter. In the cinema, it can embrace the Expressionist nightmares of Weimar Germany, the dark fairy tales of Universal and Hammer Films, the zombies of George Romero, the body horror of David Cronenberg, slasher movies and the torture-porn of the *Saw* franchise and its like. The house of horror doesn't have a dress code, and its fans don't have to think or behave in a certain way in order to be admitted; all comers are welcome. Just so long as they're willing to be shocked out of their socks, or for their spine to be tingled, or for their own mortality to be dangled before their eyes.

In short, horror covers the waterfront in subject and style, but what its many different manifestations have in common is an ability to tap into our subconscious like no other genre. Horror stories have always been a way of addressing our deepest fears and desires, those ideas and emotions it might not always be possible for us to articulate even if we wanted to. Sometimes these fears and desires are smuggled past our defenses disguised as zombies or werewolves—not in an attempt to slip one over on the censors (though there was that too, back in the day) but because it's a way for us to reflect on notions about death, decay and the human condition which in their unadulterated forms would be just too vast, distressing or embarrassing to contemplate. And maybe a tad boring, as well. Who has time for grim social realist tracts about old age and disease when Jeff Goldblum is providing a running commentary on the breakdown of his own body in *The Fly*? Who wants to struggle through an intellectual analysis of man's propensity for evil when you can read all about it in *Dr. Jekyll and Mr. Hyde*? Who wants to watch a dry documentary about consumer culture? Wouldn't you rather watch Romero's *Dawn of the Dead*, in which four people fend off flesh-eating zombies in a commodity-stocked shopping mall?

It's because horror stories tend to approach their themes more obliquely than other genres that they often succeed in getting deep under our skin where more self-consciously "serious" mainstream treatments will fail to make even the slightest dent on the surface. Horror draws on metaphors that are not polished and hermetically sealed, but misshapen or amorphous, like the monsters themselves, which leaves all the more room for us to interpret them on a personal level. Putting a name to our fears may be the first step towards mastering them, but so much horror operates in the twilight zone of the literally unspeakable that it appeals as much to the instincts as to the intellect.

But horror fans don't need to have their preferred genre validated, least of all by the self-styled arbiters of cultural taste. They are already aware that Stephen King or Ramsey Campbell offer portraits of our society and culture that are at least as evocative as the more critically respected work of John Updike, say, or Ian McEwan. The fact that most national newspaper film critics dismiss horror films with a couple of glib remarks at the end of their columns or that many literary reviewers don't even give horror fiction the time of day doesn't stop aficionados from going to see those films or reading those books. Because we're all members of a club, and we know its worth. We don't want to be part of the safe, smug, polite mainstream culture, which contents itself with splashing around in the shallows where we're used to riding the waves and plunging into the depths, where the real monsters are. We don't need to grow up and face reality, because horror is already presenting us with truths more pertinent and troubling than anything in a so-called grown-up world which refuses to acknowledge anything beyond the material and mundane. On the ocean of popular culture, we are the pirates, the explorers and the outsiders. We don't pander to the received wisdom of what art and literature should be. We know what we like. We are horror fans.

Anne Billson is a writer and photographer. She has written three horror novels (*Suckers*, *Stiff Lips* and *The Ex*) and monographs on *The Thing* (part of the BFI's Modern Classics series) and *Buffy the Vampire Slayer*. From 1992 to 2001 she was the film critic of the *Sunday Telegraph* and now writes a regular column on cinema for *The Guardian*. She lives in Paris.

# *Introduction*

This book came about by accident.

Both of us have been working in the field of genre journalism for some time. We write reviews, articles and interview people for a living—or, at least *one* of our livings (others including fiction writing and editing, as well as teaching). But neither of us had thought about compiling our interviews until a colleague said to us one day: "I guess at some point you'll put some of these together in a book, right?"

So that was it; that was the day *Voices in the Dark* was born. We already had a number of interviews completed—as anyone who works in the non-fiction world knows, you always end up with more than actually sees the light of day—but we thought it would be nice to complement this with some brand new interviews just for the book. So, while some of the material in this book has been seen, often only in part, before, there is just as much, if not more, that hasn't.

It then became a question of how we could make our book different from the other interview books that are out there. The answer to that was to make it a book of interviews of people involved in the horror scene across the board, featuring writers, directors *and* actors (originally we hoped to include FX people as well, but time and space considerations wouldn't allow it. These key personnel may warrant a book all their own, at some point in the future?). If we ourselves are fans of a particular writer, and director and actor, then it makes sense that there are fans out there who have similar interests. (Although some of the people featured here do more than one of these jobs, such as write *and* direct, we've included them in the category they're probably best known for.)

If we've done our job correctly—asking the right questions and including only the information relevant to the task at hand—you should find insights into the creative minds of those who provide and help create the books, television programs and films horror enthusiasts have enjoyed and continue to enjoy every single day, from their backgrounds and early influences, to why they undertook specific projects.

We're very grateful to all the interviewees, for their time and their candid answers, and especially to Anne Billson for agreeing to contribute the foreword for the book.

Finally, thanks to you—the reader and follower of horror in all its forms. We hope we've given you something here that you won't find in other such books: rare and unique glimpses into the dark we all love so much.

# PART ONE

*Writers*

# Clive Barker

Clive Barker was born in Liverpool, England, in 1952. He began his creative career there, writing, directing and acting for the stage, before moving to London. Since then, he has penned such bestsellers as *The Books of Blood, Weaveworld, Imajica, The Great and Secret Show, The Thief of Always, Everville, Sacrament, Galilee, Coldheart Canyon*, and the highly acclaimed fantasy series *Abarat*, for which he has produced numerous paintings. As a screenwriter, director and film producer, he is credited with the *Hellraiser* and *Candyman* pictures as well as *Nightbreed, Lord of Illusions, Gods and Monsters* and *The Midnight Meat Train*. Clive lives in Los Angeles, California.

---

*In the back of* **The Thief of Always,** *there's a picture of you as a little boy. Were you always off on flights of fancy like Harvey in that book?*

Yes. That was down to David Dodds, who used to be my personal assistant and later went back to his profession of nursing—he's in America now, doing nursing, which he loves. But for 13 years he was my personal assistant and he said, "You know, you should put a picture of yourself as a kid into the back of the book." And there was one picture which my Dad took in which I have my short haircut and round National Health glasses; they used to be made of pink plastic. If you can think of one thing that was the least attractive thing to make the frames from...! This pink plastic that actually looked like, I don't know, badger vomit [*laughs*]. I was tending towards the tubby side, as Winnie the Pooh would say, and would get a little fatter before I thinned out. Obviously I got bullied and knocked about a bit for that when I got into my junior school. But yeah, I was doing my dreaming and I had all the books that were classics for all of us, sitting on my little bookcase. It was really a pride for me to be able to build up a little library like this.

*Do you ever miss your days with The Dog Company [Barker's early theater group], and do you have a desire to direct for the theater again?*

I miss communal, creative activity. That's one of the reasons why I still involve myself in some small way with producing movies; I don't think I'm going to direct a film again. So yes, I do miss it. Do I miss having cold baked beans to eat every night? No. Do I miss the sense I had through my 20s that I was wandering, that I didn't have a destination? No, I don't miss that at all. They were tough times, we didn't have any money and yet there was this urge to tell stories that came out of everyone. Really, I realized through my 20s when I'd suddenly get commissions for plays—I was commissioned three summers in a row to write plays for community theaters—that, much as I love the communal stuff, there were visions in my head that didn't get onto the stage and *couldn't* indeed get onto the stage. I was writing these small stories and had no sense, really, of how to market them or take them into the world. But I had an agent and he sent some of them off to [publishers] Victor Gollancz, and apparently Livia Gollancz—whom I've never met—read the first few stories and said, "This man is mad." So they were sent off to Sphere books, where a lovely lady called Barbara Boote plucked them from the slush pile. She called my agent and gave me—for the first three books—the massive sum of £2,000. Then for *Damnation Game* another £2,000, then for the next three books, the completion of the six *Books of Blood*, another £2,000. So I got a good £6,000 out of those seven books.

*How did it feel to see your fiction in print?*

It was amazing. There's that "pinch me" sense. Also the sense that you're getting to people who don't know you—don't know who you are, how your head works—but are now getting these images, these dreams. Over the years I've become friends with a lot of these people, and that's tremendous too. It's a very fulfilling feeling. I've had in my life two moments when I thought, wow, if I die now it's okay. One was when the first *Books of Blood* came through the door, printed. Then when, after a long period of sweat and struggle, *Imajica* was published and came through the door. I felt the same sense of completion. Maybe this is just me, but I'm always looking for a sense of how can I ever feel that a job is done and finished—and I can relax and step away. It always feels to me that there's an energy in me which is pulling me back to the desk even the moment after I've finished. But there are these lovely moments where I ought to feel the same thing; I've delivered the latest book of *Abarat* which I hope will give me that sense of completion. It'll be all right to drop a house on me if you wanted to then. But the moment passes and you go back to your desk.

**Clive Barker at FantasyCon in 2006. Photograph by Paul Kane.**

*Doug Bradley once said, about the early days, it was more about why aren't people getting it. Was that frustrating at times?*

Horribly frustrating. I remember every bad review we, as a theater company, got. I remember every bad review I, as a writer, got. Ask me about the good ones, I have more difficulty. I think that's a universal thing, isn't it? You know the names of the buggers who gave you a bad one, their addresses and how many children they have [*laughs*] and they should be afraid, they should be very afraid. No, I'm kidding [*laughs*].

*You set some of your stories in London, some of the atmospheric parts—in particular Highgate, Crouch End.*

I lived in Crouch End, I lived in a house 13 houses from where Peter Straub wrote *Ghost Story*, which is one of my favorite horror novels. And it was amazing, counting, that it should not only be the same street but 13 houses apart. Too weird. I love California and I love the life. But there are some things that England presents and gives you which only England could. And it's to do with childhood sometimes. I miss November 5 and I will usually call home on that night so I can hear fireworks going off. I miss the smell in the air around that time. The last Christmas I spent in England I was doing my final work on *Imajica* in my house on Wimpole Street, which I'd sold but had not yet vacated. I had sent my whole life in 147 boxes to America, and there

**Cover artwork by Dominic Harman for the new UK Harper-Collins edition of *Imajica* (courtesy Dominic Harman).**

was just a desk. That's not been lost, the desk—it's just recently come back into our hands again, which is wonderful. So there was just a desk, a chair and a manuscript—and what used to be called a record player ... which you wound up ... no, I'm joking [*laughs*]. It snowed that Christmas, and I was alone, I stayed with the manuscript. And I got this overwhelming sense that I was doing something terribly wrong, that I should stay here; that being in this place, looking out at the snow and finishing my book was about as perfect an experience as I could have. Then I registered, well, that's the point, idiot: That's about as good as it's *going* to get, so move on. I'd just turned 40 and I figured if I didn't go around that time, I wouldn't go at all. And I haven't regretted it because the new experiences have given me books. I don't believe I would have written *Abarat* had I not been painting in the color- and light-saturated world of California. Just as David Hockney's color sense erupted when he got out there, and I was very much following in Hockney's footsteps.

***You visited prison, thanks to Douglas Bennett, as research for* The Damnation Game. *What was that like?***

I met a fellow who was fully a foot taller than I was, who invited me into his cell, which might have been a mistake [*laughs*]. He had little marks across his neck that said "cut here." He was a huge guy, and he'd read the *Books of Blood*. I didn't ask any of them what they did, it just seemed rude: "What do you do for a living?" "Oh, I murder people." But I got insights, and this is one of the reasons why I still try and visit the places I write about. I'm writing about Hell right now [*laughs*]. You do get insights that you wouldn't otherwise get. We had two days [at the prison]. I didn't stay overnight, they don't do bed and breakfast—and there was a guard who was really very proud. He pointed out, for instance, that it looked like a church. It was built by Victorian moralists to look like a gothic church. But he then took me—and I wrote about this, got a whole story out of this—out into the hanging shed, and a lawn beyond where all the bodies of Ruth Ellis and James Hanratty and so on were buried on a sort of piece of perfect greenery, a perfect lawn with no markers. I asked him, "Why are there no markers?" and he said, "We know where they are and the Queen knows where they are, and that's all that matters. These bodies are the possession of the Crown," which I thought was chillingly strange.

*The notion of hidden realms like the ones in* Weaveworld, The Great and Secret Show, Imajica *and* Abarat *is very appealing. Is this something to do with wanting to escape the everyday?*

Why are we all here? What do we all have in common? One of the things we must all have in common is a certain sense that the ordinary day-to-day life just doesn't fulfill us. I went to fantasy books as a kid because I hated my childhood; I was bored, I was bullied, I was profoundly unhappy. And I wrote and drew as a child, a world I could step into in my imagination and say, that's *my* world; I have my secret friends. My godfather was a ship's captain—Mr. William Weatherall. I mean, can you ask for a better captain's name than Billy Weatherall? Uncle Bill would come back from his voyages and the first thing he would do was go to Clive. When I was four or five I'd give him accounts of what my friends were doing. Now I had a lot of friends, secret friends. Some of the little secret friends, believe it or not, are in *Abarat*; they remain crystal clear in my head. The older I get, the more interesting theoretical physics becomes. The more possible—I'm not going to say *likely*, but the more possible, plausible, the notion of these other worlds becomes. I'm definitely less interested in accessing what is out in space, I'm accessing through our spirit, accessing through our imaginations, the other worlds which are waiting, just out of sight in front of us. I believe that. And I think that our urge to write and read fantasy is to some extent a primal need to have that

Alternative artwork created by Dominic Harman for the new UK HarperCollins edition of *Weaveworld* (courtesy Dominic Harman).

suspicion validated. And maybe it's where we go after we die, maybe it's where we came from before we were born. Fantasy has more to do with reality than a good deal of naturalistic fiction does. Naturalistic fiction—fuck it. I live that, right? Give me something to dream for.

*There are a lot of references to the sea and oceans in your fiction: Quiddity in* **Great and Secret Show,** *the sea in* **Abarat.** *Where does that stem from?*

Well, my godfather was a ship's captain, my dad a sailor in the Royal Navy, during the war. My brother a ship's engineer. My grandfather a ship's cook; twice sunk, twice declared dead. We once found [amongst] my grandma's papers, two letters, one from the tub he worked for and one from the Ministry of Defense declaring that Albert Barker was indeed dead. And my father told us on one of the occasions, three or four months had passed and Albert suddenly appeared at the front door, with a cigarette hanging out of his mouth, said that he was home and to put the kettle on. No telegram, nothing like that, he'd simply found his way home. And presumably he still had some tales to tell

**The cover of IDW's graphic novel adaptation of** *The Great and Secret Show,* **Collected First Volume, with artwork by Gabriel Rodriguez (2006, IDW; courtesy IDW).**

when he died of emphysema, from too much smoking, before I was really smart enough, intelligent enough to figure out I should be sitting listening to him.

*Will there be another book in the* **Cabal** *series and is there any news on the extended edition of* **Nightbreed***?*

There's 25 minutes which I think are missing. The last, not particularly pleasant conversation I had with Fox on the subject went: "Yes, we have it. Of course we have it." "Well, can I have it for the special edition?" "We don't know where it is exactly, it's in our vaults or in our warehouse." And I said, "Just give me one of your guys and I'll go along with him." But they wouldn't let me do that. Fox doesn't see the upside to it.* As far as

---

*\*Since this interview took place, Clive's friend Mark Miller has been pursuing the missing footage and was told that it could be accessed "at any time," but that there wasn't a big enough audience for it. A petition on Clive's official site, Revelations, began soon after. Phil and Sarah Stokes, who run Revelations, also unearthed a 145-minute VHS workprint version of the movie from mid–1989, which is a staggering 44 minutes longer than the theatrical release.*

doing more with the *Nightbreed*, yes, characters are starting to emerge. It'll happen very, very slowly.

***Will there be another book of the art?***

Damn right, yeah. One 900-page, big, beat-someone-to-death-with-it kind of book. And it's all here, but it has to find its moments. The *Abarat* books have turned out to be more successful than I expected and are now in ... 39 languages, I think. So this has thrown me a little bit off course; I thought I had everything neatly planned. But we'll get there, we'll get there.

***Galilee** seems to reveal something of your writing process, because the character Maddox is actually writing a book. Are there parts of Maddox that are parts of you?*

Actually, the way Maddox writes the book is the antithesis of the way I write. I get to my desk between 8:30 and 9 every day, seven days a week. Maddox is kicked into it by circumstance, and I've always known somehow or other that I wanted to tell stories. Stories put order where there is disorder. Stories make sense where there is nonsense. It may be a temporary order but it's reassuring to us. Isn't that why as kids we say, "Tell us that story again, Mum?" "Tell that story again, Dad?" Because there's a comfort in knowing that the story will come full circle and come to its end again. Unhappy endings, ironic endings, that old-fashioned irony is yesterday's business. Irony is easy. Now we have to get on with the business of real solutions and real ideas. We have to be bold and courageous and vivid and a little crazy. I got through times when I was scared of the craziness in me, and I'm coming back round, full circle as it were, to be glad that there is this crazy voice in me that does these weird things. That writes this stuff in the middle of the night, so that when I get up I say "What the fuck is that?" but find that there's actually something useful there. You know, Pinhead appeared in a little sketch in the middle of the night. There are gifts given to us by our subconscious to use as the imagination.

Cover artwork by Dominic Harman for the UK HarperCollins edition of *Cabal* (courtesy Dominic Harman).

***With the 20th anniversary of** Hellraiser *having now passed, how do you feel about the whole* Hellraiser *mythos?*

I think it's amazing—and this isn't just with *Hellraiser*. What happens is that the readers and the viewers teach you what moves them, what means something to them. And there's a wonderful lack of consistency between people's enthusiasms. I love that. One person will love *Galilee*, another will think it's a piece of crap. And sometimes you feel like a football, kicked from one end of the pitch to the other. But maybe that's healthy, maybe that's what keeps you strong.

*Why did you decide to take time out from* **Scarlet Gospels** *to write* **Mr. B. Gone?**

Well, *Scarlet Gospels*, as you know, is a bloody big book. It's a very dark book, even by my standards. And I wanted it to be my definitive visit to Hell. I also wanted it to be—and it's intended to be—my farewell to Doug's Pinhead, because whenever I bring the character to mind, it's Doug's face I see. As you know, it's also got D'Amour in, so it's Scott Bakula's face I also see in that role. But I'd been working on it a long time and I'd got into a very—I'm being honest with you here—I got into a very, very dark place. There's a line from Nietzsche that often gets quoted: "If you stare long enough into the abyss, the abyss stares at you." That was what was happening. I had got into a place where I felt as though I needed to take a step away from the work and take a breather. Just because the depth of the journey was taking its toll on ... on my health, actually. And this is unusual for me, but it does reflect how dark the material is. Having decided to do that, the Devil finds work for idle hands. I'm not the kind of guy who can say, "Okay, well, I'm going to step away from this novel for a couple of months." I have to write every day; it's in my bones, I can't *not*

Oliver Parker as Peloquin, one of the monsters from Midian in *Nightbreed* (1990, Morgan Creek Productions; photograph by Murray Close, courtesy John Gullidge).

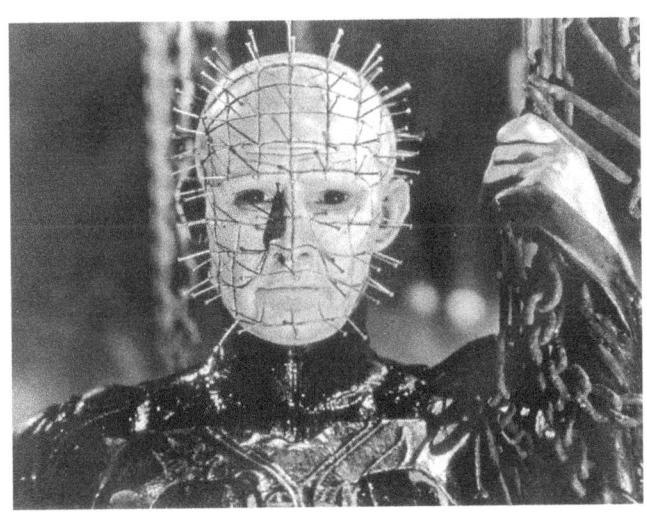

The iconic figure of Pinhead (Doug Bradley) in *Hellraiser* (1987, New World International; photograph by Murray Close, courtesy John Gullidge).

do it. So the question was: Do I start something, do I write a couple of short stories? Somehow that didn't feel right. I've had for a long time this idea of writing a book that really addressed the audience, the reader, in a way which was relatively new. I couldn't find anyone who'd attempted this before, where the book is speaking to the reader. But I thought it's such an obvious idea in one sense.

*It struck me that* **Mr. B. Gone** *is almost like second person, where you're bringing the reader into your confidence.*

Yeah. Absolutely right. In a way, what I'm doing in the book is sharing secrets, isn't it? I wanted the readers to feel as though they have been brought into the confidence of a character, Jakabok Botch, who may or may not be lying to them. Or at least polishing events a little bit. But who certainly has a tale to tell. That was the other thing I wanted to celebrate: storytelling. So rather than it simply being a series of events which take us to a conclusion, there would be little fragments of other elements, other characters that would give the reader a real sense that this is a life.

*How long did it take you to write?*

Five months. Including different drafts. I wrote it in a sort of madness. Once I started, I couldn't stop. It was strange, it was very strange. I even suspended painting for a while, which I haven't done for a long time and was not good for me physically. I actually keep fit by painting, and it wasn't good to suspend that. But Jakabok, dammit, called me back to the page. Even when I was weary, I couldn't shut him up, he was there in my head. I knew what the next sentence was, always.

*Even though he's a demon, there's something very human about Jakabok. The reality and his upbringing could have been somebody in our world.*

Yeah, that was, in many ways, the way I approached the whole endeavor. There was another version of this book that I absolutely didn't want to write, which was the one which was filled with over-the-top *Grand Guignol* scenes; very ripe, salty language. I'd done that kind of demon before. I'd also done the elegant demon, in Pinhead. I wanted this to be a man with two tails [*laughs*] and the burn marks erasing so much of what would have made him demonic. But now his past is making him hopefully a much more accessible character. Because I think if you were to meet him, you might feel the kind of pity you would feel for Quasimodo.

*He's basically carrying his emotional, internal scars on his skin.*

And it's no accident that those scars are caused by words. It's the journals that are being burned. It's his secret thoughts that are being burned, and that's the bonfire that his father left him to cook in. I think we can relate to that, all of us. The idea that our secrets can maim us, rob us of the clarity of our origins. Once we start to hide ourselves, there's no stopping us. I think one of the things that is sad about him as a character is that he never really understands who he is 'til it's too damned late.

*There's as much to hate in Jakabok as there is to love, isn't there?*

That's exactly how I feel. So you take him scene by scene, the way that we all take the ones that we share our lives with. Nobody is completely consistent. Nobody is one thing and one thing only. We live our lives in a state of constant change, constant re-evaluation if we're honest about it. We might try and paper over the cracks, if you will, and pretend that nothing more is really going on. We might say, "Oh, did I say that? I didn't really mean that. I meant...." We might try and make the inconsistencies look like consistencies, but the truth of the matter is that we are all of us changeable and the opinions we feel strongly at one point in our lives, we may come to think of completely differently at a later point. Nothing is certain, except that nothing is certain.

*We're all heroes of our own lives...*

That's right. We're writing history from our point of view, so we're bandleaders, aren't we?

*There's almost a playing down of the horrific aspects this time, isn't there?*

Absolutely, and that was a conscious decision because in the end I've been there, I've done that. What was the purpose of going back to that? On occasion, certainly when the nasty stuff starts to happen, I don't hold back. But again, you have to look at the voice of the character; the character isn't going to linger describing innards, that's commonplace for him. That was one of the places I did cut back, because I realized I was writing in the voice of Clive Barker, not in the voice of Jakabok Botch.

*Do you think that makes it more frightening, because it's like an afterthought when he mentions these things?*

I hope it does—almost nonchalant. It's not like he spends a lot of time over it. There it is, there's the cold truth of it. Next.

*Were the relationship aspects, the mother-father, his relationship with his father, based on anything you've observed yourself?*

Yes, there was a lot of stuff I've either seen or known. I don't want to say too much. It's certainly not my own mother and father. Very far from it. But yes, the cruelty of both father and mother—the cruelty of the world. This is a very dark book in that sense.

*Is there an influence in this depiction of Hell from* **Dante's Inferno**?

Yes, absolutely. I thought, well, we're not going to linger here for any length of time. So rather than spend a lot of time on creating a new Hell, if you will—which would then apply to my character to do what he would do, which is describe it; why would he describe it? it's his

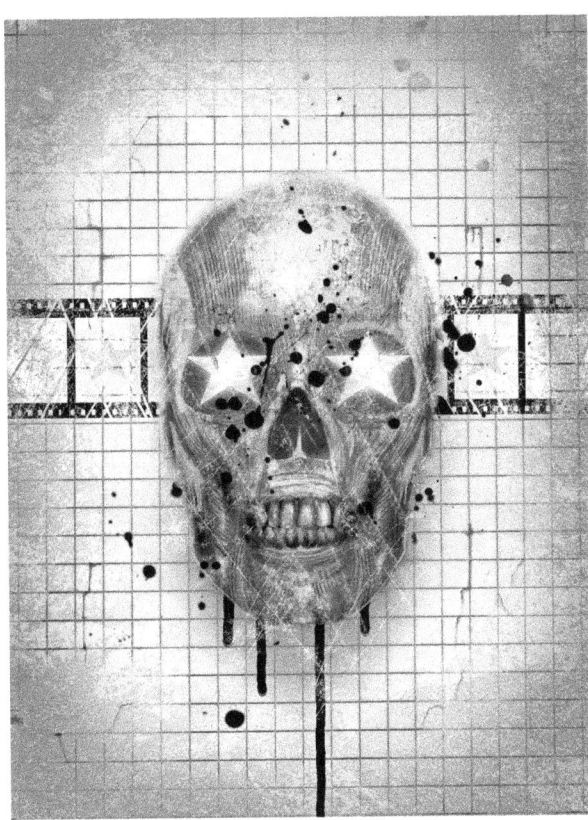

**Alternative artwork by Dominic Harman for the UK HarperCollins edition of** *Coldheart Canyon* **Dominic Harman (courtesy Dominic Harman).**

world—I decided to just reference the levels, the idea of the circles from Dante, then just move on. That wasn't the subject of the book, the subject of the book is a demon's adventures in the world.

*How do you feel the character changes as he's telling his story throughout the book?*

In one sense he doesn't change at all, because he's writing from a single point of view—and he's venting. But I think the life itself that he describes changes from being a very innocent and trusting creature in a weird way, albeit a burned and maimed creature, into being something entirely other. I mean, he has seen into the secret of Heaven and Hell. He has seen the great conspiracy. How can you ever be the same again?

*There are some great names in there. How do you come up with these?*

I'm a lover of those things. That's one of the things I keep; I've had Jakabok for a while because it has Jack in the Box in there. And it has "Jack in the Book," you see. So I liked that. I like the fact that his second name was Botch, because the homage to that was nice with Mr. B. Gone, but I am also Mr. B. So there was a nice thing going on there. The rest of it is just my love of the sounds of words.

*Did you do any sketches of the characters this time?*

No, very much not, because I thought it was important that everything be contained within the words. In fact, at some point somebody suggested that I do some illustrations, and I said, "Christ, no. Absolutely not." This is about characters who live in our imaginations, conjured through these words. I don't want to do anything that could compromise that conjuring.

*So in a sense it's the opposite of* Abarat*?*

*Exactly* the opposite of *Abarat*. Beautifully put, and beautifully observed. Not everybody would get that. It is the opposite. This is a book about the word. Where the word

Paul Kane (left) interviewing Clive Barker on stage at FantasyCon 2006. Photograph by Marie O'Regan.

comes from, where the word goes, what the word can achieve, what the word can fail to do. At one point he actually talks about what words can't do. So really in a way it's a book which I hope both celebrates The Word and also points out its liabilities—the danger of The Word.

*Finally, which are you proudest of, the theater work, paintings, fiction?*

I can't make that distinction. I am proud of staying reasonably true to my desire to make fantasy which would include my sexuality, my life, my belief about God and the Devil and all things in between. There isn't much in the worlds of the fantastic that appear on the pages of those novels that I don't in some way or another believe to be true. I might not believe it to be *literally* true in the way that something in front of me is true; but who cares whether it's literally true? What I care about is that these higher, more complicated things are used in a sense that they can be applied in some way to our lives, can change our lives, enrich our lives. And I think great fantasy and great horror fiction in some way or another draws us closer to the puzzle, the heart of the puzzle which when we wake at three in the morning in a cold sweat and think, "Oh God, I'm getting older, and I can't stop it—and my life is in chaos...." All these things that go through your head at those times, when I look for order I go to art. And I suppose I want to be somebody who has added to the list of works which can be called works of fantasy. It would be great just to be an imaginer, that would be cool.

# Mike Carey

Born in Liverpool in 1959, Mike Carey worked as a teacher for fifteen years before starting to write comics. When he began to receive regular commissions from DC Comics, he gave up the day job. Since then, he has worked for both DC and Marvel Comics, writing storylines for some of the world's most iconic characters. He is the acclaimed writer of *Lucifer* (which garnered numerous international awards and was nominated for five Eisners) and *Hellblazer* (now filmed as *Constantine*). He has also written extended runs for Marvel's fan-favorite titles *X-Men* and *Ultimate Fantastic Four*, the comic book adaptation of Neil Gaiman's *Neverwhere*, and the screenplay *Frost Flowers*, an erotic ghost story. His Felix Castor series of books include *The Devil You Know*, *Vicious Circle*, *Dead Men's Boots*, *Thicker Than Water* and *The Naming of Beasts*. He lives in London with his wife, Linda (also a novelist and screenwriter), their three children and a cat called Tasha.

---

*How did you get into writing?*

I guess it's something I've always done, on a hobby basis, going right back to when I was twelve, thirteen years old. Writing was just something I did for pleasure. But then I started to write reviews and articles for fanzines like *Fantasy Advertiser*. I sort of backed into comics through writing on an unpaid basis, just for my own fulfillment. But I think most people write because they have to. It's something inside them that comes out ... and I'm the same.

*So did you get into comics as a kid? Did you grow up reading them?*

Very much. In fact, I learned to read from comics. There was a comic called *Wham!* You know Leo Baxendale, the great British humor strip writer-artist who worked for the *Beano*, for DC Thompson, for many years? He had a falling out with them so he went to Fleetway IPC. They gave him a comic of his own, *Wham!* Then they folded that and started *Pow*, then folded that and started *Smash*, but it was always Baxendale's characters, Baxendale's vision. I was completely addicted to that stuff, from age four through to about age seven. Then my older brother, Chris, introduced me to American superhero comic books, and again it was an epiphany. I carried on reading comics passionately and constantly all the way through my childhood and into my teens. I lost sight of them for a few years round about the time I went to university, and it was Chris Claremont's *X-Men* that brought me back in. I was walking past a newsagent's when I was in Liverpool to visit my parents, and I saw an issue of *X-Men*. I didn't recognize any of the characters on the cover except for Cyclops, so I thought, "Something's obviously happened while I was looking the other way." I bought it and really, really enjoyed it. I went back and I got the whole of the Claremont run from #94 onwards—which actually cost a lot of money, more than

I could afford at the time, because they'd already become collectors' items. So I got back into the game at that point, and I've never stopped.

*You've said you got your first glimpse of Hell while your parents were working in a bakery.*

[*Laughs*] I did say that, sorry; it was a bit melodramatic. But my dad worked—as they put it—behind the ovens. He would stand behind the oven in temperatures like the stoke hold of a ship, which he also did for many years, with these enormous asbestos gloves right the way up to his elbows. He would just take out a whole rack of loaves, take out another rack, put them on another belt to be trundled away and wrapped. But he couldn't stop because there would be a backup in the machine. If the gloves slipped, he would still have to take the rack off. So he'd come home with these appalling burns. It really was like something from Dante's Inferno, because he worked 12-hour shifts. Just a horrible, horrible way to earn a living, and he did that for 30 years.

*Didn't your mother work there as well?*

She was a cleaner. "Ancillary worker," as they put it. As were two of her sisters. Walton in Liverpool was one of these places where you settle in the same street as your parents, or the next street along so there are these huge extended families—clans—living in very small areas. So yeah, most of the Careys at one time or another worked in Taylor's bakery.

*Have you always been attracted to the dark side of things?*

I've always been attracted to fantasy. Most of what I read for pleasure is weird stuff: horror, fantasy, science

Mike Carey (photograph by Lin Carey, courtesy Mike Carey).

*The Devil You Know* UK paperback cover (2008, Orbit; courtesy Sean Garrehy, Orbit).

fiction. I can read straight fiction, straight literary fiction—I did an English degree, so I have read widely in other areas. But I love fantasy, I love stuff that goes off at a right angle to reality; that's what I'm drawn to. The dark stuff is just one aspect of that.

*How did you learn to write comics in the right format?*

By looking at Alan Moore scripts [*laughs*], which was probably a mistake. I think his scripts were the first ones to appear. Because they are such beautiful literary works in their own right, publishers were quite keen to show them off. The trouble is, they're a bad model for other people to follow, because it's (A) labor intensive and (B) if you're not Alan Moore, it's probably sending you in the wrong direction because most artists have a better visual imagination than most writers. When I wrote my first comic script, *Legions of Hell*, I was literally describing where all the furniture in a room was, if people were drinking coffee I'd describe what was on the mug. It was just bananas, not trusting the artist even to wipe his own nose. That script was offered to Paul Grist, who turned it down. He said, "It's an interesting story, but what do *I* do? I'm not a machine." So that's how I learned, and then I had to unlearn it and develop a style of my own which is more telegraphic.

*So what year would this be?*

Oh, I think we'd be talking early to mid–80s. I mean, I had dabbled before then, but that was when I was first seriously trying to write full comic scripts.

*How did you first start to get published, and when did you make the transition from teaching to writing?*

It was a very slow transition because I'm just naturally cautious. I was doing some work for *Fantasy Advertiser*; I did reviews, then started writing extended articles and critical appraisals of people like [Grant] Morrison and [Neil] Gaiman. The distributor, Neptune, who'd taken over *Fantasy Advertiser*, started doing their own comics line. They asked Martin Skidmore, the editor of *Fantasy Advertiser*, to edit their comics line, Trident. So, because I already knew Martin, I thought I'd pitch him a couple of ideas: *Aquarius*—which was an embarrassing *Watchmen* rip-off—and *Legions of Hell*. I wrote the first three scripts but the company went bankrupt so the comics never appeared. But through that I met Ken Meyer, Jr., who was doing the art on my superhero story *Aquarius*, and through Ken I met Lurene Haines, who was married to Dave Dorman for many years. She did a couple of "How To" books about getting into comics. Lurene and Dave were trying to set up a comics agency called Big Time and they offered to represent me. But because the agency didn't yet exist, they basically said, "We'll do it for free, and if we get anything formally set up later you can start paying us." She found me work with Malibu and later with Caliber. So that's how I broke into the American scene. From Malibu I went to Caliber, from Caliber I went to DC because everything I brought out I was sending to Alisa Kwitney who was the editor on the last issues of *Sandman* and on the first issues of "The Dreaming." I was just saying: "I want to work for you, look at this." Which is what you have to do. I didn't stop teaching until the year 2000, and even then I only went on a sabbatical—it later turned into a permanent one. I just wouldn't let go of the salary until I had enough money in the bank to survive a year.

*What was it like to eventually be writing characters like Constantine and the X-Men?*

Fantastic! It's a dream job for me. I shouldn't get paid for it. In some ways it wasn't as easy as I thought it would be. My first-ever superhero script was actually *Firestorm*. I tried out for *Firestorm* but it never happened for various reasons. But I remember sending the first script in to Dan Rasler who was the editor, and he called me up and said, "You haven't done this before, have you?" I said, "No, I haven't." He said, "Because you've actually got 15 pages of fight scenes. You can afford to pace yourself a little bit." There are differences in the pacing, especially on a team book like *X-Men*. You've got to make sure that they all get their face time, they all get the beats that they need. With *Lucifer* it was similar; I ended up with a massive cast in the end, but I could pick and choose who was in which storyline, whereas in *The X-Men* they've all got to be there pretty much all of the time.

*You've said you had a lot of freedom when developing the* Sandman *spin-off* Lucifer. *Were you nervous about what creator Neil Gaiman might think?*

Oh yeah. I had a huge amount of performance anxiety at the start. And I think he was conscious of that. He was incredibly generous with his time, and in terms of not digging his heels in, not saying, "You can't do this, you can't do that." He just let me run with stuff. The only thing he was ever exact about was the dialogue of The Endless. He was concerned that they should sound right. When Death came in, in issue #27 of *Lucifer*, there's a sequence where Lucifer says to her, "You have no claim on me." And she says, "I never said I did and I wouldn't have anywhere to put you anyway." Neil said, "She wouldn't say that—'I wouldn't have anywhere to put you.' That suggests she has a realm; she doesn't. She moves people onwards and we never find out where she moves them to." So I had to change that line. Stuff like that, he was looking over my shoulder; the rest of the time he was content to let me do my own falling down and picking myself up. I can remember when we decided to include Mazikeen's ex-husband, Scoria, in a storyline, [editor] Shelly Roeberg e-mailed him and asked, "Is it okay if she has this backstory?" And he wrote back, "I regard Mazikeen and Lucifer as Mike's characters now, and he can do whatever he wants with them," which was incredible. I'm very grateful to Neil.

*How did you decide in which direction to take the character initially, and how much of Neil's Lucifer is in him by the end?*

That's a tough question to answer. I think there's an awful lot of Neil's Lucifer in him to begin with and I think it's really apparent through the first two years of the book, that gradually he morphs into something a little bit differ-

*Vicious Circle* **U.S. paperback cover (2009, Grand Central Publishing; courtesy Meghan Tillett, Grand Central Publishing).**

ent. He starts to become a vessel, a vehicle for me to explore ideas about free will and predestination. But certainly the initial situation, it's as Neil defined it. The fact that Lucifer rebels again, a second time, by resigning from God's plan—by walking out of Hell—is the keynote. And it continues to be throughout: Lucifer is the character who says no to God, the character who refuses to play the game by somebody else's rules, who would rather not be in the game at all than accept somebody else's rules. But while Neil's Lucifer is very much a "calling a spade a spade" kind of guy, my Lucifer becomes a bit more austere, a bit more patrician in his language, gradually.

*Neil has commented that he always said* **Lucifer** *would make a great spin-off but nobody wanted to take it on.*

Well, there is a huge problem you have when you're writing Lucifer as a protagonist, and you don't realize it until you're in the middle of a story arc. There are a large number of things that you cannot make him do. He can never be an action hero, because he only has to exert himself slightly and the opposition are swept away; you can't have Lucifer in a fight, it's inconceivable. Actually it does happen in the end, he fights Fenris, but in most of the stories Lucifer is a catalyst for other people. I think there are these big, big structural problems that you have to think your way around when you put Lucifer into a story. So that may have been part of the problem.

*And what made you say yes?*

How could you say no? It was the call I'd been waiting for all my life [*laughs*].

**Lucifer,** *and* **Sandman** *before it, are family dramas, aren't they? Is there an element of soap opera to them, do you think?*

Yes, I think there probably is, in the sense that soaps have overlapping and convoluted stories about lives going through spectacular changes. I definitely think the central theme of *Lucifer*—which is restated again and again in every arc—is parents and children. All of the most important relationships are parent-child relationships, including the God-Lucifer relationship.

*Why did you decide to have a go at a novel?*

I tried writing novels when I was much younger. Mostly I wrote the first chapter, then the first chapter again, refining and refining and never going anywhere beyond that. The only novel I managed to finish writing, between 1987 and 1990, was called *Dazzle*. It was straight science fiction, about a substance that comes to Earth in a meteorite that effectively grants wishes; it turns some people into superheroes and some people into monsters. It was a massive thing because I had no conception of what planning was. I sent it around to publishers, some of whom said, "Don't call us again or we'll kill you" [*laughs*]. Others said, "There are some good ideas here, but man, you need to learn to write, to think more about what you're doing." So I got really discouraged, threw that into a cupboard and didn't go back to writing prose again until I was writing *Hellblazer*. I'd been talking to Darren Nash, who was the editor of Simon & Schuster's Earthlight list, who then left and went to Orbit. He actually called me up and said, "Would you be interested in pitching something?" I'd been looking at the Anita Blake novels by Laurell K. Hamilton and thinking, well, actually, something set in England, against a backdrop where you've got lots of different kinds of supernatural entities woven into the fabric of everyday life, could be really cool. So I worked up the Felix Castor idea, pitched it, and three novels were commissioned. I guess it was always at the back of my mind, something I wanted to try again. I like telling stories, in lots and lots of different forms. It's one way you keep yourself fresh.

*There appears to be a definite noir influence on the Castor books. And detective classics.*

Castor's a gumshoe exorcist. I love Chandler, so I just put a lot of his beats into it. It is deliberate and I think it's a palette. Noir is just a palette of elements that you can choose from and it can be disastrous if you just pastiche what's already out there. But if you're just paying a nod here and there, I think it's very cool.

*There are certain parallels with John Constantine, aren't there?*

It's been said, yes. But I think it's possible to exaggerate those parallels too much. There are bits of Constantine, and there are bits of Lucifer in there, although they're small bits. There are bits of me, a lot of his backstory is mine, especially in the fourth book. That takes Castor back to Liverpool, to his childhood, investigating something

*Dead Men's Boots* UK paperback cover (2007, Orbit; courtesy Sean Garrehy, Orbit).

that happened to him and his brother when they were quite young. What other strands came together in Felix? I'm interested in good people who do bad things. I think that *is* a Constantine thing, yeah. That like John, Felix has done appalling things to people who he actually loves, people who love and trust him. But he carries the weight with him. He's not a ruthless, amoral bastard, he's just someone who does what's necessary and then can't work it out. He carries it around and gets more and more screwed up by it.

*Where does the interest in religion and exorcism stem from? Is that the Irish Catholic thing?*

Yeah, my Dad was Catholic, my Mum was Anglican, although they both ultimately come from Irish stock so I'm not sure where the Protestantism came from. So I come from almost a mixed race family, if you like, in Liverpool terms, because the sectarian divide in Liverpool is very real, very strong. I grew up in this situation where a lot of my Mum's family wouldn't talk to my Dad, tried to pretend he didn't exist. On the twelfth when the Orange Brigades march, you'd see violence, you'd see people throwing pepper into the eyes of the marchers. The kids who'd dressed up as William and Mary would get stuff thrown at them. So I was steeped in religion, but I always saw religion in negative terms, always saw it from the outside. I saw it as something fascinating; I could see the spiky, intense emotions that are aroused but for me it was a subject of intellectual curiosity, and I've always been mistrustful of belief systems.

*There are some terrific and quite graphic action sequences in the Castor books. How do you go about planning something like that?*

It just flows. I plan out the scenes on a sort of local level. Actually, the first three Castor novels had very, very detailed plans which ran to about 40 pages. But I wouldn't plan out the beats of an action scene, you'd just decide "That's going to happen at some point, and that's going to happen" and the rest you let come as you're writing it. For example, a fight scene from *Dead Man's Boots*, the fact that the woman is going to turn out to be a werewolf is planned, and that Castor is just going to use some foliage from a tree is planned. And the fact that Juliet is going to take frightening damage in the process. But the rest just came.

*Felix doesn't seem to be very lucky. Would you say that's a trait you share?*

I don't think it's a trait we share, but I think unlucky characters are easier to empathize with. We don't want people with perfect lives. It's one of the things I like about Tim Powers, he puts his heroes through hell and then comes up with an ending where most of the damage gets undone. Bad luck is just better from a narrative point of view. Perfection makes you envious. You can think yourself into an unlucky character's shoes. But people like the teen spy, Alex Rider; he's got it all, including a gorgeous adult woman who is his handler. It's a wish fulfillment fantasy, and wish fulfillment fantasies lose their interest really quickly, I think.

*How many books do you see it being, or are you just going to continue until you run out of steam?*

There's definitely something that happens in the sixth book which is huge, which is going to be a climax to everything that has happened so far, and I could stop at that point. Or I could go on. At this point I'd rather go on because I'm still having ideas for stories. But I think we'll sit up and have a look around after book six and see where we are, see what the sales are like and whether Orbit is still happy with me.

*How do you think Felix has changed and developed as a character over time?*

The biggest change is in book one, where he effectively starts to question,

*Thicker Than Water* UK paperback cover (2009, Orbit; courtesy Sean Garrehy, Orbit).

for the first time in his life, what exorcism means and what he's been doing. He makes the change from jobbing exorcist to somebody who protects the dead against the living; that's an important change. I think the events of book two, the fact that he betrays Rafi, lets Rafi down again by preventing Asmodeus from leaving him—I think that is an enormous turning point for him, and obviously it's a turning point in his relationship with Rafi and Pen. He's becoming less certain of himself and his own direction, of the basis of his powers and how he uses them. And he's becoming more interested in the big mysteries that he's been avoiding: Why are the dead rising, where are they coming from, where are they meant to go, what do the demons have to do with this and do they have a plan? The books are littered with characters who are convinced that there is a war coming. That there's going to be a big showdown between the living and the dead, or the living and the undead, and they're already preparing their armaments for this conflict, this apocalyptic battle. Castor doesn't endorse that idea, but I think he does become gradually aware—very much in book three and four—that there is something happening that hasn't finished happening; something that is making all these other things happen; that is making the dead rise, making the demons break the bonds of Hell and come to Earth, and he needs to find out what that is.

*There's been interest in a Castor film or TV adaptation, hasn't there? Which one would you prefer to happen?*

I think I'd prefer the TV series. What would be great, and this is what we talked about at one stage, would be turning each novel into a TV special of some kind, or two back-to-back episodes or something.

*There are parallels between Lucifer and Felix Castor in so much as they're "work for hire" and always get the dirty jobs to do.*

Yeah, that's a valid comparison. Most of my protagonists are very stubborn, willful people who follow their own line wherever it takes them. They don't compromise very easily. The difference obviously with Lucifer is, he's a force of nature. His unwillingness to bend from his own line is actually pathological, to the point where we see him in "Mansions of the Silences" sending billions of souls into the void in order to keep a promise, because he'd be lessened by breaking his word. That matters far more to him than all of those lost lives. He's only concerned about how things affect him. I've described him somewhere as a person who'd set the world on fire to light a cigarette and wouldn't think about it. Obviously Felix is far less categorical than that. He does feel a genuine sense of obligation to many people. Whereas Lucifer keeps his word because it's important to him on an existential level to do it, not to be a liar because lying demeans you, Castor tries and fails to keep his promises because he cares about those people. In terms of doing the dirty jobs, Castor does it because he has to, because they're there to do and he's not the sort of person who can shut his eyes to it. Lucifer: the jobs are dirty because of what he is. There's nothing that he wouldn't do if it serves his end, really.

*Can you tell us more about* **Frost Flowers**, *your movie?*

I normally describe *Frost Flowers* as an erotic ghost story but it is, if I'm honest, a pornographic ghost story [*laughs*]. It's about a guy who has a near-death experience, as a result of which he can not only see the dead—which is a sort of very *Sixth Sense*-y setup—but he can touch the dead as well; he can interact with ghosts. And he forms a sexual obsession with the ghost of a woman who died 100 years before. He eventually has a physical relationship with her and she gets pregnant by him. Again it's a triangular relationship because the world of the dead as presented in *Frost Flowers* is almost entirely divorced from the world of the living. Most of the dead can't see the living, in the same way as most of the living can't see the dead. They live in a world of perpetual darkness because their sight doesn't work by light, it works by some other mechanism; they don't have physical eyes after all, so it's not light reflecting off their corneas, it's something else that's going on. They can't see the sun or the sky, they can't see anything that moves, so they walk through silent streets. They can see each other, but can't touch each other. It's an afterlife of perpetual boredom, of perpetual unhappiness.

**Neverwhere,** *the graphic novel, is so different from the book and TV series. Was this a conscious thing and how well has it been received?*

Can I answer the second part of that question first? It's mostly been received very well. There were, to be honest, some people who loved the TV series or who loved the novel—more who loved the novel to be fair—who found the changes hard to take. One of the changes that was very controversial, and I knew it would be, was actually having a point-of-view character rather than an omniscient narrator. But, as I say in the foreword, the omniscient narrator works in novels, it doesn't work in comics. In comics it feels like a dated and forced device, and it actually distances you from what's going on. So I made the decision to have Richard as narrator. Some people hated that because of course it tells you that he's alive at the end. You could argue that it takes some of the force away from certain scenes. But mostly it was very well received. I mean, the question is, how do you take a story like that, which is very rich, very diverse in the novel, and make it work as a comic? In a comic you're always going to have to take short cuts, there are some things you can't play out full-length. We were told we could have between eight and ten issues, so I went for nine which was the midpoint, because structurally nine works, and I broke it down into nine chapters. We took out some minor characters who, although their roles in the book are very rewarding, don't feed into the main storyline. [As for] the other huge structural change ... it worried me that instead of the quest being a straight line, it's a loop. They meet the Angel Islington early on and they go back to him at the end, but the first time it's dead easy and the second time it's impossibly hard, and I fretted about that. So I put in that whole thing about the astral plane, that they don't meet him physically the first time around; they meet him in some kind of telepathic or soul union, and he says, "Come to me in the flesh. Come to me in Down Street where I live...." So that's a big change in the book, but I think within the structure we were setting up, it plays better that way. We were very respectful, I think, with regard to the key events and the character arcs, and I kept as much of the dialogue as I could. Again, in a novel you can have a conversation going on for a whole chapter, and if the dialogue's good, nobody minds, but you can't in a comic. So I took what I could and was sad about some of the things I had to leave out.

**You've said that there's now increasing genre freedom crossing boundaries. What did you mean by that?**

I guess, because we live in the sort of era where audiences are so used to the genre complexes, you can take their understanding for granted, and you can start to play games with it. I think it was Mark Rose who came up with this theory first, that genres progress through stages. The first stage is when you're establishing the rules and the second stage is when you can break them, because everybody knows what they are. And we're definitely, in all the main genre areas, in that second phase now. Everyone knows what the rules are, so you can just do what you like and the audiences will roll with it. I think partly this is because of the growing popularity of Eastern—Japanese and Korean—media products which have always done this, always had eclectic genre mixes. But it's wider than that, it's just a question of audience sophistication.

# *Neil Gaiman*

Neil Gaiman was born November 10, 1960, the son of David (owner of a chain of stores) and Sheila (a pharmacist). He worked in journalism for many years before turning to fiction; Gaiman has written highly acclaimed books for both adults and children and has won many major awards, including the Hugo, Nebula and Newbery. His novels include *Neverwhere, Stardust, American Gods, Coraline, Anansi Boys* and, most recently, *The Graveyard Book*. His collections include *Smoke and Mirrors* and *Fragile Things*. *Neverwhere* was turned into a BBC TV series, while both *Stardust* and *Coraline* have been adapted to the big screen. His multimillion-selling series *Sandman* was described as "the greatest epic in the history of comic books" by the *Los Angeles Times*.

---

*How did you start out as an author?*

My entire career as a published author began at a British Fantasy Society Open Night, where either Stephen Jones or Jo Fletcher—Kim Newman and I disagree on who it was—dragged me over to Kim and said we should meet. Kim started explaining, with little or perhaps no provocation, the plot of a schlocky horror novel he had decided to write about giant badgers, to be called *The Set* [*laughs*]. At the end of it, I said, "You know, I think it'd be a good idea to do a science fiction and fantasy book of quotations." And he said, "I'll do the film bit." Being Kim, of course, two days later through the post I get an outline for the book and a sample chapter. If you've ever worked with Kim, it's really scary. You'll discuss a book or something, and he just goes away and does it—normally that weekend. I'm there, walking around going, "What would be a good title?"—got to get the title just right—and Kim's written a sample chapter. We sent the outline to a few different publishers and a couple said no, but Arrow Books said yes. So, we did *Ghastly Beyond Belief*. And somewhere in the middle of doing *Ghastly Beyond Belief* I got a phone call from somebody who said, "Kim Newman writes horror books for us, he's just done a book called *Nightmare Movies*. He's suggested your name as somebody who'd like to write a rock book." I said, "Yeah, great, brilliant, I want to do the Velvet Underground book and I want to do a book on Punk...." Then there's a pause at the other end of the phone and they said, "Well, let me tell you the three books we've got: You could do the Barry Manilow book [*laughs*]; you could do the Def Leppard book; or you could do the Duran, Duran book [*laughs*]." I thought, I'm not doing Barry Manilow, even for money, and I had a writer friend who would love to do the Def Leppard so I put that his way. And I did the Duran, Duran book. I think that was actually published a month before *Ghastly Beyond Belief* so technically that was my first book.

*How did you come to work with Terry Pratchett?*

*Space Voyager* magazine assigned me to go and interview Terry. It was the first interview Terry had ever done, I think February '85. He didn't know that you're meant to keep journalists away at arm's length, and feed them crumbs, then run away very fast. So we became fast friends, and it ended up with us several years later writing *Good Omens*. Mostly because he'd phone me up, over those four or five years, and he'd say, "Which is funnier?" and he'd list two things. I'd say, "Well, you know you could do both." And he'd say, "How?" and I'd tell him. Then he'd go, "Oh yeah, I can, good," and he'd get off the phone. After a while it seemed like fun do one together.

**Author Neil Gaiman. Photograph by Paul Kane.**

*How did that actually work, writing together?*

I did all the words [*laughs*]. How did it work? It worked very well actually, mostly because at the time I was nocturnal. I'm not any more; I stopped being nocturnal about 1994 when I gave up smoking. Suddenly I couldn't do nocturnal any more. I used to work through the night, and around one o'clock in the morning I'd just light another cigarette and keep going. Then I stopped smoking and what would happen would be that I'd wake up at four or five o'clock in the morning with my head on the keyboard and 900 pages of the letter M [*laughs*]. I thought, I can't do this any more. So I would get up very late in the morning or pretty early in the afternoon and the little red light on the answer phone would be blinking. I'd play it, and a voice would say, "Get up, get up, you bastard, I've just written a good bit." I'd make a cup of tea first, then I'd phone Terry and he would read me what he'd written earlier that morning. This was 1988-ish and back then you couldn't just e-mail things back and forth, we actually had a disk that we posted. At one point I connected my computer to his via modem, these 375 board modems, and it actually would have been quicker to just sort of cough in Morse code down the phone and transcribe it. Actually, the first draft of *Good Omens* back when it was still *William the Anti-Christ* took somewhere between nine and ten weeks to actually write. Then we did another draft, then we sold it.

*When did you first meet Alan Moore?*

It was in Birmingham at a convention—I think Mexicon—and Alan actually came because Clive Barker and Ramsey Campbell, both of whom he admired enormously, were going to be there. He was a bit nervous, so I said that I'd look after him. I got to reception and there was this guy in a very natty white suit, red boots and masses of hair, and I said, "You *have* to be Alan Moore." Alan had with him—I remember getting black and white photocopies for this thing that nobody had ever heard of at that point because it wasn't even being advertised—*Watchmen* that he was doing with Dave Gibbons. He handed me the first three issues in black and white photocopies and said, "There you are, laddie, tell me what you think of this!" I curled up in a corner as a panel was going on, and disappeared into them. I'd always known he was brilliant, but at that point I knew he was a genius—and I should be much more intimidated by this man in his red boots. That was how we met, and we've been friends ever since.

*He gave you a lot of help starting out in comics, in terms of layouts and things, didn't he?*

Actually, no. He gave me enormous help in terms of moral support, but that Mexicon was where I remember saying to him, "Look, I want to write comics and I don't know how." So he grabbed my notebook and said, "All right then, page one, panel one, that's what you write. Underneath it you write what happens, what you can see.... We are looking at a room, there is a man. Underneath that, you write 'The Man' and what he says: 'Oh dear, I have hurt myself.' Then a sound effect, 'FX: Bang!' If he's thinking something, you can put, 'THINKS: My life is doomed.' Or a caption: CAPTION: Meanwhile. That's what it looks like." And that was what he showed me. I went away and wrote a John Constantine script, which was a six- or seven-page story called "The Day My Pan Went Mad," a title I lifted from Jonathan Clarkson. I sent it to Alan and he said, "Yeah, it's all right. Gets a bit bogged down at the end." Then I wrote a *Swamp Thing* story, sent it to Alan, and he said, "Yeah, it's all right." I didn't do anything with them for about a year, although the *Swamp Thing* one was eventually published in the *Midnight Days* collection 13 years after it was written. Steve Lesett and John Tottle illustrated it—which was rather good. I have no idea whatever happened to "The Day My Pan Went Mad," but Alan did actually steal some lines from it in *Swamp Thing* #51, which made me very happy.

*How did you first come to work with Dave McKean?*

After I did those first two stories, I was introduced to a man in a pub, the way these things happen. He said, "We have mutual friends." And I said, "Oh, what do you do?" He said, "I write comics." I said, "Well, I'm a journalist but I've always wanted to write comics. In fact, I've just done these two comic things...." I had a phone call from him a few days later saying, "Were you serious, do you really want to write comics?" I said, "Yes, very much." He said, "Well, I'm starting a comic and the work will exclusively be done by young, untried, fresh people. I don't want anybody who's done anything in comics before because they will bring me hackneyed work." What I didn't know was that actually the real reason why this guy wouldn't work with anyone who had been around in comics, was because they knew they'd never get paid. He was a bit of a compulsive liar, but we didn't know that. So he got together a bunch of very young, innocent, fresh-faced people, including a young art student named Dave McKean. And this guy bought—"bought" here being a general term meaning ordered and had placed but never paid for—ads advertising this magazine in *Escape*, Paul Gravett's rather wonderful magazine at the time. Paul Gravett thought, this is interesting, and came down to see what we were doing. The office space—although we didn't know it immediately at the time—was actually a telephone sales organization in Wimpole Street, from which this guy had been fired but still had the key, and knew there was nobody there on Wednesday nights. Sounds pretty odd, now I say it [*laughs*]. So Paul Gravett came down, he looked at the stuff. He liked what I was writing, liked what Dave McKean was drawing, and asked if we'd do a five-page strip for *Escape* magazine. And, enormously to his credit, a week or two later when we approached him and said we've got this thing we'd like to do that's a 48-page graphic novel about memory, called *Violent Cases*, he didn't tell us to go away, he said, "Yeah, all right." That was really how Dave and I began.

*You've said your favorite book with Dave is* **Mr. Punch.** *Why is that?*

I guess I felt like it was one of the very few things we felt like we got right. And partly that's also one of the interesting things about working with Dave. He's always on this quest for the one true way to make art; comics or film, whatever it is he's doing. I, on the other hand, tend to come at things from a slightly more lax aesthetic point of view, which consists of throwing mud at the wall and seeing what sticks, and if it looks good saying I meant to do that [*laughs*]. But Dave is always very much about the right way to do it, so we've found pieces that we're fairly happy with when we were very much starting out. Then we did *Black Orchid* which we really weren't happy with, although I learned a lot. We set ourselves a lot of constrained rules and it didn't ever really feel like it caught fire. Dave was really miserable about that. Then we did *Signal to Noise* which was fun, but because *Signal to Noise* was serialized in *The Face* the rhythms of it were very odd. So *Mr. Punch* was the first time that Dave and I had actually just done something that we felt worked.

And in *Mr. Punch* I was very happy because I got to go in and plough these peculiar childhood memories. *Mr. Punch* actually began in many ways with a very real conversation. I was at a family wedding, talking with an aunt and a distant cousin who I didn't know, and a few of these nice lady relatives from previous generations were there. The conversation somehow reached my Great Uncle Monty, who I had adored when I was a kid because he was a hunchback; it meant that even though I was only seven I could look him in the eye, which I just thought was so cool. I said, "How did he become a hunchback?" And one aunt said, "Oh, I think it was polio." The other one said, "No, it was T.B." And another aunt said, "No, no, no. Wasn't he thrown downstairs as a baby?" You go: "What?" That was where it all really began.

The other half of it was me in Greenwich, caught in a torrential thunderstorm, the kind that you just can't stand out in the street in; you flee to the nearest building. Which happened to be a joke shop. On a little shelf in this joke shop there were about five books. I picked one of them up and it was on the history of Punch and Judy from the 1920s. And the very last page—I opened it to the last page—was a summary of the plot of Punch and Judy. It just said, "Mr. Punch is left with the baby by his wife Judy, he's meant to be babysitting. He throws it out of the window and kills it. Judy comes home, remonstrating, so he kills her. A policeman comes up to arrest Mr. Punch, he murders the policeman. He goes out, meets a crocodile, is bitten to death by the crocodile, comes back from the dead in time to murder the doctor. Then a hangman tries to hang Mr. Punch and fails, and hangs himself. The devil tries to drag Mr. Punch off to Hell and is killed by Mr. Punch, who then goes off round the land bringing joy and happiness to boys and girls everywhere." [*Laughs*] I mean, as a child you see Punch and Judy, but you never really process the information; it's just an awful lot of squeaky puppets. And suddenly this thing was laid out for me and I thought, "Okay, I *have* to tell that story." So that really was the spark; it existed in the intersection of the weirdnesses of my family and small puppets murdering each other.

*How did the character of the Sandman come about?*

Necessity, I suppose, is the honest answer. We were three-quarters of the way through *Black Orchid* and DC Comics panicked. They suddenly turned around and said, "We've just realized we've got two people nobody has heard of, doing a character that nobody's ever heard of: a female character, and female characters don't sell." They said, "What we'd really like to do is give you a monthly comic to just raise your profile, and maybe give Dave like a background project to do." Which in fact turned out to be *Sandman* and *Arkham Asylum* respectively. And Karen [Berger], my editor, said, "Can you come up with any characters that you'd like to do?" So I made a great big list of characters, handed it over—phoned her up and read them off. She phoned me back a day later and said, "We don't like any of those. Furthermore, so-and-so's got *this* character, somebody's got *that* character...." Then she said, "What about that Sandman stuff you were telling me over dinner?" Because when she'd come in I'd talked about the idea of maybe doing a Sandman graphic novel that would take the old Kirby Sandman and do it much more seriously. She said, "We think maybe that would work. Why don't you just do that but don't make it the Kirby Sandman because Roy Thomas is doing some stuff with him. Just make it an original one." I said, "Okay."

That was my brief. The nature of the character wound up evolving a lot of the time from me asking myself questions like, "If this character lives in dreams, how come we've never heard of him before? Maybe he's been imprisoned. That feels right. Is he the only one of this kind? No, let's make it a family—a family would be fun." So that was the slow evolution process, and it was actually helped by the hurricane. October '87, we had a hurricane, and it occurred the day after I'd gone on the computer and written "The Sandman: A Proposal," and a major paragraph. Then we had the hurricane—I was living in a little village in the middle of the Ashdown Forest at that time—and we had no power for a week. So I would walk from dark room to dark room, lighting candles, thinking about this thing, and by the time the power went on I had the shape of the first eight issues, the first storyline. After that it was a process of discovery, but the weirdest thing about the Sandman was that it never felt like invention. It felt much more like, when you talk to a sculptor and they talk about finding the figure that was within the marble and just cutting out the bits that weren't necessary. That was what it felt like; much more like that than anything else.

*Did its success take you by surprise?*

No, because it was very, very slow. My entire career has been a bit like cooking lobsters so slowly they barely notice they've been cooked. *Sandman* came out, was a minor critical success, which I assumed meant it would be cancelled because that was what tended to happen to minor critical successes. Instead, by about issue #8 it was selling more than any comparable horror comic, about 60,000 copies. But a bog standard superhero comic at that point was selling about 100,000 copies. It took us about four years to creep up to 100,000 copies. And the point where we finally got up to 140,000 copies and feeling rather pleased with ourselves, that was the time you had this whole ridiculous image explosion and comics were selling in their millions, so again we were still sitting down there at number 98 or whatever. After that enormous boom there was a huge bust, and everyone stopped buying millions of copies as investments. It ended the first day the first person took the first box of *X-Men* #1 down to the comic shop and said, "Will you buy them? How much will you give me? You've got them on the wall there, £20 each. How much will you buy them back from me for?" And they said, "Do you know how many boxes of those we have in the back?" Suddenly everything popped. It got to the point where I looked around and discovered everything was selling 80,000 copies, then it was selling 60,000 copies. But we were still selling 100,000 copies because we were selling to readers.

Then there was the fact that we had the trade paperbacks, which was kind of unheard-of back then. It seems pretty logical now, but at the time, if you wanted back issues of comics you went and looked on the walls in the comic shops, in the small ads. So we were in print and the collections were out, and stayed in print, then started selling more and more each year. A few years ago, 2003, I was in Paul Levitz's office at DC Comics, the publisher, and there were figures on his desk. He said, "Hey, do you want to know how many Sandman books actually sold last year?" I said, "Sure." He said, "All right, as long as you don't try and think this has anything to do with your royalties..." [*laughs*]. I said, "Fine, whatever...." And we sat there going through all of his reports for the year with a little calculator and discovered that in 2003—which is a fairly average year for Sandman—about 310,000 *Sandman* graphic novels had sold in America alone. That's rather a lot. It means every three and a half years, a million graphic novels get sold. So the success has been so slow and steady over the years, it just sort of quietly grew.

*What's your favorite Anansi story?*

I like the story of Anansi and the Moss-Covered Rock—which I've never retold—and the one about the Tiger's Balls—which I retold in *American Gods*. I just got a letter from someone telling me that when they heard the story of Anansi stealing Tiger's testicles, it was actually Tiger's Sandwiches that Anansi stole, and why would I feel the urge to make such a nice clean story dirty like that...?

*Just to turn one of the Book Club discussion questions in* Anansi Boys *back over to you: What do you feel the book says about today's multicultural society?*

Not a lot. I've mostly been interested in the reactions of readers, and the idea of default skin color for people in books. The default skin color in *Anansi Boys* isn't white.

*It says in the interview at the back that you didn't really have any nicknames yourself, but have you ever given any to anyone else?*

None that have stuck.

*The initial spark for* The Graveyard Book *was a mixture of* The Jungle Book *and seeing your son playing in a graveyard, wasn't it?*

It was. It was one of those, "How do you get your ideas?" and two things come together. Really it was just watching a boy in a graveyard and thinking you could write something

The UK cover of *Anansi Boys* (2006, Headline; courtesy Caitlin Raynor, Headline Books).

like *The Jungle Book*, in that it's a small child whose family.... I always assumed his family had been killed. But he wanders in the jungle, is adopted and brought up by wild animals and taught the things that wild animals know. I thought, "I'll do something where a kid wanders into a graveyard and is brought up by dead people and is taught the things that dead people know. And I won't do it as a pastiche, I'm not going to rewrite Kipling poetry into 'This Is the Law of the Graveyard' or whatever. I'm going to do something that uses *The Jungle Book* almost as a wall to bounce my ball off."

*"The Witch's Headstone" chapter was a published short story.*

That was the first one I wrote, my experiment to find out if it worked or not. I'd been doing a number of things over the years that were essentially what I described to my editor as five finger exercises for *The Graveyard Book*. I did a story called "October in the Chair"; I did a wonderful little comic they've just made a film out of with Gahan Wilson, called *It Was a Dark and Silly Night* about these kids having a party in a graveyard. You're just sort of figuring it all out, how you play this, how you do living and dead people together on the same page. What would I like my dead people to be: How do you suspend disbelief when you have the living and the dead on the same page? So I was figuring that out for myself with those things. I tried starting *The Graveyard Book* a couple of times before; I'd always start at the beginning, and it never really worked. So I thought, "I'll start in the middle, and see how that works—just plant my flag." And actually it worked beautifully. It gave me a shape.

*What was the impetus behind having two different illustrators, Dave McKean and Chris Riddell, working on two different versions?*

It was a particularly brilliant idea from the lovely Sarah Odedina, my editor, who said, "Look, you've written this book that adults love and children love." And this is from the publisher of *Harry Potter*. She said, "It's really hard to get adults into the kids' part of a bookshop. What I'd like to do is bring out two different editions and have one that is very obviously a chil-

Dave McKean's cover artwork for the UK hardback edition of *The Graveyard Book* (2008, Bloomsbury; courtesy Kate Harvey, Bloomsbury Books).

dren's book and one that is essentially an adult book—and get them shelved in different places and have two different ISBNs." So that's what she did.

*What is it that's so appealing about graveyards and ghosts, especially this time of year?*

I think graveyards are appealing, frankly, at any time of the year. There is no wrong time to be in a graveyard. Well, actually....

*Midnight?*

I was thinking that the last time you're in one is possibly a wrong time [*laughs*]. But times when you can walk out under your own steam ... I think graveyards are beautiful, I fall in love with graveyards. The combination of wilderness and the tangled mess of ivy. Highgate Cemetery West is one of the most beautiful places in London. Hackney Park Cemetery, Stoke Newington, is absolutely gorgeous. Just a little magic place in the middle of Stoke Newington. *The Graveyard Book* is those places. I borrowed the topography of the Glasgow Necropolis—

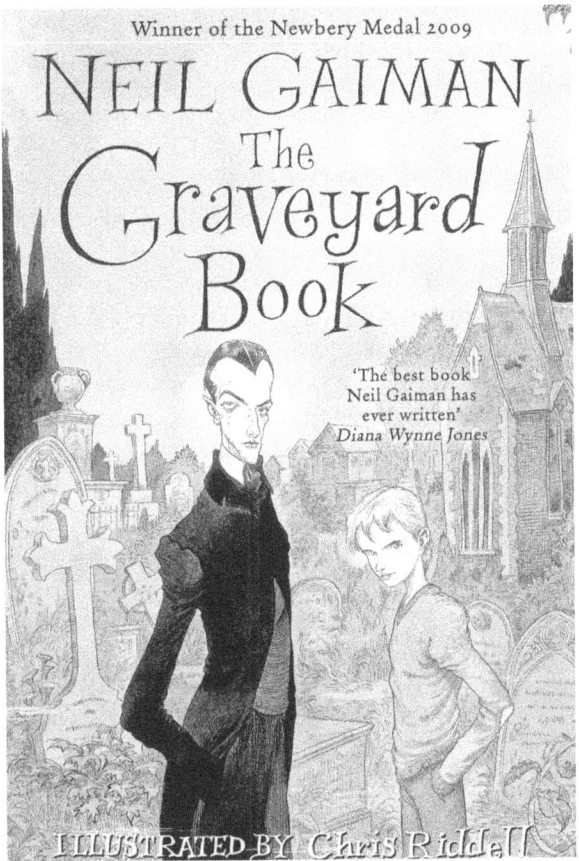

Chris Riddell's cover artwork for the UK hardback edition of *The Graveyard Book*. (2008, Bloomsbury; courtesy Kate Harvey, Bloomsbury Books).

the idea of it on a hill looking out over the city. Very much from going, "I love that. I'll take that thing and put that in my graveyard." I stole from every graveyard I loved, a little bit here and a little bit there. I basically stole the Egyptian Avenue from Highgate because I just liked the idea of that: We've got this impressive Egyptian thing, we're going to do this. But what's interesting is that they weren't actually the only place in London doing Egyptian things. They went mad for Egyptian stuff briefly in the Victorian era, so I thought, "I like the idea that somebody with a smaller graveyard, this company somewhere further up north went, 'We'll do that too.'"

*There are definite parallels between* **The Graveyard Book** *and* **Stardust** *in terms of a coming-of-age story-rites of passage.*

I don't know. Maybe you're pushing and maybe you're not. That's the kind of thing where you'd have to write the little essay and I just read it and go, "Oh, they've got a point." [*Laughs*] I don't think of them that way, because I think of *Stardust* as a book about a boy becoming a man; it is very much about an 18-year-old boy approaching manhood. And *Stardust* begins at that moment where Tristan leaves home, where he crosses the wall, where he sets out to become an adult. That's the moment at which *The Graveyard Book* ends. Yes, they both have that arc, but *Stardust* would be in that sense the next one on from Bod's story.

*There's a connection in that they both are trying to find out what their pasts are.*

Yes, and of course in *Stardust* the reader knows an awful lot more than any of the characters do. In *The Graveyard Book*, the characters—or some of them—know much more than the reader does. You're down at Bod's level for a lot of the time, and when you're not you're looking at things from outside. And you don't get very much additional information. I suppose part of it is the idea of writing something differently, from a different time. Stylistically it's very different, but I think it's also fun that way because I wanted *The Graveyard Book* to be a book of continuous discovery, and a book of continual conceptual breakthrough. It's about learning stuff, it's about having a family and understanding what your family is, and understanding that parenthood, for example, is something that—intrinsically—if you do it well, you've made yourself redundant. You are out of a job at the moment you have done your job properly. If you don't do your job properly, you might end up being a parent for life. If you've done your job properly, then there will come a point where they go away.

*Were you happy with the finished version of* Stardust*?*

Yeah, I guess. It's not something that actually, truth to tell, impinges on my universe very much. The best part of it is that the book suddenly found itself in print even in places where it had gone out of print or had never been published, in 30 or 40 different languages. The film was an international hit and it was hugely popular in the UK, which was just lovely. So in England, in particular, people now sort of think they know who I am. "Oh yeah, you're the bloke who did *Stardust*.... You didn't write it, did you, but you wrote the book *Stardust* was based on." When we were making the film, I remember turning to Matthew Vaughn and saying, "Look, I have no idea if you're making something that's going to be commercially successful or not. And I don't know if it's going to be a big hit. But I do know it will be beloved by people. You're making a film that for some people, for the rest of time,

The UK paperback cover of *Stardust* (2005, Headline; courtesy Caitlin Raynor, Headline Books).

will be their most beloved film." He did, and I think that's really sweet. There are people who cannot watch it enough, cannot experience it enough; they love it.

*Why didn't you write the script for the film yourself?*

Didn't want to. Partly I didn't want to because Matthew had a film in his head that he wanted to make, and I thought I would do much better by finding somebody that Matthew could work with. So I suggested Jane [Goldman], got her the job, and was terribly happy that I had Jane on board. I think we were all much happier for it. It's not an easy thing adapting something you've already done. One reason why it's not easy is that sometimes you simply can't think outside the box. You went through here to get there, and you just can't nip 'round the side. You can't turn it around and see it from a different angle. I'm now meant to be working on *Anansi Boys* as a film, which I *am* writing myself, and it's hard. But the main reason I'm doing

Michelle Pfeiffer as Lamia the witch in the movie version of *Stardust* (2007, Paramount Pictures).

that is because there was a BBC version that I really wasn't comfortable with. Didn't like the World Service Version of *Anansi Boys* very much. I just felt like it sort of missed the point. I sat there at the read-through, with some of the best actors in England—amazing black actors, and Matt Lucas, who's not black—just going, "I would love this cast to be doing *Anansi Boys* like it is in my head." That was the point where I wound up agreeing. I phoned a friend and said, "Can I do this with the BBC?" Got a phone call back from the BBC saying, "Let's talk about this because we think it would be great." Immediately followed by a phone call from Hollywood, from a producer who I knew and liked, saying, "I was on tour with such-and-such a star and I picked this up in an airport bookstore to read. I got halfway through it and thought, 'Oh my God, this is a movie,' gave it to the star and he says so too, and we wanna make it."

*Was that the impetus for* Neverwhere *the film as well? The BBC thing in the '90s?*

*Neverwhere* the film just sort of lurches, but yes. With *Neverwhere* I would love to see it done right. There was a point in about 2000 where I walked off *Neverwhere*, and they got someone else in to write it. Then a couple of years ago somebody found my script and went, "Oh, this is brilliant." It suddenly came back from the dead, this script—and nobody could remember why they *hadn't* liked it.

Neil Gaiman signing books at Forbidden Planet during the *Anansi Boys* tour. Photograph by Paul Kane and Marie O'Regan.

*Were you happy with the finished version of* Beowulf*?*

Happiness is relative. There's so much amazing stuff in *Beowulf*, there is this part of me that just went, "I wish they'd actually just shot the script as written with actors." Having said that, had they shot it with actors I wouldn't have been going, "You know, I got to write the first cartoon for adults, released on a mass scale internationally that got to be the #1 film in the world and the #1 film in America, and also has made whatever it is...." And nobody particularly noticed that I got to write the biggest animated film for adults that anyone's ever done. There's a very small number of animated films made for adults, and this is the first one to actually be released, not as a little underground thing and not just as an arthouse thing; this was actually properly released. I don't know that anybody noticed that. I wish somebody had actually said that, because that was something I was astoundingly proud of.

*Do you think it might be because the animation is so close to how the actors look?*

I think that's definitely part of it, with the exception of course of our Beowulf [*laughs*]. Ray [Winstone] loved it. "I got so buff, I been working out." First time I met him, he said, "Ere Neil, I just finished the script. You know what I like best about it? All the fuckin' swearing." And I had to explain that I'd just been sitting in a room taking out all of the swearing. Every "fuck" had just been replaced by something slightly more Anglo-Saxon.

*Which books are you the proudest of?*

That's hard. I'm very fond of *Coraline* just because it managed to be this thing I wanted it to be when I sat down to write it, despite the fact it took about ten years to write. And towards the end when I didn't have any time to write it, but really wanted to, instead of reading before bed, I had a notebook by my bed—I'd write 50 words of *Coraline*. Whatever else had been going on, that was the last thing I'd do at night. I'm pretty fond of *Coraline*, I'm pretty fond of *Anansi Boys*, just because I decided it would be fun to write a book that would create some type of human happiness. Just leave people feeling better at the end than they did at the beginning. I think it probably does that. But apart from that, mostly I look at my books—any tome you could mention—with enormous dissatisfaction. It's like looking at a photograph of yourself, and somebody goes, "What a great photo." And you go, "My nose is in a really funny position. And I have five chins" [*laughs*]. But mostly what I see when I look at stuff that I've written: You see the flaws, you see the faults, and you're also horribly and profoundly conscious of how very far what you wrote actually was from the flawless, perfect, pristine, magnificent, beautiful book it was in your head before you started. My next book is going to be so good [*laughs*] until it's written, and then I'll ruin it. But the things in my head are really great.

# *James Herbert*

James Herbert was born on April 8, 1943, in the East End of London, the son of street traders. His family lived at the back of Petticoat Lane in Whitechapel—once the stalking ground of Jack the Ripper. At age ten he won a scholarship to St. Aloysius Grammar School in Highgate, and at sixteen he went to the famous Hornsey College of Art, where he studied graphic design. He subsequently joined a leading London advertising agency, where he worked his way up to the position of Group Head-Associate Director. By the age of 28, he'd secretly started writing a novel, *The Rats*. Once it was finished, he submitted the manuscript to six publishers on the same day and within three weeks he had received three replies. Two turned the novel down, while the other bought it for publication. Since 1974 he has reigned as Britain's leading author of chiller fiction, with more than 20 novels to his credit, including *The Fog, Fluke, Shrine, Moon, Creed, Portent, Others, Once, Nobody True* and *The Secret of Crickley Hall*. His books have sold more than fifty million copies world-wide.

---

*For* **The Secret of Crickley Hall**, *what made you return to the theme of ghosts?*

Just the idea. An idea came up and that was it. I'm trying to remember now exactly when I thought about the evacuee kids. I was an evacuee myself: At one year of age, I was taken out of London. And I think I must have read something about those days and it prompted an idea of an orphanage, kids being killed. I'd always sworn that I'd never write anything about kids being hurt in any way, and I stuck with that for years, but I changed my mind because the idea seemed so good.

*What is it about the supernatural that you find so appealing?*

It's just interesting, because we don't know what is there. We don't know any answers, we can only speculate. So for me—it lets my mind run free and I can write whatever comes out. It also takes you away from the mundane existence of life.

*So the scope's broader for writing?*

The scope *is* broader, yeah. You can bring any sort of genre under that umbrella of horror. It can be a thriller, it can be humor, it can be historical, there's all kinds of things you can do with horror, so that's why it appeals to me.

*I read somewhere that you had about 1000 ideas for the book but only a small percentage made it in there.*

Yes, I had 1575, I think—and I used most of them, actually. But there were very small ideas and big ideas as well. Like a person should wear a certain hat, that might be one idea. Then a really significant plan or plot switch would come along, and that would be

James Herbert in his office (photograph © Terry O'Neill, courtesy Katie James and Fiona Carpenter, Pan Macmillan).

another idea. So I had lots of those and just used the ones that came up. It was like doing a jigsaw puzzle and joining all the parts.

*You've based locations in your novels on real places, which of course is the basis for the book* **James Herbert's Dark Places.** *Was Crickley Hall based on a real place in Devon?*

No, absolutely not. In fact, I went really against the cliché of the old manor house with turrets. I have used so many old houses in that fashion, and they were creepy in themselves; I wanted this one to be just plain, no romance, nothing overtly sinister to it; just an odd building. It's only when you get inside Crickley Hall that you see there's a lot more to it, it's a lot more sinister than you imagine.

*Have you ever had any ghostly experiences yourself?*

Yes. Only one, unfortunately, years ago in Marbella. I was in a friend's villa—the friend was David Moores, who was the chairman of Liverpool football club. And he was talking, this was about two or three o'clock in the morning, and behind his shoulder was an open doorway, and something walked past. Another friend who was sitting alongside me said, "Did you see that?" I said, "No." Then two minutes later, something walked past the door again. This time I saw it, and my friend saw it again as well. I rushed out into the hall to confront it, because I thought, "Hell, if I'm going to see a ghost, I'm going to see it properly" [*laughs*]. So I rushed up the stairs, in the brilliance of a marble hallway, but there was nothing there. It was gone. Our wives had all gone to bed—it was one of these drinking evenings that turned into late night drinking—and it was just the menfolk downstairs, and there was no one else around in the house.

I questioned the wives the next morning, asked them if they got out of bed for anything last night, did they go down to the kitchens, because we thought it might just have been one of the girls walking by. But no, they swore it wasn't them. It wasn't, because I would have recognized them anyway, but we were just making sure. But that's the only ghost I've seen. I mean, I stood in that hallway and I shouted, I called to it. I just wanted it to come back so I could really see what it was all about, but unfortunately that was it; it was gone. But it couldn't possibly have been anybody else.

*Did you find out anything about the history of the place afterwards?*

No, the place was fairly modern. The only thing was that it had these great Spanish doors, with all these carved figures, naked figures up to all kinds of things—it was all sort-of Aleister Crowley stuff. And the builders had brought them, and the buyer had bought them for the house, so they were the only really old things in there. They were obviously a doorway to a brothel years ago, and my friend wanted them in when he had the house built. But that's the only history the house had. It wasn't what you'd expect for a ghost.

**Crickley Hall** *deals with the period of World War II. Is this a fascination with you?*

Yes it is, because I was born during the war, just towards its end. I've always found that period between the '30s and '60s fascinating, because such a lot went on. We advanced so much; there was the big war and other wars around the world; there was food rationing and gas masks that people had to carry about with them. So that just seemed very interesting to me. And when I was a kid, because of where I lived in the East End of London, we were sent away as children to foster parents for a couple of weeks every year because our parents couldn't afford to take us themselves. There was a company called the Country Holiday Fund, a charity, and they sent us away

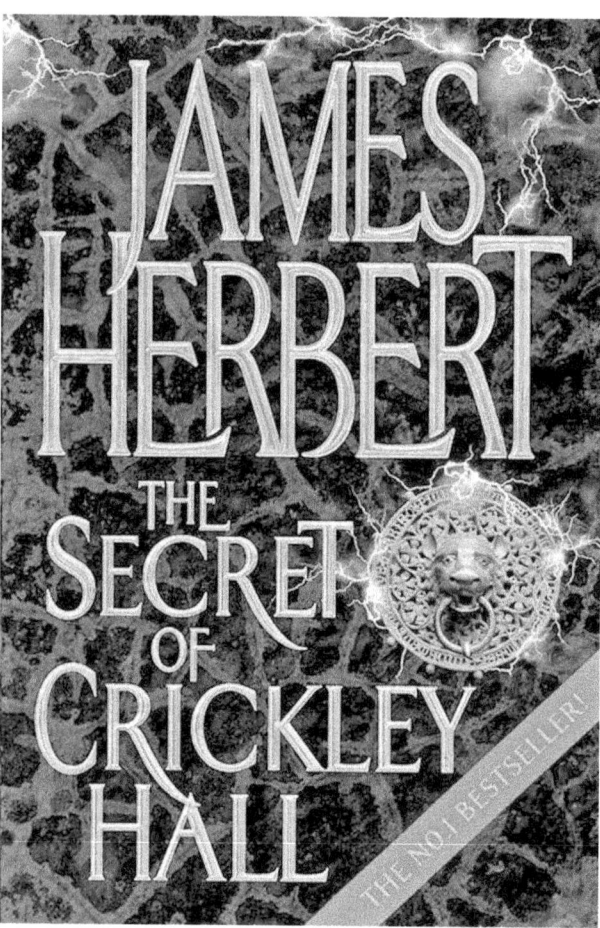

*The Secret of Crickley Hall* (2007, Macmillan; courtesy Fiona Carpenter, Pan Macmillan).

to these different places. And I'd never liked any of them, so I guess that also stuck in my mind—being an evacuee.

*The short cut through a bombed-out churchyard with your brother had a profound effect on you, didn't it?*

It was just very creepy. A journalist asked me one day, what was my childhood like and what sort of things would have led me towards horror? And that was just it, we used to come home from the cinema—a run of about two miles, I guess—and at the end it was through this old bombed-out churchyard where the tombs were askew, the crosses were almost on the ground or leaning over so far and it was just a very, very creepy place. And we used to dare each other to run through it—we didn't do it every time, just occasionally when we felt brave.

*You were already in a successful advertising career. What was the impetus for becoming a writer?*

None really, it's just that I enjoyed writing. And there were plenty of copywriters at my agency who were writing their manuscripts—the great book that would take them out of advertising. So I just thought one day, "I'll try that myself." I used to write a lot as a kid, and I thought I'd try to write a book. It was as stupid as that [*laughs*]. Naïve to imagine that I could actually get published by doing one book. Fortunately that was exactly what happened, I did the book and it got published. So then I became a writer. Five years later, and with five books behind me, I became a fulltime writer.

*A combination of ideas that inspired* **The Rats.**

Yeah, it was the old Bela Lugosi *Dracula* film where a thousand rats were outside the manor, staring into the house with red eyes—which was very visual to me. It was also from the circumstances where I used to live, where I was brought up in the East End of London, where there were lots of rats. All sorts of things went into that book, strangely enough. There was my little blast against nuclear war, messing around with nuclear bombs, that could do things, and that's how the rats mutated, of course. There was also my angst

*The Rats* (1999, Macmillan; courtesy Fiona Carpenter, Pan Macmillan).

about the government, and the elite of our society—that they would find shelters for themselves, they would build shelters just for themselves, and the rest of us would be left to our own devices if the bombs ever dropped. So that's the whole irony of the trilogy of *The Rats*, that at the end in *Domain*, which is the last book in the series, the group gets to this bunker near the Houses of Parliament and they find it's been wiped out by rats. The people who created the whole thing through nuclear power, allowing squalid surroundings, encouraging rats, importing rats—they got their comeuppance. That's what was running along in my mind, although basically it was just a story—something I enjoyed doing—and I let all my anger flow [*laughs*].

*How did you celebrate when you actually had your first book accepted?*

How did I celebrate? Well, I went into work and said, "Good morning, hacks," to all the copywriters [*laughs*], and then we all went for a beer at lunchtime. And that was it, really.

*We have to ask about Rumpole [from* **Fluke, The Magic Cottage, Once***]—will we be seeing him again in any books?*

Who knows, he may turn up again in some new book, I don't know—that's the only way I can answer it. I've no plans for him to turn up. It'd be nice to have him as a sort of running figure throughout the books, but I can only do it when the story calls for it. John Woo—the Chinese director—always has white doves in his films. I can't do that, nor can I do a Hitchcock and appear in every book [*laughs*]. I don't make plans like that, the future's the future and I let it come along as it does.

*What do you make of current horror films, like* **The Ring, Saw** *and* **Silent Hill***?*

I'm not too keen on horror films, believe it or not. There are so many trashy ones around. Some [horror films] I really like and others just leave me—I can't even say cold—they just leave me flat, you know, nothing. And too much gore, because it's done to death, literally, it's just gore for the sake of gore. I know I do that myself, or used to—I used to do it a lot, the first few books. But I just get really tired of that now. It's been done, we've been there, let's move on.

*So you find the creepy ones more effective, like* **The Sixth Sense***, that kind of thing?*

Yeah, exactly—well, *The Sixth Sense* was based on an idea of mine for *The Survivor*, where the guy is dead all the way through but we don't know it. And I've found that with quite a number of films, they've taken my idea and based another story around it. It was the same with *The Others* ... there've been quite a few and it just makes me grin, and grimace as well. So yeah, some films come off, some films are really good. *The Ring* was a terrific film, I enjoyed that. When they did it as an American movie, it was awful—the Japanese version was so much better. I think the Japanese can do these things much better than we can, they're somehow more creepy.

*Are there any of your own books that you'd still like to see filmed?*

Oh, well, every one [*laughs*]. Yeah, it's so disappointing for me that in this country I've only had four films made, when old Steve in the States—Steve King—every book he's done gets turned into a film. It'd be lovely for that to happen, but it just doesn't happen over here. I usually have huge climaxes in my book, big final disasters, and we don't have the money to shoot them. So it's unfortunate. But yes, I'd like to see a film of *The Fog* actually, but I'd like it to be *my* film of *The Fog*. And *Nobody True* I'd like to see filmed. They paid a lot of money for the rights to it and then never filmed it, they couldn't get it to work somehow. That was disappointing. But my agent told me years ago, "Jim, you're a writer. Getting it filmed, that's just a bonus. Consider yourself a writer," and it's quite right. I've been through so many contracts and deals for filming, and they never seem to work out. There are always problems with financing the movie; and that's actually happened with virtually every book. So I don't even get excited when I hear about it now, if somebody wants to option a book for film.

*Is it true that the inspiration for* **The Fog** *was a really boring presentation?*

It wasn't an inspiration, it just gave me one idea: What if the man who happened to be my creative director in advertising ... he was talking to us, I was getting very bored in the big meeting, and I thought, "Wouldn't it be funny if he did something really weird now, while we're all sitting here listening to him jabber on? What if he went over to the window and he just jumped out? What would we do? And what if we looked across the street and other people were jumping out of windows?" So that inspired the idea, it set something clicking in my mind and I thought, "What could cause something like that, that madness?" And then I thought, naturally, chemical gas of some kind—so that came to fruition. *The Fog* became the book.

**Professor of parapsychology David Ash (Aidan Quinn) in the movie version of** *Haunted* **(1995, October Films; courtesy John Gullidge).**

**Fluke** *was your attempt to do a* **History of Mr. Polly** *kind of story.*

I think I've said at some stage or other, *The History of Mr. Polly* is one of my favorite books. And when I did *Fluke* I thought to myself, "This is a kind of *Mr. Polly* book." But it didn't directly inspire it at all.

*And the publishers wanted to put a rabid dog on the cover, didn't they?*

Oh yeah, that's very true. They got the editor to take me to lunch, and he brought the manuscript along. He turned the first page and there were great blue lines across the page, crossing out sentences and things; I couldn't believe it. And he said, "Can't we have the dog a bit more aggressive now?" I said, "No, it's not that kind of dog." In the end I got really angry with his comments, we got to about page three, and he got a bit flustered and he made an excuse to rush off to the loo. I took the manuscript, flicked through it and there were markings and crossings-out all the way through, and bits added to it. And I was mad, you know? I said, "You don't want to publish the book as it is, then don't publish it!" But of course they published it. I think that book flummoxed everybody, they expected another really graphic horror story. Whereas *Fluke* was ... almost a children's story. But I wanted to stretch my wings, see what I could do as a writer. It didn't sell as well as the others at first, though over the years it's caught up and surpassed some of the others.

*It's probably one of your most loved books.*

Right, well, there's something lovable about it.

*You've mentioned that out of all your novels your least favorites are* **The Jonah** *and* **Moon**.

I didn't say they were my least favorites, I thought they were not as big as the others. I just felt they were small-scale ideas, they weren't sort of ... I don't know, blockbuster, if you like to use that word. They were fairly quiet books for horror, but they were just different again. But when I think about my books, and I rarely do, I tend to think of the big ones, like *The Ghosts of Sleath* and *The Rats* and *The Fog* of course, and now this one, *Crickley Hall*. So I didn't say that. I mean, I'm disappointed in every book I do, always am, always will be—I'll never get it exactly right. I don't know about *The Jonah* and *Moon*, I just didn't love them as much as the others for some reason, mainly because I went over to the Channel Islands to do *Moon*, and it was very lonely over there, a very lonely existence without my wife and kids—they came over later. And with *The Jonah* I went up to Suffolk on my own and scouted the territory around there, found a way of smuggling in drugs, but it was very bleak—and I found then that the whole story was bleak. In fact, both stories are bleak, and that's probably why.

*The Spear* (1978, Macmillan; courtesy Fiona Carpenter, Pan Macmillan).

*Some of your books have had thriller elements, for example* **Sepulchre** *and* **The Spear**, *and fantasy like* **The Magic Cottage** *and* **Once**. *Is it that flexibility in horror that attracted you to it?*

Exactly, yes. It's a very large umbrella under which you can have many, many genres. It just depends how the mood takes me. It could be a straight detective story; there's a lot of humor in *Fluke*; *Creed* is humor. I can be flexible and bring in all sorts of elements. It's not fashionable to call them horror stories any more, which is quite ridiculous. One of my publishers years ago invented the description "Chiller," a cross between Thriller and Horror, a creepy yarn or whatever. So that's the word we tend to use now, Chiller. Horror's gone down one of these roads where it's had a bad patch. I'm lucky and Stephen King is lucky, that we appeal to a broader audience. It's not just the people who like horror who read our books, they seem to get something else from them. So that's kept us going. But it's a shame because there are so many good writers around in the horror genre, it's a great shame they're just not even getting published nowadays.

*The City was great. Have you thought about doing any more graphic novels?*

That was a one-off. It was just an idea out of the blue one day, a publisher came to me and asked if I would do a graphic novel and I said no, I was busy on a new book. But the more I thought about it, I realized that with the *Rats* trilogy I had a bit more left over to go in, and that was the future. So I thought, "What a great idea. I don't actually want to write the book, but I could bring it out as a graphic novel and that would be great, it would get it out of my system and it would just be a new medium to try." So we did that, and there were great illustrations by Ian Miller. It sold really well. *The Dark Knight Returns* was out by that time, the new Batman that people were waiting for, and apparently *The City* outsold that three to one. Therefore I should have been encouraged to write more, but I wasn't, because with *The City* I actually drew all the frames, and then Ian did his own finished drawing. I just didn't fancy sitting down and drawing these frames again. It was something I'd ventured into, enjoyed doing, but that was it. A spin-off from writing, and it was done, so why do it again? But who knows, one day.

*The Dark* (1999, Macmillan; courtesy Fiona Carpenter, Pan Macmillan).

*At the end of* The Dark *people go on to a higher state of awareness, as they do in* Nobody True. *What are your own personal thoughts about what lies beyond death?*

Well, I know that nobody knows [*laughs*]. Therefore I can speculate as much as I like. But I do genuinely believe in an afterlife. I think this is not it, this can't be just what it's all about, there's got to be something more and we're given clues here and there—

people who claim to have seen their father who's died recently ... I think they're little clues that there is something else going on, but we don't know what it is. Faith healers and clairvoyants, I think a lot of them are very genuine, and something definitely happens with them, their minds go onto a higher plane. A lot of charlatans just make money out of the business, but there are enough good ones to outweigh that. So yeah, I kind of go along with that. I'm a Catholic anyway, so I believe in God.

*Which character that you've created has been your favorite?*

Probably Fluke. Second to that would be Joseph Creed, who is such an out-and-out bastard [*laughs*]. He's such a cynic, but I really loved doing him, I loved writing about him, because he did all the things the hero's not supposed to do. It was my resistance to the normal type of hero, that this guy could be so weak and devious, and totally cowardly. It just gave me a kick to write about him, so he's another favorite character.

*What's an average writing day for you, if there is one?*

I start late, around ten. I work 'til lunchtime, then I'll have lunch and read the morning paper. Then I'm back in the study at about half past two, and I work on 'til six o'clock. And that's the weekly job. I used to work seven days a week, but I don't any more, thank God. I've kept it down to five days. Sometimes Saturday I have to answer mail, fan mail and stuff, and all that keeps me very busy, contracts and business dealings. It's not just writing, a whole lot more is going on. But that's okay because I can handle that, because I did have two jobs at one time, one in advertising and one as a writer, and I was able to do that for five years.

*Are you still writing by hand?*

Yep, I find that the contact with the page is good for me. I've always written with a jumbo pen, Pentel, and with a jumbo pad from W.H. Smiths. It's always worked for me so I see no reason to change it. It might be unlucky for me to do it straight onto a computer.

*If it ain't broke, don't fix it [laughs]. I believe* **Others** *was based on a true story?*

Somebody told me of a hospital not far from where we lived—this was when we lived in the East End—where they used to keep deformed babies, toddlers, in a special isolated ward and nobody knew they were there. I always wondered, "What happens to these people when they grow up, or do they grow up? Where do they live, why don't we see more of them?" 'cause there's a hell of a lot of malformed kids that we don't know about. I found a book on that type of thing, a horrible book, it's not one you can buy off the shelves, but it showed me examples of the kind of mutations that can happen to human beings. So yeah, the premise for this was absolutely true. There are places where these kids are brought up or just allowed to die, and I wondered why we didn't know more about it—and why shouldn't those people be a part of society along with the rest of us, although they're different? I mean, everyone is disparate in their own way.

*Do you still believe that Bjork is part fairy?*

Oh that was a joke [*laughs*]. I'm glad you caught it though, not everybody got that.

*Does writing still give you that same buzz as when you first started out?*

Oh yes. It's very, very satisfying. Trouble is, it's very wearing as well. It's like having a fifteen-round fight with Sonny Liston, the heavyweight boxer. When I'm finished I'm totally drained and it takes me a while to get over it. That only lasts a short time and then I'm up and ready for the next one. When I see [a finished novel] in the bookshops I love it, especially if they're in a pile or all lined up together. They always look good that way. So yeah, I still get that thrill. I still get involved in the advertising, where it should go and the actual design for the posters, I'm very much involved in that part of things. So that's what I mean, it's not just writing books, other things come into it.

*Your novel* **Nobody True** *concentrates on out-of-body experiences. What first got you interested in that?*

For me, that's been around for a long time: What happens after you're dead. Many things could happen—you could go straight to Heaven, I wish [*laughs*], or your soul could just wander, lost, for a long period of time, then you're reborn. Who knows? Who cares? But again, it just seemed like a good vehicle for horror, this guy who's lost his body and he can't get back into it because it's gone, it's dead, it's cut up, and he's doesn't know what to do or what he's doing, and it's just an intriguing idea for me.

*Could you sum up what horror means to you personally?*

Let me see now, he says looking out of the window at all these acres of forest [*laughs*] and his garden....

*Not the most horrible of views, is it?*

And the three guitars up against the wall there [*laughs*], yeah, what's horror mean to me?, let me think.... No, obviously I wouldn't have written books if they weren't going to be sold in big numbers, because my job in advertising was big anyway—sorry, it sounds very boastful, but that's just the way it was. I had a great job in advertising, but I had so much energy in those days, so that's why I started writing books on the weekends. And I found that I loved it as a medium, I just got into it so much. I've loved every page I've written, not because it was well-written, in fact just because it was a page of thoughts and interesting ideas, hopefully. Yeah, it was nice to explore the supernatural and the paranormal—things that we really don't know about—and I really like researching into that. But I don't go mad over it, I'm not a fanatic, I'm not obsessed by horror, not at all. Once I leave the study at night, that's it, that's James Herbert left behind me. I always have ideas at odd times of the day, but I don't go around thinking macabre thoughts. I'm pretty normal.

*Is that because you're getting it all out on the page?*

I guess it must be, I guess it must be...

# Joe Hill

Joe Hill was born and grew up in Bangor, Maine. His first book, *20th Century Ghosts* (originally published in 2005 by PS Publishing), collected fourteen stories of the weird and the fantastic. Several stories were reprinted in various Year's Best anthologies while the book itself won the Bram Stoker Award for Best Fiction Collection, as well as the British Fantasy Award for Best Collection and Best Short Story for "Best New Horror." Joe is the past recipient of the Ray Bradbury Fellowship, the A.E. Coppard Prize for Long Fiction in 1999 for "Better Than Home," the 2006 winner of the William Crawford Award and the 2006 World Fantasy Award for Best Novella for "Voluntary Committal." His first novel, *Heart-Shaped Box*, was published by William Morrow in the U.S. and Victor Gollancz in the U.K. in 2007. He has more recently been working on an IDW comic series called *Locke and Key*, plus more books for PS: *Gunpowder* and its sequel *Slave Girls of Gunpowder*, as well as another novel, *Horns*. Joe lives in New England with his wife, three children, and enough pets to crowd an ark.

---

*In the intro to your collection, Christopher Golden asks, "Where the hell did this guy come from to just pop up fully formed like this?" and that's probably how it seems to most readers, who hadn't heard your name because they don't buy small press magazines. But it took you about ten years, didn't it?*

Yeah, that's about right. My first published story was in 1994. I won't care to say where it was published or what the title was, because that story never needs to be seen again [*laughs*]. And then a couple of short stories that are in *20th Century Ghosts*, "Better Than Home" and "Pop Art," existed in first draft, I want to say in 1995 or 1996. But they took a while to take shape and find their place, to get published in their markets. So yeah, some of the earlier stories in *20th Century Ghosts* are really over ten years old.

*So how much influence would you say the small press had on your career?*

Well, I wouldn't have any kind of career without the small presses. And I don't think I'm the only writer that's true of. I think a lot of writers have—especially more recently—struggled their way up because there were people in the small presses, publishers, who wanted to lace their fingers together and give them a boot up. I have to say, the small press is sort of in its glory days right now. Part of it is that the small presses really do produce books that are just as handsome, or sometimes even more handsome, than mainstream releases. And I think the big mainstream publishers have a tendency to go with what's safe over what's fresh. But what's safe isn't really safe. What's familiar a lot of times isn't really what people want, so the small press will sometimes take a chance on that edgier

**Joe Hill (courtesy Mickey Choate and Joe Hill).**

story and that different novel, and sometimes that's just what people are ready for. I can think of several who've come out of the small presses and are delivering work that people are really excited about. I think that Kelly Link is the biggest example, but certainly in genre fiction there's Brian Keene, whose first couple of books were for small presses and then he went to Leisure horror in the States and then I think I heard he's got a new book and is doing very nicely. So it's the small press community that's provided a network of support for him to go somewhere. I mean, I had a great experience with PS Publishing, everything went perfectly—I can't imagine a better experience, a better first experience for anyone for their first book.

*And the book did incredibly well, didn't it?*

It's been a really fun, really surprising ride. I'm glad people found their way to it, and it's exciting that it was reviewed well. And it was published by William Morrow/Harper-Collins in the U.S. and Gollancz in the U.K.

*Why do you think it's so hard to make the jump from small press to mass market? Relatively few writers make it.*

I think it depends. You'll have to be ready for a really unsatisfying answer—the better your questions are, the less likely it is that I'll say anything even remotely intelligent [*laughs*]. Some writers *have* made the jump from small press to big press, especially recently. I think it tends to be if a small press work is released and generates excitement, then the mainstream presses notice. I think there has been some good, idiosyncratic work that's come up in the small press that's attracted notice—or is noticed, but only, when you're talking about genre fiction, within the narrow range of the genre fiction community, as opposed to leaping out and getting some attention from a larger audience. I think the great thing is that there are a lot of writers who continue to be intent on doing small press work, and that makes good sense because you can continue to take chances, do different things and try different forms and genres in a small press that you might not get anywhere else. That's what it was made for. You certainly can take risks where you might not be encouraged otherwise.

*You've written both mainstream and genre fiction, yet you seem to keep being drawn back to genre fiction. Why do you think that is?*

When I started writing short stories, almost all of them were sort of literary mainstream fiction. I loved a lot of those stories, and I think the editors who looked at them also liked them, but I didn't sell a lot of 'em. What I kept hearing back was, "We really like the quality of the writing here, but the story itself doesn't excite us." And I couldn't ever blame the editors for sending them back because those stories never excited me either. At the time I was reading a lot of Bernard Malamud. I still read a lot of Malamud, and I read his essay "Why Fantasy?" in which he talked about how while all literature is make believe, Fantasy is actually more valid comparable to realism. He talked about how the walls of Norman Mailer are as purely imaginary as the walls of Lewis Carroll. They're both invented worlds, the product of pure fantasy. So he was making an argument that you could introduce a ghost into a story, or an angel, and there was no reason not to do that because that could have power. I read that and thought, "Yeah, I believe that 100 percent." Not long afterwards I wrote "Pop Art," and it was the most fun I'd had writing anything, ever. It was just a blast from start to finish. I wrote it very quickly, and the guy who published it was excited about it. People seemed to respond to it in a way they hadn't responded to my other stuff. And eventually I started thinking it was a healthy thing to let my freak flag fly, to explore weird concepts because it was something I was having fun with. The interesting thing is, now I've written all these ghost stories and all this strange fiction and everything, and the last two stories I've done have been a bit more realistic. A story

**Vincent Chong's artwork for the first edition of Hill's collection *20th Century Ghosts* (2005, PS Publishing; courtesy Peter Crowther, PS Publishing).**

I have coming up in *Postscripts* is still a sad story but it has no supernatural elements. The novel I'm working on now has no supernatural or fantasy elements. So maybe it's a periodic thing where occasionally I really want to write something weird and strange and explore those kinds of concepts, and other times not.

*You've been quoted as saying, "If you publish a story in a genre magazine it's fantasy, but if you publish it in a literary journal it's magical realism." Why do you think readers of literary journals find that difference in description necessary?*

I think the labeling game is more important to publishers than it is to writers and readers in a way, although we're talking about the difference between fantasy stories and mainstream literary stories. "Pop Art" was published in a mainstream literary market, "20th Century Ghost" was published in a mainstream literary market—it was published in *High Plains Literary Review*. I didn't look at those stories when I wrote them and say, "Now I'm doing genre stories." I still felt that what I was aiming for was a story about character and ... I don't want to sound all self-important here, what am I saying? [*Laughs*] I certainly didn't think that it was just a straight genre story, I did think that it would have appeal to the average literary reader.

*It's just where to put it on the shelf, people like to know.*

Yeah, but I do think that a lot of the stories I was selling to literary markets in America, I was then selling to genre markets in England. I don't know why that is. I do think this is a great time for genre fiction, a great time to be writing strange stories and surreal stories and magic realism. Fantasy—the genre forms of fantasy, mystery and horror and science fiction—has been invited back into the literary mainstream in a way that it hasn't in years and years. You know, back in the '30s and '40s *The New Yorker* would publish ghost stories, like Shirley Jackson's "The Lottery." And you would see writers—established, respected literary writers—who wrote ghost stories and strange stories in addition to more typical literary offerings. Then I think genre got a bad name for years and years, but what you've seen recently is writers like Michael Chabon who's written some outright fantasy and some novels that play with fantasy motifs; Jonathan Letham, whose hard-boiled crime story was "Motherless Brooklyn" and he did a superhero story which was called "The Fortress of Solitude"; Kelly Link, who I think *Time Magazine* had shortlisted as one of the five best young writers of her generation. And all these people playing with genre elements but getting literary credibility, with respect of critics and being talked about at the universities and so on. So I think there's a chance now for an interesting cross-pollination going on where if you're a genre writer, if you've always written genre stuff, literary readers aren't as afraid of that. I think if you're a literary writer and want to try something different and explore genre, that you won't be spit on and shunned for that.

*What films and books would you cite as having a significant influence on your writing?*

I think that in the short stories, especially early on, I was really reading a lot of Bernard Malamud. There's a collection of all his gathered stories, *The Complete Stories of Malamud*. Some of those stories I read two or three or four times, and I'd go through them with a highlighter and underline, to try and figure out how he'd achieved an effect. Kelly Link wrote a story called "The Specialist's Hat," and that's one that I made a real study out of. It was fascinating—I still feel it's almost like a perfect pocket watch. It's amazing to take it apart and look at all the gears packed inside it. With the novel *Heart-Shaped*

*Box*, one of the two things that I really had in mind was a novel by Charles Portis called *True Grit*—it was made into a movie starring John Wayne. The novel's pretty stunning. It's about this 14-year-old girl named Mattie Ross, who is extremely precocious and has a lot of hard bark on her, she's very rough-edged and cunning and everyone is a little bit frightened of her. She goes out to get revenge on the man who shot down her father, and she falls in with this drunk, burned-out federal marshal with an extremely ugly temper, and the two of them go on the hunt. The story really examines the road story, and the way that two difficult outsiders gradually fall in love with each other, and come to trust each other and care about each other.

There's a little bit of that in *Heart-Shaped Box*, in which you've got the lead character, Judas Coyne, and he's living with this much younger woman, a Goth who he calls Georgia to remind her what state she came from. They're playing with fate to keep on constantly reminding her of her past as opposed to who she wants to reinvent herself as. When you first meet them they seem very hostile to each other; they seem like maybe sort of ugly, bitter, angry people. Maybe you're half-rooting for bad things to happen to them, I don't know. But as the story goes along, I think it's a similar kind of journey, where they open up to each other. One thing which is great about a road trip story is that putting people on the road gives them an excuse to talk to each other and gradually strip away those layers and get past what the surface mask is, and that's always interesting.

The other thing that was really a big influence was, I was reading a lot of *Swamp Thing* by Alan Moore while I worked on *Heart-Shaped Box*, and I just love Swampie. The last half of the book winds up being set down south. Someone said to me, "You're a Northerner. Did you do a lot of research about the South?" And I said, "Yeah, I read about 40 issues of *Swamp Thing*." [*Laughs*] My version of the South is basically the version that you get in that comic book, to the point where Jude's hometown I named Moore's Corner to refer to where I got all my ideas from. But basically everything I learned about Louisiana I learned about from an Englishman from Northampton. Never been there [*laughs*].

*Is that what sparked* **Heart-Shaped Box***, then, the characterization? The characters of Georgia and Judas?*

I think originally I was trying to figure out how to work the Internet into a ghost story. I had noticed that there was this interesting and disturbing trading of cult items online. Just recently I saw a thing about a guy auctioning off his own soul. And I was thinking, "Boy, your idea's stale—someone tried to auction off his own soul three years ago, this guy's gotta get a new act." People have sold tons of items. One thing that comes up for sale about once a year, is a book that's actually bound in human skin. The disturbing thing is that someone is selling that stuff, because if someone has something they think they can make some money from, they sell it if they don't want it. What's weird is to think about who's buying it. So I had this idea of a guy being foolish enough to buy a ghost online. A lot of ghost stories are about people making purchases they shouldn't have made, buying things ... you know, buying *that* house, the house in Amityville. They think they're just getting the five bedrooms and the backyard, and in fact they're getting the horrible past that has happened to that house.

So what attracted me was the concept, but I thought it would just be a short story. I thought that Jude would buy this ghost online, as a joke, as a stunt, then realize after the ghost has come to his house—after he'd realized it was real—what a mistake he had made, but it was too late and the ghost was gonna ... eat him for breakfast [*laughs*]. That's how I thought the story would go, and that it would be done in 30 pages and I'd sell it to Andy Cox at TTA Press. But what happened was, Jude realizes about 15, 20 pages into the story that he's been tricked into buying a ghost. The woman who sold it has secret motives and he confronts her about it, and she starts laughing at him, saying, "You're gonna die!" This is the part in the story where Jude should have melted down and gone into a panic. But he didn't. As I was writing it, I found him getting calmer. And suddenly he took control of the conversation, setting the woman who's sold him the ghost back on her heels. From there on out, he just constantly proves to be more resourceful and clever and nervy than I expected him to be. So as I wrote I became interested in who he was, and how he had wound up where he was. When we meet Judas, we meet this angry, isolated 54-year-old rock star, who's had 30 years on

The UK hardback cover for *Heart-Shaped Box*, with cover artwork and design by Edward Bettison (2007, Gollancz; courtesy Jo Fletcher, Gollancz).

the pop culture rollercoaster. He's got this rock star name, Judas Coyne—no one has a name like that, that's not a real name. So I got interested in who he had been before he was Judas Coyne and how he had wound up in this place. The story becomes a mystery—not a whodunit but a who-*is*-he? I would say that the story started with the concept but that the concept only in a weird way interested me for about two and a half days, then what kept the thing going was my interest in Jude ... and my interest in Georgia, who also has her share of secrets and is not who she first appears.

*You've kind of answered our next question there; we were going to ask, do you like to plot things or let them grow?*

I think that outlines are the tool of the Devil. I try to stay away from a set idea about what should happen in the story. What I really aim for is to get a character that excites me personally—one that springs to life and has a unique way of looking at the world—and then get that character facing down some kind of threat. Then you've got something fun to write because you kinda just sit back and let that character get on with things in his or her own personal way.

*Neil Gaiman described* Heart-Shaped Box *on his journal as so nightmarishly moreish that he wound up reading it cleaning his teeth, and that it's the best debut novel since* **The Damnation Game.** *How did you feel when you heard that?*

I love Neil Gaiman, I've been reading him since I was 14; I got to spend some time with him at FantasyCon 2006 and what a privilege. The great thing is when you get emotionally attached to a writer, you get ideas about who that person must be. And a lot of times when you meet that writer, then you're completely shattered and disappointed because it turns out to be a boorish, nose-picking twit—it shatters all your illusions about things. In fact, Neil Gaiman turned out to be just the sweet and thoughtful guy I thought he would be. As thoughtful and as witty a guy as I thought he would be. It's really exciting to have written something that someone I'd been attached to in terms of reading his work since I was in high school, to have written something that he enjoyed is a real honor and really exciting. I knew he had a copy of the book, and I got an email from him saying how much he was enjoying it, and I spent the rest of the day hovering around in this happy trance with this big, stupid grin on my face.

*And there's going to be a film of* Heart-Shaped Box, *isn't there?*

Possibly. I think there's a decent chance. Just because someone buys the rights to make something, doesn't mean they're actually *going* to make something, so it's hard to say. It will be interesting to see what they do if they do make a film out of it.

*Is it something you'd like to script yourself?*

I was asked if I wanted to essentially take a stab at the screenplay, and at the time I decided not to, because I'm on the hook for another book for William Morrow/Harper, and I had some other stuff I wanted to work on. I'd spent a long time working on *Heart-Shaped Box*, so it was like, okay, time for a change. I've already said and done everything interesting I could possibly do with these characters. Maybe it would be interesting if somebody else took it and ran with it, and did their own thing. I still think that was a pretty good decision, actually. I'd love to do some screenwriting some time, but I think at this particular moment probably not.

*Any idea who you'd like to see script it, ideally?*

Well, I know that they've already assigned a guy. He's a young guy, and he's certainly got a reputation for having done some interesting work—but I don't know that much about his work. I couldn't say how many films, how many screenplays he's actually had produced. I think it's all still in the early stages and all sort of pie in the sky until you've actually got people in front of the camera and you're filming something. I should mention, though, that there's actually another film project. My short story "Pop Art" actually looks like it's going to be a short film [by] a young Englishwoman named Amanda Boyle. Again, it's the same kind of deal until they're actually filming something, I don't know whether anything's going to happen, but she certainly seems to want to make it and has most of her financing lined up.*

*Which do you find more disturbing, quiet horror or the more in-your-face shock horror?*

This is probably an awful, terrible thing to say, but as a rule I don't find shock horror that disturbing. I really tend to find it kind of funny, actually. I still think the high moment

---

*\*Pop Art has since been completed and has had screenings at the Bird's Eye View Festival in London, the Ann Arbor Film Festival in Ann Arbor, Michigan, the Dresden Film Festival in Dresden, Germany, the Atlanta Film Festival in Atlanta, Georgia and the River Run Film Festival in Winston-Salem, North Carolina.*

in the history of shock horror is *Evil Dead II*, which plays like a 90-minute Three Stooges [short] with blood going everywhere. I love quiet horror when it's something like *The Haunting of Hill House*, as long as quiet isn't a euphemism for boring. Sometimes someone will say they've done something that's quiet horror and what they really mean by that is there's 250 pages of them just spinning their wheels while nothing happens. But something like *The Haunting of Hill House* casts this uneasy spell over you from the first sentence, and you just float through it while things get worse and worse. For me, I don't really think there's any gain in just being shocking for the sake of being shocking. What I will say is that what I'm absolutely terrified of, the thing that worries me the most, is losing the interest of the reader. I don't want to be boring. If I'm boring, there's always something good on TV. So you want to get the story right up front, something in the first sentence, in the first paragraph, that introduces the threat or creates the situation in an interesting light and then hopefully keep people going.

The poster for Amanda Boyle's adaptation of *Pop Art* (2008, Film London; courtesy Maggie Ellis and Jo Cadoret [Film London], Amanda Boyle, Helen Giles, Kate Meyers and Tracy Brimm [Forward Films]).

*Is the cinema Rosebud in "20th Century Ghost" based on a real one, or a mixture of cinemas?*

Every small town has a place just like that. I got the idea of a specific theater, but the theater in the book is similar to a theater I know and love.

*You reference Jack Finney in "The Black Phone." How big an influence was he on your work?*

I don't know how big an influence he is at this point; it's been a long time since I've read anything by him. It's scary how much great work is out there, especially within the genre of fantasy and horror; it's depressing how much great work is out there that seemed really important in the moment, but now people have gradually let slip away and forgotten about. People still remember *The Body Snatchers* because [there's a movie version] about every decade, but he did a lot of work; he didn't just do that novel, he did a lot of great stuff. And I think that *I Love Galesburg in the Springtime* is a great collection and compares with classic Bradbury collections like *The October Country*. Bradbury's stuff is never ever going to be out of print. He's such a remarkable writer. But there are other writers—guys

The character Art brought to life in *Pop Art*, directed by Amanda Boyle (2008, Film London; courtesy Maggie Ellis and Jo Cadoret [Film London], Amanda Boyle, Helen Giles, Kate Meyers and Tracy Brimm [Forward Films]).

like Finney—who also did interesting, fascinating work. A lot of that Jack Finney stuff I was crazy for when I was in high school.

*You mention* **The Body Snatchers***; do you have a favorite film version of it?*

I think the original [*Invasion of the Body Snatchers*, 1956] is the really scary one. I do think that there's been a number of readings of this and they've been getting increasingly bad. But yeah, I'd go with the first one. I like all those black-and-white scary films, not that they're all that scary—especially if there are giant ants wandering through them. I'll tell you something, I love a certain kind of old horror. *Heart-Shaped Box* in many ways echoes this old horror film which is called *Night of the Demon* [a.k.a. *Curse of the Demon*, 1957]. Structurally it's a very similar kind of story, and *Night of the Demon* is based on an M.R. James short story that I've never read called "Casting the Runes." In *Night of the Demon*, there's a skeptic who doesn't believe in the supernatural [Dr. John Holden played by Dana Andrews] and he publicly ridicules a guy like Aleister Crowley [Julian Karswell played by Niall MacGinnis] who passes the skeptic a parchment with runic symbols. The protagonist starts to see this demon that breathes smoke getting closer and closer to him, and gradually he comes to realize that he's only got a certain amount of time to get rid of the parchment—to give it away to someone else before this thing gets him. And it turns into this tremendous chase, trying to figure out where this Aleister Crowley figure has gone, so he can give the parchment back to him before the demon tears him apart. It's a great, great chase—very creepy and lively. And in some ways the plot of *Heart-Shaped Box* echoes that in that the black suit—the dead man's suit that Judas ends up acquiring—is a little bit like the parchment. He finds himself in a similar kind of fix. They have their differences too, but I definitely thought of *Night of the Demon* more than once while I was working on *Heart-Shaped Box*.

*It's interesting how many times "Casting the Runes" has been reworked: You've mentioned* **Heart-Shaped Box***, but there's also Muriel Gray's* **Furnace** *and Christopher Fowler's* **Rune***.*

The really embarrassing thing is that I haven't read the original. I haven't really read that much M.R. James, I've read a couple of short stories but it's a hole in my education;

I should really go back and read some. I like that Adam Nevill story which was written in the style of M.R. James, which was in *Best New Horror*, "Where Angels Come In." He's pretty good, that was a really memorable short story.

*"Black Phone"—you've mentioned that short story kept wanting to be a novel. Do you think you'll ever go back and rework it or expand it?*

No, because I think that there are too many elements of that story which are too familiar, too clichéd. I think it works at the size it's at. At that size I was able to keep it so that it feels fresh and interesting, but I think spread across two or three hundred pages, too many of the things that are off-the-shelf would begin to seem trite. We've got this child serial killer—how many times have we seen that character? I had that tendency, especially when I was younger, for stories to run too long. "Better Than Home," the baseball story in *20th Century Ghosts*, was originally 120 pages first draft. And it became a lesson on economy; I sort of learned about economy while I was working on it, because you can't really do anything with a 120-page story, especially with no publishing credits. There was just nowhere to go with it, so I figured I had to make it shorter if I wanted to try and sell it. So I began looking at things like: Can I take these five pages and make them one paragraph? Can I take these three pages and make them one sentence? So that went from 120 pages to 80 pages, 60 pages, and finally I got it down to 37 pages, and I couldn't strip away any more without it starting to affect the story. That happens to lesser degrees with other stories; I think even now it's pretty typical for a first draft of mine to be 60 pages. For a while there I was in a good groove and I think I brought in two or three stories in a row that were like 40 pages. But, as I was finishing off, there's a kind of twist in the end with the last stories of *20th Century Ghosts*; they started to bloat again, to run out of control. I think I was just getting bored of writing stuff in the short form and I was really eager to get on to a novel. I think I had two before *Heart-Shaped Box* which started as short stories and I quickly began to see a potential there for a whole novel. And two times I held off: With "Black Phone" and "The Cape" I held off, and didn't let them become novels. Then the third time in the collection, I allowed it to go long and that's the one that turned into *Heart-Shaped Box*.

**Hill accepting the British Fantasy Award for *20th Century Ghosts*. Photograph by Paul Kane.**

*Regarding your story "Last Breath": If you could capture anybody's last breath, whose would it be?*

Hmm. ... it's such a morbid thing to own [*laughs*]. Anyone's last breath to have on my shelf? Probably Charles Addams, because I saw the whole story as being like a Charles

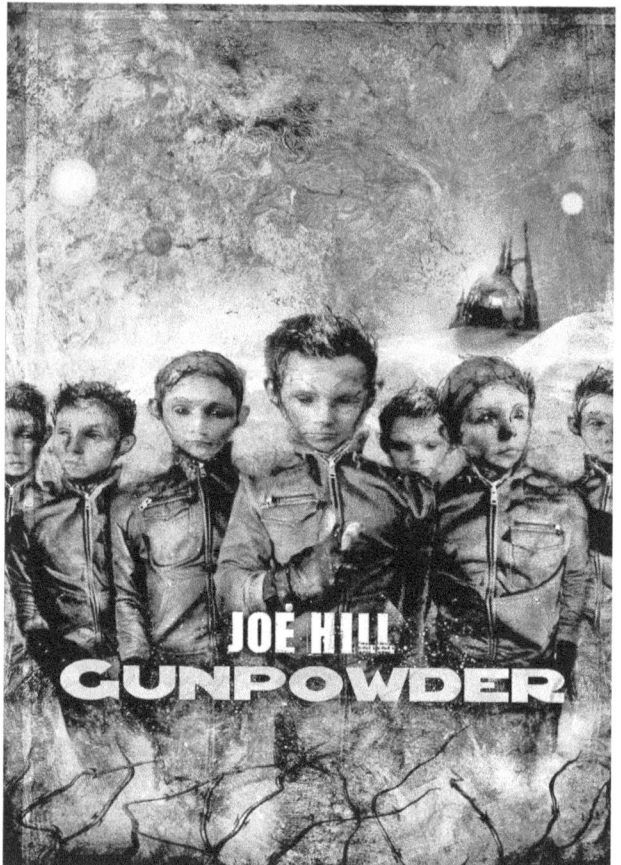

One of Hill's latest ventures, the novella *Gunpowder*, with artwork by Vincent Chong (2008, PS Publishing; courtesy Peter Crowther, PS Publishing).

Addams cartoon. It was kind of like a test to do in words what he would do in a single picture. I was going for that morbid, Charles Addams, Addams Family–type gothic humor. With his sense of humor, I think he'd appreciate having his last breath stored as some sort of bizarre memento ... or maybe not, I don't know [*laughs*].

*"My Father's Mask" is quite a surreal story. What was the inspiration for that one?*

I think I was really trying to figure out, how does Kelly Link write these great weird ones? And the inspiration was: I've gotta try one! Other than that ... people often talk about how horror stories are like nightmares. But they really never are, and I thought it would be really cool to try and write something that had a solid narrative, but to try to see how close I could structure it to feel like something in a nightmare. I don't know if I came very close, but I just wanted to see what would happen. Because what happens in a weird story like that is you have 90 percent realism, and then a scene of the fantastic. "20th Century Ghost" is primarily a realistic story, built around this one fantastic moment where in 1944 this kid sits down in a movie theater next to the ghost of a girl. Everything else about the story, about where this guy's life took him and the difficulties of running a small town movie theater, and people he's known over the course of his life, is realistic.

# Shaun Hutson

Shaun Huston was born and brought up in Hertfordshire. After being expelled from school, he worked at many jobs, including a cinema doorman, a barman, and a shop assistant—all of which he was sacked from—before becoming a professional author in 1982. His breakout novel was *Slugs* and since then he has written over 30 bestsellers such as *Erebus, Shadows, Relics, Death Day, Assassin, Heathen, Lucy's Child, Exit Wounds, Hell to Pay, Dying Words, Unmarked Graves* and *Body Count*. He has also written for radio, magazines, television and the Internet. At one time, Hutson was published under six pseudonyms, writing everything from Westerns to non-fiction. He continues to work under a pseudonym he will not disclose. His consuming passion is football; a Liverpool supporter for over 30 years, his allegiance borders on frenzy. He never misses a game, home or away. He lives in Buckinghamshire with his wife, his daughter and two pairs of Michelle Pfeiffer's shoes.

---

*What was the first piece of writing you ever did?*

A school play when I was about 11. Surprise, surprise, it was a Dracula story. The first bit of paid writing I ever did was my first published novel, *Blood and Honour*, a war novel published in 1982. I'd had about 40 rejections before then; everything from scripts to novels. I think I'd already written five books before one was finally accepted, so I sympathize when people tell me they keep getting stuff rejected by publishers. I know how it feels....

*Is it true that it was reading the books of Guy N. Smith that indirectly made you have a go at doing horror novels?*

Indirectly, because I read one of his books when I was eighteen and thought, "Christ, if he's getting paid to write stuff like that, I'll have a go myself." Ah, the innocence of youth, eh? It sometimes worries me now when my own readers say, "I read one of your books and decided I wanted to write." I think, shit, is it for the same reasons I started? Around the same time, I also saw the film *Cross of Iron*, directed by Sam Peckinpah, and I really wanted to write something like that. I went on to write about fifteen war novels, every one of them with a nod towards *Cross of Iron* in it.

*One of your favorite films is* **Alien***. Why is this?*

Because, in my humble opinion, it's a masterpiece. It was another huge influence on me at the time—1979. I recently saw the director's cut at the pictures and it's still a fantastic experience on a big screen. For me, it's one of cinema's faultless classics. Great script, great performances, brilliant direction. I love it. I also think it is head and shoulders above [James] Cameron's *Aliens*.

*When did the concept for* **Slugs** *first strike you?*

*Slugs* was originally going to be about leeches. However, the agent I had at the time had just read *Deathday*, which has a scene with a giant slug in it. He said, "Why not do a book all about slugs?" I thought it was a pretty dumb idea. At that time, there'd been books about cats, frogs, crabs, preying mantes, birds, spiders and fuck knows what. Also slugs can't chase people, can they? Well, not unless the people are crawling. Nevertheless, I did the research, wrote the book, and it was a bestseller, probably the book I'll always be remembered for, no matter what I've done since, and that's fine. Shows what I know about writing, eh?

**What was most disturbing was the way that the slugs, when ingested, could also turn normal people into psychopaths. Are you especially interested in how people can suddenly switch and do violent things?**

I think that we've all got a snapping point, a part of us that is on the edge, and that interests me. Everyone loses their temper but I'm interested in what sends them that bit further. Obviously being infected by mutated slugs will do it every time but, in all my other books, the characters are usually on the edge to begin with or can snap at any given moment. So can normal people, they just don't like admitting it.

**What did you think of the film version of Slugs, and are there any other books you'd like to see made into films or TV shows?**

The film of *Slugs* was good fun. I just thought at the time, "If it's good I'll say it's because it was based on my novel, if it's shit I'll blame the filmmakers...." Any writer knows that, when they sell their book for filming, not much of what he wrote will end up on the screen. It's no good bitching and whining about it, you just take the money and run and hope they do a good job. Obviously I'd like to see everything I've ever written turned into films and TV and all for huge amounts of money. If Paramount rang up tomorrow and said, "We'd like to buy the rights for all your books for an obscene amount of money and turn them into musicals," I'd be delighted. The public are not stupid enough to think that a film's bad because of the book it was based on. Besides, if the studios pay you enough, who fucking cares?

**What do you think it is about monster babies—which you drew on for Spawn—that's disturbing when used in horror fiction and movies? Is it an innocence thing turned sour?**

I'm not sure it's anything to do with innocence gone wrong. In fact, I'm probably the wrong person to ask because I never look for any deeper hidden meanings in books other than what's on the printed page. The monster kids in *Spawn* were monsters because they were reanimated fetuses. I must admit, I loved that image of the fetus at about three months with the big black eyes; the thought of three of the fucking things walking around was even better for the sake of the book. As with any horror cliché, if it's done well it's great; if it isn't, it becomes laughable. I hope I did it well in *Spawn*. However, for every great mutant baby, there's a shit one. For every *Rosemary's Baby* there's an *I Don't Want to Be Born*....

**Was Wakeley from Erebus based on anywhere in particular—and do you tend to base your locations on real places?**

Wakely was a composite of many different places. Unless my books are set in London, most of the locations are invented. Some of them, like the waxworks in *Heathen* or the funfair in *Dying Words*, are based on real places, but the others are just figments of my imagination. Some of the interiors of houses in books have been based on places where I've lived and many hotels have been based on actual places where I've stayed but, mainly, if I have to, I dream them up.

*In* **Shadows**, *you deal with the subconscious and hypnosis. Did you have to do a lot of research about this subject and what conclusions did you draw about the human mind from them?*

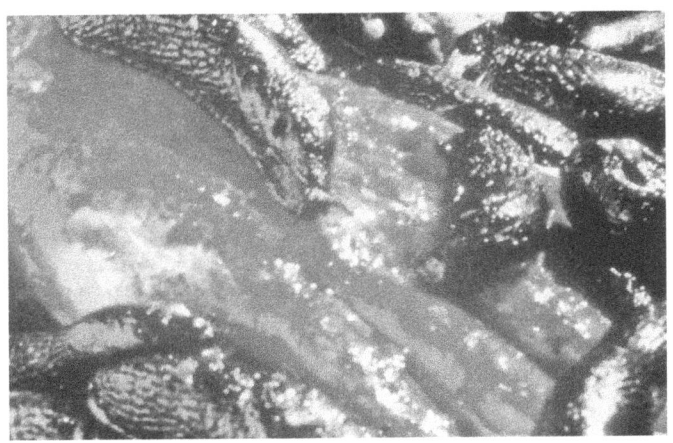

From the film adaptation of *Slugs* (1988, New World Pictures).

I went down to London to do the research, to a place called the Institute of Psychical Research, and spoke to a nice lady—who thought I was a journalist trying to write an exposé—about astral travel, hypnosis, out-of-body experiences and stuff like that. My conclusions about the human mind were pretty much made up without visiting that place, though. The human mind is capable of some amazing things and some horrible things. Pretty obvious I know but, as I said before, we all have two sides to us and sometimes the darker side is more attractive. Sorry to sound pretentious but think about it, the human mind can produce thoughts like those of Einstein or like those of Hitler.... Fuck, sorry, getting really arty-farty now, forgive me.

*You've used archaeology as a basis for a couple of your books,* **The Skull** *and* **Relics**. *Is this something that interests you, and what scope do you think there is in the past for horror?*

The archaeological aspect of those books was purely a plot device but the research was fun in both cases. Trying to mix stuff from the past with present day is good fun and it's been done to death in films and books but, if the material's there, then why not? I've got a book coming up that's set in 1812 and a few of mine have had historical connections. *Renegades* and *Nemesis* to name but two.

*If you possessed a powerful medallion like the one in* **Death Day**, *what would you use it for?*

I'd use it to make myself win about thirty million on the Euro Lottery, then I'd retire....

*Was Frank Miller from* **Victims** *named after the writer-cartoonist—and what do you make of his stuff, like* **Sin City**?

I'd never even heard of Frank Miller when I wrote *Victims*. I've never read any of his stuff. I thought the film of *Sin City* was clever but Christ did it know it. More down to Robert Rodriguez than Frank Miller though, I fear. *300* was okay. I can understand the attraction of graphic novels to filmmakers. It saves them the trouble of doing storyboards.

*Have you ever written something and thought, "No, I've gone too far" or maybe not far enough?*

I think that, after a while, if you're writing stuff like I do, it becomes impossible to tell whether you've crossed over a line of good or bad taste. Just writing in the genre shows a lack of good taste to begin with. So, if you're going to be extreme, then fuck it, go for it. I've had a couple of scenes banned before they were written, in *Erebus* and *Spawn* and, all through my career, editors and publishers have asked me to tone down violence [and] language or soften characters. No one, strangely enough, has ever asked me to cut down on the sex scenes ... weird, eh? *Deadhead* caused a terrible fuss at my publishers because of the subject matter. *Compulsion* was heavily cut. As Nick Blake I once wrote a novel called *Chainsaw Terror* that was banned outright. Killing kids in print is always a tricky area and people seem to react particularly violently if animals are hurt. You can do what you like to adults but don't hurt a fucking cat; you'll incur the wrath of the nation.

*What's your process for creating believable characters? Do you feel for them when they're in danger or going through the mill?*

Most of my characters are based on real people. All the central characters have elements of me in them. I feel what those people feel when I'm writing. The Hackets' failing marriage in *Nemesis* was horrible to write, for example. I find things like that much more disturbing than writing about violence because stuff like that's more likely to happen to people. Another relationship I found hard to write was Amy and Franklin in *Necessary Evil*. The scene where he's listening to her singing on a tape after she's been killed had me in tears. Yeah, I'm just a big softie, really. I do feel for the characters when I'm writing. You live with these people for six months or more, you start to like them. Even the rotten ones.

*What appeals to you about your recurring protagonist Sean Doyle—and what has made you use him again and again in your novels?*

Doyle's now turned up in four novels since making his debut in *Renegades* and, to be honest, at the end of the first book, as far as I was concerned, he was dead. But I had so many letters from people asking when I was doing a sequel that I checked and saw that he could actually still be alive. So, he came back in *White Ghost*, *Knife Edge* and *Hybrid*. He's so easy to write because he's so simple—not in a thick bastard way—and direct. There's no frills with old Sean. [He's] a bit like me.

*How do you feel Sean developed over time, and* is *there that much of you in him?*

There's *so* much of him in me and vice versa. I feel very comfortable writing about him and I've enjoyed writing every book he's been in. He doesn't take shit from anyone, says what he thinks and, basically, his heart's in the right place. Honest.

*You've also used policemen as central characters quite a few times. What do you think makes these good heroes to write about? And have you ever visited a police station, watched their procedures for research?*

Police are useful as central characters because they're usually on the spot when something's happened. I find the idea of the bumbling amateur sorting things out a bit irritating actually, so if you've got a police procedural novel then it's best to have a copper in one of the lead roles. Naturally I've spoken to policemen over the years for research and I visited New Scotland Yard while researching *Victims*—the Black Museum there, more specifically. Most of the stuff I need I can get from books or articles. If you start getting too technical, then readers switch off.

*You turned to thrillers more in the '90s. Was this because horror was undergoing a downward swing or just because you wanted to write more crime material? And do you think there's a natural link between the two?*

I didn't consciously turn to thrillers; it was just that the sort of stuff I wanted to write about was more thriller-based. I think all of my books have been structured like thrillers right from the beginning. The fact that the horror market was in a slump had nothing to do with it. In my opinion, horror is dead as a genre. I wish it wasn't but it's been killed by the huge amount of serial killer books spawned by stuff like *Silence of the Lambs*. The link between the two is very strong. Crime novels often become horrifying but, unfortunately, horror can't compete with human monsters. It's a real shame. It's also weird because there are so many shit horror films at the pictures but that trend hasn't spilled over into books and I don't think it ever will again. Then again, if the books mirrored some of the stuff at the pictures it's probably just as well.

**Lucy's Child** *was more psychological horror rather than the in-your-face variety. Which do you think disturbs people more? Is it better to see or not see the threat?*

*Lucy's Child* is still one of my favorite novels that I've written—sorry for the flash of arrogance there. I think the psychological horror was more effective. Certainly in films it works better with the old "what you don't see" thing. However, in books, I think you sometimes have to be a bit more full-on. As long as the violence isn't put there just for the sake of it. Same with sex and bad language. As long as those three things are necessary, then it's okay to use them. If they're put in for effect, readers will know. They're not stupid.

*The suicides of* **Stolen Angels** *were quite shocking. How hard was it to put yourself in the mind of someone forced to do that?*

It wasn't pleasant but it had to be done. I can understand how people can get to the state where they might *want* to kill themselves but actually *doing* it is a different matter. People say that those who commit suicide are cowards but it must take tremendous courage to actually end your own life. Certainly the guys in the book who killed themselves didn't have quite so much choice about it. The whole

*Dying Words* (2007, Orbit/Little Brown; courtesy Sean Garrehy, Orbit/Little Brown).

experience of *Stolen Angels* was a bit bizarre. When I first wrote it, I wasn't a father but, by the time the novel came out my daughter had been born and, flicking through it, there were bits I found very unpleasant to read again. (I know some people would say the whole book was unpleasant.) Even now, when I write about a kid being killed, I imagine my own daughter in that position. It's horrible but it helps the writing become more realistic. Sick, eh?

*Did you like the nicknames that were given to you such as "The Godfather of Gore" and "The Shakespeare of Gore"?*

I love them. It's better than being called a twat, isn't it? I think I probably have been called that too on more than one occasion, though. My favorite comment was "Britain's greatest living horror genre author." God, I love *Darkside* magazine....

*Was the story of* **Compulsion** *inspired by anything in real life?*

Not one incident in particular but a few attacks that had taken place on old people by yobs. Also I wanted to do something that had a feel of Sam Peckinpah's *Straw Dogs* to it, so things just combined to make the story. I wanted the readers to hate the yobs and then, if possible, actually pity them. I hope I managed it. Blurring that line between good and bad is very important to me. I would never have a central character in my books who was 100 percent good or 100 percent bad. After all, none of us are made like that.

*How did it feel to return to horror again with* **Hybrid** *onwards?*

To be honest, *Hybrid* was originally supposed to be a new Sean Doyle novel called *Fresh Skins* but Warners, my publishers, said they would prefer a horror novel. Well, by that time I'd written about three-quarters of the Doyle book and had to find a way of still using it. So, basically, I was left with the task of trying to "wrap a horror story around it." It turned out to be one of the most difficult books I've ever written and I was really glad when it was so well-received by readers. I didn't feel that I'd gone back to horror because I didn't ever feel that I'd left it behind. But I know what you mean.

**Twisted Souls** *deals with fear. What's your biggest fear?*

Death. Blindness. Morbid enough for you? I suppose I should say something amusing like being stuck in a room with a bunch of other authors, but I'd be lying. No, seriously, I'm terrified of death. I tend to side with Woody Allen on that one. When asked if he wanted to achieve immortality through his work he said no, he wanted to achieve it by not dying. I'll go along with that, Woody!

*Do you believe that creative gifts and inspiration come from somewhere other than inside ourselves—as in* **Dying Words***?*

Ooh, a deep one ... shit.... To be honest, I think there might be a kind of psychic price—the words of the late and very great Bill Hicks—to pay for talent. I mean, look at the number of geniuses—or whatever the plural of genius is—in history who've gone crazy. Van Gogh, great painter but fuck it, that one-eared look isn't good, is it? Nietzsche went insane. Lots of creative people drink themselves to death, die of drug overdoses or whatever. I speak as an ex-alcoholic and manic depressive; my price to pay, maybe. Probably what it is that makes creative people go loopy is that we've got more time to examine the fluff in our own navels than people with proper jobs, so we tend to attach importance to stuff that really doesn't matter.

*How did it feel to receive death threats because of your work?*

Well, it's nice to know people care enough to threaten to kill me, I suppose. Writing the stuff I write, I guess it goes with the territory. No point getting worked up about it. I'm sure people who write books about interior design get readers threatening to come round and decorate their living rooms ... or maybe not. The thing is, whatever I write is going to annoy, infuriate or offend someone somewhere—if I'm doing my job right—and it's no good worrying about how people will react. You just do it and keep your head down.

*You're a regular visitor to prisons to give talks. Have you had any experiences there you can tell us about? Any unusual prisoners that might be fans?*

Harold Shipman loved *Compulsion*. No, just kidding.... Yes, I do talk to prisoners. They're great audiences; I mean, where are they going to go? You always get one trappy bloke, an old lag who thinks he'll take the piss, but I find that telling that guy to shut the fuck up as quick as possible usually gains respect, shuts him up or gets you "stabbed up with a shank." Again, only kidding. It's weird, because I know that the guys I'm talking to are convicts, they've broken the law or they wouldn't be where they are. But they're incredibly honest—emotionally—and genuinely interested. From what many of them have told me, the problem with some other authors who've done prison visits is that they get too bloody literary and arty-farty and talk down to the prisoners. Big mistake.

*What is it in particular you love so much about Michelle Pfeiffer's footwear?*

They're exquisite. She's exquisite. So are her feet.... Oops, sorry, got carried away there. I happen to think she is one of the most underrated and brilliant actresses ever to grace the screen, apart from being one of the most stunningly beautiful women I've ever seen so, when the chance to buy some of her shoes came along, I thought, "Why not?" I was also offered one of her T-shirts but declined—and no, this wasn't by some L.A. burglar, it's a reputable shop in London that sells film star memorabilia. I've got lots of stuff to do with Peckinpah films—none of Sam's shoes, though, thank God—so, when a couple of pairs of Michelle's shoes came on the market I didn't hesitate. Surely it's no worse than a *Star Wars* fan buying a model of Darth Vader, is it?

*You've written a screenplay for a movie called* **Box**. *Can you tell us anything about that?*

A mate of mine who's got his own production company called October 11 Pictures rang me one night and said he had an idea for a film. We talked for about an hour and I eventually came up with the screenplay for *Box*. But I can't tell you anything about it because it's unmade as yet and I get nervous about things and don't like talking about them until they've happened. Ask me when it gets released.

*In* **Unmarked Graves** *you deal with an African version of voodoo called Uthalande. Was information on this hard to come by?*

Research varies dependent on the subject matter. I didn't find the research for *Unmarked Graves* to be as hard as it was for something like *White Ghost* or *Exit Wounds*, which concerned the Triads and the Yardies respectively. You just have to dig around, excuse the pun, until you find what you want.

*The subject of racism underpins everything in* Unmarked Graves. *Is this a subject you feel strongly about yourself?*

I feel strongly about people who can't mind their own business and if that includes not being able to see past the color of someone's skin, then yes. And it works both ways. People are intolerant regardless of their color. I wanted to show that racism can be a two-way thing, not just directed at non–English people. Racism of any kind is wrong, whether it's white against black or black against white. Having said that, anyone is entitled to have an opinion on the matter, it's just a question of how they express it. I believe in live and let live. As long as people's beliefs don't damage the way I live, then that's fine.

*Did you have to do much research on the journalism aspects—relating to Nick Pearson—for the book?*

I wanted to be a journalist when I left school but, other than that, the character of Pearson was a relatively easy one to write. Originally, he was going back to Darworth because of the death of his father and there was a big subplot about that, but that got cut out in the rewrite, thanks to my agent. As did the fact that Pearson had once had a relationship with the detective's wife ... a character who was removed from the book completely.

*You've used cemeteries in your books, especially the desecration of them. Are these places you ever visit yourself for inspiration?*

They're classic settings in a horror film, aren't they? The cemetery scene in *Unmarked Graves* was my homage to *The Plague of the Zombies*, the Hammer film from the sixties. I love that film. I do find cemeteries very restful, though. I love old churches too. If I was the sort of guy to sit around meditating, that's probably where I'd do it.

*Are you a fan of zombie movies in general?*

No, I can't stand zombie movies. The only one I really like is *Plague of the Zombies*: very stylish like so many of the Hammer films. I know this is heresy to horror fans but I'm not too fond of Romero's *Dead* films either. Sorry.

*Unmarked Graves* (2007, Orbit/Little Brown; courtesy Sean Garrehy, Orbit/Little Brown).

*Do you prefer Lucio Fulci movies, or maybe the remakes of Romero's films?*

*City of the Living Dead*, *The House by the Cemetery* ... no, sorry, not for me. I've seen them obviously, years ago, but I wouldn't want to watch them again. I think the remake of *Dawn of the Dead* was far superior to the original. I know horror film fans will be sharpening their wooden stakes as I speak, but I thought Zack Snyder's film was better than Romero's in every way. More heresy for you, I also thought the remake of *The Hills Have Eyes* was better than the original. Oops ... right, that's me now hated by every horror film fan on the planet I reckon. Don't even ask me about the remake of *The Texas Chain Saw Massacre*.

# Joe R. Lansdale

Texas-born Mojo storyteller and scriptwriter Joe R. Lansdale has written more than 30 novels in all genres, including crime, western, horror and pulp adventure. The author of *Act of Love*, *The Nightrunners*, *Cold in July*, *Blood Dance* and the *Drive-In* series, he is also known for his novels about two unlikely friends, Hap Collins and Leonard Pine, who live in a town in East Texas and find themselves solving a variety of often violent or macabre mysteries. The series began with *Savage Season* (1990); *Vanilla Ride* (2009)—previously referred to as *Blue to the Bone*—is the most recent title in the ongoing saga. He has also written scripts for comic books and animated television shows, including *Batman*; his short story "Incident On and Off a Mountain Road" was adapted for an episode of the first season of TV's *Masters of Horror* series. Lansdale is the winner of numerous HWA Bram Stoker Awards, the British Fantasy Award, the MWA Edgar Award, the American Mystery Award, the Horror Critics Award, the "Shot in the Dark" International Crime Writer's award, the Booklist Editor's Award and the Critic's Choice Award. His novella *Bubba Ho-Tep* was filmed by Don Coscarelli in 2002, starring Bruce Campbell, and became a surprise hit and critics' favorite.

---

*You lived on a hill near a drive-in theater when you were very little. What effect did this have on you?*

Yes, I did live on a hill overlooking a drive-in, and there, the cartoons and movies I saw, but did not hear, were like magnificent gods. Many of the movies were black-and-white and the cartoons were Warner Brothers, as I recall. They're the ones I remember. We had windows that we looked out of, and my dad worked nights, days, a lot, and at night my mother and I would put chairs to the windows and she would tell me what they were saying. Years later, watching the cartoons for myself, I was shocked to realize they were saying totally different things than what she told me. Anyway, it was an experience that, along with the books of course, put me on the path toward being a writer.

*You've said before that Jack Finney and Richard Matheson taught you to write. What was so personally important to you about their material as a developing writer?*

Finney and Matheson are among many writers who taught me to write. Edgar Rice Burroughs gave me my deepest love for fiction, though before I found him I was already pretty passionate. I loved Rudyard Kipling's *The Jungle Book* and the short stories, and I loved the *Iliad* and the *Odyssey*, Greek myths, fairy tales, you name it. I had been introduced to Matheson first through scripts he did for the *Twilight Zone* TV show, and the same goes for Charles Beaumont. Later, because of that, I read them, and Matheson led me backwards to Finney and their influences, like Robert Nathan, a neglected author. I branched out to other authors then, and in the short time I attended the university—three universities, no degree—I read Hemingway and Flannery O'Connor and Steinbeck and Fitzgerald and so on. I can't list all the writers who have influenced me. Robert Bloch, Ray Bradbury, William Goldman, as well as a number of offbeat novelists like Robert Jones and others, who are not on the radar.

*You originally wanted to be a science fiction writer. Why did this change?*

I still love SF, and have written some stories that could qualify, at least on some level, as SF; novels too, like the *Drive-In* books, all three. *Zeppelins West* and *Flaming London*, and the eventual sequel, *The Sky Done Ripped*. Numerous stories have been SF, though I've only appeared in maybe one traditional SF magazine. Perhaps another, but I can only remember one, and it was a collaboration, and it was an online magazine. Some of the stories that have appeared on *Subterranean Online Magazine*, like "Surveillance," are SF in nature. But I'm not science- or technology-oriented. I was more a *Galaxy* kind of guy, which had a lot of sociological, anthropological, and psychological SF stories. I read all the others, and had read a large amount of SF until the early eighties. I was reading other things as well, and somewhere in there, SF shifted and I shifted, and though I still love it, I read only a bit of it now, but do read a lot of books that are marginally SF. I still think of myself as having an SF writer's heart, and I certainly am best friends with its cousin, contemporary fantasy, whimsy, absurdist fiction, and horror.

Joe R. Lansdale. Photograph © Silvia Baglioni (courtesy Silvia Baglioni).

*At what point did you start to get your stories out there and how did that feel?*

I started selling in 1973, but it was non-fiction, an article I wrote for *Farm Journal* with my mother, under her name, O'Reta Lansdale. It was a letter article, and we were paid for that. Then it won a prize as best article, and I was really hooked. I wrote non-fiction off and on for the next few years, and in the mid to late seventies started selling fiction. Then in 1981 I sold two novels, one under a pen name, and they sold almost back to back. I went full time. It was a struggle until about 1986, but then some of the oddball stories I had written during the early eighties, that had been passed on by many editors, began to sell. The momentum has grown from year to year.

*"Land of the Stone-Age Cannibals" was your first story. What was that about and what was the impetus for writing it?*

I had written a play before that about a dog who talked like Maxwell Smart. I don't remember much else about it, except when I read it aloud the kids went wild. Same for the short story. This gave me another love. Reading aloud, performing in a way. I went to a special class not connected to the school. I believe the teacher's name was Miss Sessions. I went there to learn how to memorize poetry and pages from books, and I was in a play as the star, Santa Claus, Jr., that was allowed to be performed at the school. I learned to read aloud from that lady, and I seemed to have a knack for it. At the time I had a knack for memorization. I tend to do most things off-the-cuff now, but she taught me how to write speeches and how to deliver them. I think it was one of the most important things I ever learned, and it was not taught in the public school. I wonder whatever happened to her. This was in Mt. Enterprise, late fifties or early sixties. She and a lady named Sharon Ditforth, a high school teacher, were two of the most important teachers in my early life. Sharon taught at Gladewater High School, and she gave me a real love for Shakespeare. My mother had already nourished this, but Sharon made me understand it. She took our class to see *Romeo and Juliet*, the movie of that time, and she taught The Beatles as poetry. She was ahead of her time in her approach to teaching, and in the long run she was either fired or got tired of fighting the school board. She left. Hell, I think she became a lawyer. That was a loss. I never finished my college courses, but one teacher, Professor Jeff Banks, taught classes in mystery and detective fiction—Mickey Spillane, Westerns, etc.—and he gave me an insight into those genres I hadn't had before. He also put in my hands books of all kinds, and I devoured them ravenously. I still communicate with him and love him like an uncle.

*Do you have a favorite story you sold in your early days?*

I was very fond of "White Rabbit" at the time. I don't think it holds up as well as later stories, but I was leaving some of the old me behind and finding the new me with that one, and I polished that approach with "Fish Night." But the first story of mine I wrote that I thought was really what I wanted was "The Pit," though it was published well after it was written. "Night They Missed the Horror Show" is my most important story, and I have fond memories of it. The first story that really got me attention was "Tight Little Stitches in a Dead Man's Back." Still a favorite of mine.

*You mentioned discovering Edgar Rice Burroughs. Which stories most influenced you, do you think?*

I love Edgar Rice Burroughs. I think reading some of the stories now, a feeling is lost. But he was magic when I was a child, and the best of his work is still magical. The book that hit me hard and changed my life, took my ambition to be a writer [up a] notch, was *A Princess of Mars*. I adored this book, and loved the Martian series. I loved the Pellucidar series, and then there was Tarzan. *Tarzan of the Apes* is my favorite of those books, and others like *Tarzan the Terrible* and *Tarzan at the Earth's Core* are favorites as well. That's why it was so pleasing to get the job to finish the last Tarzan book in Burroughs' vault. He had part of it written, and I finished it. It was fun. Maybe not his best work, or mine, but he wrote what he wrote late in his career when Tarzan may have felt like more of a burden than a blessing, so he didn't give me his best opening to work with. I had to change it because he whacked a lion or some sort of big cat on about every other page, it felt like. Not literally, but there was so much of that, and no one got anywhere; frankly, a lot of it was boring, and that wasn't ERB's style. But we all nod. Still, it was an honor and it was great to have that opportunity. I can't tell you what Burroughs meant to me in my pre-teens and then early teens. He is to this day my sentimental favorite writer.

*Universal movies and the Roger Corman movies were an influence as well, weren't they?*

I *loved* Universal horror films and Roger Corman films. I saw most of them on TV, and a few of the Corman things at the theater, and later at the drive-in. I loved the fact they were stories I wasn't getting anywhere else, tales of the fantastic and of monsters. And I was a big fan of American International films. They did stuff kids and teenagers wanted to see. I was always drawn to that sort of thing, and I can't tell you why. It's just there. Books and films helped me escape from a world where everyone seemed interested in car engines and factory jobs. No problem with that, but it wasn't my cup of tea. My father and mother were great in supporting me to do that sort of thing, to pursue writing and reading and film. It was a wonderful escape. As I grew older and got into martial arts, I suddenly fit in better with those around me, but my interest and ambitions were frequently different, and sometimes even at odds with those around me. The films and books helped take the edge off of that.

Corman's films were a big influence on my novel *The Drive-In*, as were films inspired by his films, descendents so to speak. I loved all manner of horror films though, and the *Twilight Zone* television show, and *Thriller*. They pleasantly warped me as a child.

*Mucho Mojo* (1994, Cemetery Dance Publications; courtesy Richard Chizmar, Cemetery Dance).

*You've described your fiction or voice as "Texas Weird." Can you explain what you mean by that?*

Texas is a state of mind, but much about Texas is bigger-than-life, mythological, and odd. Or at least Texas writers see the odd in it, that's what I mean. I think of Flannery O'Connor, talking about Southerners, and she said, "We still know weird when we see it." One thing is, I'm really East Texas Weird. East Texas is vastly different from the rest of the state and is more in line with the South regionally; rich of trees and water and dark places. It lends itself to gothic fiction. Bring in the influence of the rest of Texas, the tall tales, the black folklore, and you got East Texas Weird.

*How did the characters of Hap and Leonard come to you initially, and how do you think they changed over the course of the novels they feature in?*

I wrote a stand-alone novel for Bantam, and I wanted to do a kind of Gold Medal novel. I had done one, *Cold in July*, and *Savage Season* was in that vein. I was heavily influenced at that time by Gold Medal books of the fifties and sixties, and I wanted to do an updated version of those type stories. Three years later, Hap started talking to me again, and I wrote *Mucho Mojo*, my favorite of the series, and then he wouldn't shut up. After six books he went silent, but I'm writing a new one now, *Vanilla Ride*. It picks up pretty close to the last one, *Captains Outrageous*. I'm just now getting their stories piped into my subconscious again. Okay, I'm going to be honest. I haven't seen them in awhile, and Hap, who is a friend, and Leonard, a sometime friend, spent a weekend at our house and told me of their most recent exploits.

*You've written some of the* **Batman** *animated adventures. Had you always been a fan of the Dark Knight?*

Bob Wayne, a friend of mine from Texas, works at DC. He put in a good word for me, and I had written a couple of *Batman* short stories for anthologies, and maybe by then the *Batman* novel. Anyway, DC told Warner and I got a call from Michael Reeves, who was the story editor, and went after it. I also wrote a *Batman* novel and a children's book about Batman. I have never done a comic about him, however. Maybe someday.

Bruce Campbell as Elvis in the movie adaptation of *Bubba Ho-Tep* (2002, MGM).

*You've also written for* **Superman: The Animated Series.** *Which of the two heroes do you prefer?*

Batman is my favorite, hands down, but when I was first starting to recognize superheroes, when I was maybe seven or eight, I liked Superman best. Before that, I read funny animal comics, stuff like that. I went nuts for all the superheroes, but Batman, he was and *is* my favorite.

*What gave you the impetus to put together Elvis, JFK and a mummy in* **Bubba Ho-Tep***?*

I had long wanted to write something about Elvis. My sister-in-law went to school with him in Mississippi, and my brother had met him; my brother had tried to have a career at Sun Records, so I had that connection. My brother, by the way, is about 17 years older than I am. Anyway, I loved mummy movies and my mother, due to a severe accident, had to be in a rest home for a while. Listening to the occupants of the home mixed with the other two things, so when I was asked to do a story about Elvis, it came out.

*How did the movie version come about?*

Don Coscarelli latched onto it and, with his usual enthusiasm, just stayed latched until it got made.

*Was it ever discussed that you'd write the screenplay rather than Don?*

He asked me to do it, and I turned it down. I didn't think a good movie could be made of it, I was busy at the time, and Don couldn't pay a lot for the screenplay. He was working on a shoeshine and a prayer. I looked at an early draft and made some suggestions. They didn't move him until Bruce made the same suggestions. It turned out great.

*How did you feel about Bruce Campbell taking on the role of Elvis?*

Bruce was perfect. There was supposed to be a sequel, and at one point I was going to write the screenplay, but there were time conflicts, and Don wrote the screenplay with Steve Romano. Bruce passed on the project, and now it's in limbo. I don't know if it'll ever be made with another actor. It could be, but ... like James Bond, we still talk about Connery. Honest opinion, I don't think there *should* be a sequel.

*"Incident On and Off a Mountain Road" began as a throwaway story, didn't it?*

That was a story I came up with to fulfill a contract with Dark Harvest for a *Night Vision* book. I was to be one of three writers, and I believe we each did 20,000 words. I just started writing, playing about with an idea about a woman driving late at night on a dark road, and the story jumped out. I wrote another story for the anthology titled *Love Doll*, but the publisher didn't like it, so it was cut, and I sold it elsewhere; it's been reprinted numerous times. Odd how stories get published and how they survive. Some stories I've written I really like, but they don't get a lot of play. Some that I think are entertaining but not my best, get a lot of paper and Internet time.

**The Mummy (played by Bob Ivey) stalks an old folks' home in** *Bubba Ho-Tep* **(2002, MGM).**

*Would you class "Incident..." as a traditional horror story turned on its head?*

The TV film version is more horror-oriented than the story, which was horrific enough. But it was more psychological and creepy and suspenseful than horror. I love the other, out-and-out horror, but it wasn't that way. They were true to the story, but they brought out the horror more, added in some purely horrific scenes like the eye drill. The eye thing, about the eyes being cut out, was in the story, but the drill scene wasn't. But it was pretty faithful, and I thought their expanding on the back story was great. My son Keith and I went up to Canada when they were filming it. We stayed several days. It was a lot of fun.

*Where did the original idea for "Moonface" come from? Was there any influence from monsters of the past?*

I don't know where the original idea came from. The Phantom of the Opera may lurk within his genetics. But I can't be sure. Leatherface might be there as well.

**Act of Love** *was one of the first serial killer books. What was the spark for that one, and do you see yourself as being partly responsible for the rise in that subgenre's popularity?*

*Act of Love* (1994, Cemetery Dance Publications; courtesy Richard Chizmar, Cemetery Dance).

There were serial killer books before mine. *Psycho* is a big one. I was just part of a wave, a new approach to it, and I happened to be one of those on the tip of the wave. I think it influences a lot of people, if what they tell me can be believed. It laid the groundwork for some novelists, but it was just that it was time for that kind of novel to rise and I was there along with some others. It had impact, but it was part of a collective impact. It's pretty dated now, and at the time it seemed way ahead in tone. What made it different was the combination of genres: police procedural, horror, exploitation, action-adventure, mystery, black hero; not new, but still uncommon. A heated-up writing style. It is probably one of the early Splatterpunk novels, as is *The Nightrunners*, though it took years for it to be published. It was written right after *Act*. My novel was influenced by other graphic novels that weren't crime novels, like the *Gladiator* series, and Edge Westerns. Richard Laymon's *The Cellar* predated mine. It wasn't a serial killer novel, but I think that novel and mine helped form part of what became the new movement in horror. Again, I say part. I, on the other hand, may have written some Splatterpunk material, but don't see myself as a Splatterpunk, as I wrote all manner of things, and that was only a small part of my output. I could be called a horror writer, a western writer, a crime writer, a non-fiction writer, mystery writer, and so on, and they would all be accurate at a moment in time, but the only proper title is writer.

*You've said you see your stories cinematically in your head and generally, especially with shorts, you don't plot in advance. Why do you think this process works for you?*

I normally don't plot in advance, but there have been a few that jumped full-blown into my head as a plot. Mostly I find the plot as I go. It usually works fine, but there have been a few times when it didn't, and when I reach halfway with a book I usually start to panic, but finally it all comes together. I mostly do one draft and a polish, but the last novel I did I wrote three drafts, and one of those drafts was published in Italy, before I was really finished with it, and it was a bestseller there. I guess it turned out all right. That hasn't happened to me in thirty years or more. I was really out there without a map and without an impulse sometimes. It came out all right in the end, but I fought it and wrestled with it and got some good notes from my editor, and finally got it done. But, there are no absolutes in writing. What works one day doesn't work every day.

*Some of your fiction—and horror in particular—features black humor. Do you think there's a definite link between horror and comedy?*

I learned about the connection between horror and humor from Robert Bloch and others. But he was the main one. He was, early on, my favorite horror writer, so it was great when he called me a born storyteller. He and I were just starting to know each other when he became ill and died. We exchanged a few cards, and we had talked at conventions, and Rick Klaw and I bought one of his stories to adapt to comic form for *Weird Business*. He struck me as a great guy, and he's got a lot of people he influenced running around now, writing stories.

*Writing dialogue—is this something that comes to you naturally as a writer or do you have to work hard at it?*

Dialogue comes pretty easy for me, though now and again I find myself revising it. Mostly though, it just arrives on schedule like a bus. Now and again, the bus is a little late, but so far, it's always shown up.

*You've long been involved with the Horror Writers Association. When and how did you first become a member?*

I really am not that involved with HWA. I went for years not being a member. Rick McCammon had the idea for it, but most people forget my wife founded it. She did the first newsletters with Xerox and manuscripts. I helped and Melissa Hall helped and Rick helped and others helped, but she was the one behind it. She worked hard to put the things together and gave the organization its base. Dean Koontz then got involved and asked if he could invest some of his money to make it more professional. And he did. I was a member for years, then I felt I wasn't really getting anything from the organization, and I could do for writers without being a member what I could do for them as a member. I did hold offices in the organization. I don't even remember what offices. Anyway, if you think HWA, my wife is the one who is responsible for the early organization, and gave it its legs. Last couple of years I've been asked to join and did, but I no longer feel like I'm a big part of the organization. I don't belong to much of anything like that. The Writers' Guild, Thriller Writers, and if I don't remember to pay my dues, I won't belong to that.

*Is there still any possibility of Ted Tally's script for* **Mucho Mojo** *being filmed?*

I guess there is. It's a good script and I like that book a lot, think it's the best of the Hap and Leonard books, and once in a while someone nibbles at picking up that script again and going at it, but, it's an expensive script. Ted won the Oscar for the *Silence of the Lambs* script and he's worth some money now.

*Are there any particular short stories or novels you'd like to see filmed? A lot have been optioned.*

A lot of my novels and short stories would make good films or episodes. I did the screenplay for *The Big Blow*, which Ridley Scott has now, but who knows if it will be made, and if it will be made with my script. Mine's called a rewrite, so I have another writer attached to it who wrote an original script that has nothing to do with mine, which is straight from the book. Hollywood is interesting. *A Fine Dark Line* has been scripted, and Adam Friedman and I are trying to get that one going, and right now that looks very possible. *The Bottoms* is about to be optioned, if nothing goes wrong, so that could happen with me doing the script. My brother and I wrote a throwback to those old horror and western films called *Hell's Bounty* we would like to see done, and we did a very shoestring sort of script called *Deadman's Road* we'd like to see done. It was designed to be done with Bruce Campbell on a solid, but not extreme budget. But, who knows.

*Writer of the Purple Rage* (1994, Cemetery Dance Publications; courtesy Richard Chizmar of Cemetery Dance).

*How did* **The Big Blow** *pass from David Lynch to Ridley Scott?*

Neal Edelstein worked for Lynch and talked him into picking it up for a couple to three years, then he moved on with it to Scott, and there it rests for the time being.

*How important has the support of your family been over the years?*

My family has been the perfect support system. That's the best I can say it.

*How did it feel to be the Grand Master at 2007's World Horror Convention?*

That meant a lot to me, and it was a surprise. It was a great moment. When my name was called and the people in the room stood up and applauded, I teared up, but in a manly way, of course.

*How have your writing methods changed over the years? Do you write less per day, polish what you've written right away?*

I write less per day, but I get better results. Three hours a day is about average.

# *Graham Masterton*

Graham Masterton was born in Edinburgh in 1946. His grandfather was Thomas Thorne Baker, the scientist who invented Day-Glo and was the first man to transmit news photographs by wireless. Graham trained as a newspaper reporter, then went on to edit the new British men's magazine *Mayfair*, where he encouraged William Burroughs to develop a series of scientific and philosophical articles which eventually became the novel *The Wild Boys*. At 24, Graham became executive editor of *Penthouse* and *Penthouse Forum* magazines and began writing a bestselling series of sex "how-to" books including *How to Drive Your Man Wild in Bed* which has sold over three million copies worldwide. His debut horror novel was the bestselling *The Manitou* (1976), a chilling tale of a Native American medicine man reborn in the present day to exact revenge. It was subsequently turned into a movie starring Tony Curtis, Susan Strasberg and Burgess Meredith. Since then Graham has published more than 50 horror novels, including *Charnel House, Mirror, Family Portrait* (based on *The Picture of Dorian Gray*), *Walkers, Spirit, Manitou Blood, Trauma, Edgewise* and *The 5th Witch* and the YA horrors *Rook, The Terror* and *Demon's Door*. Three of Graham's stories were adapted for Tony Scott's horror TV series *The Hunger*, and "The Secret Shih-Tan," starring Jason Scott Lee, was shortlisted for a Bram Stoker Award by the Horror Writers Association. Another short story, "Underbed," was voted best short story by the Horror Critics Guild. Altogether Graham has written more than a hundred novels ranging from thrillers (*The Sweetman Curve, Ikon*) to disaster novels (*Plague, Famine*) to historical sagas (*Rich* and *Maiden Voyage*—both appeared on the *New York Times* bestseller list). He and his wife Wiescka live in Surrey, England.

---

***In* Edgewise, *you use the Native American myth of the Wendigo, and you've used various aspects of Native American mythology before—*Rook, Manitou *etc. What is it that keeps drawing you back?***

What interests me about Native American mythology is that it is relatively unexplored in modern fiction—unlike vampires and werewolves and zombies—and that it varies so much from tribe to tribe and area to area. Some tribes have mischievous and unruly demons, such as Coyote, while others have demons who can go through frightening transformations, such as Changing Bear Maiden, who could turn into a bear and snap men's necks. Then there are terrifying demons like the Eye Killers, who can kill you just by staring at you without blinking. Like European demons, all of these creatures and their behavior carry strong moral messages, which of course are very important to any horror story. Another reason I like to use Native American mythology is that it's so closely connected with American locations: It is bound into the trees and the rocks and the rivers, and it has always been important to me to set a story in a believable and realistic location ... especially when the story is going to stray so wildly beyond the bounds of probability!

*You visited Japanese mythology in* **Tengu** *and* **Night Warriors**. *Did you find many similarities between the two cultural mythos?*

Japanese mythology does have some parallels to Native American mythology, such as the Tengu, which like some American demons had the ability to turn itself into a bird and swoop down on villages to seize their children, or the Kappa, which is a water-demon who tricks people into entering a pond and then drowns them. But on the whole, Native American mythology tends to tell cautionary stories to protect people against their own folly. The Wendigo was a lonely, lost creature of the woods exiled for its cannibalism—a warning to the Sioux from their elders not to be tempted to eat each other when the harsh winters brought near-starvation.

*What do you think is the appeal behind the current U.S. trend to remake popular Japanese genre movies, such as* **Ringu** *and* **The Eye**?

I think that Japanese horror movies have a dark and frightening atmosphere which U.S. moviemakers find difficult to create themselves. I thought the remake of *Ringu* was very good, but the remake of *Dark Water* lost all of the desperation and sheer creepiness of the original.

*In* **Edgewise**, *the chief protagonist Lily Blake is a single mother intent on getting her abducted children back. Did you find writing from the female point of view difficult?*

I have written numerous books from the female point of view—both historical sagas and horror novels—

Graham Masterton (courtesy Graham Masterton).

*Edgewise* (2008, Leisure Books; courtesy Tracy Heydweiller, Dorchester Publishing).

and I find no difficulty with it at all, although only women can judge how successfully I do it ... or not! What I like about writing from the female point of view is that there is often a conflict or a problem in women's lives apart from the principal conflict with which they have to deal in the story. Maybe they are doing a job that men consider unsuitable, or maybe their male colleagues think of them as inferior, or are constantly hitting on them. So there is an added tension and depth to the story which gives it increased believability and interest.

*What was the inspiration for FLAME (Fathers' League Against Mothers' Evil)?*

FLAME is a homicidal version of those pressure groups of divorced fathers who try so hard to gain access to their children, and are prevented from doing so by obstructive or uncooperative mothers.

*Conscience is a theme in* Edgewise. *Lily is guilt-ridden over her husband's death at the hands of the Wendigo, even though he took her children; the detective, John Shooks, aids Lily because of the guilt he feels about getting her involved with George Iron Walker, who raises the Wendigo for her. Do you feel it's important to show the consequences of characters' actions—i.e., to show that nothing's really black or white, totally good or totally bad?*

The complexities of good and evil are a source of great interest to me, and I think that they make for a much more realistic story than—for instance—a totally good guy fighting a totally evil vampire. In my recent vampire novel *Descendant*, our hero is faced with the excruciating decision of killing the woman he loves ... or not. And, as you point out, both Lily and John Shooks feel guilt for what they have done, which in some ways makes them better people than George Iron Walker, who doesn't. Questions of guilt are always arising in life. In Iraq, for instance ... Saddam was manifestly an evil and repressive dictator, but was it right to overthrow him when it cost so many innocent lives?

*The book—and this is a common theme in a lot of your novels—shows that the actions themselves*

*Night Wars* (2006, Leisure Books; courtesy Tracy Heydweiller, Dorchester Publishing).

aren't evil; it's the intent behind them that is. For example, the Wendigo is only hunting what he has been asked to hunt, it is Lily who has set him on this path, out of anger and fear for her children's safety. Is this something that you believe yourself? That it's not the power, but he who wields it, that determines whether an action is good or evil?

I believe this to some extent, but I also believe that many of our actions, no matter how well-intentioned, can have catastrophic results, and I find it extremely interesting and rewarding to explore the world of unforeseen consequences. Many of my characters are fortune-tellers or clairvoyants—Sissy Sawyer, for example—but she does not always interpret the future correctly, and her errors can lead to a bad situation becoming even worse.

*Only one of your books—your first horror novel,* The Manitou—*has so far made it to the screen, although the majority have been optioned. Do you have one favorite novel that you'd like to see brought to life?*

Several of my books have almost made it … right up to the point of having directors selected and actors cast. But in the movie business you have to learn to live with constant disappointment. Jonathan Mostow [*U-571*] optioned *Trauma*, my story of a woman who cleans up after homicides, and I would very much have liked to see that make it to the screen. *Family Portrait*, my take on Oscar Wilde's *Picture of Dorian Gray*, was optioned by Gold Circle—*White Noise*, etc.—and has a first-rate script by J.T. Petty, who wrote *Batman Begins* among other award-winning screenplays. I am still hoping that this one makes it. *Ritual*, my gourmet-cannibal novel, was bought by the Italian film director Mariano Baino—*Dark Waters*, not to be confused with *Dark Water*—but that now seems to be dead in the water. I would very much like to see *Edgewise* filmed. It already has an excellent screen treatment by Fred Caruso, the producer of *Blue Velvet*, and I am, yet again, keeping my fingers crossed.

*Who would be your choice to direct it?*

The Coen Brothers.

*Director William Girdler's next film would have been* The Djinn. *How do you feel about the fact it didn't get made?*

I was talking to Bill Girdler about making *The Djinn* the week

*Manitou Blood* (2005, Leisure Books; courtesy Tracy Heydweiller, Dorchester Publishing).

before he was killed in a helicopter crash. I liked him a lot and was extremely upset when he died. In some ways it was probably a good thing that he didn't get around to making *The Djinn* in the mid-1970s because the special effects really weren't up to much in those days—vide the coconut-flake snow and plastic icicles in *The Manitou*. But there is still movie interest in *The Djinn*, so who knows?

*The idea for Misquamacus came from a real Native American sideshow act, didn't it?*

No ... the name came from H.P. Lovecraft's story *The Lurker at the Threshold* and the concept of drinking blazing oil in order to be resurrected in the future came from the Buffalo Bill Annual.

*What was it about the myth of the Manitou that attracted you to it?*

I liked it because it was wholly American ... and because no novels had ever been written about it before, as far as I knew. I also liked the idea of one's deities being inside rocks, and trees, and water, and wind, so that one would constantly be in touch with one's spiritual protectors, wherever one happened to be.

*The original ending involved Misquamacus being defeated by a venereal disease, and was rewritten when Pinnacle wanted to reissue the book. Which ending do you prefer?*

I don't have a strong preference. I changed the ending because Pinnacle wanted something more climactic—and more modern, since by the time they published, the topic of Saigon Rose was somewhat out of date. But of course one only has to look at the whirring wheels of the IBM computers in the movie of *The Manitou* to see how dated they have become. These days, the Manitou could probably be defeated by a single laptop.

*There have been four* **Manitou** *books:* **Manitou, Revenge of the Manitou, Burial** *and* **Manitou Blood.** *Are there plans for any more?*

Yes, there is a final showdown novel between Harry Erskine and Misquamacus called *The Blinding*, which is already in preparation.

*Is it true that Harry Erskine, the protagonist of* **Manitou,** *is based on you?*

To some extent I suppose all of my male protagonists are based on me. Harry's complete inability to take anything seriously is quite characteristic of yours truly.

*What made you decide to branch out into YA territory with the Jim Rook series of books* **Rook, Tooth and Claw, The Terror, Snowman** *and* **The Swimmer?**

I sensed that there was a younger market which was very hungry for horror stories, and I wanted to write stories for them that were inspirational and encouraging as well as scary. As one grows older, it is easy to let one's characters and one's point-of-view grow older, and I wanted to write something from a very much younger and less cynical angle.

*Are there any more books planned in this series?*

Two more Rook books are scheduled. The first one, *Demon's Door*, will be ready quite shortly. I *hope*, if my fingers don't fall off first.

*Is there any subject you wouldn't write about? Anything that you'd deem taboo?*

Macramé.

*Did the furor over your short story "Eric the Pie" surprise you?*

No, because I deliberately wrote it with the intention of taking horror to an extreme. It was an exercise in how disgusting I could be and get away with it, which is not as perverse as it sounds since a story as disgusting as that has to be very well written.

*What was the inspiration for your short story "Neighbours from Hell"?*

I really can't remember what inspired it except that I was entertained by the idea of moving from city to city and discovering that one was still living next to the same house. I have never roasted any of my children, so that couldn't have been it.

*You write in several genres—thrillers, historical novels, and horror—quite apart from your non-fiction books on sex and relationships. Do you have a favorite genre?*

I love writing historical sagas but they are extremely time-consuming and very hard work to research. These days I like writing thrillers that have a strong central character and only the slightest suggestion of the supernatural in them ... such as *Trauma, A Terrible Beauty*, which was set in Ireland, and *Unspeakable*, about a deaf woman who lip-reads for the police, as well as being a children's welfare officer. I enjoy creating a realistic person in a convincing setting, and putting them through all kinds of trials and tribulations. I feel a great sense of achievement when my readers feel empathy for my characters, and one of the greatest compliments I have been paid is, "What happened to them next?" I also like writing humor. I was a regular contributor to *Punch* when it was still alive and funny, as well as several other magazines.

*You've stated that you've never really felt a part of the horror genre. Why is that?*

I have never been a joiner and while I have many very good friends who happen to be horror writers, I don't feel that my work belongs exclusively to one genre. I enjoy meeting readers. My wife Wiescka and I recently came back from a wonderful promotional trip to Poland, and I have a really responsive and friendly readership on my message board at www.grahammasterton.co.uk. But I don't enjoy horror conventions, and all the paraphernalia of "fandom."

*The theme of religious or cultural differences resulting in conflict—or in atrocities and subsequent retribution—runs through many of your novels. Is religion as a force something you feel strongly about?*

I am not personally religious but I recognize the enormous and often irrational power of religion and superstition in people's lives, and I am very interested in that as a subject. Is religion a way of abnegating personal responsibility? If you do something terrible in the name of some deity or other, is it your fault or not? Answers on a surplice, please.

*Is it harder to make a horror novel believable, as the world becomes a more secular place?*

No. Quite the opposite. The world—well, the Western world—may be becoming more secular as far as traditional religions are concerned. But in their place people are looking for all kinds of mystical and supernatural solutions to their daily problems. Fortune-telling is booming, and TV series about the supernatural have never been so popular, from *Most Haunted* to *Medium*.

*How do you think the genre has changed since its last "boom" period, in the eighties?*

I think on the whole that the horror novels published today are better written and more substantial in their thinking than the novels of the late '70s and '80s. So many of those were poorly written potboilers that the genre was bound to self-destruct. I am not sure that horror movies are any better, despite the advent of CGI. I don't have any time for sadistic films like *Saw* or *Hostel*. I just find them boring.

*In* **Night Warriors,** *you visit Japanese mythology—the protagonists fight a legendary demon, Yaomauitl, on the dream plane. Although still a horror novel, there's a definite fantasy element here. Was this change in direction something you enjoyed?*

Yaomauitl is actually an Aztec demon. But, yes, I did enjoy the strong fantasy element of *Night Warriors*. It was highly entertaining and amusing to write about a dream world in which anything was possible ... although it was very important for the dynamics of the plot to make sure that there were certain firm rules which had to be adhered to. There is also a strong element in my *Night Warriors* stories of people, who consider themselves inadequate or under-achieving in the real world, finding heroism and self-fulfillment in the world of dreams. The moral of the novels is: If you really use your imagination and have faith in yourself, you can do almost anything you want to.

*There are three books in the* **Night Warriors** *series—* **Night Warriors, Death Dream,** *and* **Night Plague.** *Are there plans for any more?*

There are four now ... the latest is *Night Wars* which was published by Leisure Books, and is my personal favorite. It will probably be published in the U.K. by Severn House soon, although I don't yet have an exact date. It tells the story of two malevolent forces which are trying to enter babies' dreams at the moment of their birth, when they know all of the secrets of the universe.

*Do you believe in the supernatural?*

I have had several experiences which might be considered supernatural, even though I am very skeptical about spirits and ghosts. I saw my dead grandfather once at London Zoo, and once in a very old pub I was gripped quite firmly on the shoulder even though there was nobody within ten feet of me. On the whole, though, I am more of a believer in coincidences. I am amazed almost every day by the extraordinary chances that determine our destiny, and how our lives all lock together like the most complicated of machinery.

*In* **Mirror, Walkers, The House That Jack Built, House of Bones** *and* **The Doorkeepers,** *you deal with essentially haunted houses—buildings that are haunted by long-ago events that took place inside their walls. In* **Mirror,** *you go one step further and posit that the eponymous mirror itself is haunted. Do you subscribe to the belief that objects can resonate with a psychic echo of sorts? Or does men's evil die with them?*

I think that when we die, we die, but the consequences of our actions can live on after us. Not trapped within the walls of houses, or in mirrors, but in the effect we have had on the people we have known and the world around us.

*Is the film version of your book* **Ritual** *still going ahead?*

I have absolutely no idea. I have had no contact from the director or the producers whatsoever.

*Have you ever been interested in writing screenplays yourself?*

Screenplay writing is a very specialist skill, which I don't possess, and unfortunately don't have the time to acquire.

*If you did, would you choose the horror genre or romantic comedies?*

I would write obscure French films like *Pierrot Le Fou*, all to be filmed in black-and-white with everybody smoking a lot and making philosophical remarks such as, "I am so glad that I don't like spinach, because if I didn't, I would eat loads of the stuff, and I hate it."

*In* Descendant, *you rework the vampire myth, bringing vampires—or strigoi—to London after World War II.*

I wanted to write a vampire book that wasn't at all Gothic, with cloaks and fangs, and I wanted to set a novel in South London of the 1950s, which is where I was brought up as a boy. I also wanted to write a love story that would present its protagonist with an impossible and heart-rending dilemma. Those three elements all came together and the result was *Descendant*, which is one of my favorite novels.

*In* Touchy and Feely, *you visit the subject of serial killers, and introduce us to a new protagonist, Sissy Sawyer, a fortune-teller. How difficult did you find the research for the characters?*

I loved writing *Touchy and Feely*, and researching the characters wasn't at all difficult, because in some ways they were both me. A creative teenage idiot and an irascible middle-aged man who blames everybody else for all of his troubles. Sissy wasn't difficult, either, even though she is seventy-plus. I talked to my mother about the way she feels, and while she is in her eighties, her mind remains sharp and young, and she finds it impossible to believe that she has grown so old.

*Will we see more books featuring Sissy Sawyer?*

I have just written *The Painted Man*, a second Sissy Sawyer novel, in which Sissy is staying with her daughter-in-law, a talented forensic artist for the Cincinnati Police Department. Unfortunately one of her sketches turns out to be a little too lifelike....

*What can we expect to see from you next?*

I am working on an idea of a father-and-son team who go in search of evils never before encountered by man nor beast.

# Richard Christian Matheson

Richard Christian Matheson is an acclaimed novelist, short story writer and screenwriter-producer. He has written and co-written feature film and television projects for Richard Donner, Ivan Reitman, Steven Spielberg, Bryan Singer and many others. For TNT's *Nightmares & Dreamscapes* miniseries, he wrote the critically hailed adaptation of Stephen King's short story "Battleground" starring William Hurt and directed by Brian Henson. As a prose writer, his fiction has been published in major, award-winning anthologies, including multiple times in *Year's Best Horror* and *Year's Best Fantasy*. Matheson's stories are collected in *Scars and Other Distinguishing Marks* and *Dystopia*. His debut novel, *Created By*, was Bantam's hardcover lead, a Bram Stoker Award nominee for best first novel and a Book-of-the-Month Club lead selection. It has been translated into several languages. Matheson is considered an expert on the occult and worked with the UCLA Parapsychology Labs, investigating haunted houses and paranormal phenomenon. He also plays drums with Smash-Cut, a blues-rock-jazz band which recently recorded a live album, *Live at the Mint*.

---

*What was it like growing up with such a creative dad? Did he inspire and encourage you to go into the profession?*

He was endlessly supportive, interesting, creatively brilliant and very funny. He always took enormous interest in my early efforts and gave me gentle but honest input.

*Which of his books or stories are your favorites and why?*

I love all of his work. No genre eludes his gift.

*Did you ever want to do anything else as a job?*

I was interested in being a magician, comedy writer, psychologist or musician. In my writing, the first three come into play. And I have been a drummer almost my whole life. I always knew what I liked.

*You mention an interest in magic. Does this stem from your formative years?*

I was a child magician. Performed at birthday parties, always loved magic. Talk about trapdoor endings; magic specializes in those; a great part of its appeal.

*Where did your interest in horror come from?*

I'm not interested in horror. I'm interested in strange and dark behavior which manifests as eccentricity or insanity; there can be horrific results. I write comedy and certainly humor and horror are bedfellows. Suspense and oddity are always interesting to me. Not horror.

*For you, what is horror and what makes a good horror story?*

Horror is dark outcome. Always terrible or emotionally wrenching; often tragic. A good horror story achieves this via emotion and trauma, not bloodshed—though it may require some. I'm not bloodless in my approach but it is a tool of narrative, not a fetish.

*Were there any other writers when you were growing up who were a particular influence?*

S.J. Perelman, F. Scott Fitzgerald, Nathanael West, Richard Matheson, Thomas Berger, Roald Dahl, Robert Sheckley, Shirley Jackson, Woody Allen.

*How about film and TV influences?*

Stephen J. Cannell, William Goldman, Preston Sturges, Neil Simon, Jay Tarses and Tom Patchett, Woody Allen, Levinson and Link, Larry Gelbart.

*Where did the idea for your first story, "Graduation," come from?*

I just started writing it one night, while still living at home, and it just started pouring out. I wrote it in one sitting and ended up with 25 pages or so. It needed cutting and my dad had some great suggestions. I must have been seventeen. My first draft was too sprawling but the central conceit and acerbic tone worked. My story ideas usually result from some ironic thought or perception. I like strange juxtapositions.

*Were you drawing on anything from your own college or educational life at all?*

I hadn't been to college when I wrote it. Just making it up.

*Was the idea of telling a story in letters influenced at all by classic tales like* **Dracula** *and* **Frankenstein,** *and putting a modern spin on it?*

Not intentional. I just started writing and it came out as letters. Its epistolary form was pointed out to me by the editor who bought it.

*What would you consider your first break in TV writing?*

Writing for a '70s sitcom, *Another Day*, starring the late Joan Hackett, which aired on CBS and was very smart. Watching them shoot my script, before a live audience who got the jokes, was surreal and I was hooked.

*Dystopia*, **a collection of Richard Christian Matheson stories (2000, Gauntlet Press; courtesy Dara Hoffman, Gauntlet Press).**

*How did it feel to be working on* The Incredible Hulk? *Did you read the comics as a kid?*

I was hired with my then collaborator Tom Szollosi because we wrote quick-witted dialogue and could cook up and craft stories. The executive producer-creator of the show, Kenneth Johnson, wanted writers who got the duality: a guy turning into a big, green man though his psyche suffers. A knowing humor was vital to Kenny so the show wasn't deadly. Smart and amusing dialogue helped to create a more credible spell.

*Your first shorts appeared in places like the* Twilight Zone *magazine. How did you feel when they first went into print?*

Having people who dig the genre read your stuff and get caught off-guard feels great.

*Why did you then decide to concentrate predominantly on the TV writing—shows like* Knightrider *and* The A-Team?

It was fun, challenging and lucrative. I also found I had a taste for the producing and business side of television and often produced shows I worked for. I became sought-out for action shows because I could always think of odd ideas for episodes, strange plot progressions and offbeat dialogue.

*Which allows you the most freedom? Possibly the prose where the imagination is limitless?*

Freedom or restriction can be experienced in either. It depends on the writer.

*How did you approach writing for* The A-Team? *Was it a good experience finally working with Stephen J. Cannell?*

I *loved* working with Cannell, we remain close friends. Being head writer on *The A-Team* demanded a constant blend of efficiency and anarchy. Scheduling demands were tough, we were writing constantly to feed the camera, but the approach to the characters, stories and twists were offbeat; Cannell and Frank Lupo, who created the show, led that straitjacket march.

*How do you feel about working with characters that other people have created—for example, in shows like* The Incredible Hulk *and* The A-Team? *Does it make it easier or harder to put your own stamp on things?*

Writing other people's characters simplified the task. It's basic mimicry and I always had an ear for dialogue and characters. I also learned fast that the way to keep shows from changing my dialogue was to create phrases and lines the writing staff hadn't heard before. Coinages, metaphoric constructions, odd insights. Stuff that sounded catchy, too fresh to lose. Do that enough, it accrues, becomes a kind of stamp, I guess.

*How did it feel when Stephen King called you "remarkable" and "a writer to watch" back in the '80s?*

I felt validated in a lasting way. All positive feedback is fuel for risk.

*Your story "Red" has deservedly been hailed a masterpiece by Dennis Etchison. What do you personally think is so special about this story?*

Its lack of affect. What has happened is so awful and the telling is plain; emotionally stripped. It's a disturbing juxtaposition.

*"Conversation Piece" is brilliant. Where did you get that idea, and what made you put the story in an interview format?*

I read an interview about medical guinea pigs; how practical they are, just making a living. I'm an inveterate reader of psychology and had been thinking about compromises we all make in life, giving up parts of ourselves. The two ideas seemed to match. I chose a Q&A format to objectify the subject; it lent the coda emotion.

*Are you a fan of "body horror"—for example, the Cronenberg type of story?*

Yes. Flesh as canvas for inner suffering is a frequent theme in my stories. I find Cronenberg's work along those lines powerful and despairing.

*Would you consider a story like "I'm Always Here" body horror?*

Yes. It's about loneliness and co-dependency made visible in the flesh. Throw in some sacrifice, devotion and country music, the idea blended pretty well.

*"I'm Always Here" feeds into your love of music. Where did this love originate? And where did you get the idea to blend it with the medical technique in the tale?*

I always found the relationships of male-female acts in country music to be highly co-dependant. It's often in the lyrics of their hits. I just took it further. It struck me as a worthy irony. And I like writing in a journalistic voice; the detached insight and aloneness.

*"Dead End" has a couple's relationship mirroring the fact they're lost. How important is setting to you when writing a story, and do you enjoying linking them to characters like this?*

I believe setting should perfectly fit story.

*How closely does the world you write about in your 1993 novel* Created By... *mirror the real world of working in TV? Did you worry at all about anyone recognizing themselves in it?*

Created By... slightly exaggerates for effect. The dysfunction and agendas are accurate. I found anyone who recognized a behavior or character quirk thought I was writing about someone else ... though it was often them. Guilt and denial marry well.

*Created By* (2007, Gauntlet Press; courtesy Dara Hoffman, Gauntlet Press).

*How did it feel to be nominated for a Stoker Award for that one?*
Honored.

*How did you find the process of writing a longer piece of fiction compared to shorts? And which did you prefer?*
It was no harder, just longer. Because I'd written scores of scripts by the time I wrote the novel, plot and character development came naturally. I like them both. One is building a yacht, the other is ships in a bottle.

*Will you be writing another?*
Just finished a new one.

*You've done a bit of acting too—in* **The Shining** *mini-series. How was this experience compared to writing?*
I don't act. I wear costumes and appear in the background. Think prop.

*You co-wrote* **Full Eclipse,** *about werewolves in the police force. Where did this unusual spin on the subgenre come from?*
Again, juxtaposition. Finding fresh links between dissimilars. I don't like werewolf movies; once they turn, they seem less menacing, even with stunning special effects. It's the mid-point between beast and man, I find troubling. I fought to get that on *Full Eclipse*; partial victory.

*You were a production consultant on Dean Koontz's* **Sole Survivor.** *Are you a fan of his work? And has he been an influence on* your *work at all?*
I enjoyed the project and Dean became a friend. He's a gifted and kind man. I learned much about suspense from Dean. He's also a closet drummer which was an unexpected bond.

**Pride** *came from an idea your father had. How did you both develop this?*
It was his idea. As always, we sat together, worked it out. Our creative fusion is fast, fairly inevitable.

*What's been the exact writing process when you've worked together on projects? Has this changed from project to project?*
We talk it over, we write an outline. During this phase, we are open to all possibility. Once writing the script, he takes one half, I take the other. We write quickly, give feedback to one another on our drafts, re-write until we like it. Our working habits are highly similar.

*How did you feel about what they eventually did with* **Loose Canons** *back in 1990?*
We didn't like it. Our script was almost entirely changed. Gene Hackman was good.

*What's it feel like to know that your writings—along with your dad's—are being preserved at the Harry Ransom Humanities Research Center at the University of Texas at Austin?*
Nice to know someone is keeping track. After my house burned down and everything I had, including my writing projects, went up in smoke, I came to appreciate important things kept in a safe place.

Fangoria *magazine have said that you're more interested in the monster inside the human mind. Do you find this more frightening than (say) a slasher killer, or fictional types of monsters?*

Violence doesn't do much for me unless it reflects a psyche acting out. As for monsters, we invent them to accommodate our urges.

*You've been quoted as saying you love "trapdoor" endings in stories. Can you elaborate on that and maybe give a few examples from your own fiction?*

A trapdoor ending is a heart that stops in mid-beat. It has a paradoxical effect, making the story expand at the exact moment it stops. My story "WYOM" ends like that. I was taught how to do it by my father. It's timing; knowing which moment or word is your exit. It usually comes sooner than expected.

Two generations of Mathesons worked together in *Pride* by Richard Matheson and Richard Christian Matheson (2002, Gauntlet Press; courtesy Dara Hoffman, Gauntlet Press).

*You've done work for both the small, indie press and mass market. Which do you prefer working for?*

I like both.

*What was your experience like at Gauntlet Press? How did you come to work for them in the first place?*

First class. I met Barry Hoffman through my father. We've become colleagues and friends.

*How did you come to be involved in* **Masters of Horror**, *and how did it feel to adapt your dad's "Dance of the Dead" story?*

The creator, Mick Garris, is an old friend and collaborator. We wrote a couple of movies together and always had an easy but interesting chemistry. I suggested the story to Mick and he instantly agreed. My dad's writing is smart, compressed and remarkable; easy to adapt.

*Why did you choose the short story "The Damned Thing" by Ambrose Bierce to adapt for the second season of* **Masters**?

I didn't. The producers and Tobe Hooper chose it, asked me to adapt it. I did what I could, given budget and time constraints, but it wasn't a story I would've chosen. It was too vague, had no central hook that grabbed me. Still, it's elegant and evocative in a way the script never could be since a narrative explanation was needed to justify a one-hour film. A moody puzzle wouldn't have worked though I far prefer the mystique of the Ambrose Bierce story. Television demands explanation, which usually has a bad effect on the power of a story. Especially an enigmatic one.

*How did you approach adapting it, expanding and making it more contemporary?*

I was basically hired to expand an evocative, transparent event. To be an hour film, it needed a lot. Plot. Characters. A theme. A location. I was reading about oil in the news and thought an oil family haunted by its rape of earth, using Texas as a locale, seemed promising. Tobe liked both, so I plunged in. Had to write fast for production reasons; what else is new? I tried to minimize explanations, protect the strange, elliptical spirit of the story. Critics of the film found that approach porous and annoying.

*Are there any other stories from old masters that you might like to adapt or update?*

Many. But I won't name them; give anyone ideas. Such stories are rare.

*Was it difficult updating the short story "Battlefield" for* **Stephen King's Nightmares and Dreamscapes***?*

No. Once I decided against dialogue and thought up the Savage Commando, to add further length and twists, it was a cinch. I wrote the first draft in a few days and Brian Henson and Bill Hurt executed it as written.

*What was it like to visit the set and see William Hurt in action?*

I flew to Australia, where they filmed the episode, to watch him. It was a thrill. There were no other actors and I got to know him a bit. Some dinners, lots of interesting conversations. Very well-read. A restless, witty intellect.

*Do you have any tales you could tell us from your time as a ghost hunter?*

Along with others in the parapsychology department, I investigated over twenty haunted houses, including the house which was central in the book and film *The Entity*. We used cutting edge equipment, séances, whatever it took. I witnessed survival of the spirit, in many disturbing forms. Also witnessed the human psyche, manifesting agony; equally disturbing. I came away from it all realizing the two are often hard to distinguish. And I came away taking it more seriously than I already had. Enough so that I don't tell war stories.

*What are your own beliefs about life after death?*

I believe in life after death. My father is my wise tutor in those matters. This is earth school and we all graduate.

*Have any stories been influenced by the fact that your mother Ruth worked as a clinical psychologist? Are there any specific examples you could tell us about?*

My mother's work has taught me to never assume personal things people tell you are the whole story. There are layers, subtexts, myriad selves. If my writing has psychological complexity, much owes to her.

*You once sold gags to stand-up comics. How hard is it to write funny as opposed to writing scary material? Do you feel there's a connection between humor and horror?*

I wrote for comedians. Sold jokes, routines, observations. It's very much like writing horror, at least the way I write it: trapdoor endings, twists. Jokes depend on those. Also language is key. Exact word choice. Rhythm, of course.

*What's your personal favorite story that you've written?*

"Who's You in America" which isn't really a story, more a thought piece. I think I captured something and worked hard to get it right. A mix of melancholy and hope.

*Can you tell us more about the new novel that you mentioned earlier?*

It's about fear and hatred visiting an innocent man.

*What was the initial spark for that one?*

The title. Which I can't mention.

*When you look back on your career, is there anything you would have done differently—or anything you wish you'd done?*

Only opportunities I walked past. But I love what I do. Writing prose and scripts, playing and recording music with my band ... it's what I always had in mind.

*What aspirations do you have for the future?*

More directing. More novels. More albums. If time permits, a psychology degree, maybe performing professionally as a stage magician. Also thinking about having children.

# Steve Niles

Steve Niles is one of the writers responsible for bringing horror comics back to prominence. The success of his *30 Days of Night* comic series led to a No. 1 box office smash, with *Spider-Man*'s Sam Raimi producing, David Slade directing and Niles co-writing the screenplay. He is currently working for the top American comic publishers—IDW, DC, Marvel, Image and Dark Horse—and recent projects include *Simon Dark* with artist Scott Hampton and *Batman: Gotham After Midnight* with artist Kelley Jones. Niles has been nominated for multiple Eisner Comic industry awards and was the recipient of two Spike TV Scream Awards for Best Horror comic and Best Comic Adaptation. He also won the Scribe Award for Best Original Novel in 2007. At present he is writing a screenplay for legendary director John Carpenter based on the comic *The Upturned Stone* for Dimension. His graphic novel *Freaks of the Heartland* is being developed for film by David Gordon Green, while *Criminal Macabre* has recently been acquired by Universal. Steve resides in Los Angeles.

---

*Did you read horror comics growing up?*

Absolutely. Everybody assumes I grew up reading EC, but I'm not that old [*laughs*]. I was born in the '60s so I grew up reading *Creepy* and *Eerie*. I was much more used to horror stories, not just with a twist, but actual character development and a more involved story. Also they had those amazing European artists. I absolutely, absolutely loved those books. I even have a memory of getting in trouble for having a copy of *Creepy* #2 in church, and my mom seeing me reading it in the pew, and absolutely losing her mind; she was not happy about that. Then *Batman* was very big for me, and at the time I was reading a lot of *Batman* that was done by Neal Adams, which had unbelievable horror elements and really frightening covers. I don't know if it was a Neal Adams cover ... but I remember there was one with basically Batman walking in on Robin having hung himself. And *that's* the cover! [*Laughs*] So there was a lot of *Batman*; I thought he was pretty dark at that point. Then I read *Tomb of Dracula* with art by Gene Colan. I loved the comics, loved the magazines, absolutely loved that, along with the other Marvel monsters.

*Did you ever collect* **Fangoria** *and* **Famous Monsters***?*

Oh yeah. I had huge stacks of *Famous Monsters* and I still have all my *Fangoria*s. I wanted to get the first issue of *Fangoria* with Godzilla on the cover. We were on vacation at Virginia Beach and I was with my mom, and she has like five sisters. I said, "Mom, can I get this?" I opened it up and showed her the picture from *Dawn of the Dead* of the guy's head exploding, and was like, "And this is why." [*Laughs*] My aunts were appalled, I remember them going, "You'd buy that for him? Oh, I would never buy that for one of my children...." But my mom bought it for me. I got every single issue of *Fangoria*, at least up to issue 100 or something, off the stand. And I still have them.

*Your mom took you to see* **Alien,** *and had her head in her hands all the way through...*

Yeah, she took me to see *Alien*; she took me to see *Escape from New York*; she took me to see just every movie that she just did not want to see. I mean, her idea of a movie is a good romantic comedy. She wanted to see *Fried Green Tomatoes*, and I'm dragging her to this stuff. She was so sweet, she would watch entire movies through her fingers, covering her eyes.

**Night of the Living Dead** *was the first genre film that you saw.*

It's the first one I remember having a really big impact. There were actually other movies. There's a movie called *The Mad Room*, that I've never seen since. Stella Stevens is in it; I don't remember it well, but there was something with a dog and a severed hand in his mouth. *What Ever*

**Steve Niles (courtesy Steve Niles).**

*Happened to Baby Jane?* terrified me. But I remember being that age, third or fourth grade, nine or ten—and catching *Night of the Living Dead* on TV with a friend of mine. I thought for about ten seconds that it was a *War of the Worlds* situation. I was like, "This is news footage!" because we'd never seen anything like this. That was the first movie to kick the crap out of me. I was so scared, and then I came walking right back for more. Because as soon as daylight came I was like, "That was kinda cool!" And I wanted to get right back to it.

*So was it that sense of being scared that maybe led you to want to scare other people?*

I think that enjoyment of being scared; I get really exhilarated. Especially as a kid when you would get scared—not appalled, not disgusted, but scared. I think that's a big part of it. I think a big part of being a writer, or being any kind of creative person, is: We spend our lives taking in other people's work. And when we decide to become writers or directors, artists or whatever ... it's part of our job to regurgitate the material. So I wouldn't say that any single event made me a horror guy. Although I'm always tempted to go, "Actually, I think it was when I watched my family being murdered." [*Laughs*] But nothing like that happened; it was just sort of a slow, gradual process. Though I remember really, really responding to *Night of the Living Dead*.

*So it must have been very exciting later on when you got the chance to adapt some of George Romero's work.*

Yeah, definitely. That's just the thing about it; I know I say it time and again, but horror's just like a rollercoaster. And, by the way, you *will not* get me on a rollercoaster [*laughs*]. I won't do it, that's the kind of fear I don't need. But for some people, that's it—they get on there, they scream their lungs out, they lose their minds with horror. Then they get off and get right back on again. I love that, and I think that's a lot of what horror's about.

*You're a big fan of '50s schlock movies as well.*

Yeah. I have a big love for the rubber-suited monsters. *Monster on the Campus* is one of my all-time favorites. *It, The Thing from Another World.* Any of the AIP movies. *I Was a Teenage Werewolf...* God. Actually, *I Was a Teenage Werewolf* was a damned good movie. I watched that recently and thought, this isn't a B-movie any more. It's good, especially Michael Landon. One thing I like about a lot of those movies is they were such an obvious, direct reaction to the world at the time. It was like, obviously we're a little bit afraid of atomic bombs so every horror movie reflected that. I could go on forever with the list of that stuff.

*You've credited TV horror host Count Gore De Vol as an influence.*

Well, he was the guy presenting *Night of the Living Dead* that night. Then as guests he would have Forry Ackerman, Dick Smith, and these people who [I] never heard of; I was just a little kid. Actually I ended up basing a story called "Aleister Arcane" on him, and he did the introduction to that. So I have a very special place in my heart for Count Gore De Vol.

*You used to work in a comics shop. Did the desire to write comics come before that?*

Yeah. I completed high school but I didn't go to college, so I was basically going to be a writer or a retail clerk. I actually went to work in comic stores and video stores and book stores because I knew that stuff. So that's mainly where I would stay, because I actually had some knowledge of book stores and comic stores. At the comic store, the one I worked at, they actually put me in the back issue department because I was the only one nerdy enough to answer everybody's questions. They'd come in and ask, "Which issue did Iron Man change his armor?" And I'd go marching off to find the issue [*laughs*]. Use your skills where you have 'em.

*Where did the desire to write them stem from?*

I grew up making Super 8 horror movies, and about the time I was 19, 20, I realized I could only go so far making films this way. It was becoming increasingly more expensive, and really hard to get my drunk friends to act. It was just getting hard. But then I looked down at my storyboards and my big stack of comics in the corner and went, "Duh!" Meanwhile I'm writing prose and I'm trying all this other stuff, and it was a big slap-on-the-forehead moment where I just went, "Comics!"

*Weren't you also involved in music at that time?*

I was in a band called Gray Matter on Dischord. With Dischord, even today, you can get an album from them for $5.99, postpaid. They work like this: Do it yourself; you don't have to bow down to the corporations; you can put out your own records; you can put on your own shows; you can do your own distribution; you can handle all these things and you can do it all without ripping people off or backstabbing your best friend to make an extra dime. That's the way I've tried to live since. So when it came time to do comics, I looked around and I was like, oh, we put out our own albums, we put on our own shows,

I'll put out my own damned comic books. It's the independent spirit of Dischord that was directly responsible for me self-publishing.

*So is that where Arcane Comix came from?*

Exactly, and that's why if you look in the back of *Fly in My Eye* there are Dischord ads [*laughs*].

*Can you remember the first-ever comic script you wrote, then?*

Had to be in that *Fly in My Eye*, a terrible comic called "Bad Moon." I just didn't know what the hell I was doing.

*So how did you become involved in adapting some of Clive Barker's stories into graphic novels? Did the* Illustrator *books come first?*

It all sort of happened at the same time. Because in that first issue of *Fly in My Eye*, it was the first time Clive's art had been presented as an artist. We did a portfolio in there and I did the lithographs. What really wound up happening was, I acquired the rights to the *Books of Blood* stuff, or half of it, and Eclipse Comics got the rest. Basically I just buckled under. Arcane was started with some really good ideas. And I am many things, but I am not a businessman—I sunk that company in about a year and a half. I just paid everybody too much. So I wound up doing Clive Barker adaptations, in partnership with Eclipse. When my line went under, Mino Milani approached me. He knew I wasn't gonna make it, he took me under his wing, and we wound up doing the Clive Barker adaptations, *I Am Legend*, and Fritz Lang's *M*, which were all things I had acquired under Arcane. And we did the *Clive Barker: Illustrator* art book as well.

*So had the first* Tapping the Veins *been out by then, by the time you came along to do the other ones?*

One of the first things I wanted to do that was different to *Tapping the Vein* was, I wanted to give each story its own book; I wanted to do that because I didn't like the way they were condensing great stories like "In the Hills, the Cities." I mean, that's just a crime. We have these perfect stories. So my first ones were *The Yattering and Jack*, *Rawhead Rex* and *Son of Celluloid*, with a few shorts. But the first ones I did were the full-length ones. I believe it was *Yattering and Jack* first because I remember John Bolton sending me Chris Claremont scripts, so I could see how a comic script was written. You think it's tough now to figure out how to write comics; back then everybody wrote them differently.

*Did you have much contact with Fred Burke, who also worked on Barker adaptations at the same time?*

Oh yeah. I wound up going out to Eclipse and he really helped me out putting things together, especially the Clive Barker art book.

*Were you pleased when Les Edwards worked on the adaptations?*

Oh my God, I was just blown away. And still, the books *Rawhead Rex* and *Son of Celluloid* are two of my favorites. I wish every comic I did could be painted like that.

*How did you end up working at McFarlane Entertainment?*

Ted Adams used to be an editor at Eclipse, then he went on his separate way and I went on mine. Ted and Beau Smith, two Eclipse guys, wound up basically working for

Todd McFarlane. Beau had been after me for years, to try and get me work, and kept pushing me for McFarlane. Then Ted got me in there. I was doing episode guides for *Spawn* animated, I was doing interviews with Paul Stanley for *Kiss* magazine, and Ozzy, any gig I could get that he was giving me, tossing me a few hundred bucks. Then I went out to Arizona and met Todd and we hit it off really well; I just ended up becoming his "go-to writer guy." I wound up writing *Spawn II*, we did a couple of TV series pilots together, and a bunch of stuff. Basically, it came to a decision that I couldn't work there any more because he wanted everybody to live in Arizona. And I'm willing to make sacrifices but I ain't livin' in Arizona [*laughs*].

*And it's Ted at IDW, isn't it?*

Exactly. That's the thing, as soon as I got hired by Todd, he left [*laughs*]. So I wound up floating for a little while, and it was while I was doing *Hellspawn* for Todd that Ted called and said, "Do you have any ideas for comics that you want to do?" I just gave him my rejected pitch list—and on that rejected movie pitch list was ... *30 Days of Night*. And *he* picked it, not me. He was like, "This vampire thing in Alaska looks good." So that led to that. For me it's such a small industry. It's amazing.

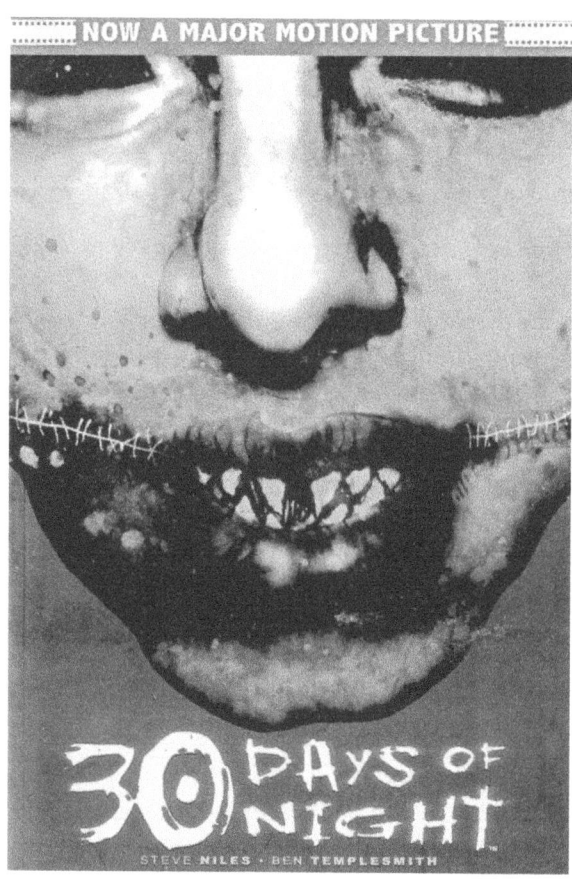

Ben Templesmith's artwork for the original *30 Days of Night* graphic novel (2007, IDW; courtesy Greg Goldstein, IDW).

*So it started out as a movie script,* 30 Days*?*

No, I only had it as a pitch. I didn't write a movie script until I got together with Sam Raimi. I had it as the basic pitch: I knew the characters, I knew the setting, I knew what was going to happen. But that's all, I hadn't written it up yet. So the first time I actually wrote it up was for the comic.

*Where did the initial idea come from?*

From a little human interest piece in a newspaper, talking about "The Town That Goes Dark." I read it and went ... vampires! Immediately. I was living in Minnesota at the time, so I just tucked it away, then I started pitching it. I pitched it to every movie company, every comic company, and they all rejected it.

*Dark Horse and Vertigo rejected it, didn't they?*

Yeah, Vertigo have rejected everything I've ever pitched them. And everything I've ever pitched them has now sold as a movie, so God bless 'em [*laughs*]. Vertigo is like my good luck charm. Maybe I write shitty pitches, I don't know. But they turn everything down.

*How did you originally get to know Ben Templesmith?*

I met him on the *Spawn* messageboards. I think one of the art directors there encouraged him to post some stuff and got him the *Hellspawn* gig, and I pushed for him for the *Hellspawn* gig. I just loved working with him, so when *30 Days of Night* came along, Ben was the first guy I thought of.

*So did you have those kinds of visuals in your head as you were writing it?*

What I love about Ben is that nobody's work looks like that. I mean, I know everyone says it's like Dave McKean, and I'm like, "What?" I can see similar techniques in there, but I think Ben has a very original style. I love the chaos, I just love the madness of some of his stuff; and I just love him for it. I just knew that Ben doesn't like to do things the way other people like to do, so we were in absolute agreement about how we wanted to approach vampires—which was that they're eating machines. They don't like people, they don't want to seduce us. They want to pop our heads and drain us. We both agreed on that, and that's what we moved forwards with.

*Was there a lot of back and forth between you two?*

Oh yeah. I didn't meet him for about two or three years face-to-face. We did most everything via IM and things like that. It was very fun.

*At what point did the relationship change between Stella and Eben from the comics to the film? It's completely different.*

I fought that from day one. And I still think I'm right. We've seen a thousand horror movies with the estranged couple brought together by horror. I love the book end and I love the idea about a loving couple. You just don't see that; it's so rare. I was outvoted by Raimi and the producers basically, and could never shake that. When you're doing movies, you've got to pick your battles, and at the time they were saying, "We're going to add a little tension between them." Okay, a little tension's fine. But it was up against the other producers who were saying, "We don't want the vampires to talk." And I was like, "Did you not read the comic book you just bought?" [*Laughs*] Those vampires are talking up a storm. They've got a whole mythology going on, so I decided at that point that was a bigger fight. So, it's just a lot of compromise. Making movies is creativity by committee most of the time, and the bigger the movie the bigger the committee. That was one of the battles I lost. The vampires talking barely made it in. We ended up inventing a language— that was David Slade's idea. In my version of the screenplay they spoke Romanian and various European languages. Still going to go with the subtitles, but they were languages we knew, which was something I liked from the comics because I wanted them to seem like they were from all over the world.

*How did you set about making Marlowe and the other vampires different from those that have gone before? Is it that sense they've all come from other places?*

Yeah. It's a pet peeve of mine, that whenever you watch the old schlock movies, every time you go to an alien planet they all have the same color hair and they all wear the same clothes. And it's like, vampires have this thing, but they're not all going to put on red capes and suits and have little doilies around their wrists. They're all going to be completely different, from all over the world and of all different ages. That was something I really wanted to portray, which I think Ben did a great job of. And in the movie they did a great job of it, too. I cannot say enough about David Slade; David Slade saved the movie. I'm very happy. We almost wound up with basically a zombie movie. Those vampires weren't talking, so that's what they would have been.

*It's a fantastic movie.*

Oh, thank you. Like I said, I'm very, very happy. I wish Eben and Stella weren't estranged, and I wish we could have had the vampire arc with the two vampires, like the comic, because I love that. I think it came across in the movie, but the vampires hide behind their mythology. They love the fact that in the *30 Days of Night* world, Dracula, Buffy, all that exists, and they hide behind that because it's so ridiculous. How would anyone believe that it exists? There are a couple of lines in there, that David got in with the Marlowe speech towards the end, and I really hope it comes across. But I miss that moment in the comic where it's the punk-ass kids who don't know any better who raid the town and then the old guard shows up going, "What the hell are you doing? [*Laughs*] Do you know how long it's taken us.... There's a reason we don't do these kinds of things." I think actually, after reading the reviews, that the audience would have enjoyed a little more info. Because I read reviews that said, "I don't understand where they came from." Even though there's a big shot of a ship [*laughs*]!

**Justin Randall's artwork for the original *30 Days of Night* graphic novel (2007, IDW; courtesy Greg Goldstein, IDW).**

*What did it feel like when there was a bidding war for the rights to* **30 Days***?*

I was just deliriously happy. Two weeks before that I had quit Todd McFarlane Entertainment because they wanted me to move to Arizona and work exclusively for them, and that would include my property. Smart move for Todd, not very smart move for me. So I walked, and I was unemployed when that happened. It just couldn't have come at a better time. It was really exciting, and I just remember not really understanding a lot of what was happening. It was really that whole year just learning the film industry and what all this entailed. So it made it very easy for me when Raimi stepped in. When Raimi entered the battle,

I just called my agent and said, "Go with him. I don't care how much money, I don't care what studio. If Raimi is attached I feel safe." It seems to have worked out, so I'm glad I did that. I may have lost a couple of million, but screw it. Got a good movie out of it.

*You're a big fan of his work, then?*

I'm a *huge* fan of Raimi, especially his early movies. I'm a huge fan of his spirit. *Evil Dead* and *Evil Dead II* are two of my favorite movies. They definitely made me want to make movies, made me want to tell stories. And with *Spider-Man* I thought he really proved how important it is to stick to the source material. When you buy a comic or a novel, especially one that has a fan following, don't go changing it. If the Fantastic Four flew by themselves, don't have them flying with Dr. Doom, that's all I'm saying. Because that's where these movies go wrong. As soon as the producers start thinking they're more clever than 50 years of fandom, they're shooting themselves in the foot. Well, that's my opinion.

*How much involvement did you have with the production as it went along? For example, were you happy with the casting?*

You know how people do those things, like dream casting? I suck at that [*laughs*]. I would have cast Walter Matthau as Eben. I don't know shit. It could actually have made a very interesting movie, watching the elderly being chased by vampires. But as each person came in, I was completely surprised. I would say the only ones who came in that I went "Yeah!" were these two: Ben Foster and Danny Huston. Danny, if you look at pictures of him when he's smiling he looks fucking evil; so I was like, "I can't wait to see him *made up* to look evil." Danny did something that was so above and beyond: He loved the comic book art of the two vampires, the groups, the two sects, and really wanted to play the part I think of what would have been Vicente. So, when the decision was made that the world couldn't handle two villains, he amalgamated the characters. If you notice, he does play it a little reckless and vicious at first, then becomes a little more responsible towards the end. And, again, God bless him for that, because I just thought it was so important to get that thread in there. I've got to admit, I know everyone was running around, screaming and yelling, when Josh Hartnett was cast—but I was like, the guy's from Minnesota, which is not only a cold weather area, but anybody born and raised there has some Native American in them. So he had the look, and I went back and looked at *Black Hawk Down* and *Lucky Number Sleven*, and I thought, "He can act, he's great."

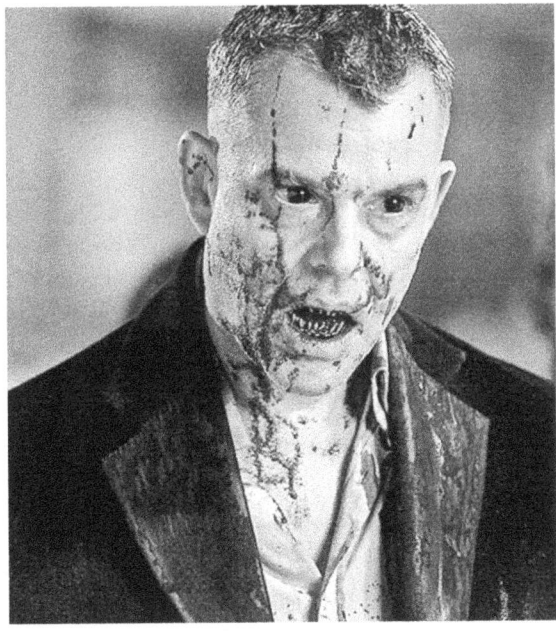

Danny Huston as the lead vampire Marlow in the *30 Days of Night* movie adaptation (2007, Columbia Pictures).

Melissa George was the only one I didn't know. I had to go out and rent some stuff, because she's done some TV things here and a lot of English movies, or Australian TV and stuff. But I thought she just knocked it out of the park. I thought she was just a great Stella.

*When you saw it for the first time, up there on the screen, how did you feel?*

Wow ... I'll tell this, I almost cried. It was great, it was beautiful. Because one of my favorite things about the story was the arctic setting; snow and horror, I just think they're great. And seeing it ... I mean, they built our town, they're our characters, and watching the stranger march in. Ahh. It was an awesome feeling, just unbelievable.

*You've described it as quite a traditional horror movie. What did you mean by that?*

Just a return to a more non-gimmick thing; I don't think you can put it in a category other than a horror movie. You could put it in "vampire movie," I suppose. But it's not going to be put under "torture porn" or "slasher" or any of these other subgenres, which I like and dislike to varying degrees. So I guess just in that way it felt like something that could be up on the horror shelf. It's a monster movie, characters in peril. It just felt more like a return to *Jaws*, *The Omen*: a straightforward horror movie with no big gimmicks.

*How did you decide which way to go with the graphic novels after* 30 Days, *with* Dark Days...?

It got harder every time. My promise was basically, if somewhere somebody could figure out the archives of my message board, they'd find after the first series, me writing: "There will be no sequel, I will not milk this idea." Yeah, I know, and now 50 books later ... big hypocrite I am [*laughs*]. But what happened was ... I got ideas. I knew I didn't want to just go around the arctic circle and have vampires attack Finland, or perhaps this poor town of Barrow get attacked every winter ... okay, this is getting old. So when I came up with the idea of Stella carrying on the story in the way she would, and that the setting would change to LA, then I started to realize, "Okay, we're on to something," and I let the characters take over. Instead of the concept of vampires in Alaska, I let the style of vampire and the characters take over. And that just led to more ideas.

*Is there a possibility that might get turned into the sequel to the film?*

There's always a possibility, but you never know with Hollywood. They might want to jump right to *Return to Barrow*. Who knows? But God, I think *Dark Days* would be a fantastic sequel. One of my favorite sequels is *Aliens*, two different movies in the same world, and I think that's what we should do with this, instead of just repeating itself.

*Who cooked up the idea to take the series into space with "Dead Space"?*

You wanna know the truth? I wanted to see weightless blood [*laughs*]. I can't claim anything more than that. Blood floating around weightless in a weightless situation is gonna look great.

*Did you have much involvement in* Red Snow?

That was *completely* Ben's. God, he did a great job. I love that thing. I thought it was really, really clever and very well executed.

*How's it been working with Jeff Mariotte on the fiction* 30 Days *books?*

Jeff was one of the original editors at IDW so he already knew the mythology really well. He was very easy to work with. I would lay out a treatment, and he would start a draft and I would start a draft. It was like a game of tennis, we'd just throw it back and forth. So we pounded out the books. I can honestly say we've not had one disagreement.

*Where did the idea for Cal McDonald come from?*

I was ... God, 17 or 18 I guess, and I fell in love with Raymond Chandler. I'd never read Raymond Chandler before and I stumbled on his stories. So naturally I started writing hardboiled stuff. And I was trying to write hardboiled detective in modern settings, but it just felt like this retro thing. So I decided to add monsters. Then I still had the same problem, it was still the hard-drinking Bogart: Sam Spade, Philip Marlowe in modern times. And it didn't work. So I ripped off his trenchcoat and his fedora, and I just gave him boots and a garage jacket. And instead of being a drunk, he's a recovering junkie. He's had substance abuse problems. That solidified it. I wrote as prose and that was the first one where it all came together. There was an earlier one called "Bakehead" but he was still in a suit; I was still trying to do the noir thing.

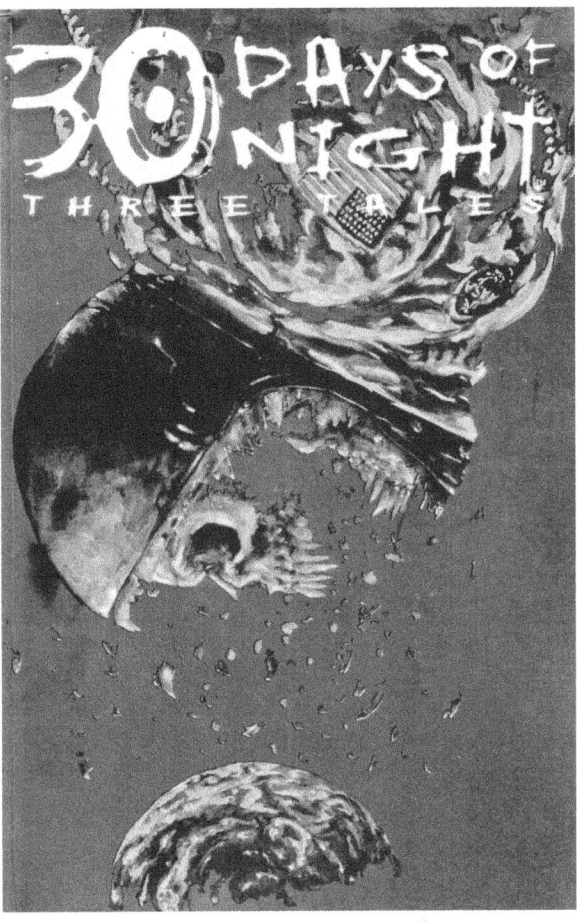

The *Three Tales* graphic novel containing the story "Dead Space" with artwork by Ben Templesmith (2006, IDW; courtesy Greg Goldstein, IDW).

When I started adding the monsters and drugs, more comedy started coming out of it. And his attitude really started to emerge. I was like, "What's this shitty attitude that came out?" That's when I was just in love with the guy, and I've been writing him ever since.

*Is he the creation you feel is most personal to you?*

Oh yeah, without a doubt. I mean, it's really funny because people think that I'm like that. And I'm like, "No, he's an asshole! I wouldn't hang out with him." [*Laughs*] There *are* certainly sides of it where I get to say things through Cal that I would never be able to say out loud. But no, he's more or less a figment of my imagination. I've had people say to me, "So, have you had those drug habits?" And I say, "No human would survive those drug habits!" [*Laughs*] If I did those things, I'd never be here. But I was in the music scene for a long time, I lost two friends to overdose, drug-related deaths. I saw a lot of this stuff and you don't need to put a needle in your arm to write about somebody putting a needle in their arm. So I did see an awful lot of what was around me.

*Is it true that Cal's ghoul sidekick Mo'lock was based on Raymond Massey?*

Not only Raymond Massey, but Raymond Massey from a very particular shot: You know the shot in *Arsenic and Old Lace* where Cary Grant and he both realize that they have a body in the window seat, and they both run for it?

**Yes** *[laugh].*

And all of a sudden he's got like Jethro pants and he's doing this run, this gangly run? That's Mo'Lock. If you could see in the early description when he comes in, it's almost like he's a marionette on strings. You can't imagine anything that thin can walk. So, it's totally based on Raymond Massey, which is very funny because if you look at the cover of *Dial M For Monster*, Tim Bradstreet totally misunderstood what I said and used Raymond Massey when he was like 60. So he was this old man sitting in a chair. That's Mo'Lock aged. But no, it was Raymond Massey from *Arsenic and Old Lace* when he was Jonathan Brewster. Cracked me up.

*There's a lot of these kinds of detectives around these days. How do you feel about the influx of all those?*

It was inevitable. They existed before and they're around now. It's just one of those things. I remember when *Buffy* came on, I was just like, "Oh Christ, that's the end of monster hunters." But there's room for everybody. The thing is, you could have another guy who writes about a monster-hunting detective, we'll both write a story and I guarantee you they won't be the same story. So I don't mind, I hope Cal has a unique voice. I think a lot more people are leaning towards the psychic detective and stuff like that, and Cal doesn't have any powers—except that he's numb, if that's a power [*laughs*]. So no, it doesn't bother me. If somebody else can get some stories out there for me to read, I'm not going to complain.

*How did you first meet Rob Zombie?*

A mutual friend introduced us, literally threw us together in a room and said, "You guys'll like each other." And we stared at each other, then went, "Hey." We started talking and sure enough found out we're from the same region, grew up in very similar music scenes on the East Coast, knew the same people, born the same year, loved the same music: it was an immediate connection. We wound up doing those two comic series together [*Bigfoot* and *The Nail*]. At the time, one of the things around us was Rob was retiring from music—that didn't last too long—and we were going to create this production company. We did the two comics and since then I've written a screenplay for *Bigfoot*.

*What's he like to work with?*

That's the funny thing. Because of his appearance and his stage persona, people think he writes with a rock or something. But he's a very wealthy fella, he's a good, smart businessman, and he's a hard worker—one of the shrewdest businessmen I've ever met. When it comes to getting work done, he gets it done, which is more than I can say for some. I've met many people who think they're rock stars and you can't get shit out of 'em, but he never missed a deadline. He was great to work with.

*I would imagine it's a lot of fun to work with him, too.*

Oh, it's total fun—he's hilarious. People might not know because he refuses to smile, but he's one of the funniest fuckers I've ever met. He's hilarious, he's absolutely hilarious.

*What were your feelings approaching writing* **Batman** *for DC?*

Well, I did *Gotham County Line* which I really enjoyed, but it was really weird. I think that's what everybody expected, a bit weird. I just figured, for a guy who reacts that badly to his parents' deaths, I don't think he has any kind of spirituality. So it was the idea that our beliefs control very much what happens in our afterlife, blah blah blah. I did that, and that was really fun. And I did a 12-issue series with Kelley Jones with a title we created: *Gotham After Midnight*. It was very exciting; it's not spooky Batman, but it looks very moody. Lots of action, lots of fun. Comics have just been so events-driven, you just can't get a decent comic these days, so Kelley and I decided to just play it very straight and give the people what they want.

*What were the influences for creating Simon Dark? He's in Gotham as well, isn't he?*

Putting him in Gotham was my editor Joey Cavalieri's idea. I've written so many stories on the Frankenstein theme that I wanted to follow it, to create a character around that, but I wanted to create a character who knows he's made up of other people's body parts, and that's *all* he knows. He doesn't know who created him, he doesn't know why he's where he is, and—as an added twist—he's 17 years old. That was the creation of the character; I wanted to start with the character itself being a mystery. Then, as it spirals out, we discover he's also very good-hearted, but at the same time capable of unbelievable violence. There's reasons for all this, some of it he just doesn't know, some of it is just ingrained in him. But the whole thing is leaning towards an expansion on the Frankenstein theme of playing God, but also the idea of playing with the supernatural in combination with science, and how dangerous that would be. All these ideas are just pushing the character forward, but what I love most about him is that he's an innocent. And when they asked if I wanted to put him in Gotham, I was like, "Yeah. You know what, you just handed me a character. Gotham is a character."

*You mentioned tackling the old monsters, like Frankenstein. You've also tackled Jekyll and Hyde.*

That was from really thinking about how medicated our society is becoming now. If we [the people of this planet] manage to live another couple hundred years, I think we'll look back and go, "Oh yeah, that was when everybody was taking drugs; everybody was using their bodies as chemistry sets." I decided how great would it be to have the idea of the scientist Dr. Jekyll trying to basically create chewable Prozak—gum that makes you happy [*laughs*]. But the biggest thing with that was the twist. When Robert Louis Stevenson wrote it, nobody could even conceive that these two characters were the same person, and that was the fun of it. Now *everybody* knows they're the same person. So what I wanted to do was have these brothers who work at a pharmaceutical company and *they* don't even know which one's gone crazy, which one's Hyde.

*How does it feel to be labeled a master of horror comics, and to have people say you've reinvigorated horror comics?*

If it's true, I couldn't be happier. Again, that's the kind of thing that makes me cry, because when I was a little kid I only dreamed of being part of the scene. I read about every period of horror—and I always wanted to be a part of it. I didn't care if I was holding cables for George Romero, I just wanted to be a part of it. If I'm even the tiniest little bit responsible for making horror comics viable again, thank you, that's wonderful. But it was a total accident, it's just because I love horror and I love comics.

# Sarah Pinborough

Sarah Pinborough was born in 1972 in Stony Stratford, Buckinghamshire, where her family have their home, and spent much of her childhood and adulthood traveling all over the world. Her father, now retired, was a diplomat and so her early years were spent trawling the Middle East, before she packed her trunk at eight years old and headed off to boarding school for a ten-year stretch, the memories of which she says still provide her with much of her material for horror writing....

She went on to teach English and write six horror novels—*The Hidden*, *The Reckoning*, *Breeding Ground*, *The Taken*, *Tower Hill* and *Feeding Ground*—plus various short stories. Her influences include Stephen King, Clive Barker, Graham Joyce, Michael Marshall (Smith), John Wyndham, Dean Koontz and Madonna. Sarah has been short-listed twice for the British Fantasy Award for Best Novel, and won the BFS Award for Best Short Story in 2009; in the same year she was nominated for a World Fantasy Award in that category. Her first thriller *A Matter of Blood* (from Gollancz) came out in the U.K. in Spring 2010 and she is also working on a series of YA books for the same publisher. She is a member of the British Fantasy Society, The Horror Writers' Association and, along with fellow horror authors Sarah Langan, Alex Sokoloff and Deborah LeBlanc, part of the writing collective MUSE. Sarah currently lives about five miles from where she was born with her cats, Mr. Fing and Peter.

---

*When did you first become interested in books and writing?*

I was always interested in books. My mum is a big reader so there were always books in the house, and she encouraged us by making sure we went to the library when we were little—a very small room in the British Embassy in Damascus!—to get out something to read on a Friday afternoon after school. I remember writing my first story when I was about five or six. I think it was a play, actually.

*What were your early influences in the fiction world, what did you like to read? For example, you appeared on the SciFi Channel once talking about Stephen King...*

I know she's out of fashion now, but when I was very small I loved Enid Blyton books. And then, when I was at boarding school, I read whatever there was on the paperback shelves in the boarding house. I found myself drawn to the *Pan Books of Horror* and other spooky short story anthologies, but I read quite widely then; Wilbur Smith I raced through, as well as various thriller authors and the usual early Virginia Andrews and so on. Then I discovered James Herbert and from there Stephen King. I won the English prize at school when I was maybe 15 and I used the book tokens to buy a stack of Stephen King books. He is a great storyteller and must have been a huge influence for writers in all genres, not just horror.

*What are some of your favorite films?*

I love a variety of films, just like most people. The *Godfather* trilogy, *The Man Who Would Be King*, *Gilda* (I'm a sucker for most of those '40s films), *The Witches of Eastwick*, *Moulin Rouge*, the *Alien* films, *The Thing* ... God, the list is endless. I just like a good story.

*What made you decide to become a writer?*

I don't think I ever decided to "become" a writer. I never thought of it as a job. I thought of it as something I did, whether it led to publishing or not. I guess when I was about 28 or 29 I started to consider the idea of getting things published.

**Author Sarah Pinborough (courtesy Sarah Pinborough).**

*Was it a conscious decision to choose horror as your genre at the beginning? Or is it just that horror is what draws you?*

I like dark subject matter and I read a huge amount of horror; the Stephen King influence draws a lot of writers of my age towards horror, I imagine. So it was probably natural to start there. I also like thrillers and fantasy and I've moved more in that direction as my writing progresses.

*You started out with short stories before the novels. Why did it take so long to return to this form? For example, most recently with stories for anthologies like* **Summer Chills**, **Hellbound Hearts** *and so on.*

I only wrote two short stories before my first novel and even now I only write them if I'm asked for one. I'm not a natural short story writer, but I do enjoy the speed of them between novels or when you're stuck in a tricky place in a book.

*How did publication of* **The Hidden** *come about?*

I was relatively lucky with *The Hidden*. I'd written it and then sent the first three chapters and synopsis to Don D'Auria at Leisure, and he emailed back and asked for the rest. Then he bought it! It took about another year for it to be published, though. I'd written the first six or seven pages a couple of years earlier and not been sure where to take it. When I found them and read them again I suddenly saw the whole story in my head.

*How did it feel when you first started to get quotes and reaction to the book from places like Horror Web and The Horror Channel?*

It's always nice to get some praise, especially for your first book—when you're still developing a thick skin and your own confidence and you don't know how people will take it. I think the *Horror Web* one I liked because I then met the reviewer at World Horror Convention 2005 in New York City and it was nice to hear the praise face to face.

*What's been your favorite quote so far? For instance, the comparison to Joe Hill was quite impressive.*

The Joe Hill comparison is great, but actually I've been happiest with the reviews that have come in for my PS Publishing novella *The Language of Dying*. It was a really personal book about growing up and loss, so the great reviews it's received have really touched me. It's also a departure from my normal writing so that was a great confidence boost, too.

*Did you draw on any real-life childhood experiences for* The Reckoning? *Was it interesting to look at how we change from kids to adults over time, and the contrast between the two?*

There weren't any real-life experiences in *The Reckoning*, that I can remember at any rate, but I did set it in a thinly veiled version of my home town. I think it was primarily influenced by Stephen King's *It*. I loved that novel and really wanted to write one of those "going home" books, but hopefully with enough new about it to make it interesting. I'm fascinated by how our childhoods shape us and how we can form truths from different perspectives, and that's what this book was really about for me.

Sarah Pinborough's first novel *The Hidden* (2004, Leisure Books; courtesy Tracy Heydweiller, Dorchester Publishing).

*How difficult did you find writing from a child's perspective for parts of the novel? Do you think your background as a teacher helped in that respect?*

I was in my first year of teaching when I wrote *The Reckoning*—I only taught for six years in total—so I don't think the teaching really made a difference. It may have done in later books but it's hard to say. I don't find writing from children's perspectives difficult; I quite enjoy it. I've just written the first of a YA trilogy for Gollancz and really enjoyed writing from young people's viewpoints.

*There seems to be an influence from John Wyndham and Jack Finney in* Breeding Ground—The Midwich Cuckoos, Invasion of the Body Snatchers, *but darker.*

Wyndham is one of my favorite authors, and *Breeding Ground* was my homage to *Day of the Triffids*. When I first wrote it, I wasn't thinking in terms of horror, rather science fiction. I guess it came out somewhere between the two.

*Why did you choose spiders?*

I can't actually remember. Just because they're so weird? And would you really want one growing inside you [*laughs*]?

*Did you find the male point of view hard to write?*

I love writing from the male point of view. I much prefer it. Most of my characters are male, and in fact in the sequel *Feeding Ground* there are no main female characters at all.

*Was* Breeding Ground *pitched as a single novel, or as a potential series?*

It was pitched as a single novel, and in essence it is. The second book doesn't lead on from the first and has different characters. Primarily because the sequel I had planned was too sci-fi for my horror editor and so I put that outline to one side and wrote a separate book. It does have more answers in it, though!

*Breeding Ground* (2006, Leisure Books; courtesy Tracy Heydweiller, Dorchester Publishing).

*Will there be any more?*

There won't be more unless I one day get to write the sequel I actually planned. The way things stand, I don't see it happening any day soon.

*Was it fun to imagine an invasion-like scenario, where our humanity is threatened?*

I think all horror and science fiction writers like to imagine a post-apocalyptic world of their own. Creating one is almost like a rite of passage, especially if you were raised on *The Stand*. It was brilliant fun to do but quite challenging.

*Have you always been interested in the supernatural and ghosts? Did this influence the premise for* The Taken*?*

I think I'll leave this question because, as I'm a horror writer, I guess we can presume I'm interested in ghostly things [*laughs*].

*The opening of* Tower Hill *grabs readers by the scruff of the neck. Do you think that's important in horror fiction?*

I was actually influenced by thrillers in the opening of *Tower Hill*. I'd just read Michael Marshall's *The Intruders*, and wanted to try out a new style. But I think *all* fiction should grab the reader by the scruff of the neck, regardless of genre.

***Tower Hill*** *is your first novel set in the U.S. Did you find it difficult writing a book set somewhere other than your home country?*

I think it would have been harder if it had been set in a country other than the States. In the U.K. we're so immersed in American references and television that it's easier to fake it. Plus, I have a lot of American friends who helped me with things I wasn't sure of.

*What was the inspiration for the characters of Jack and Gray?*

I'm not sure I had an inspiration as such. I wanted some bad guys that you sort of liked. They have a bond and are good friends, and are interesting people. I wanted to write a book where the bad guys were more fun to read than the good ones. I think I succeeded.

*You've also written a* **Torchwood** *novel called* **Into The Silence**. *What made you decide to try this?*

I did it for the money! [*Laughs*] But once I'd started I found it good fun.

*Would you like to write more books in the* **Doctor Who** *and* **Torchwood** *universe?*

*The Taken* (2007, Leisure Books; courtesy Tracy Heydweiller, Dorchester Publishing).

I'm not sure. It would depend how busy I was on other projects. But it was a good experience and I really enjoyed it.

*You've done some scripting before. Is it something you want to pursue?*

I'm currently working on a horror script with a film director I know. I'd like to do some scripting for both TV and film but these things are hard to break into properly and I have to fit them around book commitments.

*What was your motivation for writing* **The Language of Dying**?

*The Language of Dying* is a very personal book inspired by the last week of a friend of mine's life. He was diagnosed with terminal cancer and came to live with me. It was a difficult and in many ways inspiring time to live through and so the novella was quite cathartic. It's fiction with some fact woven in. PS Publishing are a dream to work with. I can't say enough good things about them, as I'm sure is the case for all their authors and artists. That's why they win so many awards.

*How did you come up with the idea for "The Confessor's Tale" for* Hellbound Hearts *[an anthology inspired by Clive Barker's original novella* The Hellbound Heart*]?*

I didn't want to write something that anyone would expect, and really liked the idea of some kind of Eastern European fairy tale that would explore how the Cenobites came to be. I woke up one morning with the first line in my head and the rest just followed.

*How did it feel to win your BFS award for Best Short Story for "Do You See" and to be nominated for a World Fantasy Award for "Our Man in the Sudan"?*

It felt really, really good—as anyone that was there could clearly see on my face [*laughs*]! The win was a surprise, and I was totally shocked to find out about the World Fantasy Award nomination. I feel very honored and I feel like my career is finally taking off a bit.

*The Language of Dying* with artwork by Mark Chadwick (2009, PS Publishing; courtesy Peter Crowther, PS Publishing).

*The children's books due out in the near future—are they still genre-related, or do they take a different direction?*

They're YA books with a 16-year-old main character and are dark fantasy, set in London. I'm really excited about them. It's a trilogy, and the first book *The Double Edged Sword* is out in July 2010.

*You've embarked on a three-book thriller series for Gollancz, the first book being* A Matter of Blood. *Why the change in direction?*

I had wanted to write a thriller for some time and luckily Gollancz have given me that opportunity. They do have a supernatural undercurrent, however.

*Can you tell us a little bit about the series?*

The male protagonist is a policeman and, on the surface, the first novel especially is a straight crime thriller. However, as he investigates three separate crimes he realizes that they might be linked, and also discovers a shadowy conspiracy that we learn more about in books two and three. I'm really proud of these books. I've never worked so hard as I did on the first one.

*How do you see your writing progressing? Will you continue to write horror when the ideas strike, or is it something you think you'll move away from?*

I think I'll definitely still write horror, especially in short fiction, but I'm enjoying doing something slightly different at the moment. I think my writing will always be dark, though!

# Part Two

*Directors*

# *John Carpenter*

John Carpenter was born in Carthage, New York, in 1948. Interested in cinema from an early age ("I fell in love with movies by *going* to the movies," he has stated), his favorites were 1950s science fiction films such as *The Thing from Another World* and *Forbidden Planet*. Carpenter went on to attend USC film school in Los Angeles, where he worked as co-writer, film editor and music composer on *The Resurrection of Broncho Billy* (1970), which won an Academy Award for Best Live Action Short Film. His first feature as director was *Dark Star* (1974). The low-budget siege film *Assault on Precinct 13* (1976) followed—inspired by *Rio Bravo* (1959)—and marked Carpenter's first collaboration with producer Debra Hill. Their pairing on *Halloween* (1978) would signify a high point in Carpenter's career; it went on to become one of the most successful independent films of all time, eventually gaining critical acclaim in the process. A string of successful and noteworthy movies came in its wake: *The Fog* (1980), *Escape from New York* (1981), *The Thing* (1982), *Christine* (1983), *Starman* (1984), *Big Trouble in Little China* (1986), *Prince of Darkness* (1987) and *They Live* (1988). On into the '90s, and *Memoirs of an Invisible Man* (1992), *In the Mouth of Madness* (1994) and *Village of the Damned* (1995) further ably demonstrated Carpenter's ability to rework classic stories and ideas, while movies like *Vampires* (1998) and *Ghosts of Mars* (2001) took supernatural elements and put them into surprising settings.

Most recently, Carpenter has directed two of the popular *Masters of Horror* episodes, and at the time of writing has two movies in pre-production: *The Ward* and *Riot*.

---

*You became friends with Dan O'Bannon, with whom you made* **Dark Star**. *Who came up with the original concept and how did you decide on the tone of the film?*

I came up with the original concept for *Dark Star*. Dan co-wrote the screenplay with me, fleshing out many of the original ideas. He also production designed the film and co-starred as Pinback. Dan contributed mightily to the tone of the film; many of the funniest moments are his ideas.

**Dark Star** *got you an agent, who told you the best way to make it in the business was to write scripts. Were there any you wrote during that time you wished you could have made?*

Yes, I wish I could have directed *The Eyes of Laura Mars*.

*When did the title of* **The Babysitter Murders** *change to* **Halloween**, *and did this significantly change what you were doing to prepare for the film?*

Irwin Yablans [the independent producer of *Assault on Precinct 13*, who went on to produce both *Halloween II* and *Halloween III: Season of the Witch* for Universal Pictures] came up with the idea to call the movie *Halloween*. This happened before shooting began.

John Carpenter publicity shot. Photograph by Sandy King (courtesy John Carpenter).

It was a great idea. I already had a general plan for the film before the title change.

*How did you attract Donald Pleasence to the part of Dr. Loomis and what was he like to work with?*

The part of Dr. Loomis was offered to both Christopher Lee and Peter Cushing. Both were screen heroes of mine. Both turned me down. Donald Pleasence agreed to do the part because his daughter, who was in a rock 'n' roll band, liked my score for *Assault on Precinct 13*. Donald and I became fast friends. I worked with him a second time on *Escape from New York* and a third time in *Prince of Darkness*.

*The signature theme—which everyone now associates with* **Halloween**—*came to you while the script was being written. What sparked the initial tune?*

The main theme for *Halloween* came

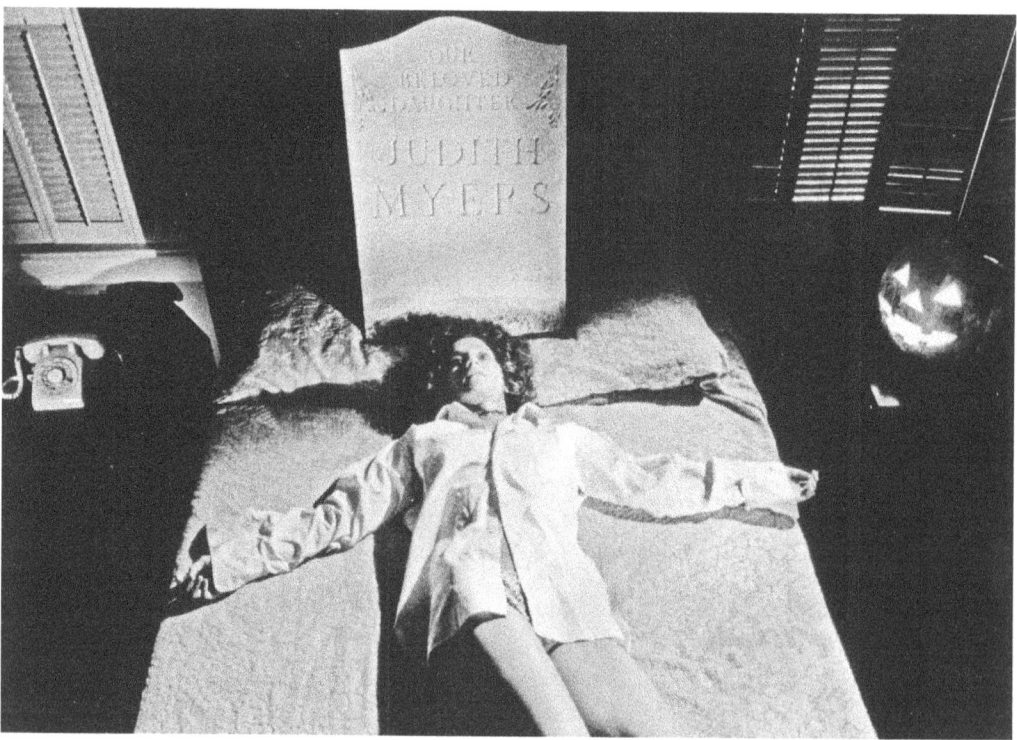

Annie Brackett (played by Nancy Kyes, credited as Nancy Loomis), a victim of Michael Myers in *Halloween* (1978, Compass International; courtesy John Gullidge).

about years before I ever got involved directing the picture. My father taught me 5/4 rhythm on a pair of bongos in my teens. That rhythm became the backbone for the *Halloween* theme.

*When did you begin to realize what an impact* **Halloween** *was having?*

I realized that *Halloween* was taking off after a review was published in *The Village Voice*. Also, Roger Ebert wrote kindly of the film. Around the time I finished directing the TV movie of *Elvis*, I began to hear about large grosses and hold-overs. It was nice.

*You were strong-armed into writing the sequel when you didn't think it needed one. Do you ever wish the sequels hadn't happened at all?*

I wish there hadn't been sequels to *Halloween* in a naïve creative sense, but I'm glad it has become a franchise because of the financial rewards I've reaped.

*How do you feel about virtually inventing the slasher genre—in spite of your movie having very little gore?*

I didn't invent the slasher genre. *Psycho* invented the slasher genre in the modern horror film.

*Okay, how about a re-invention? How did you feel about* **Halloween** *opening the door for the many slasher movies to follow?*

*Halloween* was made for very little money. This was the biggest incentive for the movies that followed.

**The Fog** *was a completely different film, a ghost story based on a California legend about luring ships to their doom. Could you tell us more about how the idea evolved and what were the inspirations?*

The idea began with just the simple image of fog upon a landscape.

*The Fog* (1980, AVCO Embassy Pictures; courtesy John Gullidge).

**Jamie Lee Curtis in** *Halloween* **(1978, Compass International; courtesy John Gullidge).**

**Janet Leigh and Hal Holbrook in** *The Fog* **(1980, AVCO Embassy Pictures; courtesy John Gullidge).**

*What was it like to work with the legendary Janet Leigh and John Houseman?*

I enjoyed working with them. Both were consummate professionals, although Houseman flubbed his lines a couple of times.

*What made you back Kurt Russell for the role of Snake Plissken in* Escape from New York, *after only working with him in the musical* Elvis? *What qualities did you see in him for this anti-hero?*

In spite of his Disney background, I saw a rage in Kurt Russell that I felt would work well as Snake Plissken. Plus, like Sam Neill and Jeff Bridges, he was my kind of actor.

*There's a reading of the movie where Snake is actually entering a kind of hellish underworld—would you go along with that?*

Yes, I would.

*What do you think people find so appealing about Snake?*

He's very cool.

*There were a fair few difficulties during the filming of your first major studio movie* The Thing, *like the weather and some of Rob Bottin's effects.*

The weather on location was miserable [Stuart, British Columbia]. The special makeup effects were frustrating. Both the weather and effects required resilience and patience.

*You've said that Stephen King doesn't translate well to the screen. Why is that? And did this affect the making of* Christine?

Most of what happens in a Stephen King story is internal.

*How did this affect your approach to filming* **Christine***?*

I simplified the story to simply a haunted car movie.

**Prince of Darkness** *had a distinctly Nigel Kneale–like quality to it—even to the point of writing it under the Alan Quatermass pseudonym. What influence did he have on your career?*

I loved Nigel Kneale's television work, as well as the screen adaptations of the *Quatermass* trilogy. I worked with him on *Halloween 3*. Let me simply say that he was a very creative writer and a somewhat angry person. He could be extremely vicious.

*How did you aim to make your version of* **Village of the Damned** *different from the original novel and the previous film version? What did you want to retain or discard?*

My version focused more on the women of the village.

**Vampires** *was probably as close to a horror Western as you've come. We got the impression you were having fun with that one.*

Yes, I was.

*Your* **Masters of Horror** *episode "Cigarette Burns" is a very unusual story. Do you subscribe to the concept of the power of cinema to affect people and make them act in certain ways?*

The screenwriters of "Cigarette Burns," Drew McWeeny and Scott Swan, are very talented and came up with a great idea for a one-hour horror tale. Personally, I'm a little dubious about the proposition that cinema—or video games or heavy metal or rap—can make a person commit violence. Violence comes from real life.

*What attracted you to the* **Masters of Horror** *story "Pro-Life" which deals with issues of abortion using the idea of a baby fathered by a demon?*

It was a Drew McWeeny-Scott Swan story again. I like their work a lot.

*Can you tell us anything more about the films that you currently have in development,* **The Ward,** **L.A. Gothic** *and* **The Prince***?*

Not until they're finished, no. [Based on information found online, *The Ward* is a thriller concerning a young woman who is

*Escape from New York* **illustrated synopsis cover (1981, AVCO Embassy Pictures; courtesy John Gullidge).**

terrorized by a spirit, written by Michael and Shawn Rasmussen and starring *Zombieland* actress Amber Head. *L.A. Gothic* is an anthology movie made up of five interconnected stories linked to a vengeful ex-priest's efforts to keep his teenage daughter safe from the supernatural evils of L.A.'s darker side, written by Jim Agnew and Sean Keller, screenwriters on Dario Argento's 2009 *Giallo*. *The Prince* has Andre Fabrizio and Jeremy Passmore attached as writers.]

# *Mick Garris*

Mick Garris is an award-winning filmmaker who began writing fiction at the age of twelve. By the time he was in high school, he was already writing music and film journalism for various local and national publications. Garris hosted and produced *The Fantasy Film Festival* for nearly three years on Los Angeles television, and later began working in film publicity at Avco Embassy and Universal Pictures. It was there that he created "Making of..." documentaries for various feature films. Steven Spielberg hired Garris as story editor on NBC's *Amazing Stories*; he wrote or co-wrote ten of the 44 episodes. Since then, he has written or co-authored several feature films (including *The Fly II* and *Riding the Bullet*) and teleplays (such as *Quicksilver Highway* and *Nightmares & Dreamscapes*), as well as directing and producing in many media: cable (including *Psycho IV: The Beginning*), features (like *Sleepwalkers*), television films (such as *Desperation*), series pilots (*The Others*), and network miniseries (*The Stand, The Shining*). He created and executive produced the *Masters of Horror* anthology series of one-hour horror films written and directed by names like John Carpenter, and George Romero. He also created the NBC spin-off *Fear Itself*.

*A Life in the Cinema*, his first book, is a collection of short stories; his short fiction has been published in numerous books and magazines. *Development Hell* is his first novel. Garris lives in Studio City, California, with his wife Cynthia.

---

*You were influenced by horror comics when you were younger—which ones in particular?*

Mostly it was *Creepy* and its follow-up, *Eerie*. I was much too young to have seen the old EC Comics that started it all, but the Warren Publishers recruited a lot of the EC artists, as well as a bunch of new guys, like Bernie Wrightson and Joe Orlando and all the others. I did want to draw comics and make animated cartoons when I was a kid. I tried to put that to use in the episode of *Tales from the Crypt* I directed, called "Whirlpool."

*You used to read* **Famous Monsters of Filmland***. How much of an impact did this have on you?*

It was a *huge* influence. Nobody I ever knew in childhood or adolescence was into horror and monster films where I lived, but I discovered this amazing magazine filled with images that just blew me away. I mean, there were the famous old Universal monsters, but also all the cheap junk that no mainstream magazine would ever have showed the least bit of interest in: *Attack of the Crab Monsters*, *X: The Man with the X-Ray Eyes*, lots of stuff like that. So I knew I wasn't the only one out there. But horror films, when I was a kid, were mostly adopted by kids who felt like they didn't belong, with the alienated, the castoffs, the unpopular. And often with good reason. I met [*Famous Monsters of Filmland* editor] Forry Ackerman on many occasions, and he was an amazing and high-spirited guy. His health was not good towards the end, but he was always good for a grin. A very sweet man.

*You mentioned the Universal films as influences when you were a kid. What exactly was it about them that made such an impression? The monsters, the fear they provoked ... assuming you were frightened of them [laughs]?*

Interesting point, as I was rarely really frightened by films. But again, I think virtually all horror fans discover the allure of horror in their youth, because they are so attracted by the symbology. I mean, what is the werewolf, really, but the metamorphosing man, growing hair in unexpected places, fighting new urges that prove almost irresistible? What is Frankenstein's Monster but the ultimate misunderstood outsider, chased by the angry mob of like thinkers with pitchforks and torches? It definitely provided a kinship, as well as offering a view of the forbidden, the dark, the rude ... and yet provided it in a safe place, like your living room.

*Did you read horror fiction when you were younger?*

I read all of Poe when I was a kid, as well as Bradbury and Matheson. Poe was where I first got a taste of the dark, in poetry as well as fiction. "The Tell-Tale Heart" introduced me to a place I'd never been before. Bradbury's voice was a unique one, and though he's not really a horror writer, he had written a lot of genre stuff, like "The Small Assassin," for the pulps. But he showed me the combination of poetry and imagination, as well as a sentimental side that I did not find in my life during my Wonder Years. And Matheson was just a great storyteller: terse, forceful and surprising. Sort of the Hemingway of Horror, I guess.

*How did the* Fantasy Film Festival *show come about?*

I was writing fiction and journalism, and not making a living at either, trying to write screenplays, like everyone else in this town. I began writing pieces for the Z Channel magazine, which was really a programming guide for the first pay-TV station in Los Angeles, even before HBO was available here. Charles Champlin, who was the lead film critic for *The Los Angeles Times* at that time, was doing interviews of a lot of actors and filmmakers for them, and I told the program director my idea, to do a similar show, but all about the SF, horror, and fantasy genres. He liked the idea, and asked me to make up a list of movies I'd like to have, and who I would get to interview if we got them. Well, months later, he had lined up a movie—not on my list, by the way—and said, "Go do it." It was *Zardoz*, and I somehow

Mick Garris publicity photograph from the set of the 2006 made-for-television movie *Desperation* (courtesy Mick Garris).

was able to contact John Boorman through his publicist or someone, and that was the first one we did.

*How did it feel to be interviewing some of the greats of the genre? Did you ever think you'd become friends with them?*

I was a very quiet and shy interviewer, as you can see on these old shows, and I was thrilled to just be in their presence, asking them questions I was interested in having answered, not the usual two minutes of talk show blather with a film clip. It was quite surprising that several of us did, indeed, become friends, though John Landis and I became friends before I started the show, as his office when he was prepping *Animal House* was next door to the office I worked at answering phones for the original *Star Wars*.

*Have you ever considered doing a reunion show, or been invited on a similar show yourself now that you're a famous director?*

Well, whether I am a famous director or not is certainly up for argument—I'd be on the opposing side, myself. I never really thought about a reunion show. The dinners we had were sort of a reunion without the cameras. I've certainly done my share of interviews in the years since, and it's quite different being on the other side of the couch. However, I am about to start interviewing horror icons for a Web and TV series we're working out now, with plans for another. Funny how sometimes you really can go home again...

*What question would you have asked yourself if you'd been interviewing?*

You've hit me with a question I just cannot answer, try though I might...

*How did you move from this into doing publicity for movies?*

At this time, there was an explosion in SF and horror genre films, and yet nobody really understood the fan base for them. Until this time, these were all thought of as movies for kids. From my show, and from being a fan myself, I knew a lot about science fiction conventions, and the fanzines, all of that sort of thing. I got a bit of familiarity because the cable system that carried my show just happened to carry cable into Beverly Hills, the Hollywood Hills, Santa Monica, all the neighborhoods where the actors and filmmakers lived. First I worked for a guy named Charles Lippincott, who created special publicity for this genre, premiering *Star Wars* at the San Diego ComicCon, things like that. I learned a lot from him. Then Avco Embassy, at the time, was getting to be the leader in independent horror films, and I met with them about being a specialist in this area. I worked on promoting *The Howling*, *The Fog*, *Scanners* and *Escape from New York* for them. They were sort of the Lionsgate of the era.

*What was it like working on* **Amazing Stories** *for Spielberg?*

Amazing [*laughs*]. He was incredibly enthusiastic and supportive and encouraging. That was my film school. Probably the most profound and influential thing he ever told me when I was prepping the episode I directed there was: "Try anything. Be brave enough to try something you'd be afraid to be fired for somewhere else. Because we're not going to fire you here." He gave me the opportunity to write for people like Joe Dante and Robert Zemeckis and a bunch of others.

*Was it daunting tackling the character of Norman Bates for* **Psycho: IV***?*

Yes, but not as daunting as working with the actor who played him. Tony Perkins had directed *Psycho III*, and wanted to direct *IV*, and the studio didn't want him to. That was an uncomfortable place to start. And he was a very complicated man: a great actor, but complicated. He would conduct very lengthy questions in front of cast and crew about things we had discussed at great length. I learned a lot from him, and liked him and respected him a lot, but he was complicated to work with. The script was written by Joe Stefano, who wrote the original *Psycho* [movie], and Hitchcock's assistant director on the original, Hilton Green, was our executive producer; a really wonderful man. We were surrounded by original props and sets from the first movie, though we shot in Florida rather than in Los Angeles. A great experience, though the film was shot very quickly—four weeks.

*How did you land the directing job on* Sleepwalkers? *Had you always been a King fan?*

I read *The Shining* when it first came out, and it was a big turning point for me. The best horror novel I'd ever read. I was an instant convert. King had director approval on *Sleepwalkers*. It came down to me and another director, and they sent samples of our work—mine was *Psycho IV*—and they actually chose the other director at first. Then there were problems in the preproduction phase, and King watched *Psycho IV* and liked it much more than he expected to, and I was conscripted into service.

Alice Krige and Brian Krause in *Sleepwalkers* (1992, Columbia Pictures).

*What was it like to work so closely with Stephen on the mini-series of* The Stand?

We became friends on that shoot. We had only met on the set of *Sleepwalkers* one day, on the day he shot his cameo. But we worked together for months on location on *The Stand*, and discovered we had a lot in common. He's a very playful guy, and loves to be on a set. It's absolutely great to be able to go to the source with a thought or a question, especially when the source is a guy like Stephen King.

*How did you keep everyone's spirits up during the long filming process?*

I think everyone was just so excited to be working on something that had such a great pedigree. Nobody thought of *The Stand* as just another job. Just the sheer scope of it was so momentous. I'm not sure everyone's spirits were up throughout the shoot, not when the location prep was two months long and the actual production another five. But we all got really close, and banded together in horrible weather and production circumstances, but with the hope that we could do this epic novel justice. I don't think anyone, even the network, imagined it could be as successful as it was.

*You and King have quite similar backgrounds. Is this one of the reasons you became friends and get along so well?*

I think so. And we have a lot of similar tastes and cultural touchstones. I don't see him nearly as much as I used to before his 1999 accident, as he lives in Maine and I live in California.

*What was your experience of working on the miniseries* **The Shining** *like? And would you do anything different if you were directing it again?*

Actually, *The Shining* was one of the best production experiences I ever had. King was around a lot, even more than he was on *The Stand*. It was mostly contained in a handful of locations, and we had close to the right amount of money to do it well. Of course, all a filmmaker can think of is how something doesn't work afterwards, but to spend time trying to reshoot something that you've finished, and spent so much time and energy on in the first place, is folly to me. You cannot second guess yourself and the shooting circumstances at the time.

*When did the* **Masters of Horror** *dinners start?*

The dinners actually started a year or two before the show began, with me contacting a dozen of the guys and trying for a week to schedule an hour that would work for everyone. It was a great time with a bunch of great people. Perhaps the funniest thing about that first dinner was how we got our name, which was a joke. There was a table next to us—and, of course, no one in the restaurant had any idea that they were sitting next to a table full of horror directors—and they were celebrating a birthday. So our table joined in singing "Happy Birthday" to them, and Guillermo del Toro stood up and said, "The Masters of Horror wish you a happy birthday!"

*At what point did you think about creating the* **Masters of Horror** *show?*

It came up after we had a few of the dinners. We all thought how great it would be to be in charge of our own destinies, creatively, which we don't get to do often. Getting everybody to sign on really didn't take long at all. All three of the companies we went to for financing were interested, but IDT—now Starz Entertainment—was ready to go immediately, so they were our patron saints.

*Your story "Chocolate" was quite an erotic one. Do you think the two things—sex and horror—go together inextricably?*

Garris on the set of the *Masters of Horror* 2005 episode "Chocolate" (courtesy Mick Garris).

I certainly think they can. For me, horror is something that resonates deep within us, and it seems that sexuality is a tremendous source of human fear and insecurity. Horror is about confronting the uncomfortable emotions and conflicts within us, and sexuality is certainly a primary candidate for that. I mean, just take a look at *Dead Ringers*, to my mind one of the greatest horror films of all time. You cannot separate sex and horror there.

*Did you enjoy turning the story into an episode?*

It was really gratifying, as it was a story I'd been trying to tell on film for over 20 years. I think a lot of people, particularly younger members of the audience, expected something more traditionally horrific, and were not enamored with the film. But it is very much the story I was trying to tell. I think the cast and crew all did a really good job with it, though it perhaps ends a bit more abruptly than I would have liked, which is entirely my own fault. I had just worked with Henry Thomas again on *Desperation* right before we went ahead with *Masters of Horror*, and he was the first actor I thought of for the role. I really thought he was perfect for it: His face is so expressive. It's an internal story, and Henry is an actor whose face shows there's a lot going on inside. Even when we did *Psycho IV*, when he was only 18 years old—hell, even when he was a child in *E.T.*—he had that quality. I like working with him a lot.

*Out of the other* **Masters of Horror** *episodes, do you have a favorite?*

That's really hard to choose. I honestly like them all, and I'm most excited about the fact that they are all so completely different from one another. That said, one of the most unique and adult and emotional is Brad Anderson's *Sounds Like*. It's a pretty amazing film. Then again, so are the others. I hope. It's really impossible to say. Each of them was made from a particular artist's perspective, and that's the important thing; giving a free voice to people who deserved not to be shackled by a studio's input. Obviously, the ones I'm closest to are the ones I did myself, but it's hard not to look at *Black Cat* or *Cigarette Burns* or *Homecoming* or any of them and not feel a sense of pride for helping bring them to the screen when nobody else would even bother.

*Where did the impetus for* **The V Word** *episode come from?*

It was a second-season *Masters of Horror* film, and I noticed that the first season was filled with sexuality and varying kinds of horror, not all of which was about building tension. I wanted to do a flat-out horror thriller, with young characters, for a change. It was fun to take the vampire ethos, throw a new spin on it—no fangs, no crosses—and to try to give it a sense of logic and fear. And to kill the protagonist, really fuck with the conventions a bit. Couldn't do that in a feature.

*What did you think of Ernest Dickerson's direction?*

Ernest is a great visual stylist; he started as a cameraman, and a huge horror fan. I really like where he took it, though, of course, I—and any other director—would have done a few things differently. I was going to direct it, if Clive wasn't able to come through with a story. He kept promising one, particularly if I was going to direct it. When he finally came through with *Haeckel's Tale*, I knew that would be my film for the second season.

*How did you approach transferring his short story "Haeckel's Tale" into a* **Masters of Horror** *episode? There were some differences between the story and script.*

There were. Originally, Roger Corman was going to direct it, and I wanted to write a Corman-Matheson-Poe style film for him, and "Haeckel's Tale" seemed just right for that. I loved the whole Frankenstein element of fooling with mankind and science and God, and things that weren't part of Clive's story. The original short story was way too short for a one-hour film, but I loved bringing all the purple period prose into play. It was a blast to write.

*How did this experience differ from working on an original Barker story for* **Valerie on the Stairs***?*

Very different experience. *Valerie* was much more difficult in a lot of ways, as there's so much that lies on the actors' shoulders, and the set was extremely complicated. Of course, it was a lot more difficult for me because I was directing; the directors are the ones who carry the burdens, so it was more complicated for McNaughton than for me to do *Haeckel*. With *Chocolate*, every bit of it was shot on location, whereas *Valerie* was shot 80 percent on the sound stage. The makeup effects for Othakeye, the sensitive nature of shooting nudity and sexuality, the many and elaborate sets, the visual effect at the end, all of them were very demanding. Plus, Clive had written a 45-page single-spaced treatment for a 60-minute film. I had to cut at least half of what he had written to make it possible to shoot. As it was, I even had to pull out scenes that were scripted because we ran out of time. Ah, the ten-day shoot...

*The ending is one of the best endings in* **Masters** *yet—the main character turns into manuscript pages. How hard was that to realize?*

It was complicated, but not incredibly difficult. I wanted something really powerful and poetic, and something you haven't seen before, when I read Clive's treatment. It was his idea to have Rob become pages of his own story, and I worked at length with Lee Wilson on the CGI aspects of it, and with Howard Berger on how to visualize the pages on Rob's skin. It was a combination of the talents of our makeup effects, visual effects, and physical effect department. Not easy, but not as difficult as some.

*Can you take us through what happened with* **Fear Itself***?*

It was a frustrating experience. When Starz decided to no longer continue with *Masters of Horror*, Lionsgate bought it. For a while, it looked like we had a deal with HDNET, another pay-TV, commercial-free network, to do the third season. When they pulled out at the last minute, I thought we were done. And, in a way, I was kind of relieved. As much as I love the show, I thought, maybe rationalizing, that we had done two years of groundbreaking horror television, and it was enough.

**Mick Garris with his wife Cynthia on the set of the 2004 film** *Riding the Bullet* **(courtesy Mick Garris).**

Then, when Lionsgate called to say they had sold it to NBC, I was ready to cut the cord, as I felt it couldn't be done well for commercial TV. I talked to the filmmakers, and they all said that we should give it a try, so I committed to it 100 percent. We developed the 13 scripts, finishing at least a first draft of each just before the writers' strike kicked in. Then I left to join the strike, and I was replaced by non-union writers. When I saw what they were doing to the scripts and the shows, and when it was clear that NBC and Lionsgate were much more creatively involved than Showtime and Starz and IDT were, I saw the writing on the wall. It broke my heart, but I just couldn't in good conscience go back to the show, when I saw that I couldn't give the creative control to the filmmakers. The show had lost its *raison d'etre*, and I just couldn't make it what it was meant to be any longer. So I gave up my baby for adoption.

*What can you tell us about* **Desperation***?*

It's a big book that I always loved, but always felt would be tremendously difficult to turn into a film. Back in 1998, we were going to do it as a feature film for New Line, but at that time, *Scream* and all the other nudge-nudge-wink-wink, self-reflexive teen horror movies became the rage, and the head of the studio decided not to invest $35 million in what we planned to be a balls-to-the-wall horror thriller that didn't fit that mold. It was on-again, off-again for years. Finally, we took it to ABC, where we'd had such a good experience on *The Stand* and *The Shining*, and they turned it down. But when both CBS and NBC were interested, ABC changed their mind, and gave it the go-ahead. But it's a different network, now that it's owned by Disney, and we had a lot of trouble with casting and scheduling. The script was basically the script that King wrote as a feature, with just a few small changes for the act structure required by television. We ended up with a great cast, with more actors that I have worked with in previous films than I'd ever had the privilege to work with before. It was an extremely difficult shoot. Everything that's complicated and troublesome and time-consuming was present in a big way: working with a child actor in most of the scenes, lots and lots of animals, stunts, driving scenes, complicated locations, visual effects, makeup effects and all. And this was virtually every day. I'm very happy with the way the film turned out, which made it doubly disappointing when ABC, in their grand Disney wisdom, decided to put it up against the next-to-last season episode of the television ratings juggernaut *American Idol*, with virtually no promotion. The audience never saw it. So, many mixed feelings about the film.

*You must have been delighted by Ron Perlman's performance as the policeman in* **Desperation***.*

I first worked with Ron on *Sleepwalkers*, where he played the sheriff. I knew how talented he was, and how much range he had, and wanted him to play Collie Entragian when we were going to do *Desperation* as a feature film for New Line back in 1998. When it finally went to ABC, they fought me on the casting, but I knew nobody could do Collie like Ron. He is certainly the highlight of the film, as he was in the story.

*Where did the idea for* **Development Hell** *come from?*

It started as a short story called "A Life in the Cinema," which was first published in a collection called *Silver Scream* that David J. Schow edited in the late 1980s. It was really a test for me; I wondered if I could write something as completely unguarded and twisted as King or Barker, and mix it in with something I was really familiar with: Make a statement on Hollywood and ego and the corrupting power of fame and fortune at the same time. I followed it with a sequel that picked up where the first one began, called "Starfucker," then a third and a fourth. Stephen King read them and said it read like a loose novel. So I decided to tighten it up into a "real" novel, and that's what led to the book as it exists today.

*Is the mutant baby based on anything in real life?*

God, I hope not... [*laughs*].

*Experiencing life in another person's body as a theme—from* Chocolate—*reappears in* DH. *What do you find so fascinating about this concept?*

I just love the idea of illustrating the loss of self, or the confusion of who we are, represented physically, as well as psychically. In *Development Hell*, the hero doesn't even have a name, his abandonment of self to the Hollywood ego is so complete. That he body-hops from one flesh puppet sheath to another just shows how lacking he is in his own humanity. In *Chocolate*, it's the fear of the loss of one's own being, and being tied to the "perfect partner" into a single being. The fantasy of finding the perfect, ideal mate is a thunderous, and ultimately tragic, journey outside of self.

*What do you personally think happens after death?*

We rot.

*Were you worried about any reactions from the real-life names you put in the book—Spielberg, Cameron, etc.?*

Well, Spielberg gave me my first opportunity as a writer, and second as a director, and I feel a great deal of gratitude for every door he opened for me. If you read the book, there's nothing even remotely negative about Steven in the novel; it's very respectful, to say the least. I don't know Cameron, and though he does rage in the novel, it's just my imagination embellishing some legendary qualities of this very talented fellow. Again, nothing really bad to say about him, either, other than that he has a temper. And what creative Hollywood type doesn't?

*How did it feel to play around with some of the ghosts of Hollywood's past, like Hitchcock?*

A total blast. I'm a student of these guys, and my respect for them is boundless. I love to transgress the rules a bit when it comes to kissing the asses of the brilliant dead.

*Development Hell* with artwork by Les Edwards (2006, Cemetery Dance Publications; courtesy Richard Chizmar, Cemetery Dance).

*Were you pleased with the finished product from Cemetery Dance, and did you like Les Edwards' cover?*

I couldn't be happier. I was deeply involved in the design of the cover myself, but I think Les' work is fantastic. I couldn't believe we got him. I was such a fan of his Marilyn Monroe cover for Clive's *Son of Celluloid* graphic novel.

*Can you tell us anything about how* **Bag of Bones** *is shaping up?*

Matt Venne has just finished a really great first draft of the script, and I am very optimistic and high on the project. It's one of my favorite King books, and I've wanted to make a film of it since I first read it.

# Stuart Gordon

In 1985, Stuart Gordon's first feature film *Re-Animator* won the Critics' Award at the Cannes Film Festival. With its stunning box office success, the movie has become a cult classic and its director has developed a strong and loyal following.

His professional career began in 1970 as artistic director of the Organic Theater Company of Chicago, a position he held for fifteen years. Gordon was able to work directly with Ray Bradbury, Roald Dahl, Mary Renault and Kurt Vonnegut, bringing their works to the stage. In 1974 he produced and directed the world premiere of David Mamet's *Sexual Perversity in Chicago*. The company performed on and off-Broadway, and toured the U.S. and Europe. Gordon left Organic in 1985 when he was offered a three-picture deal in Los Angeles after the success of *Re-Animator*. His films encompass many genres: horror in *Dolls* (1987), *From Beyond* (1986) and *Dagon* (2001); comedy with *The Wonderful Ice Cream Suit* (1998) and *Spacetruckers* (1996); crime in *King of the Ants* (2003) *Edmond* (2005) and *Stuck* (2007); and action with *Fortress* (1993) and *Robot Jox* (1990). But what all of his movies have in common is a darkly humorous point of view and a tendency to shock and surprise. Gordon is also the co-creator of *Honey, I Shrunk The Kids* (1989) and the co-author of *Bodysnatchers* (1993) and *The Dentist* (1996). He lives in Los Angeles with his actress wife Carolyn.

---

*It was your parents forbidding you to see horror films that sparked your interest in them, wasn't it?*

Yes, that's right.

*And you crept out of the house to watch* **The Tingler?**

Yeah, my brother and I went. I ended up running out of the theater and leaving him behind. He's still giving me shit about that [*laughs*].

*What sort of effect did it have on you?*

God, I had nightmares for years after I saw that movie. I never saw the end of it until a few years ago when it was shown at a film festival. I was telling Quentin Tarantino about it—and he was sitting in the seat in front of me. You know when they showed the film originally, they had these devices attached to the seats that would make them vibrate at scary moments; so I'd grab Quentin's chair and shake it [*laughs*].

*Did you experience any of those originally when you went to see it?*

Yeah, my chair started rocking and rolling, and that's when I lifted off and headed out of that theater.

*Was William Castle quite a big influence on you?*

He was, his movies were always an event; he was an incredible showman. I remember one of his movies, I was waiting in line to get in, and you'd see people being carried out on stretchers and put into ambulances. He had another movie where he was advertising it as better than 3D, the monsters really come off the screen into the theater. That was *House on Haunted Hill* and he had a thing where at a certain moment in the movie this plastic skeleton came out of a box next to the screen on a wire over the audience, and everybody started booing and throwing their popcorn boxes at it.

*Have you ever thought about doing things like that with your films?*

You know, when we first screened *Re-Animator*, we did the old routine with the stretchers and the ambulances in a screening in San Francisco.

*Is it true that in your formative years you read* Dracula *and had to sleep with the windows closed?*

That's true—where did you get that piece of information? [*Laughs*] It was in the middle of the hottest summer in the history of Chicago, so I was dying because I wouldn't open those windows.

*Obviously that had a major effect on you, reading* Dracula.

Oh yeah. Well, I used to love to read all those horror stories. I started reading Lovecraft when I was a teenager as well.

Stuart Gordon (photograph by Damon D'Amato, courtesy Damon D'Amato).

*Were there any other authors from your formative years you used to read?*

It was those Roger Corman films that got me to read Poe, and Poe kind of led me to the others. So yeah, I read them all. I read H.G. Wells, I loved all of those writers. Ray Bradbury, he wrote some scary stories too.

*You once staged a counterculture production of* Peter Pan *that landed you in jail.*

It landed my wife and myself in jail for obscenity. It was back in 1968 and it was being done as a political satire on what was going on in those days. The main event was the Democratic convention which was held in Chicago, and it ended up with the police beating the crap out of anti-war protesters. So we turned *Peter Pan* into an allegory about that. We had a scene where Wendy and her brothers fly off to Neverland by dropping acid. The show basically had a death sequence where we had a psychedelic lightshow projected onto the bodies of naked dancers. That was what got us into trouble.

*What made you decide to set up the Organic Theater Company?*

I had started a theater company when I was at college, called Screw Theater, and when I got out of school I realized I really loved theater and wanted to continue that. So Carolyn and I began the Organic Theater Company in Chicago.

*Did you ever worry about going too far with your productions?*

One of the things I've learned over time is that you should never censor yourself. We did the productions and we did crazy things, but the idea of our theater was to show the audience that it was not like watching a movie, that there was interaction between the actors and the audience. We did one production where we literally locked the audience in the theater, then grabbed people out of the audience. The people we grabbed were planted, but the audience didn't know that.

*Was any of it influenced by Grand Guignol theater?*

Very much so—we always did a lot of blood effects onstage. We once did a pirate play where we hung one of the actors upside down, slit his throat, and put a bucket underneath him. We were expecting the police for the next ten minutes.

*What was it about Lovecraft's fiction that attracted you?*

His stuff is really dark, and takes you places that none of the other writers do. His worldview is so bleak, which can be summed up by the phrase: Man is lucky to be ignorant, because if he knew the truth he'd kill himself. That's kind of Lovecraft's worldview on things. And if you're a teenager reading that, you're going, "Yes, that's right."

*Which were your favorite stories?*

My favorite story was always "The Shadow Over Innsmouth," where all the characters are turning into fish. And we were finally able to make a movie that was based on that story, *Dagon*.

*Why weren't the Organic Theater people behind you when you wanted to make an adaption of his work?*

It's funny, but by the time we got to that point, Organic had really grown; it had become an institution. The yearly budget was over $1 million and we had all these members of the community on our board. When I told them I wanted to do a horror movie, they were saying, "No, no. We don't want the Organic Theater name on a horror movie. We want to do an art film." By that point I'd met Brian Yuzna, and he had brought the financing and we were all ready to go. So I took a leave of absence from the theater and directed the movie.

*Re-Animator started out as a series for TV, didn't it?*

That was our thought, because it was written as a serial. Lovecraft wrote

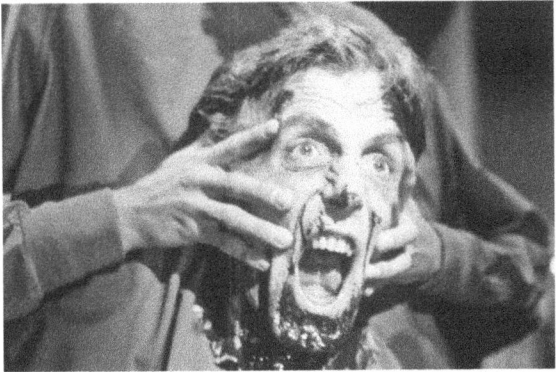

**Robert Sampson gets a head in *Re-Animator* (1985, Empire Pictures).**

it in six installments. It seemed like maybe it could be a miniseries or something. We took the first installment of the story and adapted it into a 30-minute teleplay, but no one wanted to make it. Looking back on it, we must have been insane to think anyone would. Then we thought maybe it should be an hour long, so we took the second story and combined it, but we couldn't sell that either. Then at that point I was introduced to Brian Yuzna who said, "This should be a feature." And I said, "Okay, I'll add the third story." He said, "No, no, no—add the fourth story in." So we threw them all in.

*Were there any ideas left over?*

We pretty much used everything, but there was one: There's a knock at the door, and they open up the door and there's a zombie running around on all fours with the arm of a baby in its mouth. That's one we didn't do; everything else is in the movie.

*How did you first come across Yuzna?*

I met him through a friend, a guy named Bob Greenberg, and when I think back about this, it's kind of an incredible thing because Bob had been hired by Brian to direct another film, and that project had got derailed somehow. So they were looking for something else to do, and Bob knew about the *Re-Animator* project so he suggested to Brian that we get together. I sent him the script we'd been developing and Bob was gracious enough to step aside and let me direct. I think back to that and ask, "Would I have been willing to do something like that, if I'd had my first chance to direct a picture? Give it up and let someone else direct?" It was very unselfish of Bob.

*When you first met Jeffrey Combs, what did you make of him?*

Jeffrey showed up for an audition for *Re-Animator*—that was the first time I ever saw him. He was sort of like a kindred spirit, as soon as I got to know him I realized he was exactly like the kind of people I'd been working with in the theater. Jeffrey's background is in theater as well. He has that sort of "go for broke, I'll try anything once" kind of attitude which is what I really thrive on.

*Was he well versed in Lovecraft as well?*

I don't think he knew Lovecraft, actually. It was funny, Jeffrey was not really into the horror films and was kind of disgusted by the amount of blood we were using during filming. There's a scene in the movie where a bolt-cutter cuts through the zombie and he's in blood up to his elbow and he shakes the blood off in disgust. That was genuine; that was the way Jeffrey felt about it all.

*You used the space very much like a theater set.*

There were people who said we were making movies for years except we weren't on film, we were doing them on stage, live. So what I discovered with movies was that in some ways it was actually easier than doing theater because we only did our plays in a round, a three-quarter round, and the audience could see three sides of the action, so it's much more difficult to hide the tricks. But with the movie camera you only have one audience member—and we were using techniques very similar to the ones we used on stage.

*Were you aware that the "head giving head" scene would be as infamous as it turned out to be?*

[*Laughs*] We knew that was the scene that was going to make or break the movie. It's funny because the very first piece of artwork that was ever done for *Re-Animator* was of that scene. That was the artwork Brian used to raise financing. It was done by a wonderful artist named William Stout.

*What did Barbara Crampton think about the idea at the time?*

She was very game. One of the things that a lot of people don't know is that originally I had cast a different actress to play that part. About two weeks before we were due to start shooting, this actress got cold feet. She said, "I've talked to my mother and I don't think it's a good idea for me to do this." So we recast it and that's when I met Barbara. She just completely made that part her own, and she was just a great actress. We ended up making several more movies together.

*How did the three-film deal with Empire come about?*

It was really based on the success of *Re-Animator*. After I directed *Re-Animator* I went back to the theater, to Chicago. It was several months later that I got a call saying Empire Pictures was giving Brian and me a three-picture deal. They wanted us to come to Los Angeles and get started. It was at that point I actually left the theater for good.

The catch with the three-picture deal was that we had to make the pictures in Italy. I'd moved my family to L.A. and then a couple of months later told them, "We've got to move to Rome." Which wasn't a bad thing, I mean I loved going there. But while I was in Rome working on the first film, *Dolls*, there was an article in *Newsweek* in which Charlie Band, the head of Empire Pictures, was interviewed, and he was talking about *Re-Animator* and how worldwide it made over $30 million. I had a two points profits or something, and I remember after I read it I said, "All right, drinks are on me! I'm a millionaire now" [*laughs*].

*In* From Beyond *you explored the notion that there are creatures that exist around us all the time, we just can't see them. Do you ever think this might be true?*

Well, it really *is* true. Those creatures are called germs and viruses. They're living creatures that are invisible to us. I think sometimes that was where Lovecraft was coming from, he was kind of a hypochondriac and there was this fear of invisible things that could kill you.

*Is it true that you're very squeamish when it comes to blood and gore in real life?*

Yeah, it is. My wife started laughing at me, there was this time one day when our dog stepped on a piece of glass and was tracking blood around the kitchen and I passed out. As long as I know it's fake, I'm okay, but when it's real I've got a problem with that.

*How did you approach the subject matter of* Dolls*?*

I'd read a book a few months before I made *Dolls* that I thought was fantastic. That was a

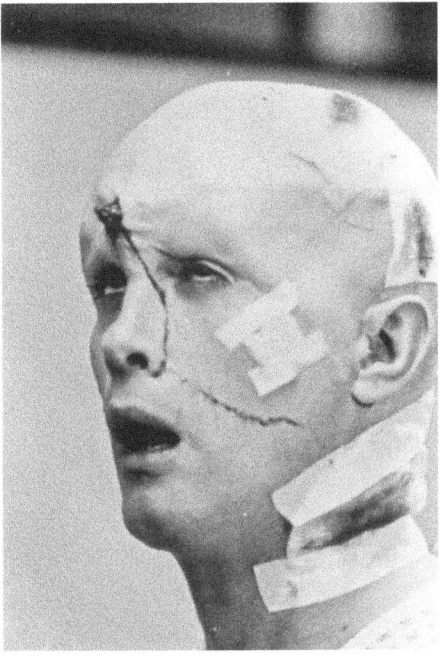

**Jeffrey Combs in** *From Beyond* **(1986, Empire Pictures; courtesy John Gullidge).**

book called *The Uses of Enchantment* by Bruno Bettelheim. It was about fairy tales and about how people are always trying to clean them up and make them less scary for children. Bettelheim said, no, no, fairy tales *should* be scary; it's a healthy thing. Children learn about life by reading fairy tales or having them read to them. And I decided to put Bettelheim's theories to the test in *Dolls*.

*There's something quite creepy about dolls, isn't there?*

Yes, it's true. When I was a student at the University of Wisconsin, they had this historical society on the top floor where there was this collection of Victorian dolls. I sat there one day drawing pictures of them and I ended up getting locked in the museum. It was really creepy, you think that they're moving or looking at you; their eyes follow you around. Those are the dolls I patterned the ones in the movie on.

*Your wife Carolyn was cast in that one. How did she take to being killed off?*

Well, I try to murder her as often as I possibly can [*laughs*]. At first she was a little disturbed by it, and she finally got around to thinking, "As long as you only do it in movies, it's okay." A few years later I did a movie and she was in it, and I *didn't* kill her, and she was very upset about that. She said, "Don't you love me any more?" [*Laughs*]

*What was it like to work with Anthony Perkins on* Daughter of Darkness*?*

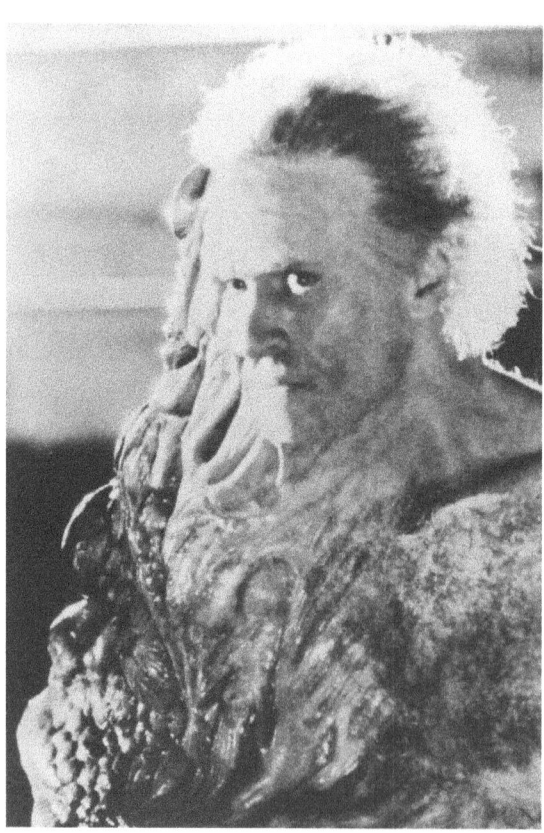

Ted Sorel as Dr. Edward Pretorius in *From Beyond* (1986, Empire Pictures; courtesy John Gullidge).

Oh, he was the best. I had such a great time with him. It was so sad when he passed away; we got to be really good friends. Very early on I introduced him to the Talking Heads song "Psycho Killer" and told him, "This song was written about you!" He was incredibly knowledgeable about horror. And he had so many great stories, because he'd worked with Hitchcock and Orson Welles; he knew everybody in Hollywood. He was a wonderful storyteller and a great man with a great sense of humor. It was a great loss, I wish he was still around.

*Was* Robot Jox *influenced by* Transformers *at all?*

Very much so. I was a big fan of those toys. I used to buy them and play with them. One of the great things about having children is that it gives you the chance to go to toy stores. I kept thinking, "Someone should make a movie about these." There were some animated adaptations, but nobody was doing live action, so I thought, "Okay, I'll do it."

*Do you wish you'd had today's technology to render the robots?*

It would have made things a lot easier; after all, that movie took three years to make. David Allen, who did the stop-motion animation work, actually took the models out to the Mojave Desert and shot them outdoors in sunlight, so that he could get the tremendous depth of field and create the illusion on camera. So the effects of the movie are astonishing but it took months for him to do that. If he'd done it in the normal, conventional way, doing it on a table on a stage, in a controlled situation, it would have been a lot easier. Everything that could possibly go wrong, did. There were dust storms and flooding—that was like a horror story.

*In your adaptation of* **The Pit and the Pendulum** *you explore Poe's fiction. In what ways does this differ from Lovecraft for you?*

Most of Poe's stories are set in the here and now. Lovecraft's work involved the idea of other dimensions, alien lifeforms and so forth. Most of Poe's stuff had to do with real people and real times. He also explores the senses; it's about characters that often have very acute senses. It means that little things can become very disturbing. Lovecraft was hugely influenced by Poe. If Poe hadn't existed, there would be no Lovecraft either.

*How did you get on with Lance Henriksen?*

Fine. He's an amazing actor, and also a method actor. He did a lot of research about Torquemada and discovered that he was ascetic, that he only drank water and only ate bread, and walked around barefoot all the time. So Lance did the same thing. Here he is in Italy, we're shooting this movie in a country that has some of the greatest food in the world, and Lance is not having any of it, not even the wine ... until Oliver Reed showed up [*laughs*]. The two of them ended up in a drinking contest, it was hilarious. Oliver drank Lance under the table. It was an amazing thing to see.

*What was Reed like as a person?*

He was wonderful too. I mean, he was completely insane. He showed up on the weekend at this castle where we were shooting and the first thing that he did was say, "Bring out every bottle of wine you've got in the castle and put it on the table." This huge banquet table. Then he proceeded to drink himself around the table. I was thinking, "Oh my God, what's going to happen when we get to Monday and we need to shoot the scene?" It was a non-stop binge that went on all weekend. And Monday morning rolled around, I went to the set and there was Oliver Reed. He was already in costume, all ready to go. He was completely sober, knew all of his lines, perfectly. It was completely incredible. His attitude was: "The weekend is my time and I can do what I want, and Monday I'm ready to work." A phenomenal guy, we had great conversations. One of the things I learned about him was that he never had appeared on stage. He started in movies at a very early age; it was actually a horror film that got him going, *The Curse of the Werewolf*, the Hammer film. But no, he'd never appeared on stage. I remember sitting around the fire with him and he was reciting Byron. It was just the most beautiful thing I'd ever heard.

*With* **Fortress**, *were you attempting to make a political statement about freedom and governments at all?*

Yeah, absolutely. *Fortress* was done at a time when in the United States they were building all these new prisons. They changed the laws so that basically anyone who committed a crime could be locked up for the rest of their lives. And there were more people in prison than there were ever before. That was very frightening. There were a lot of prisons that had been turned over to private corporations. So that was the idea that formed the basis for the film.

**Castle Freak** *brought Jeffrey Combs and Barbara Crampton back into the fold. What was it like working with them again?*

Oh, it was really great. They're both great actors. That was a movie that came together very quickly. Charlie Band financed it himself without a script. I was sitting in his office and there was a poster and it said *Castle Freak* with a picture of a guy who looked like Quasimodo whipping some naked woman who's chained to the wall. So I asked, "What's that movie about?" And he said, "Well, there's a castle and there's a freak [*laughs*]. Listen, you can do whatever you want with it as long as there are those two elements in it." I had that conversation with him, I think it was in March, and we were shooting the movie in June, so it was very, very fast. Dennis Paoli and I wrote the script very quickly—I think it's the only time I've ever shot the very first draft of a script, because it was that good.

*Why did* **Dagon** *take so long to get made?*

We'd have these meetings and as soon as we said that the characters turn into fish, the meeting was over. We had a couple of situations where the studios would say, "If you'd just make this about werewolves, you've got a deal." I had a meeting with one of the heads of the studio and he said, "Fish are just not scary." I would have loved to have got a mugshot or something and put it on his desk.

*Had they not seen* **Jaws***?*

I guess not [*laughs*]. It was just such a strange idea for them. Such a fantastic notion, but Lovecraft makes it very believable. Kind of like evolution in reverse.

Raffaella Offidani and Jeffrey Combs in *Castle Freak* (1995, Empire Pictures; courtesy John Gullidge).

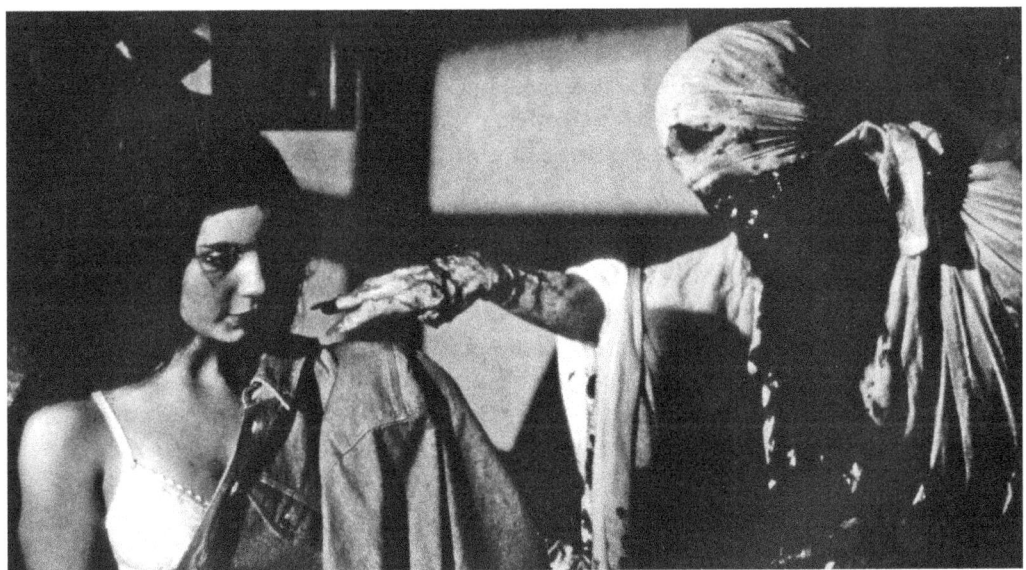

Rebecca Reilly as Jessica Dollarhide (at left) is about to be attacked by the *Castle Freak* (1995, Empire Pictures; courtesy John Gullidge).

*What was it like using more CGI on that movie?*

My feeling about computer generated effects is that it's sort of a last resort. If you can't find some way of doing it using some other technique, that's what you do. It's a tool. I don't like these movies where it's the only effect that they use. It starts to wear out its welcome and I think that's true of any effect done too often.

*You adapted another Lovecraft story for* **Masters of Horror**, *"Dreams of the Witch House." Why have you called this one of your favorite stories?*

It was also one of the very first Lovecraft stories I ever read; in fact, I think it might actually have been the very first one. That one really stayed with me, the idea of a witch coming through the wall of your room, grabbing you, pulling you out of your bed and taking you off to do terrible things. It's a terrifying idea.

*What is it about Ezra Godden from* **Dagon** *that makes him a good Lovecraftian hero? You used him here again.*

He's really a great actor—and also fearless. When we did *Dagon*, that was the most brutal shoot I've ever done to date, it had to be raining in every scene. We shot it in November so it was freezing cold; poor Ezra, he was cold and wet the entire time of making the film. But perfect Lovecraft characters are all very intellectual types and very sensitive people, and Ezra—his character, his persona—portrays that very well. He's also British, though no one seems to realize it, because his American accent is so good. He's actually from London.

*For season two of* **Masters of Horror** *you explored the world of Poe again. How did you approach this new twist on "The Black Cat"?*

My daughter Susanna is a teacher of high school English and she teaches Poe. Every year she has someone come in around Halloween to talk about Poe; so last year I came in and I read them "The Black Cat," and scared the shit out of those kids! That story is just terrifying. It struck me afterwards that it would make a great episode of *Masters of Horror*. The other thing was that Jeffrey Combs and I had been talking for a while about the idea of him playing Poe. It occurred to me that you could do that story and make Poe the protagonist. So all of that just came together and Dennis Paoli and I wrote the script again, so it came together very quickly.

*Can you tell us anything about* **House of Re-Animator***?*

Again this is one of those projects that we've been talking about for a while, but finding the money to make it has been difficult. The house in the title is the White House. And even though we have William H. Macy lined up to play the president, people are afraid I think to make that film. The story begins with the vice-president dropping dead of a heart attack, and since he's running the country, they don't know what to do. Then the CIA suggests that they might be able to use this Herbert West fellow, so that's kind of the premise. Of course things get worse and worse from there [*laughs*].

*How did Macy become involved in the project?*

I worked on *Edmund* with Bill and we were having a great time. So he said, "You know, I would love to do a horror movie." At that time I was working on the treatment for *House* and I showed it to him and he loved it, so he signed on.

*Is he a big* **Re-Animator** *fan?*

Yes. He got a chance to work with Jeffrey Combs in *Edmund* and they really liked each other too.

*Is it going to pick up from the previous* **Re-Animators***?*

In a way it will. The idea is that West and Cain are estranged, but they're forced to work together to re-animate the vice-president. I'm scripting it again with Dennis Paoli, who I did the first one with.

*Can you give us any more details about the story?*

I don't want to give too much away, but I've been talking to George Wendt about playing the vice-president, and Barbara Crampton about playing the first lady. I think that could be pretty great.

*So will she be re-animated as well?*

It's kind of a chain reaction that gets set off. When people get re-animated, they never come back quite the same. There's also the thing in the *Re-Animator* movies that their libidos are completely unleashed; that they have no control over their sex drives.

*Will it be even wilder than the previous* **Re-Animators***?*

I think it's going to be pretty wild, it really will. I think that will be the fun part about it.

*How does Jeffrey feel about coming back?*

He's excited. And Bruce Abbott is coming back as well.

*Have you been in talks with all of them about it?*

Yeah, and they really like the idea. I will give you a scoop actually, which is that in the story Dan Cain has a young son. I'm trying to convince Brian Yuzna that if there's another *Re-Animator* it should be called *Son of Re-Animator*. That would be after *House of Re-Animator*. If we're going to follow the Universal thing, we have to then do *Ghost of Re-Animator*.

*That's right, and* **Abbott and Costello meet Re-Animator** *[laughs]. How does it feel to be thinking about working on a new* **Re-Animator***?*

For me it's kind of like coming home, there's that part of it. It's such a wonderful feeling of being able to work with the same group of guys. One of the things I realized was that *Re-Animator* was one of those rare instances where everybody was on the same wavelength, which is probably the reason why it was as successful as it was. So, to be able to come back and join forces with those same folks again, is something I'm really looking forward to.

*What have you made of the other* **Re-Animator** *films that followed yours?*

I thought they had their moments, there were things about them that I liked. I liked the re-animated penis [*laughs*] and the rat. There was some good work in those. My only quibble was that they kept on referring to him as *Dr.* West and I can't imagine how he could have ever graduated.

*Is there one dream project you'd like to do in the future?*

Oh gosh—there are a lot of them. That's the thing. With the success of *300*, I've always wanted to do a sword-and-sandal movie. There's a book called *The King Must Die* by Mary Renault about Etheus and the Minotaur. I think that would make a phenomenal movie. I can't believe that no one has made that film; I think it was bought by 20th Century-Fox in the 1950s, so they own the book but they've never made it.

*What can you tell us about* **Stuck***?*

It stars Stephen Rea and Mena Suvari. It's based on a true story about a woman who hits a homeless man, and he goes through her windshield. She panics, and instead of taking him to the emergency room, she puts him in her garage—and the guy's still alive. She keeps him captive, kinda hoping he's going to die.

# Tom Holland

Tom Holland was born July 11, 1943, in Poughkeepsie, New York, the son of Lee and Tom Holland. He graduated from Worcester Academy in 1962, then attended Northwestern University in Evanston, Illinois, and the University of California at Los Angeles (where he graduated summa cum laude and Phi Beta Kappa). Tom began his filmic career writing screenplays; the first movie he wrote was *The Beast Within*, and he also wrote *Class of '84*. He acted for years under the *nom de screen* Tom Fielding; he guest starred on TV series like *The Incredible Hulk* under the name Tom Lee Holland. In 1982 he landed the job of penning the sequel to Hitchcock's *Psycho*; for his *Psycho II* script he received an Edgar Allan Poe Award nomination. His directorial debut came in 1985 with the vampire horror movie *Fright Night*, starring Roddy McDowall and Chris Sarandon. He co-scripted and directed the first in the *Child's Play* movie series in 1988, before going on to adapt the Stephen King stories *The Langoliers* for TV and *Thinner* for the big screen. He returned to the horror genre, directing an episode of *Masters of Horror*, "We All Scream for Ice Cream," in 2007. Tom Holland lives in L.A.

---

*Did you have any aspirations to be a director when you were in your formative years?*

No, I wanted to be a writer.

*What kind of writing interested you?*

Back in those days, you could only think about being a novelist.

*Any particular writers then who inspired you?*

No, I was just a prolific reader in adolescence. I loved them all. I loved science fiction. I don't remember much horror being around in those days, actually. I mean, I read the comic books, the EC *Tales from the Crypt*, and DC comic books. But in those days the comic books were considered really lower class. They weren't the art form they are today.

The magazine I remember, and I'm probably giving away my age, is *The Saturday Evening Post*. That came weekly and it was a magazine but it had entertaining short stories in it. In fact, *The Saturday Evening Post* was probably the proving ground for Hollywood screenwriters in the '30s and '40s and into the '50s. You find that if you look at a lot of those guys who were writing when I was a kid, they came out of what was called "the slicks," which were the slick magazines. They were named that because the paper was shiny and slick. That was the training ground for so many screenwriters.

*When was the first time you ever picked up a camera and started thinking about directing?*

Very early. I went to Northwestern University in the Theater School, I got hold of a 16mm camera and went out and shot dramatic shorts. That was back in the days when you had to work in film and it was very slow and laborious. Then I became an actor, and I was an actor for a long time. I started writing because I wanted to make the transition. I wanted to direct, but first I tried breaking into the television commercial world. I did a lot of that, both in front of the camera and behind. Then I figured out that if I wanted to direct I had to have a piece of material. And actually it was partially because of Jim Bridges, a writer-director who has now passed away. He did *The China Syndrome*, *Urban Cowboy* and *Mike's Murder*. Jim was writing and directing and I was at the Actors' Studio with him. I was there as an actor, but I started appearing in the playwrights' wing. They had a wing where writers could put their experimental plays up and the actors in the Actors' Studio would appear in them. So I started to meet a lot of aspiring writer-directors who were doing one-act plays. That was where I started to see there was

**Tom Holland (courtesy Kathi and Tom Holland).**

a crossover; that a lot of directors came out of being writers. So I started writing a screenplay and starved to death for a long time [*laughs*], then started to get produced.

*Was the first one you got produced* **The Initiation of Sarah?**

It was, yes. It was a Movie of the Week. I did that for [producer] Dick Berg, and the company was Chuck Fries'. That was the late '70s, it was my first credit. It became a huge success ... or rather, it got a lot of notice because it was the first "jiggle" movie—the first wet T-shirt film—and it was a Movie of the Week. In the movie, some girls end up being thrown in a fountain. That was the wet T-shirt bit and you could see their nipples. It was very shocking, and it got a lot of notoriety because of that. They remade that just recently.

*Was there an influence of Stephen King in that, with the psychic powers thing and* **Carrie** *being around in the '70s?*

I don't remember being specifically influenced by him, no. I was writing stuff that the effects people weren't able to do, I remember that. But it was about a sorority that was infiltrated by witches. No, I don't remember any King influence. That was the first credit I got in the genre, but I almost *created* the genre for television. Then what happened was, I was too out there, or too *into* the genre, and they brought writers in to smooth me out, to make it less horrifying.

*So there were people actually coming in to rewrite your material then?*

In the case of *Initiation of Sarah*, yeah. But that was why, because I was doing things like having people shapeshift, which of course you'd never seen on television [*laughs*] because there wasn't a technical way to do it back then.

**The Beast Within** *was an adaptation of an Edward Levy novel.*

This is a strange story. The novel had not been written. The producer Harvey Bernhard, who did the *Omen* series, had bought the book because he loved the title. And I believe that Mr. Levy did not finish the novel in time because he had marital difficulties, i.e., he'd gotten into a divorce. So I wrote the screenplay based on a title and there was no book [*laughs*]. That's a God honest true story. *The Beast Within* was one of the first effects movies, in the sense that it was one of the first movies where they used bladders to blow people up for the shapeshifting. That was very crude back then.

*How hard did you find it writing the sequel to* Psycho*? It must have been quite a responsibility.*

Yes, I took it terribly seriously. I was thrilled that I wasn't paralyzed with fear and I wasn't overcome [*laughs*]. I took an enormous amount of time trying to make sure that the given circumstances were faithful to the original to the best of my ability. The idea was that Norman is released, and then the relatives of his victims disagree so violently with a court letting him go that they try to drive him crazy so that he's recommitted again. One of the things that made *Psycho* the original so interesting was you had this mad serial murderer that you felt sorry for. It was playing on that vulnerability Tony Perkins had along with the madness, that makes the character resonate so much. And that is what plays in *Psycho II*; they drive him mad again, but he doesn't kill anyone until the very last moment, when he kills his mother. But he hasn't killed anybody [until then], it's just amazing. *Psycho II* was an enormous hit when it came out, a worldwide hit—it was a sleeper hit. The studio didn't expect it, they didn't know what they had. Then the film was forgotten, and I don't know when it started but for the last ten years *Psycho II* has been growing in terms of critical respect. I get more and more questions about *Psycho II*, and I find that people value it more with the passage of time.

*For your money, which is better: the film version or the Robert Bloch novel?*

It would have to be the film, wouldn't it? I mean, I think Robert Bloch was just great, and I knew him in passing and he was a terribly nice man, so I don't mean in any way to denigrate the novel. But the film, *Psycho*, the original Hitchcock film ... everything flows from that. That is what started all of it, and where we are today.

*Do you think it has to do with the iconic performance of Anthony Perkins?*

Oh God, yes. Everything stands on it, and nothing would be possible without Hitchcock's *Psycho*. It changed it all; it changed filmmaking for that matter.

*So I can imagine you would be nervous about approaching the sequel [*laughs*].*

Well, I'd only had one movie—*The Beast Within*—and I was so lucky to get

Anthony Perkins as Norman Bates again in *Psycho II* (1983, Universal Picture; courtesy John Gullidge).

that job, and I think it was because nobody wanted to touch *Psycho II*. It's hard to imagine now but in 1982 horror was banished, it was considered an exhausted genre.

*Was it more a case of that, or was it that people were just frightened to take it on because of its history?*

I suppose.... Well, I think ours started out as a cable affair—they were doing it for a cable company called Oak Communications in San Diego, and so it wasn't even a movie when it started out. It was just an amazing piece of luck on my part that they were going for the B or C team, otherwise I never would have got the chance.

*Was it due to the success of* Psycho II *that you ended up directing* Fright Night?

Oh yeah, sure. *Psycho II* started everything for me. But you had a couple of good ones in between; you had *Cloak and Dagger* which is another film I feel has been forgotten but was enormously influential in its time. That was a lot of people's favorite film when they were adolescents growing up. It was a film that wasn't a success in the theaters but became huge on VHS and on cable. But I think that film, *Psycho II*, started all of it.

*Where did the idea for* Fright Night *come from? Did you used to watch shows like that as a kid?*

Exactly. That is my homage to Peter Cushing, to all the Hammer films, and the AIP films, which are what I grew up on. There used to be, in the States anyway, on the Independent Television Channel on Friday night they'd have the horror films at like 11 o'clock. And they'd always have some corny host introducing them, like Elvira, the Vampiress, the

**Meg Tilly as Mary re-enacts the famous shower scene recreated in** *Psycho II* **(1983, Universal Pictures; courtesy John Gullidge).**

Cryptkeeper, that kind of thing. There was always a terrible, cheesy host who would introduce them. And *Fright Night* is really my homage to my childhood growing up watching horror films. It's an homage specifically to Hammer and AIP films. I named the character Peter Vincent [played by Roddy McDowall] after Peter Cushing and Vincent Price, a combination of the two [*laughs*].

*Did you have an active imagination then when you were Charlie's age?*

Oh gosh, sure I did. Well, can you think of anything better if you were a horror movie fan, than to have a vampire move in next door? Is that your idea of Heaven or what? [*Laughs.*]

*Did you ever have any of those flights of fancy when you were his age?*

I must have. I don't remember now but I must have. But there's a sense of delight, we're sitting here and we're chuckling. That's what *Fright Night* had, it had a sense of humor too.

*Were you steeped in vampire history yourself? There's a lot about vampire lore in there.*

Oh, I've read almost all the books I think. God knows, I must have been, yes, because I was into the genre. The subgenre that was created when I was growing up, of course, was zombies. But the worlds that were established when we were kids were vampires and werewolves.

*Peter makes a comment about slasher movies that were prevalent at the time and it seems like you're harking back to the old films. Which do you think was the better kind of horror?*

Obviously the old, the icons. Because at that time, everything was about the slasher movies, and the biggest thing to come along prior to that had been *Halloween* in 1978. The old horror, like vampires, had gasped their last gasp. I think *Love at First Bite* was just after that, which is a comic look at vampires with George Hamilton, and that meant vampires were dead, the genre was dead. I think *Fright Night* reinvented or revitalized the vampire genre in the mid-80s. I suppose you could say now, "What's working are the *Saw* films"—the latest one just opened to terrific business. So they don't have slasher films any more, now they're calling them torture porn. But I don't know if that's applicable to *Saw*, *Saw*'s more of a puzzle, isn't it?

*So do you think something will come along to revitalize the old kind of horror now, like* **Fright Night** *did?*

Something will, yes. And the thing is, you won't know it when it happens, because I'll tell you, when I wrote *Fright Night* it wasn't because I was trying to revitalize anything. The impulse came out of my own affection for the old icons in the genre. I loved the old fashioned horror and that's what *Fright Night* was.

*What was Roddy McDowall like to work with?*

Wonderful. The nicest man. Helpful, supportive. He'd been through everything, he knew how the system worked; he knew how hard it was to survive. He was kind ... I can't say enough good about him. He was a dear friend all the way up to his death.

*It's reflected in the parts that he plays. He always plays a really nice guy...*

As he got older, yes. I think he knew how hard it was because he'd been one of the few guys to make the transition from child actor to adult actor. There was something just nice about him, because you're in a town where nobody gives a shit about anybody. He represented the old Hollywood that I didn't know. He represented the Hollywood of the studio system. I remember him talking about how when he was 20 and MGM threw him out. He was a child and he didn't know where else to go, and told me how devastating it had been for him. So there was a lot of empathy in Roddy because of a few of the things that had happened to him in his career. A lot of them were connected with being a child actor.

*I don't know if this was true in real life, but he seemed to take William under his wing, like Peter takes Charlie under his wing in the film.*

Well, he even took *me* under his wing. He invited me to his house. He would have dinner parties—one a week—and I met Vincent Price at his house. There couldn't have been a nicer man than Vincent Price. But I met stars old and new: Walter Matthau, Lee Remick, John Schlesinger the British director. At his house I met the Hollywood that I had grown up looking up to. It was terrific.

*How would you say Dandridge compares to vampires that have gone before? What makes him different or similar?*

At the time I think he seemed so modern: Chris Sarandon. It was the first "hot vampire." He dressed in what were then the styles of the day—there was a sense of fashion to him [*laughs*]. He had a sense of humor, too.

*What's your favorite scene in the film?*

I always loved Roddy trying to make the vampire back away going up the staircase. He holds up the cross and he uses one of those great corny lines from one of the Hammer films, which is, "Back, spawn of Satan!" [*Laughs*]

*And it doesn't work...*

I was on the floor laughing when I wrote a lot of it, you know? I was tickled pink. It wasn't comedy but it was humor coming out of the reality of the situation.

*And the delivery as well.*

Yes. It's amazing that the film ever got made. You probably couldn't get it done today. So, it was just a lot of luck that it survived the system.

*Did the wolf cause you any problems during filming?*

It was hard to shoot, yeah. It took forever to get it on, the head and everything—and there's something very poignant about it. I knew I was trying to hit the horror icons of my youth, so I was trying to get a werewolf in there; I thought it was very touching. There's just a sweetness that runs through the movie. Roddy asked me for an image for Peter Vincent and I said, "He's the Cowardly Lion." Go figure: it was blessed.

*What did you think when you first read Don Mancini's script of* **Child's Play***?*

I thought it was a good concept. But I rewrote that thing from top to bottom. If you look at *Child's Play 2* you'll see a lot of the material I didn't use. My memory of it was that it was a great idea, but what happened was that whenever the boy fell asleep the doll was his alter ego. The doll got up and killed whoever the little boy was angry at. That was the original story as I remember it. I didn't think that generated enough sympathy, so I wanted a mother and a little boy in peril. That's how I came to create Charles Lee Ray and all of that.

*So they were your ideas?*

I don't really want to get into whose ideas belonged to whom. All you have to do is look at the first one and look at all the sequels, you can tell the sensibility's different.

*What kind of problems did working with a puppet and the young Alex Vincent present?*

Alex was great, but the problem with working with a little boy is that you had a limited amount of time. I think it was about five hours a day. The puppet was hell because it had no tensile strength and couldn't hold the knife in its hand. And just trying to get the eye-line so it looked like it was looking at the actors. There were a lot of problems; it was technically very difficult to do.

*What was Brad Dourif like to work with?*

Brad was great, I'd used him before on a Whoopi Goldberg movie called *Fatal Beauty*. Brad's a brilliant actor; people forget that, I think because he's done so much work in the horror medium. But look at the early credits, because there are a lot of prestige credits in there. He's a serious, heavyweight actor.

*How does it feel to have helped create this franchise that's still going today?*

It's funny, I'm thrilled—I wish I was making money off it, but I'm not. I'm thrilled for all those guys. The interesting thing is that very few people ask me about *Child's Play*. They ask me about movies that seem like they're in the past, and I think even though the first *Child's Play* was like now 20 years ago, because there have been sequels it seems like it's current. So it hasn't gotten the kind of critical acclaim my other ones have.

*Have you seen any of the toys that are based on the first movie, and have you got any yourself?*

No I don't.

*Did you get to keep anything from the film?*

No, God! And that's such idiocy on my part [*laughs*]. I didn't realize how valuable the props were going to become.

**The Tales from the Crypt *TV series came after that. Did you enjoy working on those?***

Yes, I did. All three of them [*Lover Come Hack to Me* (1989), *Four-Sided Triangle* (1990), *King of the Road* (1992)]. On one of them [*King of the Road*] I feel like I discovered Brad Pitt.

The doll Chucky from *Child's Play* (1988, United Artists; courtesy John Gullidge).

*Plus Patricia Arquette is in* **Four Sided Triangle.**

Yeah, and they're both terrific. I thought they were both talented and I really did think that they were going to become stars, both of them. They had something, you could see that in the way I used both of them. They used their sensuality and their presence.

*What made you decide to take on the mini-series of* **The Langoliers** *and what problems did the special effects pose?*

I liked the novella. I thought it was terrific. The effects: They just didn't have the money to do them properly. Conceptually the effects were fine, but they just didn't have the money to really do good effects.

*Weren't they early CGI effects?*

Yeah, very early—but they looked raw. They're too shiny and clean. They didn't give it the time or the money to really do them well. I thought the actors in the show were really terrific, but the effects are sort of tacky.

*The character interaction of the ensemble is great. Which were your favorite characters?*

I liked all of them, I thought they were all good. That was the heart of that show, the actors were all so damned good. They work so well together.

*They sell the concept, don't they?*

Yeah, they do. *Thinner* arguably is a failure, but *The Langoliers* I thought was a real success—and especially a success since we had so little money to work with. Nobody ever seems to mention *The Langoliers*, so it's nice to know that you liked it and appreciate it. It's like it never happened, very few people ever ask me about it. You know, it was a big success as a mini-series, the audience liked it. But critically nobody really seems to be interested; I think it's one of the better Stephen King pieces. But nobody seems to have noticed at all. The acting's terrific, and I wrote the script of that, the adaptation; it really is a tight piece of work. What I think is that in some ways Stephen King is the 800-pound gorilla that blots out everything. The minute you say Stephen King, it says all there is to say about it and dismisses it at the same time. There is a lot of different quality in the writing and also the execution of the pieces that have been turned into Stephen King movies.

*How long did it take to shoot?*

I don't remember now, but it was really done cheaply. We did it in a live airport in Bangor, Maine, and it had a hell of a difficult production. But it was terrifically cast, I thought everybody did a terrific job. Maybe Bronson Pinchot [playing Craig Toomey] was a little bit too big, but outside of that…. Certainly David Morse [Captain Brian Engle] is just a terrific fuckin' actor.

*Did you have to run your teleplay by Stephen King?*

Yes, I did.

*Did he make any changes to it?*

No, he was happy with it, as I understand. In the past when I've worked with Stephen, he's been nothing but supportive. I've nothing but good things to say about him.

*We've heard that from a lot of people. Obviously you're a big fan of his work.*
Yeah, he's my generation. He brought horror to the middle classes.

*Moving on to* **Thinner***: When you read the "Bachman" book, did you know it was Stephen King?*
Yes I did. I can't remember what gave it away exactly, now.

*Are you happy with how* **Thinner** *turned out?*
I'm happy with it except for the ending. The video changed the ending. That movie was a very frustrating experience. The actors, [including] Robert John Burke [playing Billy Halleck], they all did a terrific job. But the audience hated the movie. Every time we previewed the movie, they would stay with it but they hated the ending. And the ending that I had was where he literally ate the pie after he accidentally gave it to his daughter. It was a downer ending: the ending that was in the book. I always suspected that Robert John Burke did such a good job that the audience wanted him to win. Then when he lost at the end, they hated the movie because of that. I mean, that's the only explanation I have for it. I have never had a movie that has tested so obviously telling you that people hated the ending. Every fuckin' audience, no matter what I did, hated the ending. So I ended up with this screwy, not-very-satisfying ending. I think I should have gone with the original dark ending where he commits suicide after he's accidentally poisoned his daughter.

*Is there any chance of a director's cut?*
Nobody's ever asked me, so I wouldn't count on it. *Thinner* was a disappointment, in that it did not work out. Then of course when you have a movie that tests badly, you lose control of it. The studio cut it, put that ending on it. Cut it too tightly and took the humor out. It was just a flop, it wasn't a happy experience.

*Finally, what do you make of the horror genre in general, and your contemporaries working in it?*
I can remember one time at one of the "Masters of Horror" dinners, I had Wes Craven sitting to my right, Tobe Hooper sitting to my left. I had Robert Rodriguez across from me—anybody who was anybody. It felt so Goddamned nice, and it was so pleasant and not competitive and everything else. I was trying to figure out why and I suddenly realized: We're all horror guys, so by definition we're all outlaws. By definition the critical establishment of Hollywood shits all over us. I think there's a camaraderie in the genre that you don't find in the other genres.

# *William Malone*

William Malone is a Lansing, Michigan, native with Ukrainian and Irish roots. His Ukrainian grandmother, who had what he calls a "Maria Ouspenskaya quality," influenced Malone, sharing superstitions she remembered from the old country. At the age of 11 his parents bought him an 8mm movie camera. By that time, he had already become an avid movie fan, his favorites being the 1950s sci-fis and horrors; he created his own homemade 8mm versions. He also designed and built elaborate Halloween costumes, which he sold at a local store. At 19, Malone arrived in Los Angeles and took a job at Don Post Studios, one of the world's busiest mask and costume shops, attending UCLA cinema lectures by night. Within his first few years at Post Studios, he was made vice-president and head designer.

By the early '80s, the filmmaking bug was too much to ignore. His first feature was *Scared to Death* and three years later he directed the indie science fiction thriller *Creature*. Although he worked diligently in television, Malone grew frustrated with the feature film business which stalled many of his projects. He was actually going to abandon his ambitions when the chance to direct an episode of *Tales from the Crypt* cropped up. "Only Skin Deep" was nominated for a Cable ACE award and producer Joel Silver hired Malone to make his major studio debut with the remake of *House on Haunted Hill* (1999). The success of that film propelled Malone towards a second feature, the dark supernatural thriller *FeardotCom* (2002). Both gave Malone the opportunity and budget to fashion his signature horrific worlds from scratch. He was allowed even more freedom on *Masters of Horror*. Now Malone has turned again to the world of indie filmmaking for his new project *Parasomnia*.

---

*When you were little, your mother took you to see* **Creature from the Black Lagoon.** *What kind of effect did that have on you?*

I think I was probably four or five years old, and why my mom would take me to see that movie I don't know. It was 3D and everyone was standing outside in the rain waiting to get in, there was a huge line. When the Creature popped out of the screen I think I spent most of the movie ducked under the seats [*laughs*]. I'd creep up and look, it scared the crap out of me. But when I got home there was just something I really enjoyed about it. From that time on, I was hooked on that stuff.

*You've said that* **Forbidden Planet** *was an early influence too. You created a replica of Robby and you now own the original.*

I guess when I was a kid, the movies that were my main films were *Creature from the Black Lagoon*, *20000 Leagues Under the Sea* and *Forbidden Planet*. *Forbidden Planet* was probably my number one film. When I first saw it, it was kind of like when people first saw *Star Wars*. It just blew me away. I was just enthralled with Robby the Robot. Later on, when I came to Los Angeles, they had an auction. I was there to see if I could see Robby, and of course they didn't have one for sale. That gave me the idea of basically building one. The original robot ended up in a museum in Buena Park and I was able to go down there and take pictures of it. I knew nothing about plastics or forming anything, but I spent the next couple of years doing nothing but learning about stuff and building a replica. Then about 1980, the museum went out of business, and they sold the original Robby. Nobody would actually believe that it was up for sale—so I went down there and bought him for $5,000. He was in bad shape by that time, so I spent like the next year and a half restoring him. Now he's in my house [*laughs*]. I take him out of retirement every now and again. Joe Dante called me and wanted to use him on *Looney Tunes: Back in Action*, so we got the old boy out of retirement.

*When did you start to make monster masks yourself as a kid?*

When I was little, there weren't any toys like there are now. There were very few genre toys, from science fiction or horror or anything. So instead of getting toys, I'd ask my parents for clay and I started sculpting things. I made my first monster mask puppet when I was about ten or eleven. I just continued doing it as a hobby.

*Which came first, making the masks or shooting the short films?*

I think it was really about the same time, because my parents gave me a little 8mm movie camera. And what's the first thing I do? Make a monster movie. I think I made *Dr. Jekyll and Mr. Hyde*, or at least part of it anyway. I made my own Mr. Hyde mask and ran around the neighborhood taking pictures for the movie.

Director William Malone (courtesy William Malone).

*How important were magazines like* **Famous Monsters of Filmland** *and* **Fantastic Monsters***?*

A friend of mine started to visit my neighborhood, and came over one day with a copy of *Famous Monsters*. It was like a revelation, it was staggering that there was a magazine about monsters. I was totally hooked, so I got a subscription. There was also *Fantastic Monsters* and the editor was Paul Blaisdell, who of course was known for creating [the monsters for] *The She-Creature*, *It Conquered the World*, *Invasion of the Saucer Men* and all of those monster movies, I sent him some pictures of masks I had done and he asked me to do an article for the magazine. His support really launched me into the whole thing; he was a really good guy. I called him on the phone quite a number of times and he'd give me information on how to make masks. It was pretty cool. So both magazines had a huge influence on me.

**Robby the Robot, owned by William Malone (courtesy William Malone).**

*Is it true that you moved to Studio City just because of the name?*

That's true, yes [*laughs*]. I just got a map of Los Angeles when I was in sixth grade or something, and was so into the movie business. I remember coming across a place called Studio City and I thought, well they've *got* to have studios there [*laughs*]! So when I came out, I just gravitated towards it. It's actually quite a very lovely little place. There was only one studio, though, the old Republic Studio which is now CBS. And that studio's still there, actually.

*How does it feel to know that you're the one who made the original Michael Myers mask?*

Kind of crazy, really. At one point when I was working at Don Post Studios, we felt that Universal Studios were probably going to pull our license on Universal characters because they wanted to make their own, so we were looking for other things. *Star Trek* was an obvious choice, although I always thought it was kinda goofy to make a Captain Kirk mask. But we got a lifecast of [*Star Trek* star William Shatner's] head and I used that as a basis for sculpting a Kirk mask. I remember when John Carpenter and a couple of other people came in and they wanted to have it painted white; I thought, "This is pretty interesting." I just never in a million years thought that would ever be anything of interest to anyone, so...

*How much of a gamble was it for you to make* Scared to Death*?*

A *big* gamble because at the time I'd quit my job at Don Post Studios, which was very lucrative. I basically took my life savings and put them into this little movie. My friends all said I was a complete loon. It was a very scary thing to spend your own money. But it turned out well. It's not a good movie, it's a terrible film—but it did make enough for me to get my money back and launched me into making films. I think that movie made me realize how little I did know about filmmaking, so I went back and studied. But it was a great experience. I remember when I finished, I was sorry I didn't make ten of them because it actually did pretty well.

*So you must have been pleased when it got to number 16 in the national box office charts.*

Yeah, that was pretty amazing. The guy who handles my legal work called me up and said, "You've gotta check out the trades"—and I was like, "How did *that* happen?" [*Laughs*]

*How much of an influence was* **Alien** *on* **Titan Find***?*

*Titan Find*, which in the States is called *Creature*, was intended to be a riff of *Alien*. What happened was, I'd been struggling after *Scared to Death* to get another film off the ground and nobody was beating down my door. So this producer called me up and he said to me that if I could make a movie like *Alien*, he'll put up the money for it. So that's what I tried to do. [Actor] Klaus Kinski was a completely insane person. I'm sure anybody reading the book will have heard stories about him. He was probably certifiable; I had him for a week and he was just crazy. The things that came out of his mouth would embarrass a sailor [*laughs*]. Starting on Monday, I had him for a week—and by Tuesday, the crew was coming in and saying to me, "You've got to do something about this guy." By Thursday, I think, of that week I decided that the only way of dealing with him was to scream at him. And I'm not one for screaming or getting upset on set. So I winked at the cameraman, then just started screaming. He was a pussycat for the rest of the day, and then on Friday.

**The Syngenor monster attacks in** *Scared to Death* **(1981, Lone Star Pictures; courtesy William Malone).**

An astronaut about to make that fatal find on Saturn's largest moon, Titan, in *Titan Find* (aka *Creature*; 1985, Trans World Entertainment), which was hugely influenced by *Alien* (courtesy William Malone).

*How did you like filming an episode of* Tales from the Crypt, Report from the Grave, *in England?*

I shot *Report from the Grave* at Ealing Studios—which was just a great experience. I really enjoyed working with English people and shooting in England. For me it was kind of heartwarming, because the first A.D. would come up to me and say, "So, guv'nor, what's next?" [*Laughs*] It was like I was doing a Hammer film or something. I remember the door to the crypt; they said, "Yeah, this is 400 years old." We don't have that in the United States. I suppose the only negative thing was ... we were shooting in February, and for some reason I couldn't get the crew to close the door on the big soundstage. It was just freezing outside and we had this big, giant door open.

*How did you try to make your* The House on Haunted Hill *different from the 1959 original?*

I really loved the original, and I always put myself in the place of an audience. If I went to see the remake, what would I want to see? Basically the same story, only bigger and better, with more things in it. I tried to remain at least close to the spirit of the original film; that was always my intent. The only thing as a kid I was disappointed with was the fact that there were no real ghosts in it. So I thought we should at least add some real ghosts in the film; that was the major change I think I made to the film.

*What did you think of the skeleton on the wires in the original film?*

[*Laughs*] You know, I remember as a kid—I think I was about 12 years old when I saw that—we just all laughed. We threw popcorn at it. I don't think anyone ever thought that was scary, it was just goofy. Great fun.

*How would you rate Geoffrey Rush's performance alongside Vincent Price's?*

I loved both of them. Vincent Price of course was just wonderful—one of the icons of horror. I think Geoffrey did an amazing job, he actually never intended to be a Vincent

Geoffrey Rush (standing) as Stephen H. Price, with Famke Janssen, in *The House on Haunted Hill* **(1999, Warner Brothers; courtesy William Malone).**

Price model. I love Geoffrey; he's a great actor, obviously. And also very committed. I think that was the thing that surprised me, because here we are making a little remake of *House on Haunted Hill* and he's Academy Award winner Geoffrey Rush. I thought he was just going to come in and walk through this, and he didn't at all. He'd be off in his corner rehearsing, he gave it his all.

*How did* FeardotCom *come about?*

The biggest problem I have, is that I never seem to have another movie ready when I've made a film. I don't have a script ready. So on this film, I'd been trying to find something to do and I'd been offered mostly teenage slasher movies, which is not really anything I'm interested in. And the guy who produced, oddly enough, *Titan Find* called me up and said, "I want you to come and do this movie called *FeardotCom*." I said, "I hate the title, I don't want to do a movie called *FeardotCom*." He told me what the story was and I said, "Well, there could be something interesting in that." So I said I would make it, as long as he didn't call it *FeardotCom*. We got into it and wound up going to Luxembourg to shoot, which I thought was kind of an odd choice because the movie was supposed to take place in New York. Of course, the producer's telling me that Luxembourg looks exactly like New York, and I'm going, "I don't think so." So we got there and of course it didn't look anything like New York, so we ended up having to build all the sets to make it have the right look. But you never hit it exactly right, because they don't have all the little details in them. So it turned out to be a kind of weird take on New York rather than *being* New

York. With that film we had a lot of problems. During the filming I was getting script revisions which were written by like five different people and so forth. I really felt my job on that movie was damage control rather than actually making a film. A lot of people hate that movie, and that's okay. There are a lot of things in it I like, and I think that Christian Sebaldt, who shot it, did an amazing job.

I think a lot of the weather outside factors into the way that movie feels. The entire time we were there, it rained every day for months and months, which was sort of depressing—it added to the atmosphere. At the same time my mother died. It was just not a good way to be making the film. But, as I say, that's a movie you either love or you hate, which is okay.

*Were you deliberately aiming for a 1930s feel?*

Yeah, I'm a huge fan of German Expressionism—all those old films like *The Cabinet of Dr. Caligari* and *Nosferatu* and *Faust*. I really wanted the film to have that kind of a feel.

*The film's probably one of the darkest ever, literally. Was this an intentional thing as well?*

Yeah, I wanted to see what the limits were, and I think in a couple of spots I went over the edge there on the color timings a bit. It's the second movie ever made with a D.I. [digital internegative] which means transferring the film negative to a digital format and then dealing with the color timing. But I was a great believer that technology could aid the film.

*How did you approach the idea of a ghost using the Internet for revenge?*

When I first heard the idea, I thought, "That's a little goofy." Then I thought, "Well,

Twisted nurse played by Slavitza Jovan working at the asylum that becomes *The House on Haunted Hill* (1999, Warner Bros.; courtesy William Malone).

One of the ghosts from the FeardotCom website, seeking revenge because people watched her being tortured and murdered in *FeardotCom* (2002, Warner Bros./Sony Pictures Releasing; courtesy William Malone).

**Natascha McElhone and Stephen Dorff in** *FeardotCom* **(2002, Warner Bros./Sony Pictures Releasing; courtesy William Malone).**

maybe that's the challenge of it, to make it interesting." And my approach was to make it as dreamlike as possible. In fact, when I took on *FeardotCom* the idea was to make the entire film basically like a nightmare. I wanted it to be like one of those things where you wake up in the middle of the night and you think you're awake but you're actually still dreaming. That's why even in the normal scenes, everything's a little off.

*How did you like working with Stephen Dorff, Natasha McElhone and Stephen Rea?*

They were all brilliant. Stephen Rea is one of my favorite actors, he came in and gave a wonderful performance. Natasha was very committed to it. In retrospect, I think she was a little miscast. I mean, I love having her in the film, don't get me wrong, but the film should have been rewritten for her, instead of being written for somebody who was showing off how good she is at her job. Natasha has this sort of elegance and competence, so you just don't buy that with her. We tried to bend the script in her direction, but I'm not entirely sure it was successful.

*I gather you got Jeffrey Combs to deliver lines from* Re-Animator *on set.*

Yeah. I'm a big fan of that movie. Jeffrey would come onto the set and I'd go, "You're not even a half-rate scientist, get a job in a sideshow!" [*Laughs*] He was hilarious, I love Jeffrey.

*When did you two first meet?*

I'd done a show called *Perversions of Science*, which was a spin-off series from *Tales from the Crypt*—the science fiction version. Jeffrey came in and played this character who was an alien who later becomes Adolf Hitler. And we just really hit it off, I just had a great time making it. After that, whenever I was doing something, I'd call Jeffrey. He's in my most recent movie *Parasomnia*, playing a similar character to the one in *FeardotCom*, kind of a burned-out detective.

*How did your association with* **Masters of Horror** *come about?*

Mick [Garris] and I met years ago when I was working at Don Post Studios and he was head of publicity on *Star Wars*. I went up to Mick one day and said, "Wouldn't it be great if we got all the horror guys together, gather around and talk about horror films?" I don't know a lot of other directors—I know a lot of people in the business, but not directors. He thought that was a great idea, so he organized the first batch of horror dinners. Mick knew a lot of these guys, he could get a lot of them together so we could have dinner in various places around Los Angeles. We'd just show up at different places and chitchat. We'd have a great time. It wasn't always people who were on the show—David Cronenberg would show up and Mark Singer, we had a great bunch of people. Then Mick got the idea for doing the TV series and said I should come and do an episode of it. He sent me like three screenplays and the one I picked was called *The Fair-Haired Child*.

*You designed the creature for that. How did you decide how you wanted it to look?*

There was no description at all, just "a demon of some sort," and I was struggling with it. But my notion was, I wanted it to be simple, whatever it was, not one of these really complex monsters. I went back and re-read the script and there was a description of the windchime as being like Edvard Munch's *The Scream*. So I thought, "Maybe that's what the monster should look like," because I'd always thought *The Scream* was a really interesting painting, and would make a great ghost or monster or something. I sat down and did some sketches, and came up with this design fairly quickly. I sent it over to KNB to have it made up and I think it turned out really well. People were creeped out by it. I ran it for my girlfriend—she didn't know anything about the show—and when the monster skitters out, she just leaped about four feet and shouted, "What is that?" [*Laughs*] I still have the bruise marks on my shoulder.

*You mentioned* **Nosferatu** *earlier. I believe that was an influence on how you shot the movements of the creature.*

Well, that started off years ago. Of course I'd seen *Nosferatu* and I'd looked at a lot of the photographs of Joel-Peter Whitkin, who had done some blurry head things and stuff like that. At the same time I saw *Jacob's Ladder* and thought, "There's something interesting there." I'd experimented a little bit on my first *Tales from the Crypt* episode, *Only Skin Deep*, and then actually when I went to England to do *Report from the Grave* in '95 or '96, I had the idea to take that further and make a person walk in a weird way. I had the guy who plays the character from *Report from the Grave* move really slowly and shot it at a slow frame rate, and came up with some pretty interesting stuff. When it came time to do *House on Haunted Hill* I stuck it in there and I think it worked rather well. Then when we did *Masters of Horror*, I thought, "People really liked that" so I gave them some more.

*Were there any influences from Japanese films like* **The Ring***?*

Not at all. Some people have been saying that this stuff came from an Asian influence, and actually it predates all of those Japanese films. I did it first in *Only Skin Deep*, then did it in a really big way on *Report from the Grave* in '96.

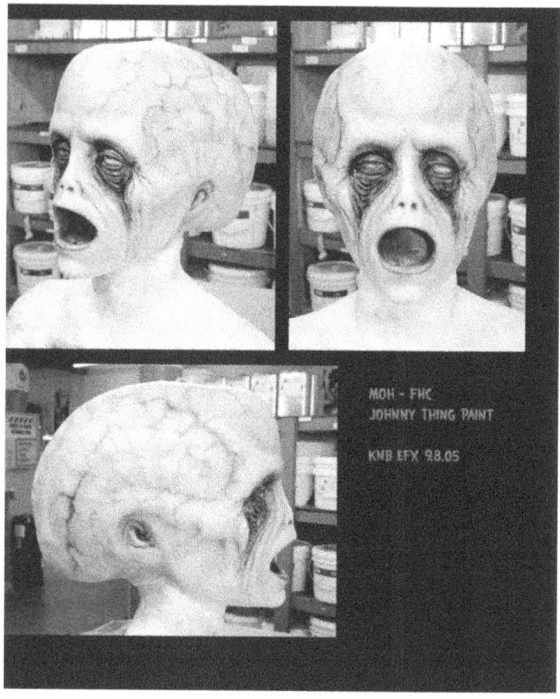

Sketch and sculpts of the creature from the "Fair Haired Child" episode of *Masters of Horror* (2006; courtesy William Malone).

*What was it about* **The Fair-Haired Child** *that attracted you?*

It had a fairy tale quality which I liked, and also, I've always wanted to make a sort of gothic horror thing which I haven't had much opportunity to do. Actually, in the original story, the two killers were country hicks and when I got the script I thought, "That's been done." I thought it might be quite interesting if we made them a little odder than that, and from a defunct music academy. So that was how that came about. And [because] I'm a big fan of classical music, I thought it would be a good opportunity to put in the film a lot of stuff that I've heard.

*What are your feelings about* **Parasomnia***?*

It's a very different movie for me. It's a thriller and a love story and it's got a lot of horror elements to it. I can't say that it's a hor-

The "Only Skin Deep" episode of *Tales from the Crypt* (1989, HBO; courtesy William Malone).

*Parasomnia* poster (2008, Rising Storm Productions; courtesy William Malone).

ror movie *per se*, but it's got a lot of really cool things in it and Jeffrey Combs comes back as a burned-out detective. Kathryn Leigh Scott, who was in *Dark Shadows*, plays one of the characters [Nurse Evans]; Timothy Bottoms plays Dr. Corso; it's a really excellent cast. Christian Sebalt who shot *FeardotCom* shot it, and I think it's really cool. It's a weird movie with a lot of bloodshed. I think the best thing I can say about it is, I can't really liken it to anything else. I don't think anyone's going to point a finger and go, "It's a rip-off of this or that." It's about a young art student [Danny Sloane, played by Dylan Purcell] who comes across this girl who's asleep all the time and he falls in love with her, then winds up taking her home, and kidnapping her. But it turns out she's got a

Patrick Kilpatrick and Cherilyn Wilson in *Parasomnia* (2008, Rising Storm Productions; courtesy William Malone).

pretty dark secret that he doesn't realize—sort of like taking the pound puppy home and finding out it's Cujo or something [*laughs*].

***Name one monster you'd like to have created and one film you'd like to have made.***

That's easy: *Creature from the Black Lagoon*. I think it's the greatest monster ever made and the underwater photography is just amazing. You know, on *Parasomnia* we had to do an underwater scene, and we had a tank—which is the most controlled situation you can have. And the water wasn't even one-tenth as clear as the water in *Creature from the Black Lagoon*. So, I don't know, they had to find the clearest springs in the world to shoot that film. It's so dreamy, there's such a sensual quality to it; it's just amazing.

# Peter Medak

Peter Medak was born in Budapest, Hungary, in 1937, and traveled to Britain in 1956 to escape from the Soviet crackdown after the Hungarian uprising against Communist rule. He soon embarked on a long and successful career in the film industry, beginning as an assistant director, then working on his first film as a director in 1968: *Negatives*, starring Glenda Jackson. He became known for films such as *A Day in the Death of Joe Egg* (1972) and *The Ruling Class* (1972) before moving to the U.S. and making perhaps his best-known film *The Changeling* (1980), a classic, haunting ghost story starring George C. Scott. Medak returned to genres such as black comedy (*Zorro, the Gay Blade*, 1981) and drama (*The Men's Club*, 1986), then returned to prominence with grittier fare such as *The Krays* (1990), *Let Him Have It* (1991), and *Romeo Is Bleeding* (1993). He also has an extensive background in television, having worked on such series as the 1980s *The Twilight Zone*, *Tales from the Crypt*, *Homicide: Life on the Street* and *Law and Order*. In 2003 he directed an episode of *Carnivàle: Black Blizzard* and more recently an episode of *Masters of Horror*.

---

*You started as a trainee in the film industry in the '50s and worked in many departments on your route to directing. Would you say that's a better grounding than today's young people get, studying it at film school?*

I think the best way to learn is to just start doing something and then work your way up. I think it's much better than film schools. Film schools are great; they didn't really exist in the '50s except in Hungary or Russia or Poland: the great film schools. The only way was to just get in and start, and survive from one job to another, and really learn from life.

*What drew you to filmmaking as a career?*

It was a combination of things. An aunt of mine gave me a 35mm handcrank projector when I was eight years old and a piece of 35mm film from a Hungarian film studio, so that was the very beginning for me. One of my best friends was a young child actor, and watching him in the theater and hanging out backstage, either the opera house or in the theater world—I think the combination of that and then seeing two or three movies when I was ten years old absolutely captivated me. I had this projector, and ever since then I wanted to make movies. And that was at age eight. During Communism it was the most unlikely gift to give to anybody, especially a small child.

*What were your favorite films growing up?*

Well, the most memorable movie was really Laurence Olivier's *Hamlet*, which I saw in 1948 in Budapest. It was that movie which completely blew me away, just as a young kid. I mean, I was a baby when I saw it. But I still remember sitting in the first row in this cinema in Budapest, watching that movie. Then after that there was a very famous Swedish movie called *One Summer of Happiness*; that movie, and a couple of French films. Then after that the Iron Curtain was closed and no western movies were allowed to be shown, except Russian or Hungarian films which were mostly propaganda films—and which, interestingly enough, were not much different from most of the commercial movies everybody makes nowadays [*laughs*]. It's just the subjects that are different.

It was an incredible time when I first came to London in 1956, having escaped from Communism—it was the end of the good old days of England, and the beginning of the great sweeping cultural change. It was a fascinating period, the early '60s—before the Beatles and all that—what London was like and the change of London. At the same time [I was] growing up in the business, going from one job to another. I was very fortunate to have been able to get in immediately. I spent a lot of time at Associated British Pathé and Pathé News. Then at ABPC studios, which then became Elstree Studios, but in those days it was a very big film studio. I became a third assistant, second assistant, first assistant; I had the chance to work with the most incredible directors and actors. For someone to come out from Hungary, from left field, and suddenly ... well, it wasn't sudden because it took about three or four years before I could get a grip on the whole thing. But in the first three years I worked through everything: editing, camera, clapperboy, cleaning the magnetic tapes and being on the dubbing stage, all kinds of stuff. But it's terribly important for a young kid to, at first hand, learn all that or witness it, be around it, not understand it, then begin to understand what it's for and how things are being made. It's a great way to learn, but today it's different because everything is much more structured for film schools. You have the advantage today of the technology and editing on computers. I partake quite a bit here in America in Writer's-Director's Lab at Sundance, which Robert Redford started 30 years ago. It's quite incredible because all the young filmmakers actually begin to make films in front of our guiding eyes. Within a month they walk away knowing quite a lot, and most of those projects get made into their first movies.

Peter Medak directing Melvyn Douglas in *The Changeling* (1980, Chessman Park; courtesy Peter Medak).

*It must be a very rewarding experience.*

Yeah, it's wonderful, a really fantastic feeling. There are a lot of film schools and film labs all over Europe which are based upon the experience of the Sundance lab, which is a very practical thing. So I'm not knocking film schools, it's just that I didn't go through that—because I couldn't, that's why [*laughs*]. It's such an ever-changing but fantastic world, making movies. It's very important for all the young filmmakers to realize that it's completely up to you to stick to your intention and be completely obsessed with it. If you are, you will get there somehow.

*Is there any director you've worked with that stands out in your mind?*

What, from years ago?

*Yes, from when you were learning.*

When I was an assistant director I had the good fortune to work with Sir Carol Reed, Fred Zinnemann, Laslo Benedek, Philip Leacock, Val Guest, and John Paddy Carstairs. I also had the great fortune to work with the most brilliant stage director in England at the time, Joan Littlewood. I did her only movie as a first assistant; she was a legend in England and her influence, particularly in the working class theater, created the most amazing changes in London and also on Broadway because of her plays. I learned everything about acting from her, she was magic. She was the most important influence in my directing career and I owe everything to her. I think it's very important, when people try to teach directing, to hand over our secrets and everything we experienced through our career. You can't really teach directing, either you have it in your soul or you don't. The only way in my mind is to take a scene, let them rehearse it, then we discuss it, then I rehearse it in front of them, they then go and shoot it and cut the scene together. We screen it and discuss it and then I screen my own scene as I insist that they choose a scene from one of my films.

Therefore they learn a tremendous amount just by looking at the different interpretations and possibilities. That is the only way to teach. We all learn by our failings and not our successes, it is most important that we all allow ourselves to make mistakes. In 1963 I went under contract with Universal Studios to start directing television but while the studio was trying to obtain my work permit they assigned me to observe Alfred Hitchcock while he was shooting his film *Marnie*. It was an incredible experience to watch that old brilliant master at work. I realized very quickly how every director works in their own different ways. Basically there are no rules in films and if you know what you are doing, and you do it brilliantly, it all works. Directing is very scary

**Medak (looking through camera lens) with cinematographer John Coquillon (in dark shirt) on location for** *The Changeling* **(1980, Chessman Park; courtesy Peter Medak).**

because you are always alone, particularly when you make your first film. It's wonderful to be able to share and hand over what you felt when you did it for the first time and what fail-safe process you created in order to survive from one day to another. To share this experience and tell them the truth of what you have gone through gives them all the freedom and comfort to take that first very scary step.

*How did you get involved with* **Masters of Horror***?*

I never did horror movies, except when I was a young assistant director in England working on some of the Hammer movies in '59, '60. I did three films with Peter Cushing, Christopher Lee, Herbert Lom, *The Phantom of the Opera* and so on. Then many years later when I was directing, I did a film called *The Changeling* with George C. Scott, which was a great classical ghost story. Then 17 years later I did *Species II* which was a science fiction horror film. I guess because of these movies, but particularly because of *The Changeling*, that's why the producers chose me. I loved the ludicrous premise of the script [for *The Washingtonians*], to presume that George Washington was a cannibal, and I thought that if I could make it funny so people realized it's really a joke, I would be forgiven for making this ludicrous statement about George Washington as well as George Bush.

*It's definitely a funny episode. Do you think the analogy to the Bush administration affected how it was received?*

I cannot answer that question as I am a totally non-political person, because when I left Hungary in 1956 I swore to myself (I was so disappointed with that entire world

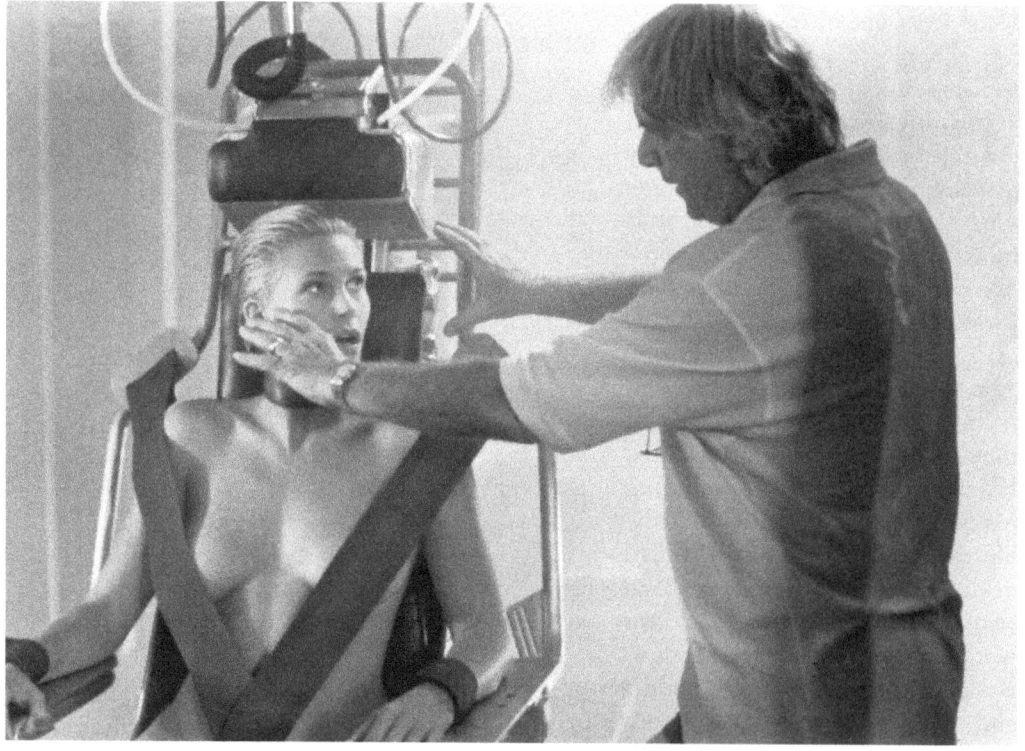

Medak directing Natasha Henstridge in *Species II* (1998, MGM; courtesy Peter Medak).

already then) that I never wanted to partake in any deep political feelings or discussions. I think it's just a tragedy to see what's happening in the world today. It is very important to make people laugh and allow them to go on in life with smiles on their faces.

*Was it hard to work within the constraints of television?*

Mick Garris and Andrew Deane, my producers, really gave me a free hand. Mick always told me never to listen to anyone: "Just listen to yourself and do whatever you want to do." It's very rare in this business to be encouraged by your producers.

*Especially in TV....*

To be given that freedom ... it's wonderful.

*I heard that when you read the script to* **The Changeling,** *you were so scared that you couldn't go downstairs to your family.*

Yes, yes, yes. I was still living in England at the time—I lived there for 36 years. We were having a dinner party and I had to read the script because the producer Joel Michaels was going to call that night. But the script really got to me and I started listening to all the creaking noises the house was making. It's great when something triggers your fantasy and you start to imagine things. I remember the same thing happened years before, when I was still an assistant director and I was trying to get a job on *The Haunting*, Robert Wise's great movie. While I was reading that script, I was so petrified I had to turn on all the lights and couldn't move in my bed. When a script scares you to that degree, then you know you're onto something great. When I read *The Changeling* it totally grabbed me and I just had to do it and I had the most fantastic and memorable time doing that film. In a way, when I did *The Washingtonians* I made it a little bit like *The Changeling*, with the little girl wandering about listening to voices in the basement and all that. I don't know, it's just something I love doing. Ever since then I've been trying to find another supernatural story and, twenty-five years later, I suddenly got a phone call from Johnny Depp's office asking if I would come and meet him to discuss a book which he just bought, a supernatural love story set in the 1920s. We immediately decided to make this movie [*Inamorata*] together, and I hope we will succeed one of these days as I will make a brilliant and very scary movie out of it. It's very hard to get good things made at the moment.

*What's* **Inamorata** *about?*

It takes place in the 1920s and it's based supposedly on a real love story between a very beautiful and wealthy medium and a young professor's assistant from a university's psychic research center. This is a supernatural

**Medak directing today (courtesy Peter Medak).**

love story; it's very sexy and at the same time very chilling in a subtle way. I'm not going to give the rest of the plot away.

*Do you prefer the supernatural to the more gory* **Hostel**-*type film?*

Yeah, I hate all that. But I love scaring people and I love doing it in a very subtle way when basically hardly anything happens on the screen but it's psychologically in the mind of the audience.

*There are rumors that* **The Changeling** *was going to be remade. Will you have any involvement?*

Yes I would, because if anybody is going to remake this film of mine which is quoted as one of the greatest ghost stories ever made, I would prefer that it is me who is redoing it.

*What was it like working with George C. Scott?*

He was absolutely magical. He was incredibly powerful and simple. I really had a memorable time with him and Melvyn Douglas, who was also a legend. Those kinds of experiences last forever, for the rest of your life. Also my wonderful D.P. John Coquillon, and my set designer Trevor Williams, who were both English, bless their hearts. The producers were great because they backed my ideas completely no matter what the extra cost, especially when I insisted on building the enormous composite set of the interior of the entire house including the exteriors. I'm extremely proud of the film, which is one of the four or five best ghost stories ever made.

*What was it like working on* **Species II**?

Well, *Species II* was quite an experience. I did it because I've never done that kind of effects-driven show, and I didn't know about special effects because every movie I did was more dependent on the performance of the actors. And I thought it would be a great chance to learn about it all. Then when I got the job I just really went at it, and it was quite a big budget—I'm not sure if we actually spent all the money [*laughs*] because I don't know where the money went in the end. But it was something I enjoyed very much, it was something I'd never done before and I like to do things which are new and somehow stretch oneself.

In every movie I do, there's always something new and unfamiliar to learn from. For the future, everything changes nearly every day and I am currently working on five different projects but it's impossible to tell which one will be next at this point. I still think it is one of the most exciting, however difficult, brilliant journeys that I could've picked for myself and I'm grateful for the moment when I look through the camera to do another set-up.

One man and his camera: Peter Medak (courtesy Peter Medak).

# *Eric Red*

Born in Pittsburgh and raised in New York and Philadelphia, Eric Red began his career in the film industry at age 19 with his urban western short *Gunmen's Blues*, shortly followed by a second award-winning short, *Telephone*, starring Bud Cort. After attending the American Film Institute, Red got his start in Hollywood by penning two classic horror thrillers, *The Hitcher* starring Rutger Hauer and C. Thomas Howell and *Near Dark* starring Bill Paxton and Lance Henriksen. The first feature he wrote and directed was the crime thriller *Cohen and Tate*, starring Roy Scheider and Adam Baldwin. That film was an official selection of the Sitges Festival in 1989.

Over the past two decades Red has written and/or directed numerous major films in the horror, thriller and western genres. His scripts include *Blue Steel* starring Jamie Lee Curtis and *The Last Outlaw* starring Mickey Rourke. He wrote and directed *Body Parts* starring Jeff Fahey, *Undertow* starring Lou Diamond Phillips and Mia Sara and *Bad Moon* starring Mariel Hemingway. Red also works in the comic and graphic novel field, where he recently created and wrote the successful sci-fi horror comic series *Containment* for IDW Publishing. Red's latest film as a writer-director is the classy supernatural thriller *100 Feet*, starring Famke Janssen and Bobby Cannavale. Red and his wife Meredith live in Los Angeles.

---

*Would you tell us a little about your influences growing up?*

I saw *Psycho* when I was nine years old. I was taken to it by my mother and grandmother, and the film probably set me on a course for life.

*What in particular stayed with you?*

I think it was the particular adrenaline level of fear that film induced in me. The death of the main character so early on in the picture scared the shit out of me and the final twist with the mother sent me running screaming out of the theater, or so I'm told.

*At what point did you decide you wanted to be involved in writing and directing films?*

It had pretty much been a goal throughout my teenage years. I got

Eric Red early on in his career (courtesy Eric Red).

serious about it when I was 19. I wrote a feature screenplay and spent about a year trying to raise the financing for it. When that didn't work, I took a look at what I had and realized I had enough to make a really solid short film, so I decided to do that. I wrote a script in about three days, a modern western in a bar, set in Jersey. I used the crew that I'd put together for the feature, and that film was kind of my film school. It was called *Gunmen's Blues*—it was basically a two-character film with two other supporting characters, about a duel between an old hitman and a young street kid who thinks he's a cowboy. I cast the late Darwin Joston, who was just a terrific actor, to play the old hitman; I noticed him in a John Carpenter film called *Assault on Precinct 13*. I liked him very much. My first short film had special effects, it had action, it had a lot of psychological drama, and I spent about a year after we shot it editing it, and it finally got national distribution on a television show back then called *Nightline*. That's what got me started.

*The initial concept for* **The Hitcher** *came from picking up a hitchhiker yourself.*

No. I'm not quite sure how that story came about. I always thought the opening of the Doors' song "Riders on the Storm" was a great opening for a film. I'd been thinking about that, and I left New York and drove to Texas. Along the way I used that as a starting point and went from there.

*The character of John Ryder—when did he start to crystallize?*

For me, characters come out of the story. With *The Hitcher* I thought it would be very exciting to set the first ten minutes in a car with a kid picking up a hitchhiker whom he realizes is a killer. The first ten pages of the script, the first ten minutes of a film, are just crucially important because that's where you grab the audience's attention or you don't. I had the kid picking up this hitchhiker and the hitchhiker telling him, "I want you to stop me," and the kid throwing him out of the car; that was the seed of the character. What I tried to do with the script was escalate the tension by having the hitcher get the kid into worse and worse problems, leading to the framing of the kid for the killings. The character of John Ryder evolved out of the story, with everything he does to Jim Halsey about making the kid strong enough to stop him, to kill him. That's where the relationship came from.

*When you sit down to write something like that, do you hear the dialogue in your head, or do you have to really work at it?*

There are certain lines that come easily, other ones are hard work. A lot of the dialogue comes from the characters and the situation. I try to figure out the conflict between the characters and then the dialogue follows from there. I try to keep it terse in film scripts.

*How did it go from there to production?*

I was very young, in my early twenties, when I wrote the script. I didn't know anybody in Hollywood, and I didn't have an agent. So I sent out query letters from Texas to basically about 300 companies that were listed in Hollywood Film Production Office. I sent one to a producer called Phil Feldman, who produced *The Wild Bunch*—I thought maybe he'd be someone who'd be interested. It actually wound up by accident going to a different Feldman on the lot, a producer named Ed Feldman, and he responded. That was very exciting. I actually got quite a large response from people I queried, agreeing to read the script. There was at the time, I presume there still is, a policy for production companies not to read unsolicited material that isn't submitted by agents. But it was not difficult to bypass all that and sell the script myself. It was a process; they bought it six months after they first got the script and optioned it, then it went into production. So things moved fast.

*When did Rutger Hauer become attached to it? I've read that you imagined other people playing John Ryder rather than Rutger.*

When I'm writing a character in a script, I never imagine an actor, unless the casting is a really specific creative component. And when I'd written that one I certainly did not see Rutger Hauer in the role.

*Sam Elliott did a screen test. What do you think the movie would have been like if he'd starred in it?*

I think he would have been great.

*Are real-life horrors, things that could happen (like picking up a hitcher), more frightening than the stalk 'n' slash scenarios?*

I try to make characters as real as possible. To imagine what a serial killer, or in other films a werewolf or vampire, would be like if they really existed. All of these characters spring from human mythology and psychology, which is why they endure in our consciousness, and I try to explore that. That's usually the way I develop them.

*How did you get on with* **Hitcher** *director Robert Harman?*

Robert was a first-time director and he had a lot of help, which he needed.

*You also built up a kind of psychological connection between the two characters. Was there meant to be a hint of the supernatural?*

No, there was nothing supernatural between the two characters. But the attempt was to create a sense that there was, yet at the same time having it all be explainable.

*The movie appeared on Bravo TV's* **100 Scariest Movie Moments.**

I'm always glad when these films connect with audiences.

*Does it make you feel proud that it's still as popular today as it was 20 years ago?*

Yeah, I think the picture holds up.

*What did you make of the 2003 sequel?*

I never saw it. It was straight-to-DVD crap. The original picture was tied up in litigation for almost 15 years, because of one of the producers, so there was no real shot to ever do anything legitimate sequel-wise. Of course, the film was remade in 2007. I hate the current remake trend, because there's no creative component involved and it's just an attempt to recycle a brand name. What I really resent is that people buy the rights to films I made and then try to attach their name to the film in a kind of ownership situation. We made *The Hitcher*

Rutger Hauer as John Ryder in *The Hitcher* (1986, TriStar Entertainment; courtesy John Gullidge).

and *Near Dark* and these were original movies. It took a lot of work and creative risk to establish the branding, so it really pisses me off when people come along and just buy the rights to the titles, trying to take authorship credit for them in the remake, counting on the short memory of audiences. It's cannibalistic, the way savages used to eat the flesh of their victims in order to gain their strength. I should also mention that the original *Hitcher* made more money than the remake did. Had to get that dig in.

*The writers of the remake seemed to follow your storyline quite closely.*

Oh, I couldn't have cared less. I was surprised and a little disappointed by the lack of quality of the remake. But to take a script we made 20 years before—I read the script because I *had* to for the Writers Guild arbitration—and not add any real new material just showed they didn't know what they were doing. I was quite taken aback by how closely it followed all of the chain of events and had the same action scenes. But I thought that at the same time the changes they did make were meretricious; they turned one character, the kid Jim Halsey, into two which really diminished the tension of the piece. If you've got a buddy on the road and you're being chased by a psycho killer, there's a lot less tension than if it's just you, just one person. And I thought they took out all the psychological level that was in the original script, so I didn't think they ended up with much. But again I haven't seen the movie so…

*What did you think of Sean Bean, who played the title role in the remake?*

He's a good actor. And I haven't seen the film so I can't say, but I think Rutger Hauer would be a pretty tough act to follow, just because of his superhuman sense of menace and physical presence that he had when back then when we did *The Hitcher*. I think it would have been pretty tough to be as scary.

*Hauer has that quality, you don't know which way he's going to go.*

Rutger as an actor had a great feel for bad guys. That was really, I think, what he did well. He could make a bad guy or an anti-hero empathetic and likable, and would steal the movie. He was certainly at his prime when he did *The Hitcher*.

*What was the experience of writing with Kathryn Bigelow like on* **Near Dark***?*

Well, we wrote the script together.

*Whose concept was it initially?*

It was both of us.

*Why did you feel the vampire mythos was ripe for reinvention at that time?*

I don't think we thought of it like that. It was just the idea of doing a contemporary vampire western and what vam-

Lance Henriksen and Jenette Goldstein in *Near Dark* (1987, Anchor Bay; courtesy John Gullidge).

pires would be like if they really existed. They would have to keep a low profile, they would have to travel, stay out of the daylight, and that sort of "American outlaw" aspect just came out of the characters organically.

*The word "vampire" is never mentioned once, though, is it? Was that a conscious thing to get away from the usual trappings of the subgenre?*

Yes, we just figured people would probably get it [*laughs*].

**Jenny Wright and Adrian Pasdar in** *Near Dark* **(1987, Anchor Bay; courtesy John Gullidge).**

*At its core, what do you feel* **Near Dark** *is about: family, love, relationships?*

Yeah, it definitely deals with the family aspect, where they take care of one another and there's loyalty. They keep together to survive, much like Jesse James and other American outlaw icons. They don't tend to stand alone.

*You've said that you didn't think the movie quite lived up to the potential of the script. Would you elaborate on that?*

Oh, I think the film lived up to the script. I wasn't happy with all the casting. I didn't care for Adrian Pasdar. His casting somewhat shifted emphasis of audience identification to the vampires. In the script they were likable, but they were still the bad guys. But I think Adrian Pasdar was uncharismatic and not enough of a young, sexy leading man. We had Johnny Depp audition for the picture and he did a terrific screen test for Caleb with Patricia Arquette as Mae that just ruled. I think the movie missed out on proper audience identification because of Pasdar's casting.

*You've mentioned the possibility of a sequel set years afterwards.*

It's been talked about, but a lot of things get talked about.

**Cohen and Tate**—*where did that premise come from?*

I'd done a few short films and I was ready to [direct] a feature after *The Hitcher* and *Near Dark*. At that point in my career I loved the whole concept of doing a tight little road picture, but a night one. The whole concept came really from the idea of two hitmen who kidnap a little kid and the possibilities in the conflict of the kid turning them against each other to survive, until the killers do what they do best and kill one another. I like taking—then and now—just a few characters and putting them in a contained psychological conflict situation. The key for me is a clean *mano a mano* confrontation.

*The tension and claustrophobia come from being in the same place.*

Yeah, which presents filmmaking challenges, because of course if you have three people in a car, you have to shoot it a little more elaborately to make it visually interesting for the audience. But it was an enthralling movie to make, basically, as first-time director. I filmed on location outside of Houston, at rural truck stops and gas stations. And working with Roy Scheider was an absolute thrill. The company didn't think that we'd get him for the movie, but I thought we would because even though the character was a bad guy and hired killer, he had kind of "samurai aspects" to him. So that was one of the most exciting aspects of making the film for me, to see Scheider bring that character to life.

*Is that always a thrill, when you see a character that you've written brought to life by a really good actor?*

Oh boy, yeah. I guess it's the difference between a play and a screenplay; because a screenplay only usually gets one shot. A play gets performed by many different actors, but with a movie you pretty much get one star, one actor who's going to embody the role. Although I've actually had the same role played twice, once by Rutger Hauer, once by Sean Bean, but from the script I've read the character is so diminished it's difficult to see it as the same thing.

*Tell us a little about* **Blue Steel.**

I had very little to do with the film. It was one of three scripts that Kathryn Bigelow and I wrote. I directed the third one, *Undertow*. Other than suggesting Jamie Lee Curtis, who was my idea for the movie, I just wrote the script. I was doing *Cohen and Tate* at the time, so had no involvement.

*In the script, was she set up as a character who becomes hardened by her experiences?*

Well, the thing with *Blue Steel* is that it was *The Hitcher* with a chick. *Near Dark* was kind of its own thing. The formula for *Blue Steel* was much simpler, although I think in some ways audiences find a woman in the victim role more palatable than a man. So I think there may have been a little more substance for Jamie Lee than there was for Tommy Howell [*laughs*]. It follows very closely that *Hitcher* type of film. It's different—it's different characters, different settings—but still follows that formula.

*Where did the initial idea for* **Body Parts** *come from?*

The story was based on a book by Pierre Boileau and Thomas Narcejac, who are two terrific French thriller authors who worked in the '50s, '60s, '70s, and were pretty much at the top of their field at the time. They wrote the novels that *Vertigo* and *Diabolique* were based on. I read a log line of this book called *Choice Cuts*, which basically involved a killer whose body parts were put onto several different people, all of whom mysteriously died. It made me want to investigate the book, so I did. It turned out this had a 20-year history of development at studios. When we finally arbitrated the writers' credit, it had been through all kinds of writers including people like Robert Benton and all kinds of incorrect story approaches. But I just thought the high concept and set-up were great, and I managed to muscle it into production over at Paramount. The thing that I love, then and now, about *Body Parts* is its combination of a psychological thriller on one hand and splatter film on the other. You have a protagonist who loses his arm and doesn't know if his personality changes come from just the traumatic accident or the fact that there was some sort of transference of the killer whose limb he has attached. That was a terrific mystery, the material presented a great opportunity for gore and action and limbs being ripped off. It was a perfect blend.

*Is it true there were some gore sequences that didn't make it into the final cut?*

There were, yes. The biggest one was a scene in which Jeff Fahey saw his severed arm on the freeway, after the crash—and a truck runs over it. It's up online so you can find it if you search on www.joblo.com/arrow, because we haven't had a special features DVD edition yet. Paramount released a bare bones DVD, although I will say that the transfer of the film itself was terrific. It looked and sounded beautiful, a fantastic widescreen anamorphic and sound dub, so I was very pleased with the DVD if not the total lack of special features.

*And was the idea rooted in a general fear of our bodies turning against us.*

Something like that. In the book that it's based on, the main character was a detective who is investigating this operation where this killer's parts were put on other people. I thought that was kind of a weak audience identification character and the fundamental flaw in the script development up to that point. The obvious point of view of the story should be someone who has, in fact, lost a limb and had it replaced. I think the premise just fired my imagination because you identify with a character who doesn't know what's wrong with him. You had this horrible accident, have someone else's arm attached and you're getting a lot angrier than you used to. Then it gave him and us the opportunity to investigate, find out the whole background and who the donor was, who the other transplant recipients were; each one of them suffered or were having different personality changes due to the transplant, some good, some bad. Is it because of the trauma of their loss of limbs or is the killer's flesh and DNA taking over? I thought the mystery had a lot of psychological legitimacy. But if the film had been done 30 years before, it would not have been able to be bloody enough. We were able to have a lot of gore—particularly for its time.

*Did you have to do a lot of research for the medical parts of it?*

Yeah. I attended a grafting operation in Toronto, at St. John's Hospital. It wasn't anything as major as the kind of operation we envisage in *Body Parts*. In fact, at the time we did *Body Parts*, those kinds of transplants were not medically feasible; the body has an immune system which rejects tissue from other bodies. But I did attend a grafting operation and observed first-hand the doctors stitching a section of the body onto a patient. They were using those giant microscopes with the twin stations that we have in the film. We actually got those machines from St. John's to use in the sequence to provide a certain level of reality. There was one interesting postscript to this movie, in terms of life imitating art. Whenever you're writing a story like this, obviously you're imagining what these things, these situations, would be like if they really happened. Remember the scene in the movie where Jeff Fahey marches into the doctor's office and demands she takes the arm off? This is a true story. Ten years later after the film came out, doctors in France were able to overcome some of the body's natural resistance to having a limb from another body put on, and performed a successful hand transplant from a donor to a recipient. Six months later the recipient went back to the doctor and demanded that the hand be taken off because he felt it belonged to someone else. So life imitated art; and we envisaged things pretty well.

*Brad Dourif's character, Lacey, was a nice counterpoint to Fahey's because he's embraced the arm, as an artist.*

Well, Lacey has nothing going for him before the transplant, he's just a kind of a hack painter. And whether it was the killer's influence on him in the new arm or simply the consequence of this incredibly traumatic maiming that jarred his creative juices, he's painting profitably and well with the new limb. So for him it's a good thing, plus he's kind of amoral; Jeff's the family man. The new arm is disrupting his life and that of his wife and children.

*How does it feel when other writers come on board to do further drafts—like Norman Snider and Larry Gross in this one?*

I actually brought them in because I didn't have time to complete the script and shoot the film. It was an unusual case where we had, once the film was set up, a start date that was just several months away. There was simply no way I could focus properly on writing the script and prep and oversee the complex production as a director. It actually was useful to have multiple writers on it.

*If you get the choice of which writers to use, does that make it easier to hand over a little bit of control?*

I supervised every aspect of the script, but I was excited to see what the writers contributed and brought to the table. And remember, this script was based on a novel to begin with. It wasn't an original screenplay. Had it been an original script, I probably would not have relinquished any writership over it, but this project began as previously existing material.

*How hard was it to find the right makeup people and to work with the prosthetics?*

Everything was carefully worked out, application time and so on. There were also elements of animatronics that we had. The special makeup effects were prepared in advance so that it was mostly ready once we got started.

*Your movies take archetypal horror subjects, like werewolves and vampires and witches, and give them a fresh spin. Has that been a conscious thing in your career?*

I like to imagine what these people or these creatures would be like if they really existed, that's the logic I go by when developing the characters. That's what excites me, I think, about mythical icons. They're all based on elements of human nature, which is why they're fascinating. My approach is always to deal with these characters as if these are real people, and events like they could really happen. Now, I'm not saying, for instance, that werewolves aren't unreal, but I approach them in as convincing a manner as possible.

*So with* **100 Feet,** *is that your take on the ghost story—to try and make that as real as possible?*

Yeah, and also it's a psychological haunting as well as a physical haunting. It's the story of a woman who's under house arrest for the self-confessed murder of her husband. She's basically sentenced for about a year to stay in the house, their house, and she's given an ankle bracelet that only allows her to move 100 feet. The husband's ghost is in the house with her, and goes at her in every way he can. And he doesn't want to kill her. I mean, *ultimately* he does, but he's trying to inflict as much punishment as possible. There were so many psychological elements to the story that were fun to work with: There's the woman's initial fear of the situation; then her finally deciding no, this is my house. I think she deserves it [*laughs*]. Finally she resolves, "I'm going to stay here, you're going to go." She has to figure out a solution to this knotty problem: how can she possibly rid herself of the spirit? It was a lot of fun to work on. It's a bit like *Cohen*. You've got basically a woman in a house with a ghost, like that film had two guys in a car with a kid, and the challenges were to make that contained situation exciting.

*It's similar to films like* **Panic Room** *and* **The Grudge**, *it has that kind of flavor to it.*

No, it's very different to *The Grudge*, for one big reason. I mean, I particularly love the original Japanese films, *Ringu* and *Ju-on*, but I guess it's very much part of that mythology over there that the ghosts in those movies are unreasonably

**Famke Janssen with Eric Red on the set of *100 Feet* (2008, 100 Feet Productions; courtesy Eric Red).**

malevolent and awful. In other words, you don't have to do anything to them, you just have to be in the wrong place at the wrong time. That's very scary and that's very evil. *100 Feet* is a different ghost story because it's very personal. Marnie [Famke Janssen] did kill her husband, and is a flawed character. She should have figured out ways to handle her domestic problems other than killing her spouse. So the ghost has what you might call a legitimate grudge, a justifiable beef. She killed him, and she was his wife. And when during the haunting his ex-wife gets involved with a local boy romantically, the ghost is not happy.

*Have you always had an interest in the paranormal?*

This one started with me wanting to do a ghost story just because it was a genre I hadn't tackled before, and I tried to find a hook for it. There were a couple of high-profile house arrests in the U.S. in the news over the last couple of years, namely Martha Stewart. I thought that whole premise was something that could be really good combined with a ghost story. The characters and story came pretty quickly out of that.

*What was Janssen like to work with?*

Total pro. Famke had a big job, she was in every scene and almost every shot, and she did one or two takes every time. She had tremendous preparation and energy, and delivered the goods.

*You've compared your new project* **Nightlife** *to* **Near Dark**. *Is that what fans can expect?*

*Nightlife* is very different from *Near Dark*, similar only in that it's a believable and convincing approach to vampires that imagines what vampires might be like if they actually existed. This one is a contemporary urban film, set in San Francisco. It's a love triangle between two sisters and a vampire. And it's a very different kind of animal, except that it's wild and realistic and very psychological.

*Your zombie graphic novel* **Containment**—*where did the idea of mixing space and the living dead come from?*

I wanted to do a space story, something set on a spaceship, and something that had not been done before. I like the idea that if you have zombies on Earth, they're only a

Eric Red today (courtesy Eric Red).

limited threat, but a spaceship is such a fragile life support system that the threat is increased exponentially. If you have zombies in a shopping mall and they smash through a wall, you go to the next room or run out into the street. But on a spaceship, if a zombie smashes through an airlock, you're going to fatally depressurize the ship, get turned inside out and die instantly. The set-up is fraught with possibilities for jeopardy. Plus, I really wanted to do a graphic novel, which was a very, very interesting but labor-intensive experience, because it's like writing a screenplay and a shot list ... you have to map all the comic panels out just like a shot list. But it was a very organic extension from directing a movie, where you design storyboards.

*Did you find it opened things up? Obviously you have to rein things in when you're making a movie, but in a graphic novel you can do much more.*

Yeah. And there's no MPAA and no ratings systems, so it's uncensored in terms of extremely graphic gore.

*Are you going to do more?*

Yeah.

*Finally, do you have any advice for people trying to break into movie writing?*

Get it done and get it read, because I think that a lot of writers don't always understand that half the job is writing the script, the other half is making sure it gets read where it needs to get read. There's a lot of hustle involved. Some writers fail to properly to push their own work and wait for somebody else, an agent or whoever, to do it. That's a mistake.

*You have to become like a salesman.*

You do. Writers shouldn't count on the quality of the script alone to get it read or made. You have to be very proactive about getting the picture set up. And here's the good news: It never gets easier.

# *Tim Sullivan*

Tim Sullivan began his career as a teenager pumping fake blood for the cult horror flick *The Deadly Spawn* (1983). This brought him to New York University where he studied film and wrote the music news for MTV. Upon graduation, Tim served in various capacities on *Three Men and a Baby*, *Cocktail*, *Coming to America* and *Godfather III*, then co-produced the independent hits *If Looks Could Kill* and *America Exposed*. In 1990, Tim moved to LA where he worked in development at New Line Cinema for five years. There he co-produced *Detroit Rock City* (1999), and also found himself yet again pumping fake blood—this time for Gene Simmons of the rock group KISS. Having formed New Rebellion Entertainment, Tim made his directorial debut with the Lions Gate horror-comedy *2001 Maniacs* (2005), followed by the hip hop fright fest *Snoop Dog's Hood of Horror* (2006). With these admittedly over-the-top, decidedly un–P.C. "splatsticks" under his belt, for his 2006 follow-up *Driftwood* the filmmaker decided to tackle another type of horror: the post–Columbine American trend of privately owned and operated "Attitude Adjustment Camps" for youths deemed troubled and problematic by their parents. A complete flip in vibe from previous efforts, *Driftwood* is a character-driven, supernatural teen thriller starring Ricky Ullman and Talan Torriero that has been described as "*Stand By Me* meets *Ghost Story*." Next up, *2001 Maniacs*; a graphic novel from Avatar Press followed by *Beverly Hellbillys*, its much anticipated and demanded sequel. After that, Sullivan will return to more subtle and elegant horror with *Brothers of the Blood*, a haunting vampire romance starring British sensation Mitch Hewer of *Skins*.

---

*How did you get into horror?*

It's interesting, I started at the tender age of five years old [*laughs*]. Here in the States, the golden age of horror was the late '60s; there was a television show called *Creature Features* that used to run the old classic Universal horror movies every Saturday night. *Famous Monsters of Filmland* magazine was in its heyday, and the Aurora monster models were more popular than ever. *Dark Shadows* was a number one phenomenon of afternoon soap opera. So I guess I was just ready for it. I caught *Dracula* for the first time on *Creature Features*, much to my parents' displeasure. And I knew in a way, because they hadn't wanted me to see *Dracula*, that it must have been some kind of Pandora's Box they didn't want me to open. But I did, and I was thrilled, scared and yet seduced at the same time, which is I guess is what vampires are meant to do to you. Lugosi worked his magic on me; it was a far cry from *Sesame Street* [*laughs*]. It was a new world for me and I wanted to spend more time in it. So I started watching *Creature Features* and *Bride of Frankenstein* followed, then *WereWolf of London*.

The next thing you know, I discovered *Famous Monsters* at the newsstand, about 1970.

I remember being fascinated because it pretty much introduced you to the people behind the monsters: the Lon Chaneys and the Karloffs, the Vincent Prices and the Christopher Lees. Not only the actors, but the filmmakers: the Tod Brownings, the James Whales, Jack Pierces and the Ray Harryhausens. And it was like, "Wait a minute, this is a job you can do?" [*Laughs*] "I can grow up and be a monster maker? For real?" So I just pursued it with a vengeance and it seemed like every way I turned, fate was helping me nurture that interest. You turn on the TV every day when you get home from school and there's *Dark Shadows*, Barnabas Collins. Then another huge influence on me was, in the early '70s they started reprinting the old EC Comics from the '50s. Amicus had made a film version of *Tales from the Crypt*, which was a British film. So this was cool because comic books were such an American tradition and creation, especially EC. They sort of had a very American film noir accent, and yet the Brits were the first to make the film version with Peter Cushing, Ralph Richardson and Joan Collins; I just loved it. Then I started reading the comic books—and they had adaptations of H.P. Lovecraft and Ray Bradbury. It encouraged me to read the original text. So that influenced my style of writing more than anything else. The EC comics—*Vault of Horror*, *Tales from the Crypt*, *Haunted Fear*—taught me how to be a screenwriter. Because, if you look at it, it's really a screenplay format. You have the exposition in the box at the top; then you've got the dialogue which is almost like in a bubble, which is how you write a script; then you've got an illustration which is like a storyboard. Little did I know it, but I was in training to become Tim Sullivan, monster maker [*laughs*].

Tim Sullivan. © New Rebellion/Tim Sullivan (courtesy Tim Sullivan).

*You started your career in your teens on the set of* **The Deadly Spawn.**

[*Laughs*] That was trial by fire. I was 15 years old and growing up in New Jersey, and it turned out that my art teacher's brother, ten years older than me, was making low-budget horror movies, right in his backyard in New Jersey. He took me under his wing; John Dods became a mentor to me. I was just willing to do anything, and he and the producers took advantage of it. It would be freezing cold weather and I'd be there lying on my back, with the Deadly Spawn puppet, trying to manipulate the wires and the rubber while they were hosing me down with water to simulate lightning and rain. And I would catch pneumonia, I'd be at death's door, but I'd show up the next day to pump the blood in another scene where I'd be covered in sticky goo that dyed my skin red for a week [*laughs*]. I was just happy, quite honestly. I wanted this so bad that I would've done anything to make movies and tell monster stories. It was just the best experience of my life. To this day, I am very close friends with John Dods and [producer] Ted Bohus. We reunited for the *Deadly Spawn* DVD so we kind of came full circle.

*What would you consider your first big break in the industry?*

I would say that had to be *Detroit Rock City*. That would be my great experience because it took my love of the rock band KISS and made that into a reality. I've been very lucky in that from the obsessions of my youth—KISS, Freddy Krueger, monsters, rock 'n' roll—I've been able to create something that I got paid for, sometimes not much but I still got paid for it. And able to make something that is out there and will last forever, like *Detroit Rock City*. To be the KISS fan who made the KISS movie: it was incredible! But having gone from the $80,000 budget of *Deadly Spawn* to twenty years later the $15 million budget of *Detroit Rock City*—it was a different playing field and it really taught me a new set of skills. After I did *Detroit Rock City* I realized that I was now in the major leagues and that it was time for me to direct my own movie.

*On your Myspace page you have a lot of pictures of celebrities you've met—Leonardo DiCaprio, Halle Berry, Clint Eastwood. Are you essentially a fanboy at heart?*

Oh, unashamedly so [*laughs*]. I don't know why, but certain people in the industry trash that. "Tim, you've gotta be careful because you come across as a fanboy." And I should be ashamed of that? Y'know what? No, I'm not. I wear it on my sleeve, I wear it proudly; a badge of honor. I am and always will be a fan. I worked with KISS, and it was hard sometimes to separate the men from the myth. Here I am directing Robert Englund and when we're working together, I can say I'm a director and I'm working with Robert on the film; but then sometimes we're sitting there having a glass of wine, and I just look at him and I go, "Fuck, that's Freddy Krueger!" I think that, quite honestly, if I have an appeal to the fans, it's that I am one of them. When I meet the people who have seen my films at festivals and conventions and on Myspace, we're speaking the same language. I don't look at them like I'm high and mighty Tim Sullivan. We're one—and that's really me on Myspace. I talk to the fans every day, I know a lot of them now and they have become friends. I was a fan, then became a journalist, and one of the best ways to get to work with somebody is to interview them first [*laughs*]. I wrote for *Fangoria* and I wanted to meet Gene Simmons so I decided to interview him. I wanted to meet Robert Englund so I decided to interview him. I turned that interview into a friendship and into a collaboration. I'm not ashamed of being a fanboy. If I was a member of KISS I'd probably be.... Well there's the God of Thunder, the Lover, the Catman, the Spaceman ... I'd be the Fanboy [*laughs*].

*What was it like the first time you met Robert?*

Actually, I knew Robert from New Line. I had worked with New Line, and it was at the Christmas party where Robert and I were off in a corner talking about horror movie trivia. Robert is an encyclopedia. Talk about a fanboy—that guy knows films inside and out, from silents to obscure Belgian horror films, to the latest cool film at the cinema last week. That guy knows everything. And we bonded there. Gene Simmons, when I first met him ... I didn't talk to him about rock, I talked to him about *Bride of Frankenstein* and *King Kong* because they were his favorite movies. So I would say that a lot of the professional relationships I have—including John Landis, Gene Simmons and Robert—are based on the fact that we are mutual fans, we're film aficionados.

*It took a long time to get* **2001 Maniacs** *to the screen.*

Yes, it was a long road. But it's funny, it's called *2001 Maniacs* because Chris Kobin and I wrote it in 2000. There was an immediate reaction, and it went into pre-production, so we figured it would come out in 2001; we thought, "How cool would that be, to have it come out in 2001?" That's why it's called *2001 Maniacs*. We had it all set up to go. On the day that we were signing the final deal with the film company, it was 9/11—and obviously we woke up to the news of what had happened so there was a lot more on our minds than *2001 Maniacs*. It turned out, though, that the company we were dealing with had their corporate office in the World Trade Center, so the deal fell apart, along with everything else. I mean, you didn't even know at that time whether you'd be alive the next day, it was such a horrible period and the last thing on anyone's mind was making a little bloody

The Reverend Jonas (Hugh Casey) in *2001 Maniacs* (2005, New Rebellion; courtesy Tim Sullivan).

monster movie. But, like everything else, you pick yourself up and life goes on. I had to really think: Do I still wanna make this movie?

And I thought, ironically, maybe this is a metaphor for 9/11. It's the story of a town that's the victim of a terrorist attack, and the Southerners in this little town pledge vengeance against the Northerners who attacked them. They become obsessed with this quest for revenge and become lost in limbo trying to avenge this attack. So I thought, "Y'know what? I'm getting a little statement out here in the guise of a splatstick," and we kept moving forward. But it seemed that every step of the way there was an obstacle. The second time I got the movie ready to go, we had cast, the costumes, the set built. Then the week before, the Santa Ana winds came along and burned down all our sets, here in California. It felt like I was never going to make this movie. But I just sat down, and finally we got third funding, and this time we found a place in Georgia, so it was either "three strikes I'm out" or "third time's a charm." Luckily, third time was a charm and the movie finally got made, three years after we set out to make it.

*How much of an inspiration was the Herschell Gordon Lewis original?*

Everything revolved around that. When I first saw Herschell's movies I was in high school. They had no grindhouse cinemas in New Jersey, they were in New York, and I used to take the train to New York and tell my mom I was going to see *Disney on Ice* or something like that, then go and see the Herschell Gordon Lewis films and the Russ Meyer films. They were not great films, let's face it: they're not really well-made, they're not really well-acted, there's a lot of things to criticize about them. But, they had an attraction. It was almost like this "I dare you to keep watching attitude" that affected me. I imagine if it affected me in the '70s it must have really blown people's minds in the '60s. I never could forget Herschell's movies, especially *Two Thousand Maniacs*. There was just something about that film, something about all these people standing around, with grins on their faces, watching all these horrible things happen. So when I decided to direct, it was perfect timing because a guy named Chris Kobin literally walked off the street into my production office and said he had the rights to remake the films of Herschell Gordon Lewis, and a light bulb went on over my head.

*Have you ever met Lewis?*

Oh yes, I've met him several times, and the guy is quite remarkable. He's a sweet guy, a marketing genius. In fact, he really made his bread and butter from doing marketing. He has retired, and he doesn't really have anything to do with films. In fact, he didn't actually have the rights to his films; those rights were held by producer David Friedman, who's like this Barnum of exploitation films. So Chris had gotten the rights from Dave. Herschell really wasn't involved in my film; he read the script and gave it the thumbs up, he basically just said, "Surprise me, go have fun with it." I don't think he expected it to do as well as it has. It's become quite a bit of a phenomenon.

*How long did* 2001 Maniacs *take?*

It took me and Chris Kobin about three weeks to write it, and we had three weeks to shoot it. I wish I had more time to shoot, but that's all we had. It's very interesting, in those six years only three weeks was spent writing and three were spent making it. The rest of the time was just trying to get it made and trying to get it filmed, and trying to promote it.

*Are you happy with the finished film?*

I'm very, very, very happy with the finished product. Because it was my first time directing, there were a lot of people looking over my shoulder. Luckily that hasn't happened with my subsequent films. Everyone has good intentions and everyone has an opinion, but I truly believe that when you're making a film, there needs to be one person who says, "This is the final decision." On the first *Maniacs*, we had a lot of people who thought they were that guy. I think the biggest concern that they had was the combination of horror and humor. Now from day one, to me, this film was a horror comedy: The whole concept was that when it's scary, it's scary, and when it's funny, it's funny. I think people were starting to second guess that. So there are some things in the film that I wish weren't, there were some things that are not in the film that I wish were. My favorite scene in the movie is not in it; it went out on DVD in the deleted scenes. It's a scene with Robert and his two sons and Jezebel; one of Robert's sons—Lester—has knitted Jezebel a little sweater, and Robert's not too happy about that: "You've done knit Jezebel a sweater? Jezebel *is* a God-damned sweater!" I love that scene and that's Robert's favorite scene, and my producers just thought that it was too funny. That's the point, it's supposed to be funny. "But this is a horror film!" "No, it's a horror *comedy*...."

My other biggest regret, the thing that really pissed me off: I absolutely hate the opening scene of the movie, because I didn't do it. I've never said this before, but at this point I'll say it, because I'm just tired of the subject. The original opening of the film was with John Landis and with Dave Friedman, the original producer. It's an awesome scene that everybody loves. What happened was, we ran out of time. I originally wrote the opening of the film to be in a classroom with lots of students and all this and all that, but when we were shooting in Georgia, we were shooting in this Civil War re-enactment town, and we had scheduled 17 days there and then the final day would be at a local college. But we were running out of time and we knew there was no way we were ever going to be able to leave the location, so I had to figure out a way to shoot that opening scene there. And we didn't have a big college classroom, there was an office that was used for the administration for the Civil War re-enactment town.

So I came up with the idea of turning this into the dean's office, and have it as quirky and creepy as possible, thunder and lightning outside, and have John Landis there; it would be sort of an homage to the *Animal House* scene where Dean Wormer is admonishing the kids. John said, "Let's have Dave Friedman there

Jaye Gillespie (center) and Robert Englund (right) in *2001 Maniacs* (2005, New Rebellion; courtesy Tim Sullivan).

and have him be this weird Prof. Lewis, as a nod to H.G. Lewis, with this trick sword." We did the scene and it was wonderful, everyone loved it. When we got back to L.A., that was one of the first scenes I cut together. But some of the producers just couldn't get away from the script, they just had it in their mind that this movie needed a bigger, more traditional opening with lots of students to show production values; "Let's show up front that we've got a big movie." I was like, "It's not a big movie, it's a small little independent remake of Herschell Gordon Lewis, and we've got John Landis for Christ's sake!" But I lost the battle. They decided that they were going to spend all this money ... I think they spent as much money on that one scene as I had taken to shoot half the film. If I ever get a chance to go back, I'd love to put that Landis scene back in the way it was meant to be. It's on the deleted scenes of the DVD, but I would love to finish it, have some ADR, some music, and put it in the beginning of the film where it was supposed to be, the way it was meant to be.

*Is there anything else you'd put in the director's cut?*

Yes there is. I was a little disappointed also with the way the character of Ricky was presented. Originally the *Camp Blood* website had attacked the film and attacked me for what they thought was a very homophobic portrayal of a gay character—Ricky as played by Brian Gross. And when you have a gay character who ends up getting rammed up the ass with a barbecue spike, you're kind of opening yourself up to criticism. Now, it upset me because I *am* gay, and that death I did design—but the death is not saying the gay guy got what he deserves. The death is a complete mockery of bigotry; these bigots are so fucked up that if they killed a gay guy, this is how they would kill him. That's what I'm saying. Well, the way I shot it, he was a playful character, and certain cuts were made against my will that turned him into a more predatory character. The perfect example of one of the things I would put back in my director's cut is when our three main heroes first arrive at the gas station. I don't think the scene works, because the scene was supposed to be poking fun at those cheesy moments in teen films when the guys first sees the girls: the cheesy music starts, the slow motion starts and you see the one girl get out of the car and she looks at the guy and the guy blushes. Then you see the other girl get out of the car and she looks at the main hero and he blushes. Then we cut to Ricky and he's like sort of grabbing the steering wheel in a very sexy way, like Jim Morrison, and he's got his black nail polish and he kind of winks, and it's a very sexy shot, and we cut to Nelson who sort of blushes and looks away.

I really like that, because first of all it tells you exactly who this guy is, and when we watch a film the audience sees the movie through the eyes of the hero. So when the hero is flirted with by a gay or bisexual character and sort of blushes and looks away, it tells our audience it's cool, this guy Ricky's cool. It's not something to be afraid of, don't be afraid of the gay guy. But what happened was, they cut those two simple frames, which changed the entire vibe of that character. They cut out the look over the steering wheel, and the reaction of Nelson. Without that, the whole joke was lost, and the whole vibe of that character was lost.

I was overjoyed with how the film turned out, and even more so considering all the pissing on the hydrants that the different producers and financiers were doing. I'm amazed how close to my vision the film actually did turn out. I thought when you make an independent film with fellow horror fans, that it would be like one big party, and I was kind of surprised. I felt the title of the film should have been *2001 Egomaniacs* [*laughs*]. When we got to the cutting room, it was like a committee meeting with 30 people in there, everybody shouting out with what they thought we should do. One of the things I really worked hard on were the murder sequences; I had storyboarded every murder years before we shot it. And the murder of Nelson, to me, it works okay. But the way it was designed and the way I wanted to cut it was so much more effective because basically, you've got a horny kid—everybody gets laid but this poor Nelson. Then the Milk Maiden [Christa Campbell] comes and that whole death, with the tube in his mouth, and the bottles, and the liquids, it's supposed to be a simulation of sex.

The whole idea is, it was meant to be the gyrating, and bucking, and she's laughing and he's gushing. The way I shot it when you see him grabbing the blanket, and his feet shaking, you're supposed to be building up to orgasm—and the very last bit is his neck bursting. Bam! The way it was 'boarded and the way it was shot, you have all these quick cuts, the rhythm. First it's slower cuts, then medium cuts and then, boom-boom, rhythm: her face, his face, the hand, this, that, then boom! His neck bursts. Orgasm! Doesn't take a genius to get that. But the "committee" decided they wanted to immediately show his neck burst, so the second after he starts bubbling, there it goes. And I was just like, "You've shot your load too early, guys." [*Laughs*] And that whole tagline, "I prefer a non-smoker!"—that wasn't me. My punchline was, you see the Milk Maiden and she's holding her bottle of acid, her jug, and she has this beautiful look on her face and she says, "I just hate a fella who can't hold his liquor." And as she says that, she moves her hand away from the jug that we thought was moonshine and the word ACID is scrawled on it. That was the tagline, and that was the payoff. They just had to put in that smoker joke. You make a film and it really does go through the hands of so many other people.

*What were your aims with* **Driftwood***?*

*Driftwood* was a wonderful experience, and everything just came together. That was in response to the trends in America post–Columbine, where you have all these Attitude

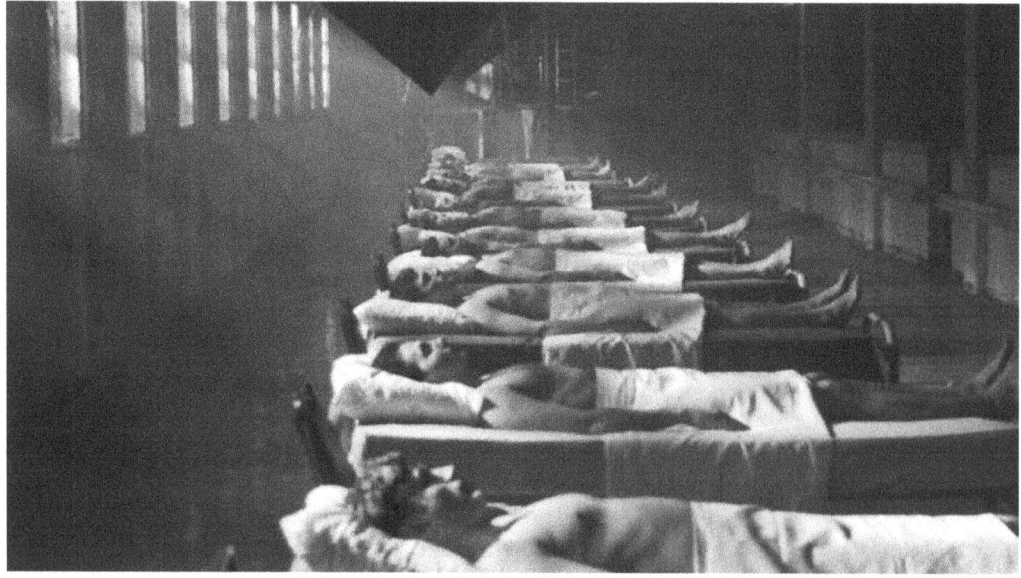

A scene from *Driftwood* (2006, New Rebellion; courtesy Tim Sullivan).

Adjustment Camps and these independent entrepreneurs who set up these camps and sell parents on the fact that, "You don't want to become the parents of the next Columbine killer!" So if you think your son may be listening to My Chemical Romance and AFI a little too much, and reading *Fangoria* or maybe likes the boy next door instead of the girl next door, then send your kids to Driftwood. And if you're under the age of 18 and your parent wants you to go on one of these things, you're screwed. These are places that completely take away your individuality, tell you who you should be, and it's just awful. I knew a kid who was sent to one of these places, I came across him in a youth group—and when he got out, the kid had his identity stolen. Maybe psychologically, having come off *Maniacs* where I'd sort of felt a victim of that, I needed to somehow tell that story. But I chose to tell it through the tale of *Driftwood*, because to me, seriously, the greatest horror is not being allowed to be who you are.

So *Driftwood* is a very character-driven story about that, and I was very lucky because I was surrounded by seasoned professionals who just believed in me, believed in the film, and decided to come down into the independent world of filmmaking from their pedestals of major filmmaking. I mean, I worked with Mike Richardson, who is the publisher of Dark Horse comics—*Sin City*,

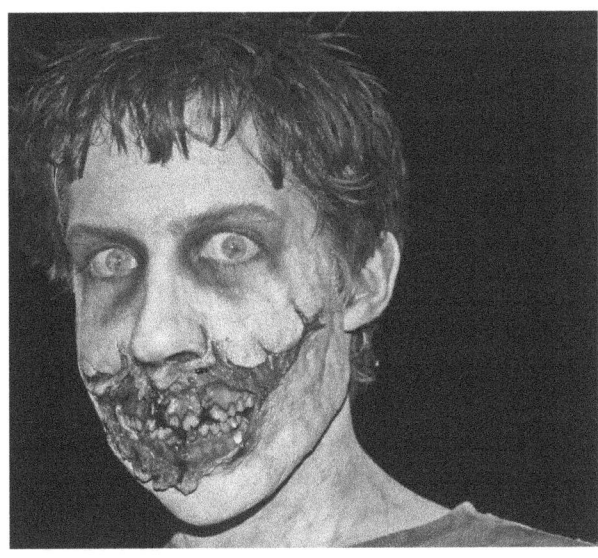

Actor Connor Ross in a *Driftwood* publicity shot (2006, New Rebellion; courtesy Tim Sullivan).

Tim Sullivan's production company is New Rebellion. © New Rebellion (courtesy Tim Sullivan).

*Hellboy* and *Alien vs. Predator*—and Bud Smith was one of the producers and co-editors of the film. Bud edited *The Exorcist, Cruising, Cat People, Sorcerer, To Live and Die in L.A.* My composer was Bill Ross, who's worked with John Williams. Every step of the way, incredible professional vets. We shot it in an abandoned juvenile prison that was 100 years old and definitely haunted. I had the best cast of young up-and-coming kids. It was just a wonderful experience and I'm very happy with how it turned out.

*What's your favorite horror movie?*

*The Exorcist.* I love it. I'm very fascinated with the concept that often the only way that we see good is to be confronted by evil.

*Where do you see yourself in a few years' time?*

People always say, "Pick somebody's career you admire and trace how they got there." Well, I look at somebody like Bill Condon, who is just a great filmmaker and a great human being and did *Dreamgirls*. Well, Bill started out doing low-budget horror movies: a great '80s cult film called *Strange Behavior*, and the follow-up *Strange Invaders*. He did *Candyman II*, then *Gods and Monsters*, and *Gods and Monsters* opened up a lot of doors for him. I would like to follow that path. I have a *Gods and Monsters* in me called *Brothers of the Blood*. It's a vampire drama, a vampire love story. I'd like to make a couple more splatsticks and then I'd like to go the way of *Gods and Monsters*.

# *Rob Zombie*

Rob Zombie is an auteur filmmaker and music artist. He has sold over 15 million albums worldwide and is one of Geffen Records' top selling and longest-running artists, winning Gold and Platinum discs. He has directed over 25 high-profile music videos and won an MTV Music Video Award for "More Human Than Human," becoming the first self-directed artist to win such an award. In 2003 he turned his hand to directing movies with *House of 1000 Corpses*, which provided horror fans with another icon in the form of Captain Spaulding (played by Sid Haig). In 2005 he released the critically acclaimed follow-up *The Devil's Rejects* and his work appeared as a trailer for a faux film called *Werewolf Women of the S.S.*, part of Quentin Tarantino and Robert Rodriguez's *Grindhouse* (2007). By this time he'd also taken on the task of writing and directing a reimagining of John Carpenter's *Halloween* for Dimension Films; it went on to take the #1 spot at the box office in its opening weekend in 2007. His most recent projects include an animated film called *The Haunted World of El Superbeasto* and *Halloween 2*, which picks up where his 2007 film left off.

---

*Where did this love of horror, and especially bizarre horror, originate?*

[*Laughs*] I'm not really sure. It's been something that has been in my life since I was such a little kid I can't even remember. In the late '60s there was kind of a big horror boom. There was a lot of the old classic stuff on TV, and there were TV shows like *The Munsters*, *The Addams Family*, *The Twilight Zone*. There was just so much horror stuff that I sucked it all up as a kid and always loved it. I don't remember ever a time when it wasn't there.

*Obviously there's influences from shows like* **The Addams Family** *and* **The Munsters** *in your work, like the video for* **Dragula** *for instance. Did anything else from the '60s influence your later work?*

I think everything influences it. The stuff that you first discover as a kid is always very significant and influential, even if you don't realize it sometimes. But I always draw on influences from back then. There's something about the first things that you're exposed to that you always, always love. Even if it's something that's crap [*laughs*], somehow it's always special to you, even if someone else hates it.

*Back then, did you have a favorite horror film?*

I think probably my favorite from back then was *King Kong*. I know that's a lot of people's favorite film but I think that might have been the first one I ever saw, so perhaps that's why. As a little kid, that just blew me away.

*Any kind of influence from your carnival background at all, especially for videos like* **Living Dead Girl***?*

That's stuff that comes into play now more than ever. As a kid I spent a lot of time on carnivals because a lot of family [members] were in that business. But when I was young, I didn't think anything of it. As a kid you're not influenced by anything, it's just your life and it just is what it is. It's only as I got older and I looked back at old pictures and books and things, that that stuff really came into play. I think whenever you sit down to work on a movie or write a script, you pull from your own life. So that's really what I'm doing with characters and situations a lot of the time.

*Which gives you more of a buzz, the performing, the writing or the directing?*

It's all incredible, because these are things I always wanted to do, and to be able to do them is amazing. I guess you probably go back and forth. If I haven't been on tour for a long time, I really miss it and really like playing live. Then if I haven't been on set making a movie in a while, I really miss *that*. But obviously I think right now making movies is a bigger thrill because it's just newer. I've been doing music for a long, long time. I mean, I've been doing movies now for almost ten years, but still, the volume of music is much bigger.

*Talking about the music, what was it like collaborating with Alice Cooper on the song "Hands of Death" ("Burn Baby Burn") for the* **X-Files** *tie-in CD* **Songs in the Key of X***?*

That was great. Those are the moments that are very exciting as you go through your career, being able to collaborate with people that you were a huge fan of. Being able to collaborate with Alice Cooper, Iggy Pop, Ozzy Osbourne, and getting to work with actors you were a big fan of, like Malcolm McDowell, these are great moments where you really feel like you've made your dreams come true, essentially.

**Musician and filmmaker Rob Zombie (courtesy Rob Zombie and Andy Gould).**

*Where did the idea for* **House of 1000 Corpses** *come from?*

That originally started off not as a movie, but as a theme park attraction. In 1999 I was working at Universal building a haunted maze for the Halloween Horror Night they do every year. I was trying to think of something to call the attraction, so I came up with this idea, "House of 1000 Corpses," and thought, "Wow, that sounds like a great haunted house." Then once I had the actual title, it started snowballing in my mind, like what would be in it, what it could be, and that just became the movie after a while.

*When did the visual image of Captain Spaulding come into your mind?*

Pretty early on. A lot of times when I'm writing a script, I do sketches of what

I think characters will look like, just for my own mind. I drew a picture of Captain Spaulding that looks almost exactly like the final character. I always wanted Sid Haig to play Captain Spaulding so I always based everything on him, even though I hadn't met him yet and I didn't know if he would do it. That was maybe around 2000.

*Is there an element of fear of clowns in there?*

I don't have any fear of clowns. I find clowns interesting because I think they're sort of scary and pathetic [*laughs*], at the same time. They're

**Captain Spaulding (Sid Haig) in** *House of 1000 Corpses* **(2003, Lions Gate Entertainment).**

depressing a lot of times, because it's a thankless job. I just think they're always fascinating.

*Do you feel that the black humor was essential in that to make the film work?*

Well, the black humor came sometimes intentionally, sometimes unintentionally. If there's one skill that you try and develop more and more as a director, it's setting the tone

**A bound Kate Norby in** *The Devil's Rejects* **(2005, Lions Gate Entertainment/Maple Pictures).**

of the film. And really trying to maintain it, because it's very hard sometimes to maintain a tone when you're shooting over weeks and weeks and weeks, and all these actors come and go, and you're shooting out of order. On that movie, it's not a comedy, but it sort of is [*laughs*]. At that point it just seemed like the most natural way for it to go, even though when I originally started I wasn't really picturing it that way. A lot of it's due to the presence of Sid Haig, who's very charismatic and funny and kind of demented. That just dictated a lot of how the movie went.

*Did the success of the character Captain Spaulding take you by surprise?*

I thought he would pop out because I knew he looked cool and he was very interesting and funny and immediately people would respond to it. I think people recognize the character more, and they don't even know which movie it's from sometimes. But the funny thing is, *House of 1000 Corpses* is almost ten years old now, and every year we sell more and more T-shirts and posters and stickers and action figures. It gets more and more popular as time goes on. I think it's the same way with Leatherface and Freddy and Jason, these characters just grow more in stature every year.

*In* **House** *and the sequel* **Devil's Rejects**, *did you always plan to add old genre stars into the mix?*

Not on purpose, but as I was writing I'd try to think, "Who do I really like, who would be good in this part?" I guess because those people were very influential to me as a kid and there were movies I loved, these were the names that came to mind. I don't really like the idea of cameos, so I never want them to play as cameos, but I'd be thinking about these people and every one of them has given at least one really significant performance in a film that is special to me. Malcolm McDowell in *A Clockwork Orange* is as great a performance as anyone has ever given in any movie. A movie like *Dawn of the Dead* is very strong to me, so working with Ken Foree is as exciting as getting some major Hollywood star, because that doesn't really matter to me. There are major people that I love, but I just go by the people I like, and they always bring something special to the table.

*You carried that over into* **Halloween** *as well.*

Yeah, some of the people in *Halloween* came back from other films. As far as new people, I've always loved Brad Dourif, Malcolm McDowell, Dee Wallace, so ... I just think of a part and go, "God, who do I love? Who's great? Oh boy, yeah." And sometimes they just come in and read for a part like Clint Howard did. He came in and read and I was like, "Oh shit, I love Clint Howard." That's why I gave it to him. Or sometimes I'd be watching a movie, like I was watching *Scarecrow*, this Al Pacino movie, and Richard Lynch pops up, so I go, "Oh my God, I love Richard Lynch!" Then I start going, "Go find Richard Lynch!" So sometimes it's just by accident.

*When and where did you see the original* **Halloween***?*

When it came out, 1978, at a drive-in. I thought it was great. Back then, there was nothing like it. It's such a simple, creepy, weird movie, but other than *Psycho* or something, there are so few movies really like that. Immediately after it there were a million knock-offs but at the time it was just a unique film. I also loved the fact that even though it was shot in Pasadena, it looked like an East Coast neighborhood where I grew up, so I could really relate to everything about the movie.

*Did you try to bring that same freshness to your film—your vision of it?*

I tried to do my version of it. Whenever you're remaking something, you're in a weird position no matter what you do. So you have to just push ahead and do what you think is right. If you change it too much, people get upset; if you don't change it enough, people get upset. So you just have to go with your gut instinct. And probably, as I look at my version of it, the first 40 minutes is very much my movie—it's totally my world. It's the second 40 minutes that's in and out of John Carpenter land.

*How did the offer of* **Halloween** *come about?*

Bob Weinstein's office called me up to have a meeting with him. I didn't know what we were going to talk about, nobody ever said. And it really wasn't about remaking *Halloween*, it was just that they owned *Halloween*. They wanted to make a *Halloween* movie whether it was a sequel or a prequel, they didn't really have an idea. They

Tyler Mane as the new Michael Myers in Rob Zombie's *Halloween I* (2007, Dimension) and *Halloween II* (2009, Dimension).

had five or six scripts they hated, mostly all sequels, and I didn't really like the idea of being involved with it because I didn't like any of the sequels to *Halloween*. I loved John Carpenter's movie but that's about it. So at first it didn't sound like a very interesting offer at all, and I said no. Then, after I'd thought about it for a long time, that's when I came up with the idea of doing a remake, but trying to make it different, because I just love the character of Michael Myers. I thought, Michael Myers is like a modern-day Frankenstein, he's such an iconic movie monster. The idea of being able to use that character became very exciting.

*You've mentioned having an emotional core to the film rather than just blood and guts.*

I wanted to make it more of a character movie about Michael Myers, because having him just be a faceless killer ... that's already been done. It was done eight times, actually. Maybe somebody else would have done it that way, I don't know. But to have no back story and just be the Shape again didn't seem that scary any more. It seemed scary in 1978 for sure, but it's just been imitated so many times and overdone. I thought, well, why don't we make him like a real kid and develop him into a real character, so when we see adult Michael there's some emotional core—even though as soon as he puts on the classic Michael Myers mask, there's such a strong history that goes with it. It kind of erases everything you think about Michael Myers because it's like Darth Vader's helmet, such an iconic thing. It has a lot of power behind it.

*Was there a conscious move away from the supernatural aspects of the original?*

I didn't want to do anything that was even slightly supernatural because I thought that was cool in the first film. It ends in a big mystery and leaves you saying, "Holy shit." But in the later films he becomes this invincible killing machine and I didn't want to do that. That was why I cast somebody who was so big, because I wanted to have someone who was physically incredibly powerful, but believably powerful, not supernaturally powerful.

*What's Tyler Mane like in real life? Because he comes across as terrifying...*

He *is* pretty terrifying-looking because he's so big. The funniest thing is when we did all the rehearsals, he wouldn't have the mask on because he hated wearing that mask. And he was scary *without* the mask because he has such an intense face. Of course he's like the nicest guy in the world, but I guess if you made him mad he'd kick your ass [*laughs*].

*What was the casting process like? Did you pick someone for Laurie who would be really small beside ... well, obviously* **everyone's** *small beside Tyler [laughs]?*

Casting Laurie was the hardest. For most of the roles I knew who I wanted; I knew I wanted Tyler right away, there was never anyone else in consideration for Michael Myers. But Laurie ... a million girls came in and read and Scout was the first person I saw. I just liked her the best. Then I thought maybe I was just excited because she was the first person I saw. So we went through so many other people, over and over, people now that have actually had hit movies, TV shows, have gone on to big things. But I still kept coming back to her. And I couldn't convince anyone of it. Nobody wanted to cast her. It was the hardest thing, but I really believed in her. She was 17 years old, so she was really like a believable teenager. I wanted someone who was 17 so when we worked together I could bounce ideas off her and go, "Is this believable?" Because nothing's worse than a 40-year-old director with a 30-year-old actress pretending to be 17, and they're trying to decide what a real teenager is like. So it was good, and that's why she has a little more attitude than the Jamie Lee Curtis version. We just made her real, and eventually I convinced everyone to cast her and now they all love her, of course.

*Did the ghost of Donald Pleasence rear its head at all when Malcolm McDowell was playing Loomis?*

Not really because there's two things: Malcolm has never seen *Halloween*, so he had no idea what Donald Pleasence had done; second of all, he knew Donald Pleasence so his idea of Donald Pleasence was the actual man, not Dr. Loomis. So he really had nothing to draw on. Any time that he seems like he veers towards it, is just coincidental.

*In casting the young Michael, you were looking for a certain quality. How hard was it to find who you were looking for?*

It wasn't too hard. Daeg [Faerch] came in with one of the first groups of kids. There were a lot of kids and they were good young actors; they just didn't have the look I wanted. They looked too "All American, Peachy Pie." The great thing about Daeg is, he was only ten years old; all the little kids in the movie were ten, except he was like a foot taller than they were, and 40 pounds heavier. So that was a godsend, because I said, "Look, I need a kid who would believably grow up to be 6'10"." And he had long hair, and just had a different look. I thought he was perfect.

*Is it true you watched Jeffrey Dahmer home movies as research?*

Yeah, I'd seen these home movies of Jeffrey Dahmer, which is what inspired me, where he was sitting at home opening Christmas presents with his parents and I think his grandmother. He'd already been killing people, but he was just sitting there having Christmas while he's got like dead bodies in his refrigerator. That's what I found interesting, the way that they disassociate themselves from the things that they do. So on the one hand they're carrying on this normal life and doing these crazy things, and they become more and more detached. Daeg was really good at that. One minute he seems really scary and manipulative, then he seems like the sweetest little kid you've ever met. And that was really important; it didn't seem put on. That's why a lot of the scenes in the sanatorium are very loose, because I just wanted to show him very slowly sinking deeper into this more comatose Michael Myers.

*You took the aspect of the masks a step further.*

Well, yeah. There was one thing, I think it works fantastic for John Carpenter's film, but I went back and watched it a million times and realized most of the events in the movie are kind of random. The fact that he steals the mask from the hardware store, the different things that happen. And I really wanted everything to have more meaning, that the mask wasn't just a random mask he stole; that the masks in general represented him detaching himself from the actual person he was and slipping deeper into this other persona. It just made everything a little bit more realistic, I thought, as far as having done the research on kids who kill and psychopaths.

*Did you find it helped or hindered, watching the original so many times?*

It actually became a problem. After a while I had to never watch it again. That's why I could tell from a lot of the reviews and a lot of the fans, they can't disassociate themselves from that movie no matter how hard they try. And I couldn't do it, either. I was trying to change it but it was so burnt into my brain, it was so hard to picture it any other way. So I just stopped watching it. As the months went by it became easier and easier to create a fresh vision. But it's hard to forget about a movie you've seen hundreds of times over the last 28 years or something. It would really be like remaking *Jaws* or *Star Wars* or some movie you've seen a million times. You just picture it a certain way.

*How did John Carpenter react when he found out about the remake?*

He was fine with it. I called him up and told him about it and he was just like, "Hey great, go for it." He's a very cool guy. *Halloween*'s front and center for everybody else, but that's a long time ago for him, and he's certainly not sitting there worrying about Michael Myers.

*How long was the shoot?*

The shoot was 38 days, which is very short. There's no room for error. And it's a pretty big movie with a lot of characters and a lot of places, so it was exhausting. We cut together a four-and-a-half-hour "Making Of *Halloween*" documentary for DVD, and the one thing that I really forgot was just how little time we made the movie in. It was just crazy. I had so much less time than I had on *Devil's Rejects*. It was just one of those projects that was always so far behind schedule, rushing to make this release date. It was just madness, total madness [*laughs*].

*Is there anything that you would change?*

I'm happy with it the way it is, but my original intention, which I couldn't get anyone to back me on, was to shoot parts one and two simultaneously. I wanted part one to end when adult Michael put on the white mask. And part two to start there. That's always going to be my great regret, because a lot of people watch the movie and go, "I love it, but it kind of feels like two movies." I know, I *wanted* it to be two movies. But it's hard to convince someone to let you make two movies. That's my only regret.

*Did you actually write the two movies and then condense it?*

When I finished the script, I realized, "This is two movies" [*laughs*], because I felt like the whole movie could have just been young Michael, then Smith's Grove, then he escapes and then it ends. He comes back to Haddenfield, then you pick it up in Haddenfield. It's a lot of material jammed into one movie so unfortunately sometimes I feel like it gets rushed in certain areas but, y'know, it is what it is.

*You and Steve Niles have worked together on two projects.*

Somebody introduced us, this was like about six years ago I think. Somebody at Dark Horse Comics, I think, said, "Oh you guys should meet, you guys would get along." And we met and did get along good, and we did two projects together, *The Nail* and *Bigfoot*, and we haven't done anything since. We might do someday, but we haven't got any plans. We still talk to each other, but I just got busy with the movie stuff and he's always busy doing comic stuff.

*Is there any possibility that either of those might be turned into movies?*

There's always a possibility of anything [*laughs*]. Never say never with anything, that's for sure.

*Is there any possibility of the* **Grindhouse** *trailer that you shot [*Werewolf **Women of the S.S.***] being turned into a film?*

Probably not. I wanted to make that into a movie and we talked about it actually, me and [Producer Harvey] Weinstein, but it's a tough one because making any kind of movie is a lot of work, and that would be a lot of work and take a lot of time. But I just really don't know if there's a market, y'know [*laughs*]. So that's kind of the trick. I would love to because I'd love to make that movie; I think it would be insane. I actually started writing the script but then I realized, "What am I doing, where am I going with this?" So I put it on hold.

*What have you got coming up?*

I've been finishing up *The Haunted World of El Superbeasto*, a project that's been going on for years. Animated movies take forever. I've been making a new album with the band. And I've been writing the script for my new movie *Tyrannosaurus Rex* which, if all goes according to plan, I will start shooting soon.

*Can you tell us anything about that?*

It's a violent action movie starring badass motherfuckers [*laughs*].

# Part Three

*Actors*

# Christa Campbell

Born in Oakland, California, Christa Campbell started her career as a pin-up model and soon after arriving in Hollywood was bitten by the acting bug. She has starred in *Bettie Page True Hollywood Story* and guest starred on TV's *Pacific Blue*, *Sabrina the Teenage Witch* and *The Jamie Kennedy Experiment*. Christa starred in her first horror film, *2001 Maniacs*, in 2005 and went on to feature in the remakes of *The Wicker Man* in 2006 and *Day of the Dead* in 2008. Christa has since branched out into action films (*Hero Wanted* [2008] with Cuba Gooding, Jr., and *Lies and Illusions* [2009] with Christian Slater) and comedy (*Finding Bliss* [2009] with Leelee Sobieski). She has also shot her first children's film, *Cool Dog*, a remake of *Rin Tin Tin*. She recently returned to horror in the sequel to the movie that started it all for her, *2001 Maniacs: Beverly Hellbillys*. She has also done pictorials for *FHM*, *MAXIM*, *Stuff* and *Playboy*.

---

*What were your ambitions growing up?*

I started out doing modeling and beauty pageants. After high school I came to Los Angeles for a New Year's Eve party, met a photographer there, and he started shooting me. Then, for me, modeling became kind of boring so I wanted the challenge of acting. I started to study and to train as an actress. It was very challenging, but exciting.

*What were your first breaks in the film industry?*

A friend of mine produced an HBO series called *Erotic Confessions*, so I did several episodes of that. But I didn't do any nudity, I would just play the maid, the friend, this and that. But it's on my résumé now, so when people go on there, they think I've done some things I haven't [*laughs*].

*Your first film role was as Bettie Page. How did you go about preparing for that?*

I actually didn't know who Bettie was at the time, but I went in and they gave me photos. And they were like, "You really look like her." Then I got a wig, a clip-on Bettie. I researched her, they gave me footage to watch, and learned about her. I kind of got hooked, she's such an amazing person. I actually met her, with Hugh Hefner up at his house. She still looked exactly the same, she hadn't had any plastic surgery or anything—but you knew it was her.

*How do you feel about being labeled a scream queen?*

I always say I'm usually not the one who's screaming, though. Usually I'm the killer in most of my films. I guess I'm a scream queen *sort of*, but I think I'm more aggressive. I'm more the vamp, the one who wants to kill these people...

*The psycho?*

Yeah, the psycho! I wanna rip people's hearts out [*laughs*]!

*Are you friends with any of the other scream queens?*

You mean like the legendary scream queens? No. I never planned to do this, it just sort of happened. It's not like I researched the horror business, I sort of just fell into it. I've just arrived and I'm like, "Who? What?" So I'm still learning myself about who's doing what. But it's a very small community, which is nice. The fans are the most dedicated I've met, ever. They know every line in every movie, it's crazy. No wonder it's so huge.

*Do you have a favorite horror actress, past or present?*

Well, now every frickin' actress wants to do horror movies, so…

*Ingrid Pitt, Jamie Lee Curtis?*

Yeah, I'd say Jamie Lee.

*Any actresses in general, any role models?*

It changes for me, but I do like women who are beautiful, but also have a strength: Charlize Theron, Angelina Jolie. They have beauty but they have a strong side, they do a variety of things. I look up to them because that's what I'm trying to do and trying to become, so those are the types of women I idolize. Strong role models. Jennifer Connolly, I love her too. But those who can act—I love beautiful women who can act. I hate seeing people who suck on screen, it's such a bummer. There are so many good actors out there, and directors have to choose *them*?

*Do you like watching horror films?*

Oh, I love it. The thing is, I could never get anyone to go and see them with me, because everyone's such a pussy. I had to see them by myself. Now that I've been behind the scenes it doesn't scare me as much so I can actually watch them—if I get them on DVD—by myself; it doesn't really bother me. I love *Poltergeist*, I know every word of the movie. For some reason, I must have been a sick, demented child, because I watched it 30 times when I was a little kid; my parents let me watch this movie, it was crazy. But I know every line in the movie, it's my favorite, so I guess I was destined for horror in some way. I just loved weird films as a child: *The Shining* and *Poltergeist*, just these creepy films. I guess I was a creepy kid in a sense.

**Actress Christa Campbell (courtesy Christa Campbell).**

*So* **Poltergeist** *is your favorite of all time?*

It is, just because it was so creepy with the kids and everything. It really affected me, it was such a psychological thriller. I had nightmares.

*How did you come to be involved in* **2001 Maniacs***?*

I originally went in and just auditioned like everyone else, and it happened very quickly. I went in on a Thursday, auditioned, and they said, "Come back tomorrow, you're perfect." I came back the next day, auditioned again, then they had me read with them and like a thousand other guys who were going to play different roles in the movie, so I knew I kinda had it. But originally I was supposed to have the mouthpiece. I was the Milk Maiden, but they had her wearing the mouthpiece. But then the writers changed it right at the last minute, and said, "No, you should have the acid jug and the character of Peaches. [Wendy Kremer] should have the mouthpiece." I thought "*Fantastic!*" I didn't want to wear that in the movie.

One of Christa's modeling shots (courtesy Christa Campbell).

*What did you think of the script?*

I loved it, and the fact that Robert Englund was doing it. I was very excited, it was the first time I was actually going away on location to shoot. I was very excited to go on location and be with a group of actors, and to go away and camp. I read the script, I loved it, and I was working. I was just so happy to be involved.

*Were you there when the set burned down?*

Yes. It sucked because they were saying, "We're shooting tomorrow" or whenever it was, November 1 or something, and the day before I get a call saying, "We're not starting for a few more months." I'm like, *what?* But it happens, especially with low-budget movies.

*How would you describe your character, The Milk Maiden?*

Sweet and innocent, who turns into a wicked, devilish killer...

*Psychopath again?*

Yeah, psychopath [*laughs*]! And that's what I wanted to portray. In the sequel I play different characters, so she changes outfits and becomes different people. I think I'm going to explore different characters in the sequel with her.

*Do you enjoy playing villainous parts?*

Yes. [*Laughs*] I like to be mean. I think because people expect me to be sweet and innocent, I just want to take all my aggression out on every man that ever betrayed me [*laughs*].

*Do you have any other funny stories from the shoot?*

This movie trained me. Basically I can do any movie now and nothing affects me, because *everything* happened on this movie. We didn't have any money on the film, so everything was pressure, pressure, pressure, and trying to get everything right. So there was drama: We had all these weird things happen, we had people passing out, going to the hospital, choking, getting into car accidents, falling into a hole, having an epileptic attack. We had so many crazy things ... Tim [Sullivan, the director] got stung by seven wasps, right before my scene! Then it was like *Dawson's Creek*, all the kids were screwing each other on set and fighting, so the producers were like hall monitors. It was pretty crazy...

*Were you disappointed when it didn't win a Chainsaw Award?*

I actually went to the Chainsaw Awards. The production value was so big and it was a real deal, so I can see why a lot of films missed out, because they had a lot of big films in there as well. They should have something for just the low-budget films. I'm a bit bummed when they put the bigger budget pictures in there from the studios to compete. But it was done really well, and I think next time we'll have a chance with the sequel and have more money shooting the film.

*And also the fan base will have built up.*

Yeah. I think because the film came, it had a buzz, and it sort of went away because our distribution was shaky at the time. But then it finally kicked in and it took a while, so there was like a pause before the moment it became a cult.

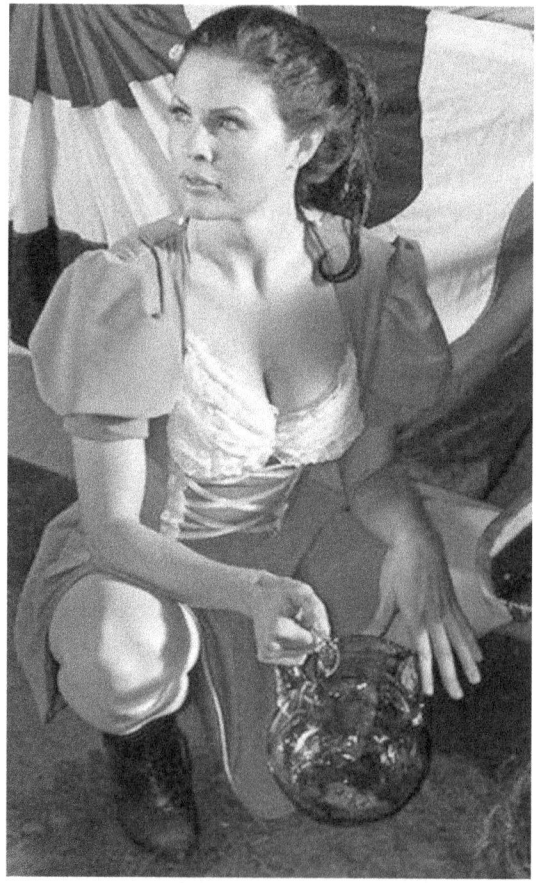

**Campbell as the Milk Maiden in *2001 Maniacs* (2005, New Rebellion; courtesy Christa Campbell).**

Campbell (right) with Robert Englund and Wendy Kremer on the set of *2001 Maniacs* (2005, New Rebellion; courtesy Christa Campbell).

*You were in* Sabrina the Teenage Witch.

That was fun, because I hadn't done too much TV. I got to be on a sitcom, I had a good time. She's really a talented young lady, Melissa Joan Hart, so it was nice to work in a different type of genre. It's comedy, and I'm not too confident with the comedy yet, I don't feel 100 percent comfortable. But it was fun. I played a total bimbo who speaks in a really high voice and I was really stupid. It was really fun. You get to play a different kind of character, so it was nice...

*How did you get involved in hosting* Thunderbox?

I shot a movie called *Red Letters* and then that film company started producing this boxing series for Fox. They asked, "Do you want to host it?" and I said, "No, I'm an actress." But they insisted, so I said all right. Actually hosting is quite hard, I thought, because you're looking directly into the camera and going, "Welcome to the show...." It was very difficult for me. But it was fun, it was a good experience. I got to travel around, and it was the highest rated show on Fox Sports for a long time in syndication. Boxers love me. I'll be in a restaurant and they'll be: "Yo, *Thunderbox!*" [*Laughs*]

*You were in* Lonely Hearts *with John Travolta.*

It was one of the most amazing experiences of my life. It took that a while to get out—it premiered at the Tribeca Film Festival. My goal in the movie was: Don't get fired. I was like, "They're going to see sexy pictures of me on the Internet and I'm gonna get fired, something's going to happen." I didn't sleep for weeks. But John was the most amazing guy—dancing, singing, hugs, kisses, all the time. Selma Hayek was great, she's the nicest. Really, really cool and down to earth.

*How did you feel when you landed the part in the new version of* The Wicker Man*?*

I was really, really excited. I got to go to Vancouver, I got to work with Nic Cage. It happened so quickly; I was auditioning for another role, then I got that one, and I got to do the opening scenes with Nic, so it was cool. I wasn't there too long, so I didn't get a chance to really hang out, but I was happy just to be there.

*Did you get a chance to talk to Nicolas?*

A little bit. But it was one of those things where he has different names on every movie set that he calls himself, like aliases. And his name was Frankenstein on the movie. So I'm sitting there, and I'm sitting in Frankenstein's chair, and I'm like, "Who's freakin' Frankenstein?" All of a sudden someone said, "That's Nic's chair! You, get out!" It was the worst nightmare [*laughs*]. I was like, "Oh no, I sat in the star's chair."

*Which version do you prefer, the original or the remake?*

There's something about the original, it was very haunting and erotic. It was different, and when they try to make remakes they don't grasp this—even with the Japanese films—that these kinds of films are more psychological. They try to remake them and they're just bloody and gory and they don't really get the haunting feeling that sits with you for days. So I think the erotic feeling I got from the original, like "Oooh, this is kind of creepy and sick" sort of feeling ... that's why I enjoyed the original. It wasn't like over the top, bloody and gory; it was subtle.

*How do you deal with the obvious male attention?*

Oh, bring it on. I need a husband. I'm taking applications [*laughs*].

*Have you got any messages for your fans?*

Yeah, I'm very excited they're interested in me and my films. It's nice to be able to travel and have other people recognize you from things. I love to meet people.

*You were in the remake of* Day of the Dead.

That was amazing, it was crazy. It was a really scary movie, like *28 Days Later*. We had fun, we shot in Bulgaria and I had to go through the different stages of makeup because I eventually turn into a zombie. I had to wear some prosthetics under my eyes, I couldn't see through these crazy contacts. Then I was like, "Fuck it, I'm gonna do my own stunts." They had stunt doubles, but they wanted to do close-ups, so I get thrown out of a window a couple of times, they tied me up and threw me across the room, and I attack people. So I had a good time. I thought, "That's what I want to do, I want to do my own stunts." I was really excited about it.

Day of the Dead *had an emotional side to it.*

It did, but I think that depends on the editing and directing [by Steve Miner]. The story was really good, and in the script it definitely did, for sure. Me and my husband [Robert Rais]—in the opening scenes you see us rushing our child to the hospital because he's sick and they quarantine the whole city. We can't get through, there are roadblocks, so we're going crazy, trying to break through to take our kid to the hospital. He goes apeshit and kills a nurse [*laughs*]. We all end up in this radio station, people are crazy and sick, and we're going nuts in the radio station. There are these kids, and they're saying, "We've been rescued, we've been rescued...." Then they turn and they're eating my husband's stomach out. All of a sudden, they turn up behind and I just attack one, and we go crazy. That's when I turn...

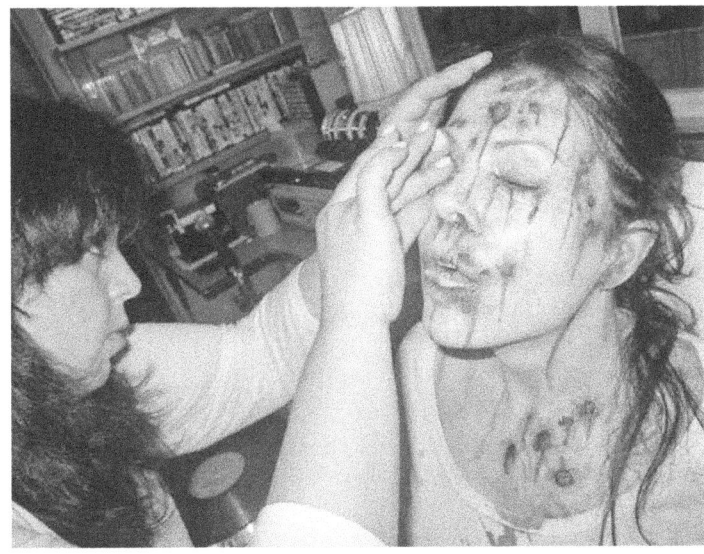

Campbell being made up as a zombie for *Day of the Dead* (2008, Millennium Films; courtesy Christa Campbell).

*You've been in a few remakes now. How do you feel about them?*

I'm just happy to have a job [*laughs*]. Part of me is saying, "Where are the original ideas?" So it's sad in a way, and I don't know if a remake is ever going to be as good because

Campbell and unidentified zombie friend on the set of *Day of the Dead* (2008, Millennium Films; courtesy Christa Campbell).

people have these expectations. I don't know if they will ever live up to the originals; there will always be critics. I mean, some of them have been good, some of them not so good. I just think that they do them because the younger kids have never seen the originals, so they remake them. And they can remake them for little money and make a lot of money because they use the name. I think in *Day of the Dead* the name itself was $1 million. But once they have the name, they already have the audience on board so it's a sure winner. That's why they're doing it.

*What's your favorite of the Romero zombie films?*

The first one. *Night of the Living Dead*.

*What can you tell us about* Revamped?

We shot *Revamped* for no money. I think Jeff Rector financed his house [to fund the production]—I know, scary. We shot this vampire movie, we'd been shooting it on weekends so it took months. I think I went off to do *Day of the Dead*, then came back and finished *Revamped*. Then they said, "Okay, we're going to have a screening, a trailer or whatever." I show up and, I tell you, it's really good! I was shocked, I was so happy.

*It looked bigger budget than it was.*

It did. It looked like it was on film, really dark, but not grainy. I was very happy. I was like, "Wow, we all look amazing in it." Sometimes if you've got a new director [like Rector], it's hard to put your whole trust into what they're doing. You know they have the passion, but sometimes, if they don't have the experience, you don't really know.

*What was* Hallows' Point *like to work on?*

Oh, that was fun. I flew out to Florida to play Tanya Graves, this reporter reporting on these deaths, crimes, whatever [*laughs*], like the Courteney Cox character in *Scream*. I was literally deliri-

Campbell in full zombie attack mode for *Day of the Dead* (2008, Millennium Films; courtesy Christa Campbell).

ous and jet-lagged, but it was really easy. I flew in for a couple of days, did it, and they were so nice and generous...

*And what do you think of Tim Sullivan's movie* **Driftwood***?*

Tim is great. I'm so proud of Tim because he really has so much passion. He's just created a whole thing for himself. We went to the premiere of *Driftwood* and it's a really great film. It's beautiful, it's amazing.

*What's in store for the Milk Maiden in the sequel,* **Beverly Hellbillys***?*

Okay, the Milk Maiden is gonna be great. In this one I'm going to play different characters; I'm myself but I'm wearing different outfits this time and I kill a lot more. There are not going to be as many characters in the next movie as far as the maniacs are concerned, just Lin [Shaye], me, Robert, and a couple of others, plus a couple of new ones. There are going to be many more killings, but my character will morph into different characters and kill in different ways, so it's not going to be the same. I think it's great and it's actually better than the original in a lot of ways. It's got a little more money and a little more time, we're going to have a normal schedule. And I think now that we've felt the characters out, now that we know who they are, we're going to really dig in and play with them.

**Campbell attending Chillerfest in the UK in 2006. Photograph by Paul Kane and Marie O'Regan.**

# Zach Galligan

Zach Galligan was born on February 14, 1964, in New York, the son of attorney Arthur John and psychologist Carol Jean. Galligan graduated from Columbia University and his early passion for acting saw him win the coveted breakthrough role of Billy Peltzer in the Spielberg-produced and Joe Dante–directed movie *Gremlins* in 1984. The film was a phenomenon and shot him to fame overnight. Galligan went on to star in the horror comedy *Waxwork* (1988) for director Anthony Hickox, before reprising his role as Billy in the smash sequel *Gremlins 2: The New Batch* (1990). Since then he has starred in movies such as *Waxwork II: Lost in Time* (1992), *Pyschic* (1992), *Warlock: The Armageddon* (1993), *Cupid* (1997), *Prince Valiant* (1997), *Infested* (2002) and *Legion of the Dead* (2005) and appeared regularly on TV shows like *Star Trek: Voyager*, *The Net*, *7th Heaven* and *Dr. Quinn, Medicine Woman*. As well as acting, Galligan now teaches at New York University and writes scripts. His latest horror venture is the ambitious independent movie *Cut*.

---

*Billy from* **Gremlins** *was into comics and drawing. Did you have any aspirations like this as a child?*

I loved drawing and I tried to. I was okay at it, but I was really pretty average. I've always been a bit of an Anglophile, so I loved Andy Capp growing up, and can draw a lot of Andy Capp and Flo cartoons. I loved *The Prisoner* so I did a long comic strip based on the opening credits, which was kinda cool.

*Which films and TV programs had an impact on you growing up, and did any of these have an influence on you wanting to become an actor?*

I'm sure a lot of it influenced me into going into acting, but there was really nothing specific. I always just liked playing pretend, and it's kind of ironic that I've done most of my work in horror and sci-fi and fantasy films because those were always my favorite genres growing up as a kid. Not that I didn't like straight drama, because I did and I do, but it's interesting that I managed to make a mark in horror films particularly.

*Does any horror or genre film jump out from your childhood?*

I was pretty obsessed with horror movies at a very young age, probably from about five or six onward. I can remember *The Blob* with Steve McQueen having a big effect on me. Particularly the beginning when they find the meteor and the old man pokes it with a stick, then it climbs up the stick and goes onto his hand. I can remember watching that on a black-and-white TV at my childhood friend's house, and that terrified me—but at the same time it excited me, so I wanted to watch more. We had a television program called *Chiller Theater* in New York, a local horror movie show. It had a piece of Claymation at the beginning; you'd see this swamp, and the word CHILLER was spelled out in this weird kind of plant life, then this Claymation arm came out of the swamp and would pick up all the letters—C H I L L E R—then sort of eat them and vanish into the swamp. There'd be this weird, creepy music, and a scary voice would go: "Chiiiillleeeer." That hand coming out of the

Zach Galligan (right) with the director of *Cut* (2010, Hawthorn Productions), Dominic Burns (courtesy Dominic Burns).

swamp when I was five, six, that scared the crap out of me—scared me actually more than the movies. All the early *Godzilla* movies I loved; there was one called *The Atomic Submarine*, a 1950s movie about this giant squid thing, and they puncture its eye at the end, to get away from the monster, and it bled. Oh, and *The Crawling Eye* and *The Creeping Unknown*, which was the first *Quatermass* movie—that scared the crap out of me. So all those late '50s horror movies. You've got to remember, late '50s—I'm four years old in 1968, so those were only like seven, eight, nine years old and that's what you'd see cycled on television.

*What did you think of the script for* **Gremlins** *the first time you saw it?*

The first time I saw the script was after I'd gotten cast in the movie. The only thing I was allowed to do was audition with the scene in which I ask Phoebe Cates out on a date. So I had really no idea; I figured the movie was going to be about gremlins, since that was the title. But from the script it was like a young guy asking a girl out on a date. So the process basically was this: I went in and met the casting director, Susan Arnold. She liked me and brought me back to meet [Producer] Mike Finnell maybe two days later. I read for him and he was great. Joe Dante wasn't there at the time because he was plane sick—he hates flying—so they called me back and put me on tape with Phoebe Cates about three or four days later, just before I went on a spring break holiday down to Fort Lauderdale, Florida. I'd auditioned with Phoebe Cates for other projects, so this was maybe the third time as local New York actors that we'd auditioned together. So I already had a bit of a crush on her and knew she was kind of a local New York celebrity, she was on the cover of *17* magazine. In the teen world she was kind of well-known by high school students. So I did the audition and when it was all over, because they had to put us on tape, they had us stand basically shoulder to shoulder. And when the audition stopped, apparently—I don't remember this—I put my head on her shoulder jokingly, and sighed like I was all lovestruck. The camera was still running and Spielberg saw that and said, "Look at him, the guy's already in love with her. Let's hire these two actors because the relationship's already there. They don't even have to pretend."

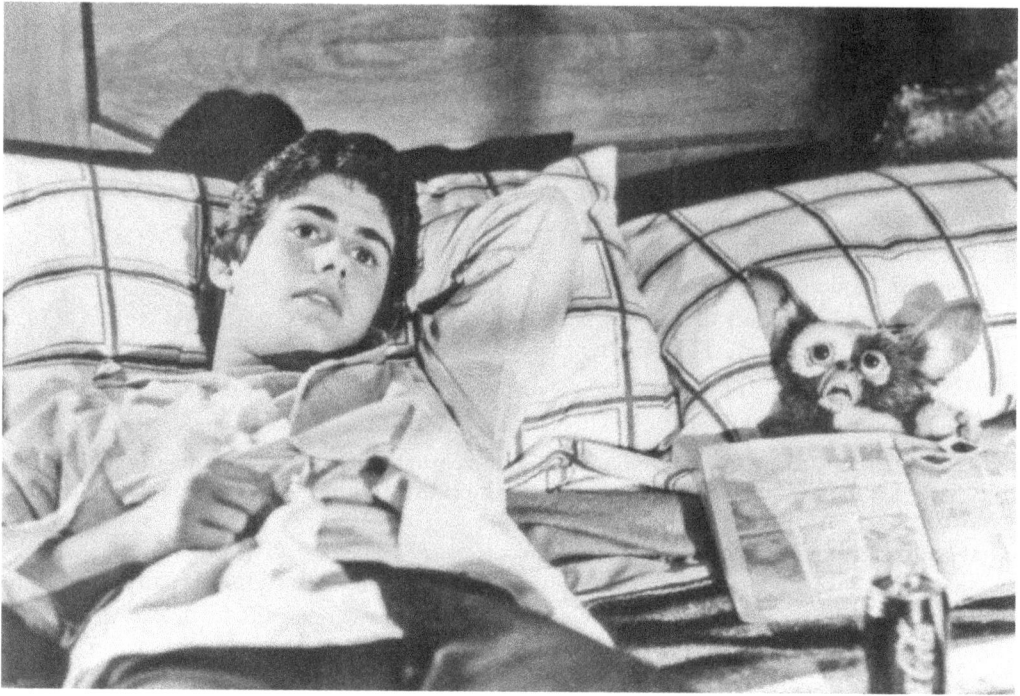

A fresh-faced Galligan as Billy Peltzer, with Gizmo in *Gremlins* (1984, Warner Bros.; courtesy John Gullidge).

*What was Joe Dante like to work with?*

Joe really hasn't changed a bit in all the years I have known him. He is a laid-back but concentrated guy who is extremely smart and knows exactly what he wants. I've yet in my lifetime to meet someone who knows more about movies and cartoons than he does. He's a complete encyclopedia. He and Mike Finnell were really, really relaxed and patient when dealing with what was essentially a group of young kids. Phoebe and myself and Judge Reinhold, we were all 19, 20, 21 years old.

*Did you get to meet or see Spielberg much?*

He was doing *Indiana Jones and the Temple of Doom* at that time, but I think they finished a little early, and he was there on the *Gremlins* set on and off for the last couple of weeks. He would watch and make a suggestion here and there towards the end, and it was all very friendly. Sometimes Joe would take the suggestion, sometimes he would jokingly tell him to go back to his own movie. It was all good fun, there was no ego head-butting or anything like that.

*Did you have any say in Billy's character, or any room to improvise?*

A little bit. Joe was open to a certain amount of improvisation. For example, the scene with the chainsaw and the bat, that was actually an idea I came up with when we were looking through the set and saw the chainsaws and baseball bat. I was going to pick up the bat anyway, to fend off some of the objects the gremlin was throwing at me. And I believe I said aloud, "Wouldn't it be cool if we could have a fight, with the gremlin with the chainsaw and me with the bat." That was all spur of the moment, so there was a little bit, yeah. With the chainsaw, for most of it they took the cutting blades off. But there was one scene where we needed to see the bits of wood flying into my face on the close-up, so they put the chainsaw on. I was instructed absolutely under no circumstances was I allowed to move the bat either to the right or to the left because they were afraid the chainsaw would bounce off and cut one of my fingers off. So there is a shot in there where the chainsaw blade is real, and it's actually cutting through the bat.

*Was it more difficult working with Mushroom the dog or the Gizmo puppet?*

Oh, much more difficult with the puppet. The dog was incredibly well trained—and actually was two dogs. There was one dog that did the vast majority of what you see in the movie. Then there was another dog that was the dog's sister from the same litter—she was a little bit heavier—and she was the stunt dog. So when the dog gets hung up in the Christmas tree lights, that's the girl, and other times it's Mushroom the boy.

*So it was trickier working with the puppet.*

There were so many different kinds of puppets. Some were remote controlled, some were animatronic so the wires would be running out of the backs of them. Also, they would have to tape the wires to my body, underneath my clothing. So they could come out of the back of the puppet, would be taped up to my arms, down my torso, down my leg, then a hole was cut in my sock, and the wires would go across the room. Different wires were controlled by different joysticks, so one person would be doing the ears, one person the nose, one the arms. They had to watch on the monitor and they'd been practicing for months to coordinate all those movements. Of course what would happen is, I would be acting with Gizmo and they would be doing the joysticks, and a lot of times it would pinch my skin or the hair on my skin underneath my clothing, and I would have to ignore all of the pinches. It was like trying to do a scene and having ten people pinching you while you're doing it. You just have to ignore it and keep going.

*Did it make it more difficult for you as an actor to interact with Gizmo?*

There were some concentration issues, but basically it made it easier because instead of acting to a CGI thing that's not there, I had the actual creature in my hands, looking up at me and smiling, making cute little gestures. The animatronics people were really quite good at what they were doing.

*So you'd prefer to do that than to work with a CG version of Gizmo.*

Sure. I think that's one of the things that's holding up *Gremlins 3*. The corporations want to do it with Joe and with Mike, but they don't want to switch. My understanding is that Joe wants to do it again, but he wants to do it with puppets instead of CGI, but the studios are saying that's three times as expensive.

*How did you get on with your fellow actors Phoebe Cates, Corey Feldman and Judge Reinhold?*

You've got to remember that Corey Feldman was what, eleven? He was fine, he was cute. He was only really there for a couple of weeks, on and off, if you added it all together. But I was with Phoebe most of the time, she was great. Judge was great. It was a really good mood on the set. Everybody had a feeling that they were making something kind of special.

*It seemed to me like a family, almost.*

Dick Van Dyke was the original first choice to play my dad. He couldn't do it because of some scheduling thing, so they got Hoyt Axton; now that he's gone, it's hard to imagine somebody else. And my mom: it's interesting because Francis Lee McCain was very similar to my real mother, so that had a lot of verisimilitude about it.

*There's a definite split in the movie, the first half being quite light while the second is darker. Which part did you prefer?*

I really don't know, because I don't think the movie could work without either half. The whole point was to lull you into this cute, sweet feeling, then just when you'd relaxed, kick you in the gut. So you need the light in order to have the dark. It's kind of a Yin-Yang thing.

*Were you impressed by the way the Gremlins were given human qualities? For example, in the bar sequence they almost seem like raucous students.*

Well, they were certainly supposed to be like rowdy troublemakers in a bar, so anything that a human would do in a bar, we tried to figure out. And we tried to give them all sorts of different kinds of archetypal things. That's why you've got that Frank Sinatra Gremlin listening to sad songs late at night on the radio. Then there's that very surreal thing where another Gremlin starts to break his reverie by coming in with the hand puppet; but of course it's a puppet with a puppet, so that was sort of surreal in and of itself.

*What's your favorite scene in the movie?*

I think the most enjoyable scene to film for me was the scene in the pool when Stripe jumps in and multiplies, because the way they did that was really impressive. We had a swimming pool in a place called the Warner Brothers Ranch, which is very near by in Burbank. It had taken them a couple of days, but they had rigged the swimming pool so that they could pump in thousands of gallons of liquid nitrogen, to cause a big chemical reaction. So, they only had enough liquid nitrogen to probably do three or four takes at the most, and we would rehearse it without pumping the liquid nitrogen in. Then we did one take, and I can remember them so vividly the clapboard in front of me, and the camera's on a crane hovering over the center of the pool and I'm supposed to be staring out, and he goes, "Look at it in horror, wait five or six seconds." Right? Pretty easy to do. So they go, "Action!" and they start pumping the liquid nitrogen into the pool. And the entire ground started shaking and trembling like an earthquake. You don't get a sense of it in the movie, but the chemical reaction was so violent the hair on the back of my neck just rose up on end.

*Did you have a favorite piece of Gremlins merchandise?*

I think being on the thermos is pretty cool. But I would probably say, when you're a kid and you grew up collecting baseball cards, to have a whole collection of packages of cards you can buy with a stick of bubble gum with your face on them, that's pretty amazing.

*Were you tempted to steal one of the Gremlins?*

It's funny you said that, because apparently the people at Warner Brothers were afraid I might be tempted, too, because all through *Gremlins* and *Gremlins 2*, when I left Warner Brothers Studios they made me open my trunk. I'm not kidding.

*How did you get involved with* **Waxwork***?*

The director Tony Hickox was a huge *Gremlins* fan. We had lunch at a place called Hugo's in Los Angeles. He can sell ice cubes to Eskimos. So basically, I was all ready to tell him, "No thank you, but I appreciate the interest." He had sketches and drawings and was so fun and convincing. And by the time the lunch was over he just really sold me on the project, so I was surprised to find myself walking out of the restaurant going, "Yeah, let's do it."

*There are quite a few differences between the characters of Billy and Mark. For one thing, Mark has a lot of money.*

Yeah, he was much more like the spoiled rich kid with the inattentive parents. But the interesting thing is, that doesn't really come into play very much in the rest of the movie. It's set up and then not really addressed, so it was kind of a difficult character to play because he was just another variation on the dashing hero.

*What was it like working with Pactrick Macnee?*

Ah, well, I grew up watching *The Avengers* so that was a huge thrill. And to find out that Patrick himself was such a nice human being. I mean, he's where you get the expression "a gentleman," he really was that. He was professional and focused, but he was kind and gracious, never talked down to us because we were young kids. He was just great.

*What was it like on set with Hickox?*

To be honest, *Waxwork II* was pretty much of a nightmare because I was in a vast majority of the movie and we had a small amount of time in which to do it. So they broke it down into A units and a B unit. And when I wasn't shooting an A unit, I was pretty much shooting in the B unit. So that was about six days a week for about four weeks, for about 14 hours a day. I'm not sure but I don't remember really having a day off during that shoot; maybe I had one. Obviously it was a lot of work, and work is fun, but the pace ... I mean, Tony was known for doing 40, 50, 60 set-ups a day. Sometimes you don't even get 60 set-ups in a *week*, so it was a lot of work and very little time off.

*Which of* **Waxwork***'s horror film homages did you enjoy the most?*

I really liked what they did with *The Haunting*. That was kind of clever. And I got a kick out of doing the *Dawn of the Dead* in the mall thing, because we got to shut down the West Side Pavilion in Los Angeles, a huge mall, and shoot in there, so that was a lot of fun.

*Was it good to get the* **Gremlins** *group back together again for* **Gremlins 2** *in 1990?*

It was definitely a strange feeling at first, because some people were there and some were missing. You know, my parents weren't featured in it, but the Futtermans were, so it was great to see Dick Miller and Jackie Joseph again. Then there were some new people, so that added a lot to it. The shooting schedule was incredibly long, about five months. What was really weird about it was, I shot a lot, and then would have long breaks. So I would do six, seven weeks in a row and then have like three and a half weeks off.

We had a ball. Me and [actor] Robert Picardo had a great time together; I love Bob, I worked with him on *Gremlins 2* and on *Star Trek: Voyager*. And Christopher Lee was in a really good mood because *Gremlins 2* was apparently his 200th movie, so we had a nice big cake for him to celebrate. You have to remember that, like all actors, his career has

**Phoebe Cates and Galligan in** *Gremlins 2: The New Batch* **(1990, Warner Bros.; courtesy John Gullidge).**

had ups and downs. I mean, the last ten years have been incredibly good for him, but it hasn't always been that way. And I think he was very, very appreciative of the level of respect that Mike Finnell and Joe Dante showed—the regard that they held him in was second to none. So Mr. Lee could not have felt more appreciated anywhere else on Earth than with two huge film fanatics like Joe and Mike.

*Did you get a chance to ask him about his career?*

Yeah, I did actually. I asked, "Two hundred movies—which one was your favorite one?" Did he *have* a favorite, or was that a ridiculous, preposterous thing to say? And he didn't hesitate at all, he said at the time his favorite performance was—and probably still is—in *The Wicker Man*. He loves that movie.

*Did you have a favorite of the New Batch of Gremlins?*

There's one that we called the Burgess Meredith Gremlin. He was like George in *Of Mice and Men*, and he had this big Lenny sidekick. I kind of liked him because he was just so grumpy and funny.

**Psychic** *was about a student getting visions from a serial killer. Do you believe in psychic phenomena?*

I went to at least three or four psychics, because I wanted to see whether they were just trying to read the people or whether anybody had any kind of ability. Most of them I found to be charlatans, but I went to one person who did something I found really

Veteran actor Christopher Lee in *Gremlins 2: The New Batch* (1990, Warner Bros.; courtesy John Gullidge).

unnerving. I sat and talked to her and she said, "It seems like you're unhappy in your relationship." And I knew not to give away things, I was very poker-faced. So I said, "Not really, why would you say that?" The truth is, the previous night I'd gotten into a big fight with my girlfriend at a place called the Soup Plantation. And this woman was touching my hand, looking at my palm. She said, "I have this vision of you and you're with your girlfriend recently. You're at a restaurant, you're arguing about something and you're sitting in a booth." Then she proceeded to give an excellent description of where I was sitting and down to what I was eating. I don't believe that anybody can predict the future, but it made me wonder if there are people who perhaps—in the same way that like a radio can tune into a station—can maybe access your thoughts? I can't explain it or understand it, unless of course she was sitting behind me in the restaurant [*laughs*].

*What was it like filming the* **Tales from the Crypt** *episode* **Strung Out?**

It was fun. It was very short, about four or five days, and I got to work with Donald O'Connor who was a legend. Patricia Charboneau, who played my wife, was terrific. I really had a good time with that. It happened very quickly. As soon as I finished the audition—and this has never happened to me before or since—they said, "Congratulations, you've got the part. Go to wardrobe." And we shot it a couple of days later. It was a very quick, solid experience and I really enjoyed everything about it.

**Cupid** *dealt with a psychological terror. What attracted you to this story?*

It was weird playing a character who was born on my birthday; I was born on Valentine's Day. And I actually think that's what helped me get the part, because I told them and they said, "Oh sure." So I took my driver's license out and they were like, "Wow, that's weird." I think, to be honest, that heavily influenced them, because it is unusual that one of the ten or twenty actors trying out for the part would actually be born on that day. It just seemed like an interesting script. I thought it was weird and unusual, and even a little distasteful in a positive way. They had me having a sexual relationship with my sister; they incorporated an incest quality to it. I thought that was very daring for the time.

**Infested *[2002] draws on people's fears of insects. Is it a fear of yours?***

When I was a kid, that *Night Gallery* episode about the earwig that crawls into the guy's head to eat his brain really, really freaked me out. So much so that this weekend I was down at my sister's country house and I saw an earwig, and that's all I could think of. I have a really visceral distaste of that particular insect. But, if you ask my wife, I'm the kind of guy who picks up spiders and puts them outside instead of stomping on them. I just really don't like killing anything if I can avoid it.

**What was it like working with the special effects this time?**

Very few of the effects were there, because they shot it on DV. So it was just a lot of pretend, to be honest. Josh Olsen, the director—I really had a feeling about him. I found him to be a great guy, super-intelligent, and the whole thing of spoofing *The Big Chill* as we were doing a horror movie was a clever little twist. I thought that he would become a director or writer of note, and lo and behold a few years later he got the Oscar nomination for *A History of Violence*. So again it confirms that I'm a reasonably good judge of ability and talent.

**You're now teaching acting and scriptwriting. That must be quite a satisfying thing to do.**

Yeah, well, I really lucked out, because I started doing it privately, and I came to the attention of a woman who cast me in an independent movie called *The Pack*, which sounds like it's a great werewolf movie, but it's actually about cigarettes. She not only happens to be a talented director, but runs a screen acting studio that's affiliated with New York University. So she had me come in and now I teach auditioning as a skill to NYU drama school students. So here I am back in my hometown, and I'm affiliated with a major university, I give grades, but the great thing is, I only work a couple of days a week and the other days I'm off auditioning, working and writing. If I get a job, I just go do it, and they let me take a sabbatical and I come back. So it's absolutely fantastic because now between my wife and myself I no longer really have to … I don't want to say "worry about money," it's not like I'm rolling in it, but I have a certain amount of financial stability that comes with having a part-time job that allows me to audition with complete confidence and to enjoy the process again, and not to need a job.

**What's the best piece of advice you give your students?**

I think the key thing is that you have to find a way to eliminate pressure from the auditioning process, so that you're acting because it's something that you love and not because it's something that you need.

**You mentioned the possibility of a third Gremlins *movie. Can you tell us any more about that?***

The only thing I'd say is that things are still very much in the talking phase. It's my understanding, and I'm not 100 percent sure of this because I haven't spoken to Joe personally about it, but I think that if there was going to be a third one, there would probably be an

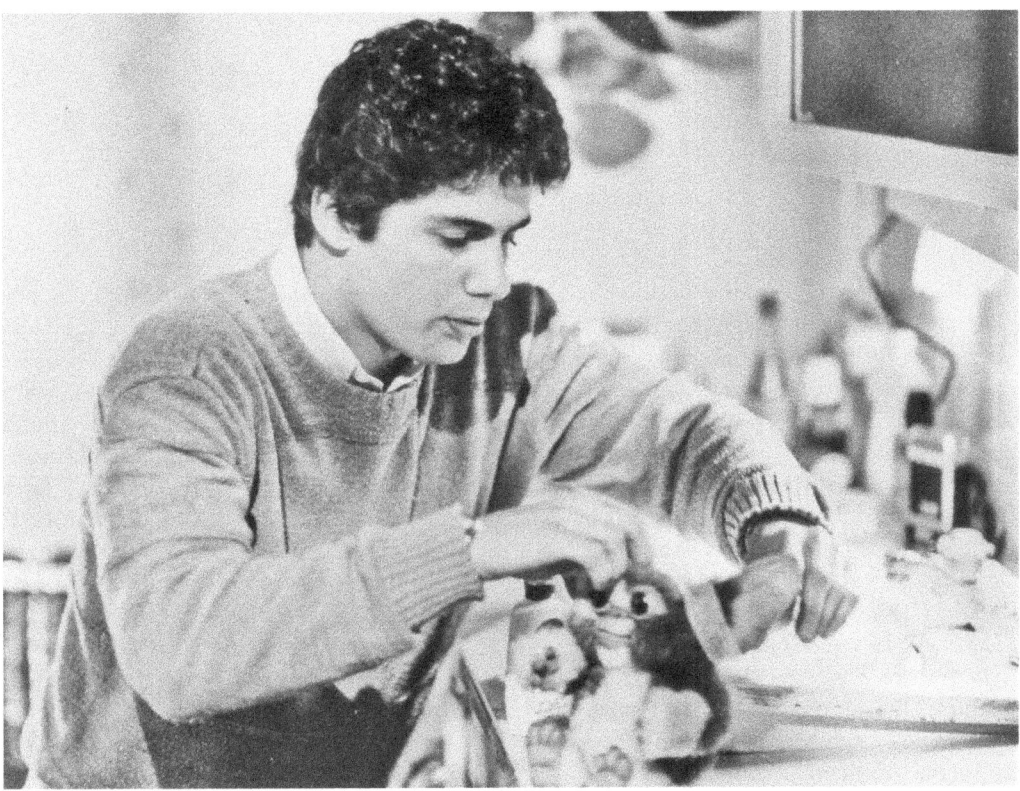

Billy Peltzer (Galligan) re-united with Gizmo for *Gremlins 2: The New Batch* (1990, Warner Bros.; courtesy John Gullidge).

insistence on the animatronics. I know that Joe and Mike are not particular fans of CGI, so that's probably a hold-up. And I think a huge thing is, what are we going to do? Where do you go? We did the first one, then we did the second one as a spoof of the first one, so where do you go with it? I have some ideas, but I'm not sure whether it's for me to say. I've always been tempted to write a spec script and just send it and say, "What about this?" So you never know...

*What do you think the enduring appeal of* Gremlins *is down to?*

I just think it deals with the duality of nature. There's good and there's bad. If you look at things like *Harry Potter*, *Lord of the Rings* and *Star Wars*, the one thing that they really have in common is: you have "good," and it's clearly delineated, and you have "bad," and it's clearly delineated. I think people enjoy that, because the majority of people believe that there is good and bad. Or maybe I should say good and evil?

# Betsy Palmer

Betsy Palmer has been working in show business for over 50 years and is still at her happiest when on the stage. Some highlights of her career include such Broadway shows as Tennessee Williams' *The Eccentricities of a Nightingale*; *Same Time, Next Year*; *South Pacific*; *Cactus Flower*; *Roar Like a Dove*; *The Grand Prize*; and *Affair of Honor*, working with stars such as David Selby, Don Murray, Ray Middleton, Lloyd Bridges, Charlie Ruggles, June Lockhart and Denis King. Her touring and regional theater work includes *Gigi*, *South Pacific*, *The Prime of Miss Jean Brodie*, *The King & I*, *Mary, Mary*, *Once More With Feeling*, *Love Letters* (with Robert Reed, Van Johnson, Eddie Albert, Gavin MacLeod, and Norman Fell) and *On Golden Pond*. She has worked extensively on television, appearing on *The Today Show*, *I've Got a Secret*, *Playhouse 90* (with Jackie Gleason and Buster Keaton), *The U.S. Steel Hour*, *Candid Camera*, *Knots Landing*, *As the World Turns*, *Columbo*, *Write Me a Murder* and *The Love Boat*, to name but a few. Her films include John Ford's *The Long Gray Line*, *Mister Roberts*, *The Tin Star*, *Queen Bee*, *The True Story of Lynn Stuart* and *The Last Angry Man*, working alongside such stars as Tyrone Power, Maureen O'Hara, Henry Fonda, Jack Lemmon, James Cagney, Tony Perkins, Joan Crawford, Jack Lord, Paul Muni, Luther Adler and Billy Dee Williams. In 1980 her role as Mrs. Voorhees in *Friday the 13th* brought her to the attention of a whole new set of admirers. She is adored amongst horror fans who turn up in droves when she makes public appearances.

---

*Your interest in acting goes right the way back to school, doesn't it?*

What happened was that, from the time I was in kindergarten to first grade, all the teachers just kept pushing me on stage. Whether I liked to show off, I don't know—who knows what it was. But all through school I was always encouraged, not so much by my family, but my teachers.

*Did you ever watch or enjoy horror films as a youngster?*

No. I went to a few movies, not a lot. My parents really wanted to control what it was that we saw. Actually, a very interesting thing—and this shows how there is an agenda you come in with and there's a plan whether you know it or not. The first two films I ever saw in my life were *Treasure Island* with Jackie Cooper and a Pearl Buck story that was called *The Good Earth*, with Paul Muni and Luise Rainer. So I ended up doing my first half-hour dramatic show in New York, a night-time show called *Hollywood Screentips*, where they took a known and an unknown, and Jackie Cooper was the known and I was the unknown. And then my first summer stock job was with Luise Rainer. I did this play, which was actually performed in Britain first with Sir Ralph Richardson, called *Home at*

*Seven* by R.C. Sherriff. It didn't do well there and it didn't really succeed here; I played a Cockney barmaid. Then I did *The Last Angry Man* with Mr. Muni.

I remember a Christopher Morley book that I adored when I was young, maybe six or seven, about a cat, called *I Know a Secret* ... and I ended up doing a game show for ten, eleven years called *I've Got a Secret*. I'm in my eighties now, and to look back on your life, especially when people interview you ... you begin to dredge these things up and suddenly you think, wow! There were little indications, little yoo-hoos coming at you all the time, even if you didn't know it then.

*How did you get into working on TV?*

I went to New York in 1951 with a friend, Sasha, after doing a couple of seasons of winter and summer stock. We went to the house of her sister, who was married to Frank Sutton—who couldn't get himself arrested in those days. I walked into their little apartment on the Friday night, and there was a man sitting

**Actress Betsy Palmer (courtesy Aine Leicht and Betsy Palmer).**

in the corner of the room and I heard him say, "She'll be perfect." And he motioned me over to where he was sitting, and there were three guys sitting on the floor. He said, "Are you an actress?" I paused, then said, "Yes." He said, "Monday go up to so-and-so's office and tell him that I sent you up for a role—and I'll call him." So Monday I went up, met this man, and he said, "Do you have a Southern accent?" and I said, "I sure enough do, honey," and he said, "You've got the job."

It was for a soap opera that came out of Philadelphia. Ernie Kovacs was at that station; it was all done in Philadelphia because it was cheaper than New York. I had a running part on a soap called *Miss Susan* with Susan Peters. Then after about three or four months the show went off the air, so I did too. But I just kept falling into work, and I did the first *Wheel of Fortune*. I ran into Peter Arnell on the street and he said, "What are you doing?" and I said, "I'm off to be interviewed for a hostess in a restaurant." He said, "Look, I've just written this game show. It's not acting, but you'd be a Girl Friday to the host on the show. Would you be interested in doing that?" I said, "Sure." So I did that show and then, of course, it became this great big thing because Merv Griffin bought it many years later and all those people have gone on to do it for many, many years. I did it for six, eight months. So that happened, and I was making some bread.

Did you ever hear the name Joe Papp? He started a big thing downtown, very big here in America. Anyway, he was the floor manager on that show [*I've Got A Secret*]. Joe went from CBS to become a big, big producer and director and an important man in theater here in the city. Things just came—I did my first Broadway show in 1954 and did television, and I was there doing these funny game shows before I ever was on the panel of *I've Got a Secret*. Never thought I'd be a panelist, just thought I'd be the Girl Friday.

*Your first movies were for John Ford? What was he like to work for?*

I was sent up to see him—he was here in New York in a hotel room—and the movie was *The Long Gray Line* with Tyrone Power and Maureen O'Hara. I liked Mr. Ford and I liked working for him, and he liked me very much. He gave me the job without reading or anything. I don't think I had done a film, it was all live shows for television in those days, which was just great because it was like the stage.

*You once starred in a theater production of* **Countess Dracula**.

I played three characters: I played Lady Alucard, the Countess Dracula and Elizabeth Von Helsing—you know, the doctor. 'Course, Van Helsing never had a wife, but when you get into those stories they make them up the way they want them to be. It's actually in print, I think people do it in stock companies and things like that. [Our production] was up in Buffalo, New York, where eventually we did the set-up to go to Broadway for Tennessee Williams' last show when he was alive—*The Eccentricities of a Nightingale*, which I had been doing out in summer stock. Actually, what happened once I was on *I've Got a Secret* was that all the summer stock and winter stock opened up for me because they wanted to see this gal they had fallen in love with on the panel. I think they showed *I've Got a Secret* in England, because I remember Arthur Treacher was the actor with the secret on the show that night, and the secret was that they were going to send me to England to cover Princess Margaret's wedding. And I did; on the Wednesday night I did the show and I had to leave with my husband—my only husband, who is now my ex-husband—the next day. That was my first trip to England, very exciting.

*Is it true that you accepted the* **Friday the 13th** *job because you needed the money for a new car?*

I was on Broadway doing *Same Time Next Year* at the time, and I had a Mercedes that I'd had for many, many years, which broke down driving home to Connecticut from the theater that night. It was a trip that usually took an hour, hour and 15 minutes, but ended up taking five hours, so I didn't get home 'til about 5:30 in the morning. So I said to myself, "I need a new car," to the universe. And I was talking to my daughter the next day and she said, "Go and look at a certain car," and I did and I liked it; it was $9,999.50. It was not considered a cheap car, but a good car. My agent called me that Friday and said, "How would you like to do a movie?" And I said, "Oh, great. I haven't done a movie since the '60s." He said, "They'll pay you $1,000 a day. It's ten days work." I said, "Great, it'll pay for my new car that I wanna get." He said, "There's one drawback." I said, "What's that?" He said, "It's a horror film...." I said, "Awww, no. No way. I have a reputation as being a game player on television anyway. I want to really be considered an actress, and now to be in a horror movie? No." Then I thought about the car and I thought about the bread, and I said, "Oh, send me the script." He sent me the script and I read it, and said, "What a piece of shit. Nobody will ever see this dreck. It will come, it will go; I'll have my money, I'll buy my little car, and that will be it...." Well, here we are, you and I are talking today [*laughs*].

To tell you the truth, I've only seen *Friday the 13th* three times in all these years. My daughter and I went to see it when it opened—she was about 18—at this movie theater in

Connecticut because that was my home at the time, on the water. It was Mother's Day, and there were six little boys in the theater and we watched them. Not a sound, not a peep, these little boys didn't react in any way. So we got outside the theater and I said to her, "Now tell me the truth, are you ashamed of your mother because of this movie?" And she said, "No. Now I don't have to explain to my friends who you are any more." So that was from her mouth to the universe's ear. Then I had to see it one night—which changed my mind about it—not too long ago, maybe two or three years, at one of those autograph-signing horror conventions; you sign your 8 x 10 glossies and people buy them and all that sort of thing. They were going to show the film, and they wanted me to introduce it and talk about it, which I did to a group of people. Then, as I was going back to my autograph table, I said to the man, "Now, when you bring me back, let me walk through the audience and say, 'I'm sorry, I lost my head!'" They took me back, but it was when I came into that scene; so I had to stand there at the back of the little theater and look at it and watch it, and enough years had passed that I said, "Ah, well, it's really not such a bad job at all." You watch a woman going insane, and I thought, "Ah, not too bad."

And people love Mrs. Voorhees, they love the character; it's so crazy. They hug me, and they put their babies in my arms, and they have photographs taken with me at these autograph-signing sessions. It's very sweet, as a matter of fact. Very dear. The interesting thing, too, is that you never see me kill anybody. I mean, I get it in the end, or in the neck should we say [*laughs*], but in this country [America] they have not shown the unedited version. The unedited version has been shown in Japan and Germany and all of that, while here they say, "Oh, we've got to edit it. We don't want our kids seeing it." What, with the war going on, and all those other movies that are so blatant? You get smacked in the face with the horror of it all. So I've made peace with it. All right, if you love it and love me, thank you. I've never received a penny; I made my $10,000, but there's never been one cent residual on the first one. I've never seen the others, and I refuse to accept and acknowledge the guy in the hockey mask. I always say to people at signings, "I don't know who he is ... I'm crazy, but I'm not insane. I would never have done what I did if it hadn't been for my little boy Jason at the bottom of Crystal Lake." And these guys who play the role ... who knows who they are, poor dears, they never get their faces seen. They come up to me—again, at these conventions—and I'm nice to them, but say as a parting shot, "No, you're not my baby. He's at the bottom of the lake." So it's all a joke, really.

*Is it true that you came up with a whole history for Mrs. Voorhees before playing her?*

Yeah. But that's the way I work as an actress. Every role I do has a history. You are somebody before you come on stage; you bring a life with you. What happened was that when I was reading the script, I noticed that at one point there was a POV and a hand with a class ring on it; which, by the way, was a hairy hand by this point—because it was a young man who assisted Tommy Savini. Tom did all the special effects; he is really a genius in his own right. So, I thought, "'class ring'—that's my time in high school, back in the '40s, and girls always went steady with someone and wore the guy's class ring wrapped up in tape, put nail varnish on it so it wouldn't get dirty, or you hung it with string around your neck." This was a time when guys and girls didn't go around making love, not the way it is now. There was no such thing as knowing about contraception and nobody wanted to get pregnant, so I figured she and the guy she went steady with—because she's wearing the ring—made love and she became pregnant. And she said to him, "I'm pregnant," and he was, "Ahh, pregnant?" So she tried to hide the pregnancy until she got into her sixth or seventh month, and had to reveal to her parents that she was pregnant. Her father threw her out of the house and said, "You tramp, get out of here. I never want to see you again." And in those days I was on the advisory board of the Salvation Army here in New York, so there would be times that I would go to the home for unwed mothers and have dinner with some of the girls there. So I figured, okay, she goes to the Salvation Army and has the baby.

So the night that I drove up, Tom started to make up my head, and the mask and all, he was showing me some Polaroids of the stuff that he had done. I'm sitting there and he had this picture and I said, "Who's this?" He said, "Well, that's your son." I said, "Really? Why does he look so strange?" He said, "He's a mongoloid." I said, "*What*? That wasn't in the script." He said, "Well, he didn't look spooky enough so we decided to do this makeup job on him." So I figured, oh my God, out of wedlock, she's pregnant, and the father throws her out, and now she has a baby that isn't really whole and wholesomely well and going to be a functioning child. She doesn't know how to earn a living, she hasn't learned any skills and all because she's just out of high school, and thrown out—the whole thing. And I thought, "Oh my God," y'know? This young woman has been pressured to get a job at this camp, washing dishes, cooking in the kitchen, so that her little boy could be with other children his age. And of course he drowns because they're off making love.

That was my autobiography for Pamela Voorhees. And that's why I justify her doing the things that she did and behaving the way that she did; she was a bit crazed.

[Director] Sean Cunningham really made you use your imagination, it's your imagination which is talking to you all the time in the film. I mean, when the little girl goes to the john and washes her hands, is that shower curtain moving? What's that voice out there in the rainstorm? All the things that are insinuated but not really enunciated, so to speak, and put right out in front. That's why I like reading. I don't go to see many movies and I don't watch TV hardly at all any more. It's just pathetic. But the idea that you're sitting there and you don't know what's coming, and you're titillated by it all. I think, of its genre, it is a goodie. I think it has to do

The *Friday the 13th* poster (1980, Paramount Pictures/Warner Bros.; courtesy Aine Leicht and Betsy Palmer).

with that; everybody gets to use their imaginations. And if we leave a few more things to our imaginations, like women who dress, but only reveal so much [*laughs*], it's much more attractive and fascinating.

*How did you get along with Cunningham during the filming?*

Got along fine, just fine. I'm just sorry I never made any money out of the whole damned thing. But I've made more than that. I really have been loved and adored, in another way, and respected all these years. It's a cult film. Who would have thought I was in a cult film, for God's sake? [*Laughs*]

*Is it true that, in a fight scene rehearsal with Adrienne King, you slapped her so hard you made her cry out?*

No, I didn't slap her that hard at all. I remember the sequence; half the time we couldn't shoot because it was snowing outside. They started it outside in the mountains in June, but by the time they got to me it was end of September, so it was cold. We were inside of this place, I remember some bales of hay and straw and things like that around, and I said to Adrienne, "Let's rehearse this little scene here." On stage, when you slap somebody you really do it, but you really know *how* to do it with your hand, and you catch them along the jawline so you don't break their jaw open. It's a technique, like one where you fall on stage, you do it a certain way so you don't kill yourself. Well, we were off in the corner rehearsing it and we got to the slap. I slapped her; not *hard*, but I think it surprised her. She dropped to her knees and said, "Sean, Sean..." and she was crying. So he came up and asked, "What's happening here?" "She hit me, she hit me...." I said, "No, no, no, no, no, we were rehearsing the scene, and I just slapped her when the slap comes in." And he said, "Oh no, Betsy. We don't really slap people." I said, "You're kidding! The camera's right there and you don't slap somebody?" He said, "No, no, we'll put the sound effect in." I said, "Isn't it going look like I'm missing her?" He said, "No, we'll shoot it in such a way that that won't happen." But that's how that happened, you see, and I still laugh about it. Adrienne's at all these autographing signing sessions, as is Ari [Lehman], the boy who played my son. They line us up together sometimes—we're the family [*laughs*], so to speak.

*It was quite a physical fight that you and Adrienne King had.*

No. Down on the beach when I'm banging her into the sand and all, she doesn't really hit me in the crotch [*laughs*]! With that oar, or whatever it was. People bring this up, they have these photographs on their phones. And I say, "Oooh, that must have smarted," when I see that oar running into my crotch, for God's sakes [*laughs*]. But no, no, no, no, no. I remember I went out to the cabin, because everything was shot right there in the compound of the Boy Scout camp, and I got out of all my wet sweaters—they had me wear a couple of sweaters 'cause I'm slender and I didn't really look like I could hawk a body through a window and all. Anyway, I was up there getting out of all my wet stuff and somebody from down below at the shoot came up and said, "Hey, hey, they're gonna chop your head off. You wanna see it?" I said, "You've got to be kidding." So I never saw how they did it. I saw a photograph in just the last few months of how the young man who played me throughout the film was wearing the sweater and they've sewn the head onto the sweater on the back of his shoulder and neck, like Quasimodo, y'know? I think Tommy was actually the one who chopped the head off. Adrienne looks like she's going to be the one that whacks me, but I think Tom did it. I think he didn't want anybody to get killed, especially his associate.

The first time we all saw it was at Paramount here in New York, at a showing for family and friends. We all invited people we knew, and the mothers and fathers of the different kids who were in the thing. I've never met Kevin Bacon. He and I have never met and he lives around the corner actually, not too far from where I live. I don't think he likes to talk about being in the film; I think it was one of his very, very early things. He's such a great actor, I love his work and look forward to meeting him one day. But we all were sitting there, waiting and waiting for this thing to happen, and Sean was evidently still putting it together and he was inserting that old sound effect of [*does noise of the tension-building sound effect "sha-sha-sha-shi-shi-shi"*]. It was brilliant, just brilliant, that sound effect.

When I was doing Strindberg's *The Father* in Philadelphia, after the theater we all would leave and go to the supermarket and get stuff for our little kitchens in the apartments we were staying in. I was pushing my little cart around and I heard behind me, "Sha-sha-sha-shi-shi-shi!" and I turned around and the guy said, "I knew it was you, I knew it was you." And that still happens, everybody does that particular sound. Again, it titillates your imagination.

*The critics hated the film at first. Is it true that Gene Siskel printed your address and encouraged people to write to you?*

I heard that. But I didn't hear it until years later. Apparently they said, "Write to Betsy Palmer, tell her how dare she!" Come on, y'know, get a grip [*laughs*]. You play all kinds of roles ... you're an actress. But people are funny.

*Why didn't you come back when they asked you to do* **Jason X** *or* **Freddy vs. Jason***?*

Well, they asked me to do three different ones, the last one being the Freddy. But, y'know, like two lines? I actually think it was dishonest to put a girl in it who supposedly looked like me and sounded like me, but all my fans say, "No, we know it's not you. We could see that right off the bat." But it's like two lines, what the hell is that? It's not a role. At least Mrs. Voorhees in the first one is an acting role. And [they offered] no money; they wanted to pay me SAG minimum, for one, two days work. I said, "Pay me what you're going to pay Freddy." They said, "Well, it's only two days work." I said, "I'll work for you 200 days. Just give me a guarantee you're going to pay me the same money as him." [*Laughs*] So I said no thank you to the whole thing.

*Have you seen the other films?*

No. Haven't seen any of them with Jason. I've only seen number one.

*Have you had any memorable experiences at conventions?*

I think the thing that's a lot of fun is when they put us up on stage. Actually there was one they did about a year ago, where they had all the women from *Friday the 13th*—all the actresses who had played in the other versions—and introduced as "Ladies of the Lake." I get very naughty when I'm in front of an audience, I say the word penis and things like that [*laughs*]—what's wrong with that? It's a word, and having been married to a doctor, you just say it. But there was one gal talking, being very coy, suggesting someone evidently had a very large ... but she would only say "equipment." So I laid it right out [*laughs*] and said, "Well, were you able to accommodate it?" The audience went crazy; they think I'm so funny ... which I am [*laughs*]. Take things sincerely but not seriously...

*Do you believe in the supernatural or psychics or anything like that?*

Yeah, I enjoy that. I listen to a radio program called *Coast to Coast*, I find it very interesting. There was a woman on last night who has an Haitian background from five generations ago, and she's of a family where all the women have been voodoo priestesses. She was very, very interesting. Of course it isn't all this crazy stuff that Hollywood has made out. As she explained it, it's a religion in itself. I'm a great believer that it's all out there the way it's supposed to be. And I like to read books that have to do with—I hate to use the word "spiritual" because it gets so misused—but that other aspect of what we really are.

**Palmer in a "striking" pose as Mrs. Voorhees (courtesy Aine Leicht and Betsy Palmer).**

*Which kind of acting do you prefer, theater, TV or film?*

Oh, theater has always been my first love. I love a living audience, and I love the whole idea of having the opportunity to do it over and over again. I go around the country and do *Love Letters*, an A.R. Gurney play, which is a man and a woman and you sit and you read a script—there's a table and chairs and a rug underneath you. You're two people who start off in the third grade together and then end up in their 60s, or even further down the line. And it's not ooey, gooey love letters at all; a couple of times I say "fuck," y'know? I've been doing that character for years now. But I don't ask for any money, I just say, "Get me there and put me up overnight or for a couple of days." I love it, and every time I do it I always find something new in her and the audience loves it. There isn't necessarily any acting, because you read it, but I play her—and your body language happens when you're into it. It's a role I really like a lot. And, as I say, it's something that's easy to do. You don't have to memorize a bunch of lines, you just get up and do it. I did some wonderful radio stuff yesterday for a man who's 96, who was a big radio producer and director in New York all those years ago. It was all about the polio vaccine, and he gives it to colleges and universities, so the young men and women and children can hear radio the way it should really be done. It's very rewarding. I feel most blessed, I really do, to be able to still be out there doing something that I like to do, allowing the universe to use you for what it is that you bring out.

# *Ron Perlman*

Ron Perlman was born April 13, 1950, in Washington Heights, New York, the son of a municipal employee mother and jazz drummer-repairman father. He attended George Washington High School and later Lehman College in New York City, graduating with a Bachelor of Fine Arts degree in Theater, and also the University of Minnesota, where he earned a Master's in theater arts. He made his feature debut in Jean-Jacques Annaud's *Quest for Fire* (1981) and made an impression as Salvatore in *The Name of the Rose* (1986) before shooting to fame as Vincent in the TV series *Beauty and the Beast* (1987–1990) alongside *The Terminator*'s Linda Hamilton. Various other notable film roles followed including Stephen King's *Sleepwalkers* (1992), *The Island of Dr. Moreau* (1996) and *Star Trek: Nemesis* (2002). He worked with director Jean-Pierre Jeunet on both *The City of Lost Children* (1995) and *Alien Resurrection* (1997). But his most successful longstanding actor-director relationship was with Guillermo del Toro on *Cronos* in 1993. This would eventually would see him taking on some of his most famous roles: as Reinhardt in *Blade II* (2002) and as Hellboy in 2004 and again in 2008. Ron has also done a lot of voice-over work, in cartoons ranging from *Teen Titans* and *Batman: The Animated Series* to *Mortal Kombat* and *Afro Samurai*.

---

*How did you get into acting?*

I couldn't do anything else; I had no other skills. If it wasn't for acting I'd be homeless.

*Did you aspire to be an actor as a youngster?*

Not really, no. I was forced into it in high school. They were having auditions for the school play and only girls showed up, so my swimming coach pushed me into going to the auditions because he hoped that maybe I could do the drama department more good than I was doing the swimming team. Since I was one of the only boys who showed up, I of course got a role, and that led me to where I am today. The play was *Thieves' Carnival* by Jean Anouilh, a French farce—sort of a fable farce, a lot of prat-take comedy.

*Did you have an interest in the horror genre as a youngster?*

Never much of a fan of horror. Strictly quote the devil that I've made so much of my living around the horror genre.

*How about fantasy, science fiction or anything like that?*

No, I always was a fan of the golden era of cinema: the John Ford movies, the Howard Hawks movies, George Stevens, Raoul Walsh, Hitchcock... Hitchcock was about as occult as I got, but it was more the Hitchcock films like *Rear Window* and *Rebecca* and things of that nature, which were more drama than anything else.

*Do you have a favorite from that era?*

I have a lot of favorite films. I think *Sullivan's Travels* is one of the greatest films ever made; that's Preston Sturges. I think the whole body of work of Frank Capra. I think I could probably name about six or eight John Ford films that would be favorites. A few Errol Flynn movies, like *Gentleman Jim*. There are tons of movies.

*Your father was a drummer. Did you have any musical aspirations when you were younger?*

Well, there was music abounding in the household while I was growing up, and my brother in fact became a jazz musician as well. But I tried my hand at it and I had no skill, and no discipline, no desire to put in the time that was necessary to master the playing of an instrument. I was more concerned with hanging out in the schoolyard and playing baseball, stuff like that.

*How did the role of Vincent in* Beauty and the Beast *come your way?*

I don't know exactly how it how came about. I had done two movies that required me to wear prosthetic makeup. One was *Quest for Fire* and, more recently, *The Name of the Rose*, when *Beauty and the Beast* was circulating the town. Rick Baker had been hired to do the makeup for the Beast and I think he recommended me because he felt as though I was comfortable doing mask work, and that I had the patience in the makeup chair to endure the hours it would take to get the job done. I read for the role and the rest is history. I remember the first day in makeup; it was one of the very last scenes of the pilot episode, where I'm dropping off Beauty after she has been underground in my world and we have begun to forge a relationship. I remember it like it was yesterday, in fact. It was 1986.

*Was that a more heavy duty makeup than your others?*

**Ron Perlman (photograph by Gordon Correll; courtesy Gordon Correll).**

Once you go through a complete transformation like that role, you're generally looking at a four-hour investment in the chair. Most of them have been between three and five hours and there's been quite a few over the course of time. But the unique thing about *Beauty and the Beast* was that it was a TV series and not a movie where after a few weeks or a few months you get to go home; this was grueling in so far as it was nine months a year for three years. You would finish one episode at 11 o'clock at night and then be back in the makeup chair at four o'clock in the morning to start a new one, without any break in between. So it was more of an endurance test than anything else.

*The makeup part of it—does it get easier or harder the more jobs like that you do?*

I think I'm finally, finally at the point where the role has got to be truly spectacular for me to want to make that investment of time. And over the years I've grown more comfortable in working without makeup. In the early days of my acting, I think the fact that I was behind the mask was very freeing. I think I was more comfortable as an actor when I was masked. But time marches on and one becomes more comfortable with one's self and now the makeup is beginning to be a little bit taxing, as I get older. I just finished seven months shooting *Hellboy 2*, having said all that, and there's an example of a role that's so extraordinary that one goes through whatever one has to in order to realize it. And there's nothing that's too difficult really because the goodness of the character far outweighs any of the negatives of getting to the set.

Perlman with Linda Hamilton in the hit TV show *Beauty and the Beast* (1987–1990, CBS).

*You invest the* **Hellboy** *character with so much emotion, the audience feels for him too. Is that difficult to do with all the makeup on?*

Well, once again in the first movie it was a Rick Baker design and the fluidity to his work is otherworldly—and frankly I don't even quite understand how it's possible where you're behind a few inches of rubber, which is an inanimate object, and yet whatever it is that you're thinking, your very thought is mirrored without any adjustment whatsoever. So I never had to make any adjustments for the playing of Hellboy. Nor did I have to make any adjustments for the playing of Vincent in *Beauty and the Beast*. Rick Baker is just such an extraordinary artist. In the second *Hellboy*, the makeup was slightly redesigned by Mike Elizalde and the good people at Special Motion, and once again it didn't require any real adjustment on my part. I mean, once the makeup was on, I completely forgot it was there and just played the character the way I would play him if I weren't wearing any makeup at all.

*Have you found a difference in makeup over the years?*

Yeah, the state of the art has refined over the years. The very first makeup I wore was in 1980 in *Quest for Fire*. They had a problem blending the edges, especially if the edges needed to be blended onto a part of your face, because the rubber wasn't quite as good or the edges weren't quite as well reproduced. Now those issues are almost ancient history.

*How did you first come into contact with Guillermo del Toro?*

Guillermo was a horror freak. He was a young Mexican filmmaker who had never directed a movie before but had made a lot of short films and a lot of TV shows, all featuring monsters and ghouls, and cadavers, and flights of fancy. Because the art of special effects makeup wasn't so well articulated in Mexico, he took it upon himself to study under Dick Smith and Rick Baker, and became a special effects makeup artist and opened his own shop, so that he could service his own inventions. So he became acutely aware of my work since I had done so much work under makeup. I had already gone through quite prominent exercises: *Quest for Fire*, *Name of the Rose* and of course *Beauty and the Beast*. And when he got ready to do his first film, which was *Cronos*, he sent me a letter and a script and it seemed as though he wanted me to participate in it, sort of as a good luck charm. I was somebody whose work he had seen a great deal of, because of the fascination with special effects makeup. I read the script and it was as unique as anything I'd ever read and we forged the relationship starting with that film in 1992. And we've now finished our fourth film together.

*Is it nice to have that kind of relationship that carries on throughout a career with a director?*

It's *really* nice. I mean, it's a privilege to have watched him evolve into a filmmaker. *Pan's Labyrinth* is as close to being a perfect film as anything I've ever seen. To be a part of his personal history is a privilege and an honor, and one that I don't take lightly. Aside from collaborations, we've become quite good friends, and there's a kind of shorthand to our work together, which is one of the cornerstones of having so long and rich a history together.

*Is that the case with Jean-Pierre Jeunet as well?*

I did two movies with Jean-Pierre, *City of Lost Children* and *Alien Resurrection*. I didn't quite span the length of time with him as I had with Guillermo del Toro or Jean-Jacques Annaud. Jean-Jacques I did three films for, including the first film I was ever in—and then one of the last films he made, which was *Enemy at the Gates*, and it was *Name of the Rose* in between. But that was another relationship that stands the course of decades, and there's a true friendship and brotherhood that lies underneath the working collaboration.

*What was the experience of working on Jean-Pierre's* **Alien** *film like?*

It was a fun movie to work on. It was six months working in Los Angeles, which is very unique these days; most of the time you're working in Canada or Eastern Europe, because filmmaking has got so expensive. And it was a great ensemble of actors, some of whom I've taken with me throughout the rest of my life as great friends, so all that was good. Sigourney Weaver was a joy. She was very generous, she had a lot of fun doing what she was doing. She didn't take herself terribly seriously, but she took the work very seriously. That's my favorite combination, somebody who works in that vein.

*What was* **Blade II** *like to work on?*

That was kind of a lark for me. You know, there's a lot of movie on the screen in *Blade II* and that was Guillermo beginning to flex his muscles as a big-time studio filmmaker, with big action sequences and an epic sweep. But my contribution to that film was minimal, and I don't remember ever breaking a sweat. There wasn't a whole lot of makeup, there wasn't a whole lot of heavy lifting. I was more of an observer on that film, watching my friend Guillermo grapple with a real genre, big-time studio machine—and watching him adapt, coming from his very humble roots as a Mexican filmmaker, scrambling for whatever dollars he could get, into someone who suddenly had all these resources. And it was a seamless transformation.

*Is it more fun to play a bad guy than it is to play a hero?*

It depends on the writing and it depends on who you're working for. But of course that's true of any character you play. It can be nightmarish if the writing is bad and the filmmaker doesn't have that *joie de vivre* that a filmmaker should have. Or it can be a phenomenal experience if it's one where a great deal of heart is exhibited along the way, and there's a great joy and a great enthusiasm to every passing day. I do like playing bad guys if they're interesting and if they're well-rounded and if they have a lot of idiosyncrasies or they have a lot of behavioral tweaks.

*So it comes down to the writing more than anything?*

It *always* comes down to the writing...

*Were you anxious or excited about taking on the role of Hellboy?*

I was very humbled by it, you know. The film languished in a studio for five years because Guillermo kept bringing up my name and the studio kept saying no. And after five years they gave him back the material and said, "Look, it's pretty clear that we're not going to come to any sort of agreement, so good luck with your project." I frankly never thought that he would ever be able to persuade a major studio to invest in someone like me who is, at best, an under-the-radar character actor who'd never really carried a movie,

**Perlman in his most famous role as Hellboy in** *Hellboy II: The Golden Army* **(2008, Universal Pictures).**

much less a franchise before. And when a studio makes an investment the size of the one that they made with *Hellboy*, it's simple mathematics, they need to have a bone fide and bankable movie star to hedge [their] bet. So when he finally was able to persuade somebody to put all those resources behind me, it occupied more the realm of fantasy, of dreams coming true than of actual investment in like, "Oh God, I hope this happens"; I never for a minute thought that it was going to happen with me. And I in fact told Guillermo that he should drop the idea of using me and make the film because it was too good to not make. But he doggedly and persistently, and patiently, waited until the opportunity presented itself. I think the opportunity presented itself more because of the triumph of *Blade II* and the fact that so many studios wanted to be in business with him, that he finally had enough influence to pull this off.

*He's got such foresight. It's impossible now to imagine anybody else playing the part other than you.*

Well, thank you. It's a beautiful character. And it's a character that means a lot to Guillermo, and certainly a lot to me. I feel lucky every day that I got to play him once, much less a second time.

*Had you read the comics before taking the part?*

I had deliberately avoided the comics and anything to do with *Hellboy*, because for seven years while he was going through this exercise—which I felt was an exercise in futility—I refused to invest myself emotionally in the idea of ever playing the role, so I steered clear of the material and never read the script until Guillermo finally called me up and said, "We did it!" Then, of course, I read everything, and became good pals with [Hellboy creator] Mike Mignola, and picked his brain for any light that he could shed on who he saw this guy as being.

*Did you notice many differences between the comic strips and the film version of the character?*

The comic character is not as multi-dimensional as the film character, he speaks in two-word sentences and never really reveals a great deal of personality. He's more a functionary, an iconic archetype, than anything else. The exercise of transferring that character into the humanity that it takes to create a film character of multi-dimensions and complex emotional schematics is quite a different exercise—and I think the genius of Guillermo's writing was adding the personality to this guy, the very complex behavioral result of the dilemma of who Hellboy is in the world.

*And of course John Myers [Rupert Evans] is not in the comics. Hellboy bounces off this character in the film.*

That was an invention of Guillermo's for the purposes of the screenplay.

*What's your favorite thing about the Hellboy character?*

His wit, his irreverence. His normalcy, his lack of the pretension that goes with being a superhero. The superheroes one sees in comic book movies are very one-dimensional, very true-blue, and almost cardboard-like, whereas Hellboy is an underachiever of gigantic proportions. Very self-indulgent, very much an adolescent. Sort of a blue collar kinda guy you'd think about having a beer with, rather than accompanying to save the world. So the personality, the wit, the humor—those are my favorite things about that guy. And also the heart. He has a heart that's exemplary, and also one that I in fact aspire to learn from.

*Do you have a favorite line from the first film?*

There were too many favorite lines to choose from to pick one [*laughs*].

*It seems as though you did a lot of physical work in the first movie.*

It *was* an arduous shoot, but when things are as arduous and long hours and difficult as the *Hellboy* movies are, then the passage of time seems to have those things fall away and one only remembers the good aspects. I don't remember *Hellboy* ever being burdensome. The second *Hellboy* is fresh—I finished it not that long ago—and it was a much more difficult shoot, but it was a four-times-bigger film, and I think a more elegant film, and a more painstaking bit of filmmaking on the part of Guillermo and the part of all of us. I think the results are going to be on the screen.

*How do you see the character developing in the second film?*

Well, the character—when the movie opens—is now married to Liz and they're living together in his little bunker underneath New Jersey, like a mile underground—and she's stuck in this little kind of bachelor pad of his which is kind of a tribute to empty pizza boxes and dirty socks, a lot of kittens and a lot of kitty litter.

*Rings very true...*

And they're fighting, they're not getting along [*laughs*]. They're like the Bickersons. So in this particular installment, Hellboy is emotionally at sea. Whereas in the first movie he was just filled with swagger and self-assurance and a lot of one-line quips, in the sequel he's grappling for his emotional stability and balance because he's desperately in love with Liz and is trying to find a way to keep her in his life. So it's a more complex Hellboy, emotionally and behaviorally.

*What's your take on the villains?*

The villains come from this world of elves that ruled the Earth thousands of years ago. There was a king of the elf world and his two offspring, a prince and princess. The prince has come back and decided to decimate the pact that the king made with the human world so that there would be peace among all of the various forms of humanity. He's a real threat and he's determined to wage a war that will exact a profound price on humanity. So that's what Hellboy's up against in the second film.

*Did you enjoy the shoot?*

I enjoyed the collaboration with Guillermo a great deal. The shoot was really, really difficult and I'm just coming out of it right now. I was challenged to the nth degree to just physically get through it. It was long, six months of six-day weeks, and it was very easy to become incredibly depleted under those conditions. But I think that the slog was well worth it.

*You play the character in the cartoons as well. What's that process like? Do all the actors get together?*

No, most of the time you're in a booth by yourself recording your lines in a vacuum, and then you have to imagine the other characters. That's just the physical constraints of doing animated work, they record characters one at a time. It's a slightly different exercise, it doesn't have the same *joie de vivre* and the same camaraderie, and the same bouncing-off-one-another. So it's a little bit more difficult in that regard.

*How did you land your part in* **Masters of Horror?**

Mick Garris directed a movie called *Sleepwalkers*, which I had a rather small role in, many years ago. Then we sort of had a reunion when we did *Desperation* together, the Stephen King mini-series for television, and had a phenomenal time working on that. That was an extraordinarily beautiful piece of material, a great adaptation by Mr. King himself. And that kind of rekindled a great fondness for one another that started back in the '80s. I happened to be on the scene coincidentally when he was getting *Masters of Horror* realized and into production. Every time they offered me an installment, it always conflicted with other work, but they finally offered me this one that John Carpenter was going to direct [*Pro-Life*]. I always wanted to work with and get to know Carpenter, and it just happened to slip into my schedule really well, so I did that.

*How did you feel about the subject matter of abortion in* **Pro-Life?**

I found the subject matter to be haunting and intimidating because the minute I read it I realized we could be asking for a lot of trouble. And I thought that the whole exercise was a bit of a tightrope walk, whereas if you went the wrong way, the other way, you would fall headlong into the abyss. But the idea of working with John Carpenter assuaged all of my fears and I figured, if this was good enough for John, it was good enough for me. I got a chance to spend some time with a real hero of mine.

*We saw a film recently called* **The Last Winter** *that you were in and were very impressed with that one. What attracted you to the role?*

The script was what attracted me—and the role. I thought it was a real thinking man's piece, and I felt that whoever had written it [Larry Fessenden and Robert Leaver] had [the same] take on horror films as Guillermo. Somebody who came to the party with a great intellectual depth and a real seriousness which was at the forefront rather than just horror for the sake of horror. There was a really important issue at the heart of the dialectic which was "The Last Winter." And of course the horror is basically an offshoot of those.

**Perlman as Brother Samuel in** *Mutant Chronicles* **(2008, Edward R. Pressman Film; courtesy Magnet Releasing).**

Perlman (center) with Thomas Jane (left) and Benno Fürmann in *Mutant Chronicles* (2008, Edward R. Pressman Film; courtesy Magnet Releasing).

There were some very sobering ideas. And then I immediately fell in love with Larry Fessenden as a filmmaker, and now Larry and I are having the kind of relationship that we referred to earlier—an ongoing relationship with lots of projects that we're doing together. I got to go to New York and be in a little mini-horror movie that he's producing and starring in. Then there's another film we're hoping to get to work on soon. So this was more than just taking a role in a film, this was finding someone who I'm enthusiastically wending my way through life with like I am with Guillermo.

*Do you both subscribe to the "less is more" idea in those horror films? That what you* **don't** *see is more frightening?*

I really hate anything that's gratuitous. To me the problem with horror, especially the horror I was growing up with, was that everything was around the stiff, and everything was around the effect of what it was going to have on the audience by the shocking aspects of whatever it was: vampires, werewolves, etc., etc. Whereas horror is the result of the underpinnings of something that has more gravitas. It relates more back to the real world. There's a smartness to it that I find riveting and compelling. Guillermo's work fits that description to a tee, as does Larry's.

Perlman today (photograph by Gordon Correll; courtesy Gordon Correll).

*We heard a rumor that you might be involved in an H.P. Lovecraft adaptation.*

Guillermo's always wanted to do this film *At the Mountains of Madness*, which is Lovecraft. And apparently he's written a role for me in there. I have not read the script, I don't know whether he's ever going to get it done; he's got so many projects and is so "in demand" right now, that it's just a question of what he prioritizes for his limited amounts of time. We'll see.

*Which part do you think has stretched you most in your career? And which part would you like to play in the future?*

Which part stretched me the most? I would have to say Hellboy pretty much is my Hamlet. All actors want to play Hamlet because it's an emotional home run, it covers every conceivable facet of the human condition and it does so in a way that's sublime and of the highest elegance and intelligence. If that's the description of a great role, then Hellboy is for me what Hamlet is to the regional six billion theater actors.

*And any dream roles?*

I've stopped dreaming about roles, because the roles that I've gotten to play have gone so far beyond anything I could possibly have dreamed, that now I'm just very content to sit and wait and see what happens. There's a movie I'm here in London for, doing post-production, which is incredibly near and dear to me, which I look forward to seeing how the world embraces—and that's called *Mutant Chronicles*. It's really the first film of someone I consider to be one of the most extraordinary and imaginative directors I've ever worked with. His name is Simon Hunter. And [based on] what I've seen in the last couple of days—I certainly haven't seen the whole film—the world is about to see something incredibly special and intelligent, and filmmaking of the highest order.

# Alex Vincent

Alex Vincent was born April 29, 1981, in New Jersey. At a tender age he won the coveted part of Andy Barclay in *Child's Play* (1988), which would launch a horror franchise that is still going strong to this day; it earned him a nomination for Best Juvenile Performance from the Academy of Science Fiction, Fantasy & Horror Films. A year later he starred in *Wait Until Spring, Bandini*, then reprised his role as Andy in *Child's Play II*. He went on to star in *Just Like in the Movies* (1992) and *My Family Treasure* (1993), before graduating from Hackensack High School in Hackensack, New Jersey in 1999. More recently he has put in appearances at many horror conventions. Alex also writes, works as a sound engineer and continues to act. He resides in the Tampa Bay area.

---

*Is it right that you got into acting because a local girl was doing it?*

Yeah, basically. I was five years old and this girl who lived down the block from me was doing commercials. I saw her on TV and that gave me the idea, it looked like something I wanted to do. So I told my mother I wanted to be in commercials or be on TV, and she said to me she had the same manager that my friends down the block had. From there I went out on a lot of auditions and I got lucky with *Child's Play*.

*Were your parents very encouraging?*

Oh yes. My mother drove me to New York City to audition three or four times a week for most of my childhood.

*How did the* Child's Play *part come about?*

I auditioned with many, many kids from New York, and I had a call-back in New York and then I had a second call-back to fly out to California to audition against, I think, one or two other guys. I did that and it went well for me. I was lucky and I got the part.

*How did you get on with Catherine Hicks?*

She was a really sweet lady, she was very nice while I was working with her when I was younger and I've been friends with her since.

*Did that help you get into the roles of mother and son?*

Yeah, I would think so. It made me comfortable, definitely.

*How was Tom Holland as a director?*

Well, he knew what he wanted and he was assertive in getting it. I think there were a couple of times when I had to be taken off the set because he was frustrated and using language which they wanted to get me away from. But to me he was really nice all the time. I had a good time working with him.

*Have you had any contact with him since?*

No, I actually haven't spoken to him or seen him since the first *Child's Play* movie.

*Did you find the scenes with Chucky, especially in the bed in the dark, scary at all to film?*

No. None of it was ever scary, it was all very fake.

*Was it weird working with the puppet of Chucky?*

No, I thought it was cool. I thought it was great how they got it to operate and I was friends with the puppeteers who operated him. I enjoyed working with them, I thought it was a good time.

*And were Brad Dourif's voiceovers dubbed on later?*

They were done first. And they got the doll to operate around the vocal track.

*Did you ever hear any of that to react to?*

Yeah, it was on playback, every take.

*The finale with the fire looked dangerous. Can you remember anything about filming that?*

The scene where they set the doll on fire? I wasn't there when they did that. It was actually the little person who played Chucky in certain scenes, and he was a friend of mine making that movie. I didn't really want to see them set him on fire [*laughs*].

Alex Vincent (right) with Catherine Hicks in *Child's Play* (1988, United Artists; courtesy John Gullidge).

*Were the filmmakers very careful not to show you any of the really scary bits?*

Actually they were. I don't think I ever saw the melted Chucky, while we were filming.

*Do you think it would have bothered you at that age, or would it have all been part of the make-believe?*

I probably would have been fine with it. I liked all the special effects.

*Are there any other interesting stories from that set you might be able to remember?*

No, not really. I was six years old; it's hard to remember too much [*laughs*].

*You look more confident on* **Child's Play 2**. *Was this more to do with having more experience as an actor or the direction you were given?*

It was definitely having more experience and knowing the role, coming back and knowing what I had to do. And I was a little older too, I think I had a better concept of it, for the second one.

*What did you think of the director, John Lafia?*

I thought he was good, he was a very nice guy. I remember playing with him off set.

*Did you like the way that they brought back Chucky?*

Yeah, I thought that worked well.

*Were you pleased to get top billing on the credits of this one?*

I don't know if I thought much of it at the time. I was happy that my name was first, sure.

*Were there any major differences on that set from the first one?*

Well, it was at Universal Studios—that was the biggest difference. I used to love Universal Studios on the tour on the tram and all this was in the middle of all of it, so that was exciting.

*What were Jenny Agutter and Gerrit Graham like to work with?*

Gerrit Graham I didn't really work with too much. I had a couple of scenes with him, but didn't really spend much time with him. Jenny I got along good with. I didn't spend as much time with her as I did with Catherine, but she was very nice to me.

*Have you ever bumped into either of them again?*

No.

*You seemed to get along well with Christine Elise [Kyle]. Were the scenes with her fun?*

Yeah, I enjoyed working with her and hanging out with her. The whole time I was filming the movie, I spent a lot of spare time with her. She was really sweet. I never saw her again either, sad to say.

*Do you have any memories of filming the scenes in the cellar where you face Chucky?*

Yeah, I have vague memories of it. I remember that battery-operated knife that I had. But nothing really sticks out as a big memory from that.

**Chucky attacking young Andy Barclay (Alex Vincent) in** *Child's Play* **(1988, United Artists; courtesy John Gullidge).**

*Was that a real knife or a fake one?*

Yeah, it was a real knife.

*What was it like being on the Good Guy factory set?*

That was really cool. It was a huge set, they had all those fake Chucky boxes everywhere, and it was exciting to do that stuff. The scene where I melt Chucky down—it wasn't even really hot, but it was made to look like hot melted wax. I remember pulling that thing down and shooting that. It was one of the most fun times I had, I think, making the movie.

*So the makers weren't too concerned this time about showing you the melted or burned dolls?*

No, I think I saw the Chucky doll after they'd melted him down when they exploded it. I thought it was cool-looking. It was fun. They had some behind-the-scenes footage of me doing that on that day, and I remember I had a great time shooting that scene.

*So that didn't gross you out at all?*

No, I thought it was really, really cool.

*How many times did you have to do the scenes on the rollers?*

I don't remember. It was definitely fun. I think it came out pretty funny-looking, you get a chance to almost laugh a little bit, and then Chucky comes up and scares the heck out of you.

*And what was it like filming the scene where you crawl through the eye-punching machine?*

I think I remember being worried about that a little bit. But it wasn't that big a deal. The shot where they show my feet narrowly making it through—I don't think they were my feet, I think they were actually the feet of Josh, my stand-in.

*Did you have any contact with second unit director [and designer of Chucky] Kevin Yagher?*

Yeah, Kevin Yagher's a great guy, a great friend of mine. He's married to Catherine Hicks, and I went to their house not so long ago. They're really good friends. I hope to see them again soon.

*How did you feel when you heard they were making a third one so soon after the second?*

I think originally I thought I was going to be in it, but when they told me I wasn't, I was pretty disappointed.

*You've seen* Child's Play 3. *How did you rate Justin Whalin as an older version of Andy?*

He did a good job. I don't know if he looked so much like I did when I became his age, but I think he did a good job with it.

*Would you have done anything differently if you'd had the chance to play him?*

It's hard to say, because the script was ahead of my age at that time. I was ten years old only, so I'm not sure how anything would have been different.

*Say they'd made the film later when you were old enough.*

I don't know. I would have done my best and that's all. I don't really know how it would have come out in comparison with Justin Whalin's performance.

*What do you make of the way the franchise has progressed with* **Bride of Chucky** *and* **Seed of Chucky?**

It sort of became a comedy, which I think was kind of expected. That was the only way you could really carry it on. Same thing with the Freddy movies and the Jason movies, they've gotten a little more progressively funny instead of scary. And I think the idea is, if you want to keep the story going, you have to pretty much be able to make fun of yourself before anyone else can. So I think Don Mancini had a lot of fun with it, making it a comedy, and they're successful and that's good. But they're a completely different kind of movie.

*Which ones do you prefer, the harder-edged ones or the more comic?*

I'm happy to have been part of it when it was a horror film.

*How do you feel about the sheer amount of merchandise that's been associated with* **Child's Play?**

It's good for them, it's only made the films more popular. There are some cool Chucky dolls out there. It makes more people think of the movies, I guess, so it's good for them.

*Do you see a lot of it at conventions?*

Yeah, people sell Chucky dolls and stuff. I think it's cool that it keeps people into it.

*Do you have a favorite doll?*

Not really. I think the McFarlane dolls are pretty good.

*Did you get a chance to take any of the Chucky dolls or any other souvenirs?*

I wish. I would have sold them on eBay if I had [*laughs*]. But no, I never got to take any of them home.

**Andy Barclay (Vincent) in the Good Guy factory in *Child's Play* (1988, United Artists; courtesy John Gullidge).**

*Now you're very interested in music. How did that begin?*

I listen to music a lot, I've always enjoyed it. I played piano a little bit when I was younger and I still play a little bit, a little guitar. I'm not really a great musician; I write lyrics and I like music a lot. I'd like to get better at it. I was in a band for a little while but it didn't work out—but maybe again in the future it might.

*Have you ever considered doing film music?*

Actually, a lot of the stuff that I have made is computer generated music, and does sound a lot like film soundtracks. I think if I spent more time on that I would actually probably be pretty good at it. But I don't know if that's something I'll end up doing or not.

*We love your guitar with the Chucky face on it.*

That's not actually mine, it's owned by the artist. Brooks is his name. He makes guitars for all the horror legends, like a Jason guitar and a Freddy guitar, and they're really cool.

*Do you know how much it's worth?*

I don't know. I don't think he's selling it really; he collects them, he's got a lot of them. It's just something he does, it's a hobby of his.

*Is there any possibility of Andy coming back for a future film? We read that you'd mentioned it to Don Mancini, and that the fans are asking for him to come back.*

The fans that I meet at conventions have been saying that for years. That's one of the most popular, most common things that they say. I had some e-mail correspondence with

Don, just catching up basically, and I said to him, "If you ever feel like bringing my character back, I would be interested." But I don't know if that's going to happen, I don't know that he really has any plans for Andy. I don't know if there's anything he'd really want to do with the character at this point.

*It'd be a great comeback, like the* **Phantasm** *films where the original actor comes back to play the lead.*
Well, if he ever mentions it to me, I'd be interested in it. But nothing so far.

*Do you have any other acting roles coming up? Anything you've auditioned for?*
I haven't auditioned for many years. I live in New Jersey and auditioning in New York is pretty challenging and not something I've really been committed to do. If I move out to California, then that would be a different story. There have been some independent films that I've been offered roles in, most of which have fallen apart thus far. But we'll see what could happen in the future and I'd consider doing a lot of work if it was offered to me.

*Would you be more drawn towards the horror genre?*
I wouldn't mind either way. I like horror films; that's why I like horror fans, I think. Horror fans really appreciate the genre a lot, so I'd be happy to make another horror film. But I'd be interested in anything, I suppose, if I enjoyed it.

*Does it impress you, the way Chucky fans remember scenes from the films and quote lines from them?*
Oh yeah. I'm a fan of things too—I'm a fan of several things. There are people I'd be excited to meet and things that I would want to say. So I completely understand the other side of it.

*Can you give us any examples of people you'd like to meet?*
I've met a lot of people I've wanted to meet in my life. I suppose there are a few others I'd really like to meet. I got to meet Trent Reznor, and that was probably the most exciting for me. But I want to meet a few others: Howard Stern, Keifer Sutherland—they're two of my favorites—and Jack White.

*Is there anything planned for the twentieth anniversary of* **Child's Play***?*
We're doing a 20th Anniversary DVD of the first *Child's Play* film. I'm going to be doing a commentary on it, an on-screen interview, and then I'm going to the Monstermania convention in Cherry Hill, New Jersey. Catherine Hicks and Chris Sarandon are going to be there and we're going to do a Q&A panel for the fans. They're recording that for the DVD also. So it's going to be good.

*What do you think it is about Chucky that's made him such a popular, enduring horror icon?*
He can scare you and he can make you laugh. I think the concept of a doll coming to life; a lot of people grew up with dolls and they can understand the fear that would be involved in one coming to life and trying to kill you, then replace your soul with his. I think it's appealing to a lot of fans because they hadn't really seen anything like that. Maybe only in their imaginations could they picture something like that happening. A lot of people are scared of dolls, but it's the fact that he can walk and he can talk, he's independent, he has a mind of his own. That's exactly what scares people about the idea.

# Index

*The A-Team* (TV series) 90
*Abarat* 7–12, 16
Abbott, Bruce 142
Abbott and Costello 143
ABC 130
ABPC studios 166
Academy of Science Fiction, Fantasy & Horror Films 239
Ackerman, Forrest J 98, 124
*Act of Love* 70, 76
Adams, Neal 96
Adams, Ted 99, 100
Addams, Charles 59–60
*The Addams Family* 191
Adler, Luther 220
ADR 187
A.E. Coppard Prize 50
*Affair of Honor* (theater) 220
AFI 189
*Afro Samurai* 229
Agnew, Jim 122
Agutter, Jenny 241
AIP Films 98, 147–148
Albert, Eddie 220
*Alien* 61, 97, 156–157
*Alien* (film series) 109, 232
*Alien Resurrection* 229, 232
*Alien vs. Predator* 190
*Aliens* 61, 104
Allen, David 139
Allen, Woody 66, 89
*Amazing Stories* 123, 125
*America Exposed* 181
*American Gods* 28, 33
*American Idol* 130
American Mystery Award 70
Amicus 182
*Anansi Boys* 28, 33, 37–39
Anchor Bay Entertainment 174–175
Anderson, Brad 128
Andrews, Virginia 108
Andy Capp 210
Angel Islington (*Neverwhere*) 26
*Animal House* 125, 186
Annaud, Jean-Jacques 229
*Another Day* 89
Anouilh, Jean 229
*Aquarius* 20
Arcane, Aleister (character) 98
Arcane Comix 99
Argento, Dario 122
*Arkham Asylum* 32
Arnell, Peter 221

Arnold, Susan 211
Arquette, Patricia 151, 175
*Arsenic and Old Lace* 106
*As the World Turns* 220
Ash, David (*Haunted*, *Ghosts of Sleath*) 45
Asmodeus (Felix Castor series) 25
*Assassin* 61
*Assault on Precinct 13* 117–118, 172
Associated British Pathé 166
*At the Mountains of Madness* (film) 238
*The Atomic Submarine* 211
*Attack of the Crab Monsters* 123
Australia 94
Avco Embassy 119–121, 123, 125
*The Avengers* 215
Axton, Hoyt 214

*The Babysitter Murders* 117
Bachman, Richard 152
Bacon, Kevin 226
*Bad Moon* (film) 171
"Bad Moon" (comic strip, *Fly in My Eye*) 99
*Bag of Bones* (film) 132
Baino, Mariano 83
Baker, Rick 230–232
Bakula, Scott 13
Baldwin, Adam 171
Band, Charles 137, 140
Bangor, Maine 50, 151
Bantam (publishers) 74, 88
Barclay, Andy (*Child's Play* & *Child's Play 2*) 239, 242–245
Barker, Clive 7–8, 10–11, 15–16, 29, 99, 108, 113, 129–130, 132, 128
Barrow (*30 Days of Night*) 104
Bates, Norman (*Psycho* films) 125, 146
Batman (character) 47, 74, 96, 107
*Batman* (comic) 96, 107
*Batman Begins* 83
*Batman: Gotham After Midnight* 96
*Batman: The Animated Series* 70, 74, 229
"Battleground" (short story, Stephen King) 88
Baxendale, Leo 18
The BBC 28, 37

Bean, Sean 174, 176
*The Beast Within* 144–146
*The Beatles* 72, 166
Beaumont, Charles 71
*Beauty and the Beast* (TV series) 229–232
Benedek, Laslo 167
Bennett, Douglas 9
Benton, Robert 176
*Beowulf* (film) 38
*Beowulf* (poem) 1
Berg, Dick 145
Berger, Howard 129
Berger, Karen 32
Berger, Thomas 89
Bernhard, Harvey 145
Berry, Halle 183
Bettelheim, Bruno 138
"Better Than Home" (short story, Joe Hill) 50, 59
*Bettie Page True Hollywood Story* 201
The Bickersons 235
*The Big Blow* 78
*The Big Chill* 218
*Big Trouble in Little China* 117
Bigelow, Kathryn 174, 176
*Bigfoot* 106, 198
Billson, Anne 1–3
Bjork 48
"The Black Cat" (*Masters of Horror*) 128, 141
"The Black Cat" (short story, Edgar Allan Poe) 142
*Black Hawk Down* 103
*Black Orchid* 31
"The Black Phone" (short story, Joe Hill) 57, 59
*Blade II* 229, 232, 234
Blaisdell, Paul 154
Blake, Anita (character, Anita Blake books) 22
Blake, Lily (*Edgewise*) 81–83
*The Blinding* 84
*The Blob* (1958) 210
Bloch, Robert 71, 77, 146
*Blood and Honour* 61
*Blood Dance* 70
*Blue Steel* 171, 176
*Blue Velvet* 83
Blyton, Enid 108
Bod (*The Graveyard Book*) 36
*Body Count* 61
Body Horror 91

247

*Body Parts* 171, 176–177
*Bodysnatchers* 133
Bogart, Humphrey 105
Boileau, Pierre 176
Booklist Editor's Award 70
Boorman, John 125
Boote, Barbara 8
Botch, Jakabok (*Mr B. Gone*) 14–16
Bottin, Rob 120
*The Bottoms* 78
Bottoms, Timothy 163
*Box* 67
Boyle, Amanda 56–58
Bradbury, Ray 50, 57, 71, 124, 133–134, 182
Bradley, Doug 8, 13
Bradstreet, Tim 106
Bram Stoker Award 50, 70, 80, 88, 92
*Breeding Ground* 108, 110–111
Brewster, Charlie (*Fright Night*) 148–149
*Bride of Chucky* 243
*Bride of Frankenstein* 181, 183
Bridges, Jeff 120
Bridges, Jim 145
Bridges, Lloyd 220
Brother Samuel (*The Mutant Chronicles*) 236
*Brothers of the Blood* 181, 190
Browning, Tod 182
*Bubba Ho-Tep* 70, 74–75
Buck, Pearl 220
Buckinghamshire 61, 108
Budapest, Hungary 165–166
*Buffy the Vampire Slayer* 2, 102, 106
Bulgaria 206
Burgess Meredith Gremlin (*Gremlins 2: The New Batch*) 216
*Burial* 84
Burke, Robert John 152
Burns, Dominic 211
Burroughs, Edgar Rice 70, 72–73
Burroughs, William 80
Bush, George 168
Byron, Lord 139

*Cabal* 11–12
*The Cabinet of Dr. Caligari* 159
Cable ACE Award 153
*Cactus Flower* (theater) 220
Cage, Nicolas 206
Cagney, James 220
Cain, Dan (*Re-Animator*) 142
Caliber (comics company) 20
Cameron, James 61, 131
Camp Blood website 187
Campbell, Bruce 70, 74–75, 78
Campbell, Christa 188, 201–205, 207–209
Campbell, Ramsey 2, 29
Canada 76, 232
*Candid Camera* 220
*Candyman* 7
*Candyman II* 190

Cannavale, Bobby 171
Cannell, Stephen J. 89–90
"The Cape" (short story, Joe Hill) 59
Capra, Frank 230
*Captains Outrageous* 74
Carey, Mike 18–19, 21
Carpenter, John 96, 117–118, 123, 155, 172, 191, 195, 197, 236
Carroll, Lewis 52
Carstairs, John Paddy 167
Carthage, New York 117
Caruso, Fred, 83
Casey, Hugh 184
"Casting the Runes" (short story, M.R. James) 58
Castle, William 134
*Castle Freak* 140–141
Castor, Felix 18, 22–25
*Cat People* 190
Cates, Phoebe 211–213, 216
The Catman (KISS) 183
Cavalieri, Joey 107
CBS 89, 130, 155, 221, 231
*The Cellar* 77
*Cemetery Dance* 73, 76, 78, 131–132
Cenobites 113
CGI 86, 129, 141, 151, 213, 219
Chainsaw Awards 204
*Chainsaw Terror* 64
Champlin, Charles 124
Chandler, Raymond 23, 105
Chaney, Lon 182
*The Changeling* 165–170
Charboneau, Patricia 217
*Charnel House* 80
*Child's Play* (film series) 144, 243
*Child's Play* 149–150, 239–240, 242, 244–245
*Child's Play 2* 149, 239, 241
*Child's Play 3* 243
*Chiller Theater* 211
Chillerfest 209
*The China Syndrome* 145
Chizmar, Richard 73, 76, 78, 131
"Chocolate" (*Masters of Horror*) 127, 129, 131
"Chocolate" (short story, Mick Garris) 127, 131
*Choice Cuts* 176
Chong, Vincent 52, 60
*Christine* (film) 117, 120–121
Chuck Fries' (production company) 145
Chucky 150, 240–245
CIA 142
"Cigarette Burns" (*Masters of Horror*) 121, 128
*The City* 47
*The City of Lost Children* 229, 232
*City of the Living Dead* 69
Claremont, Chris 18, 99
Clarkson, Jonathan 30
*Clive Barker: Illustrator* 99
*Clive Barker's Books of Blood* 7–9, 99
*Clive Barker's Tapping the Vein* 99
*Cloak and Dagger* 147

*Coast to Coast* (radio show) 227
*Cocktail* 181
*Cohen and Tate* 171, 175–176, 178
Colan, Gene 96
*Cold in July* 70, 74
*Coldheart Canyon* 7, 15
Collins, Barnabas (*Dark Shadows*) 182
Collins, Joan 182
Collins, Hap & Pine, Leonard (*Savage Season Vanilla Ride* aka *Blue to the Bone, Vanilla Ride, Captains Outrageous*) 70, 74, 78
Columbia Pictures 103, 126
Columbia University 210
Columbine 181, 188–189
*Columbo* 220
Combs, Jeffrey 136, 137, 140, 142, 160, 163
ComicCon, San Diego 125
*Coming to America* 181
*Compulsion* 64, 66–67
Condon, Bill 190
"The Confessor's Tale" (short story, Sarah Pinborough) 113
Connolly, Jennifer 202
*Constantine* 18
Constantine, John 20, 23, 30
*Containment* 171, 179
"Conversation Piece" (short story, Richard Christian Matheson) 91
*Cool Dog* 201
Cooper, Alice 192
Cooper, Jackie 220
Coquillon, John 167, 170
*Coraline* 28, 38–39
Corman, Roger 73, 128, 134
Correll, Gordon 230, 237
Coscarelli, Don 70, 75
Count Gore De Vol 98
*Countess Dracula* (theater) 222
The Countess Dracula (*Countess Dracula*, theater) 222
Cox, Andy 55
Cox, Courteney 208
Coyne, Judas (*Heart-Shaped Box*) 54–55, 58
Crampton, Barbara 137, 140, 142
Craven, Wes 152
Crawford, Joan 220
*The Crawling Eye* 211
*Created By* 88, 91
*Creature* (aka *Titan Find*) 153, 156–157
*Creature Features* 181
*Creature from the Black Lagoon* 153, 164
*Creed* 40, 46
Creed, Joseph (*Creed*) 48
*The Creeping Unknown* 211
*Creepy* (comic) 96, 123
*Criminal Macabre* 96
Critics' Award, Cannes Film Festival 133
Critic's Choice Award 70
Cronenberg, David 1, 91, 161
*Cronos* 229, 232
*Cross of Iron* 61

Crouch End 8
Crowley, Aleister 42, 58
*Cruising* 190
The Cryptkeeper 148
Crystal Lake 223
Cunningham, Sean 224–226
*Cupid* 210, 217
*The Curse of the Werewolf* 139
Curtis, Jamie Lee 119, 171, 176, 196, 202
Curtis, Tony 80
Cushing, Peter 118, 147–148, 168, 182
*Cut* 210–211

*Dagon* 133, 135, 140–141
Dahl, Roald 89, 133
Dahmer, Jeffrey 197
Damascus 108
D'Amato, Damon 134
*The Damnation Game* 8–9, 56
"The Damned Thing" (short story, Ambrose Bierce) 93
"Dance of the Dead" (short story, Richard Matheson) 93
Dandridge (*Fright Night*) 149
Dante, Joe 125, 154, 210–213, 216, 218–219
*Dante's Inferno* 15–16, 19
*The Dark* 47
Dark Horse (publishers) 96, 100, 189
*The Dark Knight Returns* 47
*Dark Shadows* 163, 181
*Dark Star* 117
*Dark Water* 81, 83
*Dark Waters* 83
*Darkside* (magazine) 66
*Daughter of Darkness* 138
D'Auria, Don 109
*Dawn of the Dead* (1978) 2, 69, 96, 194, 215
*Dawn of the Dead* (2004) 69
*Dawson's Creek* 204
*A Day in the Death of Joe Egg* 165
"The Day My Pan Went Mad" (comic script, Neil Gaiman) 30
*Day of the Dead* (2008) 201, 206–208
*The Day of the Triffids* (novel) 111
*Dazzle* 22
DC Comics 18, 20, 31, 33, 74, 96, 107, 144
DC Thompson 18
"Dead End" (short story, Richard Christian Matheson) 91
*Dead Men's Boots* 18, 23
*Dead Ringers* 128
*Deadhead* 64
*The Deadly Spawn* 181–183
*Deadman's Road* 78
Deane, Andrew 169
*Death Day* 61, 63
*Death Dream* 86
Def Leppard 28
del Toro, Guillermo 127, 229, 231–238
*Demon's Door* 80, 84
*The Dentist* 133

Depp, Johnny 169, 175
*Descendant* 82, 87
*Desperation* (novel) 130
*Desperation* (miniseries) 123, 124, 128, 130, 236
*Detroit Rock City* 181, 183
*Development Hell* 123, 130–131
*The Devil You Know* 18–19
*The Devil's Rejects* 191, 193–194, 197
D.I. [digital internegative] 159
*Diabolique* 176
*Dial M for Monster* 106
DiCaprio, Leonardo 183
Dickerson, Ernest 128
Dimension (film company) 96, 191, 195
Disney 120, 130
*The Djinn* 83–84
"Do You See" (short story, Sarah Pinborough) 113
Dr. Corso (*Parasomnia*) 163
Dr. Doom 103
*Dr. Jekyll and Mr. Hyde* (novel) 1
Dr. Loomis (*Halloween* films) 118, 196
Dr. Quinn, Medicine Woman 210
*Doctor Who* 112
Dodds, David 7
Dods, John 182–183
The Dog Company 7
*Dolls* 133, 137–138
*Domain* 44
Don Post Studios 153, 155, 161
Donner, Richard 88
*The Doorkeepers* 86
Dorff, Stephen 160
Dorman, Dave 20
Douglas, Melvyn 166, 170
Dourif, Brad 150, 177, 194, 240
Doyle, Sean (*Renegades, White Ghost, Knife Edge* and *Hybrid*) 64, 66
Dracula 61, 102
*Dracula* (film, 1931) 181
*Dracula* (novel) 1, 89, 134
"Dragula" (song, Rob Zombie) 191
*Dreamgirls* 190
"The Dreaming" (*Sandman*) 20
"Dreams in the Witch House" (short story, H.P. Lovecraft) 141
"Dreams in the Witch House" (*Masters of Horror*) 141
*Driftwood* 181, 188–189, 209
*The Drive-In* 73
*Drive-In* (book) 70, 71
*Dying Words* 61, 63, 65–66
*Dystopia* 88–89

Ealing Studios 157
The East End, London 40, 42, 48
Eastwood, Clint 183
Ebert, Roger 119
EC Comics 96, 123, 144, 182
*The Eccentricities of a Nightingale* (theater) 220, 222

Eclipse Comics 99
Edelstein, Neal 78
*Edgewise* 80–83
Edinburgh 80
*Edmond* 133
Edwards, Les 99, 131–132
*Eerie* (comic) 96, 123
Elise, Christine 241
Elizalde, Mike 231
Elliott, Sam 173
Ellis, Ruth 10
Elstree Studios 166
Elvira 147
*Elvis* (film) 119–120
Empire Pictures 135, 137–138, 140–141
*Enemy at the Gates* 232
Engle, Captain Brian (*The Langoliers*, miniseries) 151
Englund, Robert 183, 186, 203, 205, 209
Entragian, Collie (*Desperation*, miniseries) 130
*Erebus* 61–62, 64
"Eric the Pie" (short story, Graham Masterton) 85
*Erotic Confessions* 201
Erskine, Harry (*The Manitou*) 84
*Escape* (magazine) 30
*Escape from New York* 97, 117–118, 120–121, 125
E.T. 128
Etchison, Dennis 90
Evans, Rupert 234
*Everville* 7
*Evil Dead II* 57, 103
*The Ex* 2
*Exit Wounds* 61, 67
*The Exorcist* 190
*The Eye* 81
*The Eyes of Laura Mars* 117

Fabrizio, Andre 122
*The Face* (magazine) 31
Faerch, Daeg 196–197
Fahey, Jeff 171, 177–178
"Fair-Haired Child" (*Masters of Horror*) 161–162
*Family Portrait* 80, 83
*Famine* 80
*Famous Monsters of Filmland* 96, 123, 154, 181
*Fangoria* (magazine) 93, 96–97, 183, 189
Fantastic Four (characters) 103
*Fantastic Monsters* 154
Fantasy 1, 7, 10–11, 17, 19–20, 28, 46, 52–53, 57, 71, 86, 109, 124, 210, 229, 234, 239
*Fantasy Advertiser* 18, 20
*The Fantasy Film Festival* 123–124
FantasyCon 8, 16, 56
*Fatal Beauty* 150
*Faust* 159
*Fear Itself* 123, 129
*FeardotCom* 153, 158–161, 163
*Feeding Ground* 108, 111
Feldman, Corey 213

Feldman, Ed 172
Fell, Norman 220
Fessenden, Larry 236–237
*FHM* 201
Fielding, Tom (Tom Holland) 144
*The 5th Witch* 80
*Finding Bliss* 201
*A Fine Dark Line* 78
Finnell, Mike 211–213, 216
Finney, Jack 57–58, 70–71, 110
*Firestorm* 20–21
"Fish Night" (short story, Joe R. Lansdale) 72
Fitzgerald, F. Scott 71, 89
*Flaming London* 71
Fleetway IPC 18
Fletcher, Jo 28, 55
Florida 126, 208, 211
*Fluke* 40, 44–46, 48
*The Fly* (1986) 1
*The Fly II* 123
*Fly in My Eye* 99
Flynn, Errol 230
*The Fog* (film, 1980) 117, 119–120, 125
*The Fog* (novel) 40, 44–46
Fonda, Henry 220
*Forbidden Planet* 117, 153
Ford, John 220, 222, 229–230
Foree, Ken 194
*Fortress* 133, 139
Foster, Ben 103
"Four-Sided Triangle" (*Tales from the Crypt*, TV series) 150–151
Fowler, Christopher 58
*Fragile Things* 28
Frank Sinatra Gremlin (*Gremlins 2: The New Batch*) 214
Frankenstein (character) 89, 107, 124, 129, 195
*Freaks of the Heartland* 96
*Freddy vs. Jason* 226
*Fresh Skins* 66
*Friday the 13th* (1980) 220, 222, 224, 226
*Fried Green Tomatoes* 97
Friedman, Adam 78
Friedman, David 185–186
*Fright Night* 144, 147–148
*From Beyond* 133, 137–138
*Frost Flowers* 18, 25–26
Fulci, Lucio 69
*Full Eclipse* 92
Fürmann, Benno 237
*Furnace* 58
FX 3, 30

Gaiman, Neil 18–22, 28–29, 38, 56
*Galaxy* 71
*Galilee* 7, 12–13
Galligan, Zach 210–212, 216, 219
Garris, Cynthia 123, 129
Garris, Mick 93, 123–124, 127, 129, 161, 169, 236
Gauntlet Press 89, 91, 93
Geffen Records 191

Gelbart, Larry 89
*Gentleman Jim* 230
George, Melissa 104
Georgia (*Heart-Shaped Box*) 54–55
German Expressionist Cinema 1, 159
Germany 1, 56, 223
*Ghastly Beyond Belief* 28
*Ghost of Re-Animator* 143
*Ghosts of Mars* 117
*The Ghosts of Sleath* 46
*Ghost Story* 8, 181
*Giallo* 122
Gibbons, Dave 29
*Gigi* (theater) 220
*Gilda* 109
Gillespie, Jaye 186
Girdler, William 83
Gizmo (*Gremlins*) 212–213, 219
*Gladiator* (series) 76
Glasgow Necropolis 35
Gleason, Jackie 220
The God of Thunder (KISS) 183
Godden, Ezra 141
*Godfather* (trilogy) 109
*Godfather III* 181
*Gods and Monsters* 7, 190
Godzilla (character) 96
*Godzilla* (film series) 211
Goldberg, Whoopi 150
Goldblum, Jeff 1
Golden, Christopher 50
Goldman, Jane 37
Goldman, William 71, 89
Goldstein, Jenette 174
Gollancz 50–51, 55, 108, 110, 113
Gollancz, Livia 8
*The Good Earth* 220
*Good Omens* 29
Gooding, Cuba, Jr. 201
Gordon, Carolyn 133, 135, 138
Gordon, Stuart 133–134
Gordon, Susanna 141
*Gotham After Midnight* 96, 107
*Gotham County Line* 107
"Graduation" (short story, Richard Christian Matheson) 89
Graham, Gerrit 241
Grand Guignol 1, 14, 135
*The Grand Prize* (theater) 220
Grant, Cary 106
Graves, Tanya (*Hallows' Point*) 208
*The Graveyard Book* 28, 33–36
Gray, Muriel 58
*Gray Matter* 98
*The Great and Secret Show* 10–11
Green, David Gordon 96
Green, Hilton 126
Greenberg, Bob 136
Greenwich 31
*Gremlins* 210–212, 214–215, 219
*Gremlins 2: The New Batch* 210, 214–217, 219
*Gremlins 3* 213, 218
Griffin, Merv 221
Grindhouse 185

*Grindhouse* (film) 191, 198
Grist, Paul 20
Gross, Brian 187
Gross, Larry 178
*The Grudge* (2004) 179
*The Guardian* (newspaper) 2
Guest, Val 167
Gullidge, John 13, 45, 118–121, 137, 173–175, 212, 216–217, 219, 240, 242, 244
*Gunmen's Blues* 171172
*Gunpowder* 50, 60
Gurney, A.R. 227

Hackensack, New Jersey 239
Hackman, Gene 92
Haddenfield 198
"Haeckel's Tale" (*Masters of Horror*) 128
Haig, Sid 191, 193–194
Haines, Lurene 20
Halleck, Billy (*Thinner*, film) 152
*Halloween* (1978) 117–119, 148, 191, 194, 196–197
*Halloween* (2007) 194–195
*Halloween II* (1981) 117
*Halloween III: Season of the Witch* 117, 121
*Halloween 2* (2009) 191
*Hallows' Point* 208
Halsey, Jim (*The Hitcher*, 1986) 172
Halsey, Jim (*The Hitcher*, 2007) 174
Hamilton, George 148
Hamilton, Laurell K. 22
Hamilton, Linda 229, 231
Hamlet (character) 238
*Hamlet* (film) 165
Hammer Films 1, 68, 139, 147–149, 157, 168
"Hands of Death" ("Burn Baby Burn") (song, Rob Zombie & Alice Cooper) 192
Hanratty, James 10
Harman, Dominic 9–10, 12, 15
Harman, Robert 173
HarperCollins 9–10, 12, 15, 51, 56
*Harry Potter* (series) 34, 219
Harryhausen, Ray 182
Hart, Melissa Joan 205
Hartnett, Josh 103
Hauer, Rutger 171, 173–174, 176
*Haunted* 45
*Haunted Fear* (comic) 182
*The Haunted World of El Superbeasto* 191, 198
*The Haunting* (1963) 169, 215
*The Haunting of Hill House* 57
Hawks, Howard 229
Hayek, Selma 206
HBO 124, 162, 201
HDNET Channel 129
Head, Amber 122
"Head giving head" scene (*Re-animator*) 136
*Heart-Shaped Box* 50, 53–56, 58–59

*Heathen* 61–62
*Hell to Pay* 61
*Hellblazer* 18, 22
*The Hellbound Heart* 113
*Hellbound Hearts* 109, 113
Hellboy (character) 229, 231, 233–235, 238
*Hellboy* (film) 190, 229, 234–235
*Hellboy 2: The Golden Army* 231, 235
*Hellraiser* 7, 12
*Hell's Bounty* 78
*Hellspawn* 100–101
Hemingway, Mariel 171
Hemmingway, Ernest 71, 124
Henriksen, Lance 139, 171, 174
Henson, Brian 88, 94
Henstridge, Natasha 168
Herbert, James 40–41, 49, 108
*Hero Wanted* 201
Hewer, Mitch 181
Hickox, Anthony 210, 215
Hicks, Bill 66
Hicks, Catherine 239–240, 243, 245
*The Hidden* 108–110
*High Plains Literary Review* 53
Highgate & Highgate Cemetery 8, 35, 40
Hill, Debra 117
Hill, Joe 50–52, 59–60, 110
*The History of Mr. Polly* 45
*A History of Violence* 218
Hitchcock, Alfred 44, 126, 131, 138, 144, 146, 167, 229
*The Hitcher* (1986) 171–176
*The Hitcher* (2007) 173, 174
*The Hitcher II: I've Been Waiting* (2003) 173
Hitler, Adolf 63, 160
Hockney, David 9
Holbrook, Hal 120
Holland, Kathi 145
Holland, Tom 144, 145, 239
Hollywood 37, 78, 104, 125, 131, 138, 144, 149, 152, 171–172, 194, 201, 227
*Hollywood Screentips* 220
*Home at Seven* (theater) 220–221
"Homecoming"(*Masters of Horror*) 128
*Homicide: Life on the Street* 165
*Honey, I Shrunk The Kids* 133
Hooper, Tobe 93–94, 152
*Horns* 50
Horror 1–3, 9, 17, 19, 28, 32, 40, 43–44, 46–47, 49, 51, 53, 56–58, 60–63, 65–66, 68–71, 73, 76–78, 80–81, 83–89, 93–94, 96–98, 101, 104, 107, 108–109, 111–112, 114, 119, 121, 123–130, 133–136, 138–139, 142, 144, 147–150, 152–154, 157, 161–162, 168, 171, 173, 178, 181–183, 186–187, 189, 190–192, 201–202, 210–211, 214–215, 218, 220, 222, 223, 229, 231, 236, 237, 239, 243, 244, 245
The Horror Channel 109

Horror Critics Award 70
*Horror Web* 109
Horror Writers' Association (HWA) 70, 77–78, 80, 108
*Hostel* 86, 170
*The House by the Cemetery* 69
*House of Bones* 86
*House of 1000 Corpses* 191–194
*House of Re-Animator* 142
*House on Haunted Hill* (1959) 134, 157–158
*House on Haunted Hill* (1999) 153, 157–159, 161
*The House That Jack Built* 86
Houseman, John 120
Houston, Texas 176
*How to Drive Your Man Wild in Bed* 80
Howard, Clint 194
Howell, C. Thomas 171, 176
*The Howling* 125
Hugo Award 28
*The Hunger* (TV series) 80
Hunter, Simon 238
Hurt, William 88, 94
Huston, Danny 103
Hutson, Shaun 61
*Hybrid* 64, 66

*I Am Legend* (comic) 99
*I Don't Want to Be Born* 62
*I Know a Secret* 221
*I Was a Teenage Werewolf* 98
IDT (now Starz Entertainment) 127, 130
IDW 11, 50, 96, 100, 102, 104–105, 171
*If Looks Could Kill* 181
*Ikon* 80
*The Iliad* 70
"I'm Always Here" (short story, Richard Christian Matheson) 91
*Imajica* 7–10
*In the Mouth of Madness* 117
*Inamorata* 169
"Incident On and Off a Mountain Road" (*Masters of Horror*) 70
"Incident On and Off a Mountain Road" (story, Joe R. Lansdale) 70, 75
*The Incredible Hulk* (TV series) 90
*Indiana Jones and the Temple of Doom* 212
*Infested* 210, 218
*The Initiation of Sarah* 145
*The Intruders* 111
*Invasion of the Body Snatchers* (film, 1956) 58
*Invasion of the Saucer Men* 154
Iron Walker, George (*Edgewise*) 82
*The Island of Dr. Moreau* 229
*It* 98
*It* (novel) 110
*It Conquered the World* 154
*It Was a Dark and Silly Night* 34
*I've Got a Secret* 220–222

Jack the Ripper 40
Jackson, Glenda 165
Jackson, Shirley 53, 89
*Jacob's Ladder* 161
James, Jesse 175
James, M.R. 58–59
*James Herbert's Dark Places* 41
*The Jamie Kennedy Experiment* 201
Jane, Thomas 237
Janssen, Famke 171, 179
Japan 223
*Jason X* 226
*Jaws* 104, 140, 197
Jekyll and Hyde (characters) 107
*Jekyll and Hyde* (short film, William Malone) 154
Jeunet, Jean-Pierre 229, 232
*Jezebel* (2001 Maniacs) 186
JFK 74
*John Carpenter's Vampires* 117, 121
Johnson, Kenneth 90
Johnson, Van 220
Jolie, Angelina 202
*The Jonah* 46
Jones, Kelley 96, 107
Jones, Robert 71
Jones, Stephen 28
Joseph, Jackie 215
Joston, Darwin 172
Joyce, Graham 108
*The Jungle Book* (novel) 34, 70
*Ju-on* 179
*Just Like in the Movies* 239

Kane, Paul 8, 16, 29, 38, 59, 209
Keaton, Buster 220
Keene, Brian 51
Keller, Sean 122
Kilpatrick, Patrick 163
King, Adrienne 225
King, Denis 220
King, Stephen 2, 44, 47, 88, 90, 94, 108–110, 120, 126–127, 130–132, 144–145, 151–152, 229, 236
*The King & I* (theater) 220
*King Kong* (1933) 183, 191
*The King Must Die* 143
*King of the Ants* 133
"King of the Road" (*Tales from the Crypt*, TV series) 150
Kinski, Klaus 156
Kipling, Rudyard 34, 70
Kirby, Josh 32
KISS (band) 181, 183
*Kiss* (magazine) 100
Klaw, Rick 77
Kneale, Nigel 121
*Knife Edge* 64
*Knightrider* 90
*Knots Landing* 220
Kobin, Chris 184–185
Koontz, Dean 77, 92, 108
Kovacs, Ernie 221
Krause, Brian 126
*The Krays* 165
Kremer, Wendy 203, 205
Krige, Alice 126

Krueger, Freddy 183, 194, 226, 243, 244
Kwitney, Alisa 20
Kyle (*Child's Play 2*) 241

*L.A. Gothic* 121–122
Lacey (*Body Parts*) 177
Lady Alucard (*Countess Dracula*, theater) 222
Lafia, John 241
"Land of the Stone-Age Cannibals" (short story, Joe R. Lansdale) 72
Landis, John 125, 183, 186–187
Landon, Michael 98
Lang, Fritz 99
Langan, Sarah 108
*The Langoliers* (minseries) 144, 151
*The Langoliers* (novella) 144
*The Language of Dying* 110, 112, 113
Lansdale, Joe R. 70–71
Lansing, Michigan 153
*The Last Angry Man* 220–221
"Last Breath" (short story, Joe Hill) 59
*The Last Outlaw* 171
*The Last Winter* 236
*Law and Order* 165
Laymon, Richard 77
Leacock, Philip 167
Leatherface (*The Texas Chain Saw Massacre*) 76, 194
Leaver, Robert 236
LeBlanc, Deborah 108
Lee, Christopher 118, 168, 182, 215–217
Lee Ray, Charles (*Child's Play* series) 149
*Legion of the Dead* 210
*Legions of Hell* 20
Leicht, Áine 221, 224, 227
Leigh, Janet 120
Leisure (publishers) 51, 81–82, 84, 86, 109–112, 109
Lemmon, Jack 220
Lesett, Steve 30
Lester (*2001 Maniacs*) 186
*Let Him Have It* 165
Levinson & Link 89
Levitz, Paul 33
Levy, Edward 145–146
Lewis, Herschell Gordon 185, 187
*Lies and Illusions* 201
*A Life in the Cinema* 123
"A Life in the Cinema" (short story, Mick Garris) 130
Link, Kelly 51, 53, 60
Lionsgate 125, 129–130, 181, 193
Lippincott, Charles 125
Littlewood, Joan 167
Liverpool 7, 18, 19, 23, 41, 61
"Living Dead Girl" (song, Rob Zombie) 192
*Locke and Key* 50
Lockhart, June 220
Lom, Herbert 168

London 7, 8, 18, 35, 40, 42–43, 56–58, 62–63, 67, 86–87, 113, 141, 166–167, 238
*Lonely Hearts* 205
*The Long Gray Line* 220, 222
*Looney Tunes: Back in Action* 154
*Loose Canons* 92
Lord, Jack 220
*Lord of Illusions* 7
*Lord of the* Rings (trilogy) 219
Los Angeles (L.A.) 7, 67, 96, 117, 122–124, 126, 133, 137, 144, 153–155, 161, 171, 187, 215, 232
*The Los Angeles Times* 28, 124
"The Lottery" (short story, Shirley Jackson) 53
*Love at First Bite* 148
*The Love Boat* 220
*Love Doll* 75
*Love Letters* (theater) 220, 227
Lovecraft, H.P. 84, 134–137, 139–141, 182, 238
The Lover (KISS) 183
"Lover Come Hack to Me" (*Tales from the Crypt*, TV series) 150
*Lucifer* 18, 21–22
Lucifer (character) 21–23, 25
*Lucky Number Sleven* 103
*Lucy's Child* 61, 65
Lugosi, Bela 43, 181
*The Lurker at the Threshold* 84
Luxembourg 158
Lynch, David 78
Lynch, Richard 194

*M* (comic) 99
MacLeod, Gavin 220
Macnee, Pactrick 215
Macy, William H. 142
*The Mad Room* 97
Maddox (*Galilee*) 12
Mae (*Near Dark*) 175
*The Magic Cottage* 44, 46
Magnet Releasing 236–237
*Maiden Voyage* 80
Mailer, Norman 52
Malamud, Bernard 52–53
Malibu (comic company) 20
Malone, William 153–160, 162–163
Mamet, David 133
*The Man Who Would Be King* 109
Mancini, Don 149, 243–244
Mane, Tyler 195–196
Manilow, Barry 28
*The Manitou* 80, 83–84
*Manitou Blood* 80, 83
"Mansions of the Silences" (*Lucifer*) 25
Maple Pictures 193
Margaret, Princess 222
Mariotte, Jeff 104
Mark (*Waxwork/Waxwork II*) 215
Marlowe (*30 Days of Night*) 101–102
Marlowe, Philip 105
*Marnie* 167
Marnie (*100 Feet*) 179
Marvel Comics 18, 96

*Mary, Mary* (theater) 220
Massey, Raymond 106
*Masters of Horror* 70, 93, 117, 121, 123, 127–129, 141–142, 152–153, 161–162, 165, 168, 236
Masterton, Graham 80–81, 85
Matheson, Richard 70–71, 89, 93, 124, 128
Matheson, Richard Christian 88–89, 93
*A Matter of Blood* 108, 113
Matthau, Walter 103, 149
*MAXIM* 201
*Mayfair* 80
Mazikeen (*Lucifer*) 21
McCain, Francis Lee 214
McCammon, Richard R. 77
McDonald, Cal (*Criminal Macabre*) 105–106
McDowall, Roddy 144, 148–149
McDowell, Malcolm 192, 194, 196
McElhone, Natasha 160
McEwan, Ian 2
McFarlane, Todd 100
McFarlane Entertainment 99, 102, 243
McKean, Dave 30–32, 34, 101
McNaughton, John 129
McQueen, Steve 210
McWeeny, Drew 121
Medak, Peter 165–170
*Medium* 85
*Memoirs of an Invisible Man* 117
*The Men's Club* 165
Meredith, Burgess 80
Mexicon 29
Meyer, Ken, Jr. 20
Meyer, Russ 185
MGM 74–75, 149, 168
Middleton, Ray 220
Midian 13
*The Midnight Meat Train* 7
*The Midwich Cuckoos* 110
Mignola, Mike 234
*Mike's Murder* 145
Milani, Mino 99
The Milk Maiden (*2001 Maniacs*) 188, 203–204, 209
Miller, Dick 215
Miller, Frank 63
Miller, Ian 47
Miller, Mark 11
Miner, Steve 206
*Mirror* 80, 86
Misquamacus (*The Manitou*) 84
*Miss Susan* 221
*Mr. B. Gone* 13–14, 16
*Mr. Punch* 31
*Mister Roberts* 220
Mojave Desert 139
Mojo 70
Mo'lock (*Criminal Macabre*) 106
Monstermania, New Jersey 245
Moon 40, 46
Moonface (*Incident On and Off a Mountain Road*) 76
Moore, Alan 20, 29–30, 54
Moores, David 41

"More Human Than Human" (song, Rob Zombie) 191
Morley, Christopher 221
Morrison, Grant 20
Morrison, Jim 187
Morse, David 151
*Mortal Kombat* 229
*Most Haunted* 85
Mostow, Jonathan 83
*Moulin Rouge* 109
MPAA 180
Mrs. Voorhees 220, 223–224, 226–227
MTV 181, 191
*Mucho Mojo* 73–74, 78
Munch, Edvard 161
Muni, Paul 220–221
*The Munsters* 191
Murray, Don 220
MUSE 108
Mushroom (dog, *Gremlins*) 213
*The Mutant Chronicles* 236–238
MWA Edgar Award 70
My Chemical Romance 189
*My Family Treasure* 239
"My Father's Mask" (short story, Joe Hill) 60
Myers, John (*Hellboy*) 234
Myers, Michael (*Halloween* films) 118, 155, 195, 196–198
Myspace 183
Mystery (genre) 53, 72, 76–77

*The Nail* 106, 198
*The Name of the Rose* 229–230, 232
*The Naming of Beasts* 18
Narcejac, Thomas 176
Nash, Darren 22
Nathan, Robert 71
NBC 123, 130
*Near Dark* 171, 174–176, 179
Nebula Award 28
*Negatives* 165
"Neighbours from Hell" (short story, Graham Masterton) 85
Neill, Sam 120
Nelson (*2001 Maniacs*) 187–188
*Nemesis* 63–64
*The Net* 210
*Neverwhere* 28
*Neverwhere* (film) 37
*Neverwhere* (graphic novel) 18, 26
*Neverwhere* (TV series) 28
Nevill, Adam 59
New Line Cinema 130, 181, 183
New Rebellion Entertainment 181–182, 184, 186, 188–189, 204
New York 110, 158, 171–172, 185, 211, 221–222, 227, 229, 237, 239
*New York Times* 80
New York University (NYU) 181, 210, 218
Newbery Award 28
Newman, Kim 28
Nietzsche, Friedrich 13, 66
*Night Gallery* 218
*Night of the Demon* (aka *Curse of the Demon*) 58

*Night of the Living Dead* (1968) 97–98, 208
*Night Plague* 86
"Night They Missed the Horror Show" (short story, Joe R. Lansdale) 72
*Night Vision* 75
*Night Warriors* 81, 86
*Night Wars* 82, 86
*Nightbreed* 7, 11–12
*Nightlife* 179
*Nightline* 172
*Nightmare Movies* 28
*Nightmares & Dreamscapes* 88, 94, 123
*The Nightrunners* 70, 76
Niles, Steve 96–97, 198
9/11 184–185
*Nobody True* 40, 45, 47, 49
Northwestern University 144
*Nosferatu* 159, 161
Nurse Evans (*Parasomnia*) 163

Oak Communications 147
O'Bannon, Dan 117
O'Connor, Donald 217
O'Connor, Flannery 71, 73
*The October Country* 57
"October in the Chair" (short story, Neil Gaiman) 34
Odedina, Sarah 34
*The Odyssey* 70
*Of Mice and Men* 216
O'Hara, Maureen 220, 222
Oleson, Eben (*30 Days of Night*) 101–103
Oleson, Stella (*30 Days of Night*) 101–102, 104
Olivier, Sir Laurence 165
Olsen, Josh 218
*The Omen* (1976) 104, 145
*On Golden Pond* (theater) 220
*Once More with Feeling* (theater) 220
100 Feet 171, 178–179
*100 Scariest Movie Moments* (Bravo) 173
*One Summer of Happiness* 166
O'Neill, Terry 41
"Only Skin Deep" (*Tales from the Crypt*, TV series) 153, 161–162
Orbit/Little Brown (publishers) 19, 22–24, 65, 68
O'Regan, Marie 38, 209
Organic Theater Company of Chicago 133, 135
Orlando, Joe 123
Osbourne, Ozzy 192
Oscar (Academy Award) 78, 117, 158, 218
Othakeye ("Valerie on the Stairs," *Masters of Horror*) 129
*The Others* (film) 44
*Others* (novel) 40, 48
*The Others* (TV series) 123
"Our Man in the Sudan" (short story, Sarah Pinborough) 113

*Pacific Blue* 201
Pacino, Al 194
*The Pack* 218
Page, Bettie 201
Palmer, Betsy 220–221, 224–227
*The Pan Books of Horror* 108
Pan Macmillan 41–43, 46–47
Pandora's Box 181
*Panic Room* 179
*Pan's Labyrinth* 232
Paoli, Dennis 140, 142
Papp, Joe 221
Paramount 62, 176–177, 224, 226
*Parasomnia* 153, 161–164
Pasadena 194
Pasdar, Adrian 175
Passmore, Jeremy 122
Patchett, Tom 89
Pathé News 166
Paxton, Bill 171
Peaches (*2001 Maniacs*) 203
Pearson, Nick (*Unmarked Graves*) 68
Peckinpah, Sam 61, 66–67
Peloquin (*Cabal/Nightbreed*) 13
Peltzer, Billy (*Gremlins*) 210, 212, 215, 219
Pen (Felix Castor series) 25
Perelman, S.J. 89
Perkins, Anthony 125, 138, 146, 220
Perlman, Ron 130, 229–231, 233, 236–237
*Perversions of Science* 160
Peter Pan 134
Peters, Susan 221
Petty, J.T. 83
Pfeiffer, Michelle 37, 61, 67
*Phantasm* (film series) 245
*The Phantom of the Opera* (character) 76
*The Phantom of the Opera* (film, 1962) 168
Philadelphia 171, 221, 226
Phillips, Lou Diamond 171
Picardo, Robert 215
*The Picture of Dorian Gray* 80, 83
Pierce, Jack 182
*Pierrot Le Fou* 87
Pinback (*Dark Star*) 117
Pinborough, Sarah 108–110
Pinchot, Bronson 151
Pinhead 12–14
Pinnacle (publishers) 84
*The Pit and the Pendulum* (1991) 139
Pitt, Brad 150
Pitt, Ingrid 202
*Plague* 80
*The Plague of the Zombies* 68
*Playboy* 201
*Playhouse 90* 220
Pleasence, Donald 118, 196
Plissken, Snake (*Escape from New York* & *L.A.*) 120
Poe, Edgar Allan 124, 128, 134, 139, 141–142, 144
Poland 85, 165
*Poltergeist* 202–203

Pop, Iggy 192
"Pop Art" (short story, Joe Hill) 50, 53, 56
*Pop Art* (film) 56–58
*Portent* 40
Portis, Charles 54
*Postscripts* 53
*Pow* 18
Power, Tyrone 220, 222
Powers, Tim 24
Pratchett, Terry 29
Presley, Elvis 74–75
Price, Stephen H. (*House on Haunted Hill*, 1999) 158
Price, Vincent 148–149, 157–158, 182
*Pride* 92–93
*The Prime of Miss Jean Brodie* (theater) 220
*The Prince* 121–122
*Prince of Darkness* 117–118, 121
*Prince Valiant* 210
*The Prisoner* 210
"Pro-Life" (*Masters of Horror*) 121, 236
Prof. Lewis (*2001 Maniacs*) 187
PS Publishing 50–52, 60, 110, 112–113
*Psychic* 216
*Psycho* 76, 119, 126, 144, 146, 171, 194
*Psycho II* 144, 146–147
*Psycho III* 125
*Psycho IV: The Beginning* 123, 125–126, 128
Purcell, Dylan 163

Quasimodo 14, 140, 225
Quatermass, Alan 121
*Quatermass trilogy* 121, 211
*The Queen Bee* 220
*Quest for Fire* 229–232
*Quicksilver Highway* 123
Quiddity 11
Quinn, Aidan 45

Rafi (Felix Castor series) 25
Raimi, Sam 96, 100–103
Rainer, Luise 220
Rais, Robert 206
Rasler, Dan 21
Rasmussen, Michael & Shawn 122
*The Rats* 40, 43–44, 46–47
*The Rats* (trilogy) 47
*Rawhead Rex* (comic) 99
Ray Bradbury Fellowship 50
*Re-Animator* 133–137, 142–143, 160
Rea, Stephen 143, 160
*Rear Window* 229
*Rebecca* 229
*The Reckoning* 108, 110
"Red" (short story, Richard Christian Matheson) 90
Red, Eric 171, 179–180
*Red Letters* 205
Redford, Robert 166
Reed, Carol 167

Reed, Oliver 139
Reed, Robert 220
Reeves, Michael 74
Reinhardt (*Blade II*) 229
Reinhold, Judge 212–213
Reitman, Ivan 88
*Relics* 61, 63
Remick, Lee 149
Renault, Mary 133, 143
*Renegades* 63, 64
"Report from the Grave" (*Tales from the Crypt*, TV series) 157, 161
Republic Studio 155
*The Resurrection of Broncho Billy* 117
*Revamped* 208
*Revenge of the Manitou* 84
The Reverend Jonas (*2001 Maniacs*) 184
Reznor, Trent 245
*Rich* 80
Richard (*Neverwhere*) 26
Richardson, Mike 189
Richardson, Ralph 182, 220
Ricky (*2001 Maniacs*) 187
Riddell, Chris 34–35
Rider, Alex 24
"Riders on the Storm" (song, The Doors) 172
*Riding the Bullet* 123, 129
*Rin Tin Tin* 201
*The Ring* 44, 161
*Ringu* 81, 179
*Rio Bravo* 117
Rising Storm Productions 163
*Ritual* 83, 86
*Roar Like a Dove* (theater) 220
Rob ("Valerie on the Stairs," *Masters of Horror*) 129
Robby the Robot 153–155
*Robot Jox* 133, 138
Rodriguez, Robert 63, 152, 191
Roeberg, Shelly 21
Romano, Steve 75
*Romeo and Juliet* 72
*Romeo Is Bleeding* 165
Romero, George A. 1, 2, 68–69, 97, 107, 123, 208
*Rook* 80, 84
Rook, Jim (*Rook, Tooth and Claw, The Terror, Snowman* and *The Swimmer*) 84
Rose, Mark 26
*Rosemary's Baby* 62
Ross, Bill 190
Rourke, Mickey 171
Ruggles, Charlie 220
*The Ruling Class* 165
Rumpole (character, *Fluke, The Magic Cottage, Once*) 44
*Rune* 58
Rush, Geoffrey 157–158
Russell, Kurt 120
Russia 165
Ryder, John (*The Hitcher*) 172–173

Sabrina the Teenage Witch 201, 205
*Sacrament* 7

Salvatore (*The Name of the Rose*) 229
*Same Time, Next Year* 220, 222
Sampson, Robert 135
*Sandman* 20–22, 28, 31–33
San Francisco 134, 179
Sara, Mia 171
Sarandon, Chris 144, 149, 245
*The Saturday Evening Post* 144
Savini, Tom 223, 224, 226
*Saw* 1, 44, 86, 148
Sawyer, Sissy (*Touchy and Feely, The Painted Man*) 83, 87
*Scanners* 125
*Scarecrow* 194
*Scared to Death* 153, 155–156
*Scarlet Gospels* 13
*Scars and Other Distinguishing Marks* 88
Scheider, Roy 171, 176
Schlesinger, John 149
Schow, David J. 130
science fiction (SF) 1, 22, 28, 53, 71, 111, 117, 124–125, 144, 153–154, 160, 168, 229
Sci-Fi 111, 153, 171, 210
Sci-Fi Channel 108
Scoria (*Lucifer*) 21
Scott, George C. 165, 168, 170
Scott, Kathryn Leigh 163
Scott, Ridley 78
Scott, Tony 80
*Scream* 130, 208
*The Scream* (painting, Munch) 161
Screen Actors' Guild (SAG) 226
Screw Theater 135
Scribe Award 96
Sebaldt, Christian 159, 163
*The Secret of Crickley Hall* 40–42, 46
*Seed of Chucky* 243
Selby, David 220
serial killer 59, 61, 76–77, 87, 146, 173, 216
*Sesame Street* 181
*17* (magazine) 211
*7th Heaven* 210
*Sexual Perversity in Chicago* 133
"The Shadow Over Innsmouth" (short story, H.P. Lovecraft) 135
*Shadows* 61, 63
Shatner, William 155
Shaye, Lin 209
*The She-Creature* 154
Sheckley, Robert 89
Sherman, Liz (*Hellboy* and *Hellboy II*) 235
Sherriff, R.C. 221
*The Shining* (film) 202
*The Shining* (miniseries) 92, 123, 127, 130
*The Shining* (novel) 126
Shooks, John (*Edgewise*) 82
"Shot in the Dark" International Crime Writer's Award 70
*Shrine* 40
*Signal to Noise* 31

# Index

*The Silence of the Lambs* 65, 78
*Silent Hill* 44
Silver, Joel 153
*Silver Scream* 130
Simmons, Gene 181, 183
Simon, Neil 89
Simon & Schuster 22
*Simon Dark* 96, 107
*Sin City* 63, 189
Singer, Bryan 88
Singer, Mark 161
Siskel, Gene 226
*The Sixth Sense* 25, 44
*Skins* 181
*The Skull* 63
*The Sky Done Ripped* 71
Slade, David 96, 101–102
Slasher Films 1, 93, 104, 119, 148, 158
Slater, Christian 201
*Slave Girls of Gunpowder* 50
*Sleepwalkers* 123, 126, 130, 229, 236
Sloane, Danny (*Parasonmia*) 163
*Slugs* 61–63
"The Small Assassin" (short story, Ray Bradbury) 124
*Smash* 18
Smith, Beau 99–100
Smith, Bud 190
Smith, Dick 98, 232
Smith, Guy N. 61
Smith, Michael Marshall 108
Smith, Wilbur 108, 111
Smith's Grove 198
*Smoke and Mirrors* 28
Snider, Norman 178
*Snoop Dog's Hood of Horror* 181
*Snowman* 84
Snyder, Zack 69
Sobieski, Leelee 201
Sokoloff, Alexandra 108
*Sole Survivor* 92
Son of Celluloid (comic) 99, 132
*Songs in the Key of X* 192
Sony Pictures 159–160
*Sorcerer* 190
"Sounds Like" (*Masters of Horror*) 128
*South Pacific* (theater) 220
*Space Voyager* (magazine) 29
The Spaceman (KISS) 183
*Spacetruckers* 133
Spade, Sam 105
Spaulding, Captain (*House of 1000 Corpses*) 191–194
*Spawn* (animated) 100
*Spawn* (novel) 62, 64
*Spawn II* 100
*The Spear* 46
Special Motion (FX) 231
*Species II* 168, 170
Sphere (publishers) 30
*Spider-Man* (film) 96, 103
Spielberg, Steven 88, 123, 125, 131, 210–212
Spike TV Scream Awards 96
Spillane, Mickey 72
*Spirit* 80

Splatterpunk 76–77
Stalk 'n' slash 173
*The Stand* (miniseries) 123, 126–127, 130
*The Stand* (novel) 111
*Stand By Me* 181
Stanley, Paul 100
*Star Trek* 155
*Star Trek: Nemesis* 229
*Star Trek: Voyager* 210, 215
*Star Wars* 67, 125, 154, 161, 197, 219
*Stardust* (film) 36–37
*Stardust* (novel) 28, 35–36
"Starfucker" (short story, Mick Garris) 131
*Starman* 117
Steinbeck, John 71
Stern, Howard 245
Stevens, George 229
Stevens, Stella 97
Stevenson, Robert Louis 107
Stewart, Martha 179
*Stiff Lips* 2
Stokes, Phil 11
Stokes, Sarah 11
*Stolen Angels* 65–66
Stout, William 137
*Strange Behavior* 190
*Strange Invaders* 190
Strasberg, Susan 80
Straub, Peter 8
*Straw Dogs* 66
Strindberg's *The Father* (theater) 226
Strode, Laurie (*Halloween*, 2007) 196
"Strung Out" (*Tales from the Crypt*, TV series) 217
Stuart, British Columbia 120
*Stuck* 133, 143
Studio City, California 123, 155
*Stuff Magazine* 201
Sturges, Preston 89, 230
*Subterranean Online* (magazine) 71
*Suckers* 2
Sullivan, Tim 181–184, 186, 188–189, 204, 209
*Sullivan's Travels* 230
*Summer Chills* 109
Sundance 166
*Sunday Telegraph* 2
Superman 74
*Superman: The Animated Series* 74
"Surveillance" (short story, Joe R. Lansdale) 71
*The Survivor* 44
Sutherland, Keifer 245
Sutton, Frank 221
Suvari, Mena 143
*Swamp Thing* 30, 54
Swan, Scott 121
*The Sweetman Curve* 80
*The Swimmer* 84
The Syngenor monster (*Scared to Death*) 156
Szollosi, Tom 90

*The Taken* 108, 111–112
*Tales from the Crypt* (comic) 144, 182
*Tales from the Crypt* (film) 182
*Tales from the Crypt* (TV series) 123, 150, 153, 157, 160–162, 165, 217
Tally, Ted 78
Tampa Bay 239
Tarantino, Quentin 133, 191
Tarses, Jay 89
Tarzan (character) 72
*Tarzan at the Earth's Core* 72
*Tarzan of the Apes* 72
*Tarzan the Terrible* 72
Taylor-Compton, Scout 196
*Teen Titans* 229
"The Tell-Tale Heart" (short story, Edgar Allan Poe) 124
Templesmith, Ben 100–101, 104–105
*Tengu* 81
*The Terminator* 229
*A Terrible Beauty* 85
*The Terror* 80, 84
"Texas Weird" 73
Theron, Charlize 202
*They Live* 117
*Thicker Than Water* 18, 24
*The Thief of Always* 7
*Thieves' Carnival* (theater) 229
*The Thing* 2, 109, 117
*The Thing from Another World* 98, 117
*Thinner* (film) 144, 151–152
*30 Days of Night* (books) 104
*30 Days of Night* (comic) 96, 100–102
*30 Days of Night* (film) 103
*30 Days of Night: Dark Days* 104
*30 Days of Night: Dead Space* 104–105
*30 Days of Night: Red Snow* 104
*30 Days of Night: Return to Barrow* 104
Thomas, Henry 128
Thomas, Roy 32
Thorn, Tristan (*Stardust*) 35
3D 134, 153
*Three Men and a Baby* 181
*Thriller* 73
Thriller (genre) 1, 40, 46, 65, 80, 85, 108–109, 111, 113, 121, 128, 130, 153, 162, 171, 176, 181, 203
*Thunderbox* 205
"Tight Little Stitches in a Dead Man's Back" (short story, Joe R. Lansdale) 72
*Tin Star* 220
*The Tingler* 133
*Titus Andronicus* 1
*To Live and Die in L.A.* 190
*The Today Show* 220
*Tomb of Dracula* (comic) 96
Toomey, Craig (*The Langoliers*, miniseries) 151
*Tooth and Claw* 84
*Torchwood* 112
*Torchwood: Into the Silence* 112

Torquemada 139
Torriero, Talan 181
Torture-Porn 1, 104, 148
Tottle, John 30
*Touchy and Feely* 87
*Tower Hill* 108, 111, 112
*Trauma* (novel) 80, 83, 85
Travolta, John 205–206
Treacher, Arthur 222
*Treasure Island* (film, 1934) 220
TriStar Entertainment 173
*True Grit* (novel) 54
*The True Story of Lynn Stuart* 220
TTA Press 55
20th Century–Fox 11, 143, 205
"20th Century Ghost" (short story, Joe Hill) 53, 57, 60
*20th Century Ghosts* 50, 52, 59
*28 Days Later* 206
*20000 Leagues Under the Sea* 153
*Twilight Zone* (magazine) 90
*The Twilight Zone* (TV series) 70, 73, 165, 191
*Twisted Souls* 66
*2000 Maniacs* 185
*2001 Maniacs* 181, 184–186, 189, 201, 203–205
*2001 Maniacs: Beverly Hellbillys* (working title for *2001 Maniacs: Field of Screams*) 181, 201
*Tyrannosaurus Rex* 198

Ullman, Ricky 181
*Ultimate Fantastic Four* 18
*Undertow* 171, 176
United Artists 150, 240, 242, 244
Universal Films 1, 73, 96, 117, 123–124, 143, 146–147, 155, 167, 181, 192, 233, 241
University of California–Los Angeles 88, 153
University of Minnesota 229
*Unmarked Graves* 61, 67–68
*Unspeakable* 85
Updike, John 2
*The Upturned Stone* 96
*Urban Cowboy* 145
*The U.S. Steel Hour* 220
*The Uses of Enchantment* 138

"The V Word" (*Masters of Horror*) 128
"Valerie on the Stairs" (*Masters of Horror*) 129
Vampire 80, 82, 87, 100–104, 128, 144, 148–149, 173–175, 178–179, 181, 190, 208, 237
*The Vampiress* 147
Van Dyke, Dick 214
Van Gogh, Vincent 66
Van Helsing, Professor Abraham 222
Van Helsing, Elizabeth (*Countess Dracula*, theater) 222
*Vanilla Ride* 70, 74
Vaughn, Matthew 36–37
*Vault of Horror* (comic) 182
Venne, Matt 132
*Vertigo* 176

Vertigo comics 100
Vicente (*30 Days of Night*) 103
*Vicious Circle* 18, 21
*Victims* 63–64
*Village of the Damned* (1995) 117, 121
*The Village Voice* 119
Vincent (*Beauty and the Beast*, TV series) 229–231
Vincent, Alex 150, 239–240, 242, 244
Vincent, Peter (*Fright Night*) 148–149
*Violent Cases* 31
"Voluntary Committal" (novella, Joe Hill) 50
Vonnegut, Kurt 133
*Voodoo* 67, 227
Voorhees, Jason 194, 223, 226, 243–244

*Wait Until Spring, Bandini* 239
*Walkers* 80, 86
Wallace, Dee 194
Walsh, Raoul 229
*War of the Worlds* 97
*The Ward* 121
*Warlock: The Armageddon* 210
Warner Brothers 66, 70, 74, 158–160, 212, 214, 216–217, 219, 224
Washington, George 168
"The Washingtonians" (*Masters of Horror*) 168–169
*Watchmen* 20, 29
*Waxwork* 210, 215
*Waxwork II: Lost in Time* 210, 215
Wayne, Bob 74
Wayne, John 54
"We All Scream for Ice Cream" (*Masters of Horror*) 144
Weatherall, William 10
Weaver, Sigourney 232
*Weaveworld* 7, 10
Weinstein, Bob 195
Weinstein, Harvey 198
*Weird Business* 77
Welles, Orson 138
Wells, H.G. 134
The Wendigo 80–83
*Werewolf of London* 181
*Werewolf Women of the S.S.* 191, 198
Werewolves 1, 80, 92, 140, 148, 178, 237
West, Herbert (*Re-Animator*) 142–143
West, Nathanael 89
West Side Pavilion, Los Angeles 215
Westerns 61, 72, 77
Whale, James 182
Whalin, Justin 243
*Wham!* 18
*What Ever Happened to Baby Jane?* 97
*Wheel of Fortune* 221
"Where Angels Come In" (short story, Adam Nevill) 59

"Whirlpool" (*Tales from the Crypt*) 123
White, Jack 245
*White Ghost* 64, 67
*White Noise* 83
"White Rabbit" (short story, Joe R. Lansdale) 72
Whitkin, Joel-Peter 161
"Who's You in America" (short story, Richard Christian Matheson) 95
*The Wicker Man* (1973) 216
*The Wicker Man* (2006) 201, 206
*The Wild Bunch* 172
Wilde, Oscar 83
William Crawford Award 50
William Morrow (publishers) 50–51, 56
Williams, Billy Dee 220
Williams, John 190
Williams, Tennessee 220
Williams, Trevor 170
Wilson, Cherilyn 163
Wilson, Gahan 34
Wimpole Street 9, 30
Winnie the Pooh 7
Winstone, Ray 38
Wise, Robert 169
*The Witches of Eastwick* 109
"The Witch's Headstone" (*The Graveyard Book*) 34
*The Wonderful Ice Cream Suit* 133
Worcester Academy 144
World Fantasy Award 50, 108, 113
World Trade Center 184
Wright, Jenny 175
Wrightson, Bernie 123
*Write Me a Murder* 220
*Writer of the Purple Rage* 78
Writers Guild 174
Wyndham, John 108, 110
"WYOM" (short story, Richard Christian Matheson) 93

*X: The Man with the X-Ray Eyes* 123
*The X-Files* 192
*X-Men* 18, 20–21, 32

Yablans, Irwin 117
Yagher, Kevin 243
*The Yattering and Jack* (comic) 99
*Year's Best Fantasy* 88
*Year's Best Horror* 88
Yuzna, Brian 135–137, 142

*Zardoz* 124
Zemeckis, Robert 125
*Zeppelins West* 71
Zinnemann, Fred 167
Zombie, Rob 106, 191–192
*Zombieland* 122
Zombies 1–2, 68, 80, 102, 136, 148, 179–180, 206–208
*Zorro, the Gay Blade* 165

www.ingramcontent.com/pod-product-compliance
Ingram Content Group UK Ltd.
Pitfield, Milton Keynes, MK11 3LW, UK
UKHW050537150426
5217IPUK00026B/1969